Ma   or IT

An Inte

Wendy Currie

Senior Lecturer
The School of Management, University of Stirling

PITMAN
PUBLISHING

London · Hong Kong · Johannesburg · Melbourne · Singapore · Washington DC

PITMAN PUBLISHING
128 Long Acre, London WC2E 9AN
Tel: +44 (0)171 447 2000
Fax: +44 (0)171 240 5771

A Division of Pearson Professional Limited

First published in Great Britain 1995

British Library Cataloguing in Publication Data
A CIP catalogue record for this book can be obtained from the British Library.

ISBN 0 273 60700 6

10 9 8 7 6 5 4 3

Typeset by M Rules
Printed and bound in Great Britain by Clays Ltd, St Ives plc

The Publishers' policy is to use paper manufactured from sustainable forests.

CONTENTS

6   Outsourcing: the New IT Strategy

9 Managing IT in the Private and Public Sectors: Evaluation, Performance Measurement and Control

12 Organisational Learning as a Competitive Strategy

13 Summary and conclusions

Index

ACKNOWLEDGEMENTS

I would like to take this opportunity to thank all the individuals who agreed to be interviewed for the various research projects covered in this book. In particular, I am indebted to the managers and staff at the following organisations who agreed to be interviewed on several occasions: The Royal Bank of Scotland, Merrill Lynch, The Bank of Scotland, The Canadian Imperial Bank of Commerce, Societe Generale, Continental Bank, Standard Life, Scottish Widows, GEC, Ferranti, British Aerospace, Rolls Royce, The Ford Motor Company, Pirelli, Sony, Mitsubishi Heavy Industries, Mitsubishi Bank, Yamatake Honeywell, Lothian Regional Council, Stirling Royal Infirmary, Scottish Office, and Lothian Computer Services Unit, among others.

The following funding bodies are also thanked for supporting the various projects covered in this book. They are the Science and Engineering Research Council (SERC), the Nuffield Foundation, the Chartered Institute of Management Accountants (CIMA), the Carnegie Trust and the Scottish Higher Education Funding Council (SHEFC).

I would also like to acknowledge the work of the following academic colleagues who have influenced my own ideas on the strategic management of IT. In alphabetical order they are Peter Armstrong, Barbara Farbey, Michael Earl, Andrew Friedman, Robert Galliers, Rudy Hirschheim, Mary Lacity, Henry Mintzberg, David Targett, Geoff Walsham, Malcolm Warner and Leslie Willcocks.

Thanks are also expressed to Takeo Yoshikawa, James Algie, Arthur Money, Ian Glover, Colwyn Jones and Bob Hart for their interest in my work. I am also grateful to Colin Bryson for his help on the survey research.

I am also greatly indebted to Jonathan Seddon whose in-depth practical knowledge of managing information systems projects has been invaluable to this study.

CHAPTER 1

Organisation, Management and IT: Themes and Perspectives

Introduction

The view that Information Technology (IT) is becoming increasingly important in organisations is now widely accepted in the literature (Allen and Scott-Morton, 1994. Benjamin et al, 1984. Davenport, 1993. Grindley, 1991. McFarlan, 1984. Parsons, 1983. Porter and Millar, 1985. Remenyi, 1987. Robson, 1994. Synot, 1987. Wiseman, 1985. Wysoki and Young, 1990). Some commentators even suggest that IT is now firmly on the boardroom agenda where it is discussed together with land, labour and capital (Guest, 1994). Others predict a future where every organisation, irrespective of its mission or role, will critically depend on IT in every functional area. The rapid information flows enabled by state-of-the-art technology will engender organisational redesign as fewer managers and clerical staff will be needed for executive and administrative decision making (Burrows, 1994).

The critical role ascribed to IT in both private and public sector settings is based upon two popular precepts. First, that IT is a strategic device which, if deployed effectively, can sustain and improve the competitive advantage of a commercial organisation (Porter, 1985. Porter and Millar, 1985). This is perceived as crucial to business survival as companies are faced with the choice to automate or liquidate. Against a background of intense global competition, the emerging markets of central and eastern Europe and the Pacific/Asian region, deregulation and privatisation, and new rules of competition in the free trade areas of the European Union and elsewhere, it is little wonder that managers look towards IT as a device to enhance corporate performance. Even in the public sector, IT is now seen by many as crucial in the pursuit of efficiency improvements, rationalisation and restructuring (Currie and Bryson, 1995).

Second, the normative literature argues that IT is most effective when aligned to the corporate strategy (Jarpenpaa and Ives, 1993). Here, IT is seen as instrumental in achieving improved information flows, better service to customers, greater internal efficiencies in the form of cost control, and headcount reduction (specifically middle management positions) (Dopson and Stewart, 1993). Arguably, the link between competitive advantage and IT and the assumption that an alignment between IT and business strategy will generate performance improvements is one which has been overstated in both the academic and business/trade literature.

In recent years, a new management *philosophy* has emerged in the form of business process re-engineering (BPR). BPR is designed to create, among other things, more effective communication channels and the instantaneous transfer of information (Davenport, 1993. Henderson and Venkatraman, 1994. Earl, 1994). Essentially, BPR assumes that organisations should constantly seek out new and improved methods and techniques for the management of core and service business processes. IT is therefore an appropriate tool to effect such changes, and this in turn reinforces the link between IT and competitive advantage.

A review of the literature shows that stories relating to competitive success through IT are well documented (Wiseman, 1985. Porter, 1980. Porter and Millar, 1985. Remenyi, 1987. Robson, 1994). Whilst it is outside the scope of this book to discuss all of them fully, some examples include: the SABRE system – American Airline's reservation system which ultimately became a computerised reservation system (CRS); the American Hospital Supply's ASAP order entry and inventory control system and the United Service Automobile Association in which the Automated Insurance Environment (a collection of telecommunications systems, databases, expert systems, and image-processing technologies) were used to 'consistently outperform its insurance industry rival in service quality, premium growth, and profitability' (Hopper, 1990, p. 118). Other examples include the use of IT to sustain competitive advantage at Otis Elevator (Loebbecke, 1992) and the Singapore TradeNet system 'because it established lines of communication, clear objectives and user involvement in project management' (Willcocks and Griffiths, 1994).

But against a background of literature which assumes a relationship between competitive advantage and IT, there are many other studies which suggest that IT is under-utilised and poorly managed by all commercial and non-commercial sectors (Sauer, 1993. Henderson, 1990. Avison et al, 1988. *Computer Weekly*, 1989). Indeed, empirical evidence to this effect seems to be growing. In the case of TAURUS (Transfer and Automated Registration of Uncertificated Stock – a city-wide, large-scale IS development project which failed in March 1993 at an estimated overall cost of £400 million), the overwhelming conclusion shows the failure to be directly attributable to poor management practices which, in turn, led to a major technical malfunction (Currie, 1994a).

IT disaster stories are perhaps more common than the management textbooks would lead us to believe. Indeed, the simple prescriptive, menu-driven approaches to IT strategy formulation suggest that project managers and IT strategists need only follow a simple formula to achieve competitive success. Whilst this is not to decry the intellectual exercise of attempts at IT strategy formulation, the transition from the strategy phase (the vision) to implementation (the reality) is arguably fraught with problems and more challenging than most managers would care to admit (Currie, 1994a. Sauer, 1993). To this effect, some writers would argue that strategy formulation is not a scientific endeavour, but instead a dynamic process which is subject to many conflicting interpretations from stakeholders and onlookers (Walsham, 1993. Mintzberg, 1993).

This chapter begins our discussion of management strategies for IT by considering some of the recent technical changes from mainframe to client-server. The general message is that IT continues to confront managers with a formidable challenge, and this is not helped by the speed at which new technology is introduced into the marketplace. Moreover, the ongoing developments in new technology call into question some of the traditional strategies and methodologies for managing change. For example, the notion that IT strategies should follow a linear path is perhaps outdated when we consider the significant changes in IT over the last two decades ; in particular, the move from mainframe systems to PC-based systems. An important issue here is not only that IT specialists continuously need to update their skills to meet technical challenges, but that managers should equally reassess their own learning needs to enable them to effectively co-ordinate and control IT projects. Old formulas for IT strategy development may thus be inappropriate and outdated for the new PC-based IT environment. This may also apply to the strategies hitherto adopted for mainframe systems, particularly in the area of legacy system maintenance (Case, 1993).

This chapter begins by considering some of the key developments which have taken place in the IS field over the last fifteen years. The discussion is intended for the lay person, though it is recognised that some technical terms need to be defined and interpreted. The purpose of including a technical section is to demonstrate how IT has changed over the years, and why these changes pose fresh challenges to managers and staff.

Following this discussion, an attempt is made to clarify some of the key issues in the field of managing technology. Here we consider a range of relevant questions under particular subject headings. These questions are developed from an interdisciplinary literature review of the IS field. The concluding section gives a brief outline of the remaining chapters of the book. The case studies at the end of each chapter are intended to provide practical insights into some of the key management issues. As far as possible, they represent the subject matter contained within the chapter. Whilst the case studies offer no practical solutions, they highlight the many difficulties inherent in managing IT in contemporary private and public sector organisations.

Key developments in corporate information systems in the last two decades

Fifteen years ago the PC was considered an executive's toy. It was expensive, slow, limited in what it could do and esoteric in its operation. It was assumed that the only way data would ever be stored and managed was through a mainframe connected to dumb terminals. A dumb terminal is a workstation which merely displays data, but contains no processing power or logic. All the programs which manage the input of data operate within the mainframe. An extreme example of this is where a time delay of several seconds occurred between entering an instruction on the keyboard and seeing it displayed on the screen.

A mainframe is an expensive item of hardware and absorbs a large proportion of the annual IT spend. As a company's central data store, it represents a reliable repository which has massive disc input/output capacities, effective database management systems (e.g. IBM's DB2) and robust system management facilities. Any data which is to be stored is usually entered via a dumb terminal. An exception is when magnetic discs are loaded into the mainframe. Since the dumb terminal has no processing power, all validation and analysis of data must occur on the mainframe. Figure 1.1 shows a typical mainframe/dumb terminal set-up.

Most applications are written in COBOL. An estimate in October 1993 was of 150-200 billion lines of COBOL code world-wide (Case, 1993. Sinur, 1994). Today this

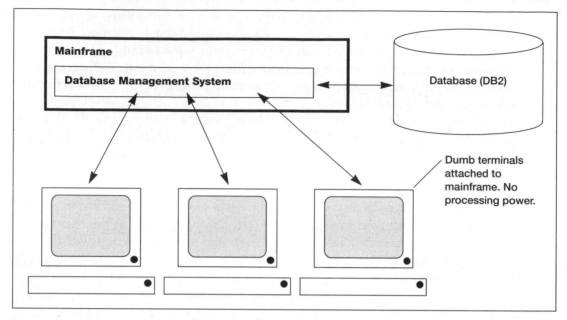

Figure 1.1 Structure of mainframe, database and dumb terminals

represents a legacy of monolithic mainframe applications. Case (1993, p. 2) recently claimed that, 'During the next five years, the majority of development resources will be deployed to maintain legacy applications'. A legacy system is an information system which was not recently developed yet continues to be used and maintained by the organisation. Many legacy systems in the form of mainframe computers pose problems since their maintenance requirements are formidable both financially and technically.

From mainframe to PC?

Throughout the last fifteen years, spectacular development progress has been made to the PC in terms of performance, data storage, reliability and usability. The first computer sold commercially presented no real strategic benefits to a company. Today the performance and capability of a PC has enabled it to play a central role in an organisation's activities. Table 1.1 shows a comparison between an early computer and one today.

Data storage for a PC is improving continuously. Whilst the example in Table 1.1 shows a 1994 PC having a 320M bytes (320,000,000) hard disc, optical storage discs now exist which are capable of holding 2G bytes (2,000,000,000) of data. These discs are in fact smaller than the 32M bytes hard disc found in the 1984 PC. This is shown by the changes to the floppy diskette. Whilst the above 1994 model can store 10% more on half the diskette area, 2.88M bytes 3.5″ diskettes are now becoming common. This represents an improvement in storage per area unit of almost 2.5, and all at the same cost! Due to the amount of code associated with some of today's applications (help files, debug tools, libraries of common utilities etc.) software is not always installed from diskette. Microsoft's Visual C++ version 1.5 is one of many which supplies all of the code on a

	1984 PC	1994 PC
Cost	£2000.00	£2000.00
Processor and Speed	Intel 80286 – MHz	Intel Pentium – 100 MHz
Random Access Memory (RAM)	512K bytes	8M bytes
Monitor	Color Graphics Adapter (CGA). 16 colours	Super Video Graphics Adapter (SVGA) and 2.0M bytes of video memory giving about 1.6 million colours
Hard Disk	32M bytes	320M bytes
Floppy Drive	5.25" 1.2M bytes	3.5" 1.44M bytes

Table 1.1 Changes to the personal computer over the past ten years

compact disk. Rather than install the 100M+ bytes associated with this package, personal computers are able to access 600M bytes of read only optical storage.

This is part of the multi-media capabilities of the PC. True stereo sound can now accompany moving high-quality graphical images. Whilst such programs are very memory hungry and processor intensive, the availability of high storage capacity disks and low-cost memory makes this a reality.

The monitors of the 1984 PC were basic in design and display. Unable to support more than sixteen colours and graphical images they presented an obstacle to the development of a user-orientated environment. Today, monitors have become very sophisticated. Using a super video graphics adapter (SVGA), dedicated memory and their own processor, images containing over 1.6 million colours at a very high resolution can be displayed (somewhat more colours than the human eye can detect). Such displays represent images in 'true colour', having greater depth and resolution than a photograph.

The use of random access memory (RAM) has been the key in enabling such developments. For example in 1984 it cost almost £300.00 to increase the 512K of RAM to 640K (i.e. by 128K). In 1994 the same amount could buy 4M bytes, representing a thirty-fold cost/performance improvement. The initial limit of 16M bytes to the RAM has increased to 128M bytes. This is essential if the high-resolution graphical images are to be manipulated at reasonable speeds.

The processor speed of the 1994 computer appears to be about fifteen times faster. This value, measured in hertz, represents the number of cycles the processor makes in each second and thus dictates the speed at which the entire system operates. It is analogous to the heart which beats slowly when we rest and pumps hard when we run to catch a bus. This calculation is misleading, since the Pentium processor is over 300 times faster than the 80286 chip. This is because the processor is capable of executing two instructions and retrieving four times as much data at once, as well as decreasing the time taken for any calculation by a factor of five. Performance improvements do not stop here. DEC have launched a 300 MHz chip (Stammers, 1994) which extends PC capabilities even further.

It is not only the hardware which has seen major developments over the past two decades. Programming software and operating systems have also changed. The original disc operating system (DOS) limited how much data could be stored on a hard disc and how files were managed and discs maintained, and optimised the use of system memory and the operating speed of programs. As the processor changed and became more powerful and hardware capacities increased, DOS changed to maximise its functionality. For example, only 32M bytes could be stored on a hard disc. Now the only limit is the size of the hard disc itself. Storage has been improved by DOS programs which can seemingly double the space on a hard disc.

The user was originally faced with a command line prompt (that is C:\>) where program names were typed to begin them. This meant that only one program could be run at any one time. When running, the screen display was not user friendly. For example, running a word processor such as WordPerfect® 5.0, the user was presented with a blue screen and the cursor positioned at the top left hand side. Any action to the typed text had to be set up using various key strokes. Microsoft radically changed the way PCs presented data by a software package called Microsoft® Windows™. Running from the DOS command prompt it took control over how the system operated. It enabled users to run numerous programs at once (only limited by the system's memory) which were driven by the mouse or keyboard. The screen was changed from standard ASCII text to a graphical (WYSIWYG – what you see is what you get) display. This meant that users could look at multiple word processing documents (WordPerfect for DOS was limited to two) and many other applications (e.g. spreadsheets, electronic mail, databases and drawing packages) all at the same time. Figure 1.2 represents three applications (WordPerfect, Excel and Visual C++) all being used at the same time (multi-tasking). This PC screen is called a desktop and is meant to represent all of the tools a user will have on their desk.

IBM have brought out a replacement for the existing DOS software called OS/2 (operating system 2). Instead of needing to run DOS before MS Windows, OS/2 combines these two systems with a new operating environment. Unlike DOS which used 16-bit processing, OS/2 is able to make full use of the 32-bit Intel processor. This represents a substantial increase in system performance. Microsoft have a similar product called Windows NT (new technology) but this can only be used on servers. Servers are the data repositories in client-server networks. They are discussed below. Microsoft have a replacement for DOS/MS Windows called Windows 95. This is to be released in the middle of 1995.

Software developments have enabled programmers to write systems which interact dynamically with others. For example, a set of results within a spreadsheet can be inserted into a document, and when their values change they are automatically altered when the document is viewed. 4GLs have been written to reduce screen prototyping and development time by removing much of the complexity required for a Windows system. One example is a 'data aware' field. By setting the database and column to be used, this field will automatically populate itself. In other words all of the values which this data field should show are handled with a minimum of coding by the programmer. The programming functions which a 4GL use combine many allied functions into one. In a 3GL, such as C ++, several calls are required to send a message to the screen's objects. With a 4GL, they are all combined into a single function call. The increased productivity of using a 4GL offers many benefits to the developer/programmer:

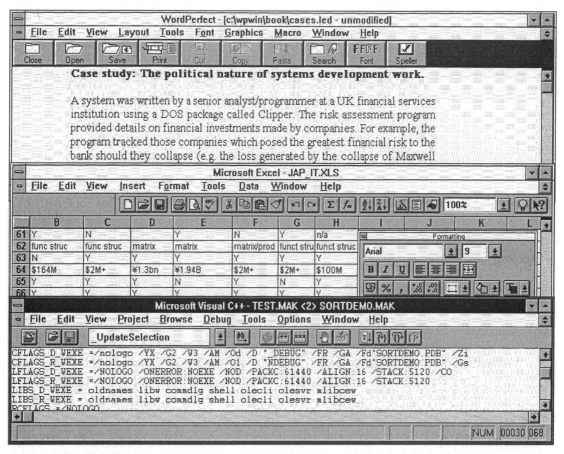

Figure 1.2 Operation of different applications within a MS Windows™ environment (multitasking)

- by reducing the lead time to write a program, any alteration to the functional specification (e.g. what the proposed system is intended to do) will not be as costly compared to a system written in a 3GL
- total development costs are reduced because of the time reductions in developing the system
- end users can be more closely involved in the systems development process

Another development to the programming language is object orientation. If many data fields share similar properties such as size, content and text colour, and respond in similar ways to events (change to red if the number content is less than 0), then they can all be derived from one class. This class defines all of the events which affect instances of itself. An instance refers to the data field which has been derived from a class of data fields. This instance can also be called an object. All the functions and variables which are defined within a class can be inherited by any other class. This means that a function which is defined in one class can be called by another class without having the code repeated.

A definition of object-oriented programming is defined by Gietz (1993, p.545) as follows:

'Unlike traditional structured programs, whose elements are tightly integrated into the whole, an object-oriented program is composed of independent software modules called objects. Each of these modules has its own job and is (ideally) solely responsible for managing how this job is done. Collectively, the objects do the business of the program in much the same way that different departments of a company do the business of the company.'

Looking at Figure 1.3, a class ndfBase has been defined for a numerical data field. A function which is to be shared by each field derived from this class is defined in the class itself. This function CheckValue alters the colour of the text displayed. Because of inheritance there is no need to code this function in any of the derived instances. Using object-oriented methods, the amount of programming code in addition to its maintainability is significantly reduced. Although more analytical work is required to set up these classes, substantial benefits accrue at the programming stage.

This methodology offers three development advantages:

Re-use: Developers are able to build blocks of code which can be used in many different applications. These are called libraries and are dynamically linked (DLL).

Productivity: A wide range of productivity improvements such as reduced code development times, delivery costs and performance.

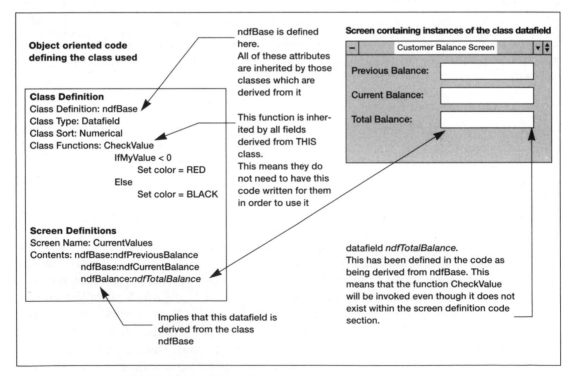

Figure 1.3 Development using object-oriented techniques

Communication: Objects bridge the gap between the problem domain (the business) and the solution (information systems). The communication is improved because the system reflects the business model.

Object orientation is not specific to a 4GL, for example Visual C++ is a 3GL. However, the use of a 4GL provides high-level visual interface for code generation, speed, intuitiveness and ease of use. By using a 4GL an average productivity improvement of 2.5:1 over 3GLs is achievable. This is due to factors such as:

- The screen is displayed in WYSIWYG format. This applies to the development of printed material which includes graphical images and varying font types and sizes.
- 4GLs have pre-built code libraries of high-level functions which ease the interaction between disparate developments.
- Non-procedural rules have been specified, such as data type validation for a users entry.
- A self-contained, interpretative edit-debug-compile-test environment, compared to a pre-compile, compile, link and test cycle for a typical 3GL

Client-Server development

Using a PC as a standalone tool does not give a large corporation any real competitive advantage because all its data is not accessible by any other machine. This has been overcome with the use of local area and wide area networks (LANs and WANs). A LAN connects PCs in the same physical area (a London office) whilst the WAN connects LANs in distributed areas (offices in London, Birmingham and Glasgow). The use of such networks is fundamental to the operation of client-server applications.

One facet of client-server technology is in the form of distributed processing where computing activities are shared amongst networked computers. This is shown in Figure 1.4.

In the LAN, the server is a powerful PC and holds the database used by the client machines. For example, if all of the clients are running a MIS then the database which is used by each application is stored and managed on the server. This data is managed through co-operative processing. Any information which is held on the client machines cannot be accessed by any other. The client terminals are responsible for managing the screen display (GUI), the interactive dialogue between the end user, validation of all the data which is entered, and any local computations required. As such, each client provides a networked interface which can communicate with the server. The database server is responsible for storage, security, integrity and the input/output of stored data. Under this arrangement the operation of the application is maximised. All data-intensive tasks are off-loaded to the server whilst doing as much processing as possible on the client.

The benefits of distributed databases can be seen as:

- the decision of where to place the client application is independent of where the data is stored
- a database can be moved without affecting user applications
- hardware and software from different manufacturers can be used

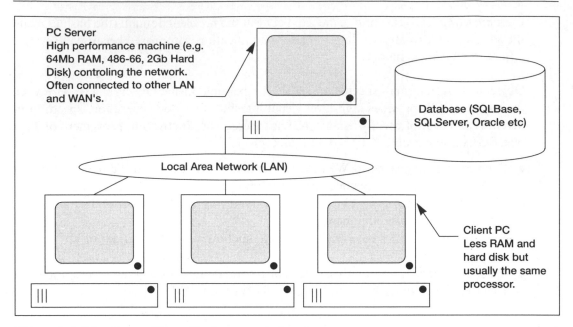

Figure 1.4 Structure of the client-server network

- if a server goes down only its clients are affected, not the entire organisation. This can be seen as an improvement to the systems availability.
- the application's hardware can be closely matched to its operational requirements. Applications which manage large databases or graphical images need far more RAM than those which perform a minimal amount of calculations.

Much work has so far been done in estimating the cost of client-server applications. Experience has shown that such networks cost considerably more than the conventional approaches available (i.e. standalone or bespoke systems). It has been estimated (Dec and Miller, 1994) that the average cost of running 5,000 client workstations over a five-year period was $48,000. This is substantially more than the very best PC currently available. Such costs reflect the price of the server which is operating ($68,000–80,000), maintenance, wiring and communication, purchased applications, end-user labour, network management, user training, application development, labour, professional services, client hardware and software.

In a recent survey (Dec. 1993) it was observed that '... 70 percent of respondents indicated that their client-server developments had gone beyond the "information gathering" and "seriously considering" stages. Thirty six percent were developing pilot client-server applications whilst 30 percent were building them'.

The key justification for client-server is the benefit to end users. The end user is seen to be more productive, responsive and collaborative. Client-server applications are best evaluated holistically.

Figure 1.5 shows a matrix which illustrates the organisational use of IT. The matrix is intended as an ideal type which locates the use of IT in four quadrants. Here, it is postulated that client-server is maximised at professional/managerial levels which undertake

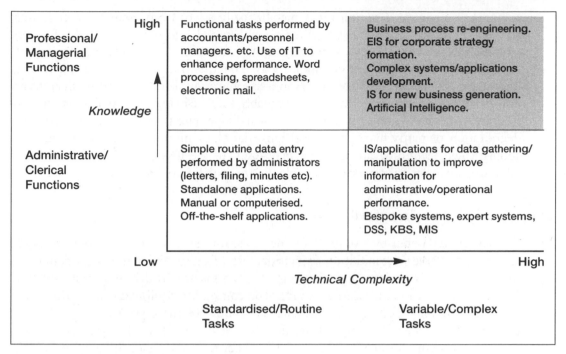

	High	Functional tasks performed by accountants/personnel managers. etc. Use of IT to enhance performance. Word processing, spreadsheets, electronic mail.	Business process re-engineering. EIS for corporate strategy formation. Complex systems/applications development. IS for new business generation. Artificial Intelligence.
Professional/ Managerial Functions *Knowledge*			
Administrative/ Clerical Functions		Simple routine data entry performed by administrators (letters, filing, minutes etc). Standalone applications. Manual or computerised. Off-the-shelf applications.	IS/applications for data gathering/ manipulation to improve information for administrative/operational performance. Bespoke systems, expert systems, DSS, KBS, MIS
	Low ⟶ High		
	Technical Complexity		
		Standardised/Routine Tasks	Variable/Complex Tasks

Figure 1.5 The organisational use of IT

complex and variable tasks. This quadrant encapsulates ambitious management change programmes such as business process re-engineering (BPR). Here it is contended that professional/managerial functions require a high level of knowledge in addition to utilising state-of-the-art technology. Client-server can greatly enhance the usability of complex technical applications to maximise productivity. Key to their success is a rigorous design and development cycle undertaken by users, developers, analysts, programmers and project managers. Client-server technology is only likely to be successful if it is embraced by a significant proportion of organisational members.

The quadrant which represents standardised/routine tasks carried out by administrative/clerical functions includes expert systems, knowledge-based systems and decision support systems. However, once expertise, knowledge and structured decision processes are contained within an application/program, it is likely that non-experts will be able to use and understand it. Knowledge levels of administrative/clerical functions are traditionally lower than their professional/managerial counterparts. However, as knowledge becomes contained within DSS, KBS and expert systems, it is likely that non-professional/managerial staff will be able to execute these technical applications. Conversely, the quadrant representing professional/managerial functions undertaking standardised routine tasks will require a competent level of professional knowledge to be able to use specific technologies (e.g. the accountant using a spreadsheet, the social scientist using a statistical package, etc.). Technical complexity may be low, and it is likely that, in some instances, professionals and managers may not even use a PC to undertake their work.

The fourth quadrant is where administrative/clerical functions use technology for standardised and routine tasks. These individuals will also use a word processor or spreadsheet package. Examples may include using a word processor to enter student names and addresses. Clearly, no professional knowledge is required here. Equally, administrators and clerical workers may or may not use a PC to undertake their work, though this is becoming less common today. This quadrant represents a low level of knowledge and technical complexity. However, some administrative/clerical functions are now using more complex technologies. Arguably, this is closing the gap between the professional/managerial and administrative/clerical divide. This is likely to be reflected in the degradation of many managerial positions. For the containment of knowledge into sophisticated technological packages may result in the loss of professional status as administrative/clerical personnel are able to exploit these applications.

Stages of IS development

A much quoted paper by Nolan (1974) identified four stages in the development of the IT function. These were initiation, expansion, formalization and maturity. Initiation was the rationale behind selecting the first computer. This is usually driven by cost reduction. Expansion represents the rapid expenditure on computing equipment. Formalization is the action by managers to curb the excess spending of the expansion stage. Finally, maturity represented the stage where, the 'dust having settled', the systems began to operate in an economical way. This model was later revised (Nolan, 1979) to include the phases of control, integration and data administration to replace that of formalization. This was to represent the transition from management of the computer to management of the data. Since the publication of Nolan's work, other writers have stressed that most empirical tests have not confirmed the hypotheses which support the model (Friedman, 1994). Moreover, the model was developed two decades ago, and the assumptions behind it need some revision in the light of contemporary technical, organisational and managerial change.

A significant development is the rapid expansion of the PC market. It represents high-performance/low-cost technology which is readily integrated into the business structure and corporate architecture. The original use of the computer (particularly the mainframe and dumb terminals) was predominantly to save money by replacing labour-intensive clerical operations. This was met with resistance as people felt threatened by the automation of their work. During this period, there was little user involvement as systems were generally imposed upon the work force by the centralised IT department.

Since then, a wave of new technologies have entered the marketplace and been implemented in a range of private and public sector organisations. Whilst the contentious issue of job reduction through technology continues to be debated, the emphasis at the present time seems to be on the development of computer applications to generate enhanced information to users, for example MISs for marketing managers to provide a statistical analysis and associated trends in consumer behaviour using thousands of records. This type of activity is clearly dependent upon the development of software for a specific application, which presents useful information to a business area. The advantage of such a system is its flexibility in data manipulation. Here the PC is the appropriate tool since it enables the individual to work on a specific applications package which may be tailored to the business.

The operation of a character-based dumb terminal is not comparable to a high-performance graphical PC screen. The movement is now away from centralised databases to a distributed client-server environment. Key to the rapid application of the PC has been the growth in suppliers. Supported by the hardware reliability and software capabilities they were able provide competitive alternatives. This forced the PC market to become highly competitive and resulted in the market moving away from the traditional mainframe applications. Today users are entering an employment market where computers are now established. Rather than sabotaging any attempt to install them, they accept that training is the only way to remain in employment.

Nolan's (1979) second model showed the way the computing department changed its direction from maintenance to data management. Today, within even small companies, separate areas are responsible for such activities, namely the database administrator, network administrator, help desk, system development and testing.

Friedman (1994) has presented an updated model of these phases of the information system department. He presented an argument that there were two general strategies for managing IS specialists. The first was *responsible autonomy* where little control was placed upon the 'creative' flair of the programmers. For this to work he suggested that employee loyalty was rewarded by employment security, social rewards and so on. The opposite to this was to impose *direct control* on the employee's work. Work was divided into small tasks removing as much individual creativity as possible. Financial and job threats were used to motivate employees. A mixture of these controls would then be applied as the case demanded.

A significant development in the last decade has clearly been the degradation of job security in the IT profession. Even industry leaders such as IBM announced a 30,000 redundancy scheme in 1992. In addition, the current wave of IT outsourcing is likely to shrink, or even eliminate, IT departments (*Computing*, 1994), particularly in the public sector. The IT outsourcing phenomenon will undoubtedly have significant effects on how contract IT professionals are managed. For example, individuals on short-term employment contracts will need to be given new incentives by managers to maximise their performance. Responsible autonomy is an interesting concept, although in the context of outsourcing, it is likely to take on new meaning. For example, individuals seeking contract IT positions may seek to present themselves as *portfolio workers*. In other words, they will demonstrate a wide range of skills which they have acquired from a number of commercial or public sector settings. It is also likely that IT contract managers will become more widespread in the next few years. These individuals will similarly present themselves as having managed large-scale complex IT projects, possibly focused in one sector.

Conversely, direct management control may become more difficult as companies move towards outsourcing. This concept is also at odds with the view that organisations should encourage learning and creativity. Indeed, research suggests that the process of applications development is dynamic and dependent upon individual flair, and not one which is necessarily amenable to direct management control (Currie and Bryson, 1995).

Recently, Friedman (1994, p. 142.) commented that recruitment to IT departments favoured people '...with more generalist backgrounds. Traditional computer science and engineering qualifications have been giving way to degrees in liberal arts, social science and especially business studies.' Whilst this policy has been adopted by a number of large corporations, the assumptions which underpin it are questionable in the light of the many IT applications development failures. Clearly, there are likely to be different management styles and priorities between IS and non-IS managers (Galliers, et al, 1994) and more empirical research is needed which examines the link between managerial background and IT project performance.

Recent interviews with analyst/programmers in the private and public sectors shed some new light on the generalist-technologist divide (Currie and Bryson, 1995). Here it was found that IT staff working for non-IS managers (those without an IS/IT background) were highly critical of the latter's management style, priorities and judgement. Many analyst/programmers suggested a crisis in management control given that they believed they were effectively *managing themselves*. Part of the crisis in management control is due to the vast changes in technology over the last twenty years. This leaves some managers conceptually redundant in regard to ascertaining appropriate methods and techniques for managing their *high flyer* IT staff.

The development cycle has also changed dramatically. Using the early languages (e.g. COBOL) the ratio between writing code and doing analysis and screen design was about 8:1. Today the ratio is now about 1:1. This is due to the use of 4GLs which provides enhanced functionality and user involvement throughout the development process. By no means is this process linear, rather it is multi-staged and iterative. The user involvement in the screen development is represented by the circle on the right hand of Figure 1.6. The postulation that client-server IS development is an iterative and not linear process will clearly have significant implications for management and organisation. These issues will be discussed in the following chapters.

Key questions in the management of IT

It is suggested that the subject of managing IT is more appropriately researched through an interdisciplinary framework. This presents researchers with the challenge of seeking out new literature from a variety of disciplinary fields. Although the subject of managing technology is a relatively new area, it seems that most studies are concentrated under at least seven areas. The key questions relating to these areas are as follows:

Technical
1. What are the important new developments in IT?
2. What technology is needed to facilitate BPR? (Earl, 1994)
3. How should legacy systems be maintained? (Sinur, 1994)
4. What are the phases of IS development? (Friedman, 1989, 1994)
5. Is the development of IT evolutionary or revolutionary? (Forrester, 1980, 1985)
6. Why do information systems fail? (Sauer, 1993. Currie, 1994a. Ewusi-Mensah et al, 1994. Mitev, 1994. Willcocks and Griffiths, 1994)

Strategy
1. Should organisations develop a clearly defined IT strategy which is aligned to the corporate strategy? (Earl, 1989. Henderson and Venkatraman, 1994)

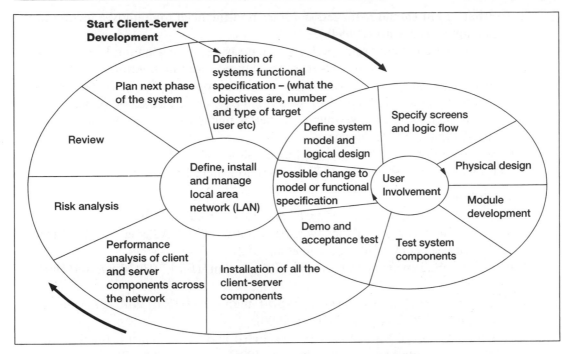

Figure 1.6 Complex development process for client-server systems

2. Are IT strategies best described as formal-rational and deliberate, or *ad hoc*, emergent and fluctuating over time? (Mintzberg, 1993)
3. What is the relationship between business process re-engineering (BPR) and IT strategy? (Davenport, 1993)
4. What is the most appropriate duration for IT strategies? (e.g. long, medium or short term) (Currie, 1989)
5. How can IT sustain and improve competitive advantage? (McFarlan, 1984. Porter, 1985)
6. Should IT be outsourced? (Lacity and Hirschheim, 1993)

Structure
1. How should the organisation be structured to facilitate the IT strategy? (Davenport and Short, 1990)
2. Should organisations have a centralised or decentralised IT department? (Kaestle, 1990)
3. How does IT affect the structure of an organisation? (Keen, 1981. Ein-Dor and Segev, 1982)
4. Should IT be a profit or cost centre? (Bryson and Currie, 1995)
5. What is the relationship between structure and size of the organisation? (Woodward, 1958. Pugh et al, 1969ab)

Evaluation
1. What are the most appropriate quantitative methods and techniques for evaluating IT (e.g. ROI, payback, DCF, etc)? (Farbey et al, 1993, 1994. Dugdale and Jones, 1991)

2. To what extent should managers consider non-financial (qualitative) factors in the evaluation of IT? (Currie, 1994b)
3. What are the most important performance measures for evaluating IT in relation to the business (e.g. increased market share, reduced lead times, improved information for decision making, the creation of new business opportunities)? (CIMA, 1993)
4. What are the political processes of justifying IT to senior managers? (Currie, 1989)
5. How can technological investments be better understood through a strategic cost analysis? (Shank and Govindarajan, 1992)
6. Can IT enhance profitability? (Lincoln and Shorrock, 1990).
7. Can IT reduce costs? (Nolan, 1977. Porter and Millar, 1985).

Managerial

1. Should an organisation appoint an IT director? (Grindley, 1991)
2. Should technical or general managers be in charge of IT? (Adler et al, 1992. Morone, 1993. Benbasat et al, 1980. Boynton et al, 1992).
3. Is senior management commitment to IT important? (Earl, 1989. Rowe and Herbert, 1990)
4. How can organisations develop hybrid managers? (Earl and Skyrme, 1992. Meiklejohn, 1990. Palmer and Ottley, 1990).
5. Has the knowledge gap between the generalist and IT specialist created a crisis in management control? (Currie and Bryson, 1995)
6. What is the most appropriate way of interpreting information systems? (Walsham, 1993)
7. What are the political processes of managing IT? (Davenport et al, 1992. Markus, 1983. Frost and Egri, 1990)
8. What are the key IS management issues of the next five/ten years? (Galliers et al, 1994. Hutchinson and Rosenberg, 1994).

Cross-national comparisons of managing IT

1. Is it possible to identify more effective methods and techniques of managing IT from cross-national comparisons? (Currie, 1994b)
2. Are Japanese management practices effective for managing technical change and innovation? (Fruin, 1993)
3. Can Japanese practices be transferred to the West for performance improvements? (Jones et al, 1993)
4. Are IT skills shortages, training strategies and HR practices similar world-wide?

Organisational learning, knowledge and skills development

1. What is a learning organisation? (Garrett, 1987. Stata, 1989. Maccoby, 1993. Garvin, 1993. Senge, 1990)
2. How can managers exploit organisational knowledge to achieve competitive advantage? (Tricker, 1992)
3. What is explicit and tacit knowledge? (Nonaka, 1991)
4. What skills are needed for today's high-tech companies? (Thamhain, 1993).

The above questions are an attempt to unravel some of the important themes and questions relating to managing technology in contemporary private and public sector organisations. They are by no means exhaustive.

This book discusses many of the issues relating to the above questions, but cautions that no easy answers are possible. On the contrary, the interdisciplinary approach appears to raise more questions about the pitfalls of introducing IT, and as a consequence, rejects over-simple explanations of IT strategy formulation and implementation.

Chapter two introduces perhaps the most prolific theme on the subject of IT. Here we consider the relationship between competitive advantage and IT, and the work of Porter (1985) and others is introduced. The discussion cautions against over-simplistic notions that IT can achieve almost automatic competitive advantages for companies, given that not all IT applications are needed for this purpose. Chapter three continues the theme of competitive advantage and IT by considering some of the strategy literature. Here it seems that many writers have superimposed the models used in the general strategy literature on IT. In this context, many writers talk optimistically about the importance of devising an IT strategy to sustain or win competitive advantage. Chapter four introduces another popular topic on IT which concerns investment appraisal and evaluation. In short, an important issue is that managers have difficulties in both justifying IT investments to senior executives and evaluating IT projects (pre- and post-implementation). Chapter five looks at the role of the IT professional, and how IT staff fit within the wider organisation. In particular, the chapter looks at the skill requirements to manage IT specialists and discusses the viability of the hybrid manager.

Chapter six considers a growing interest in the IT field – IT outsourcing. It discusses some of the recent literature on this subject and questions whether outsourcing is the right way forward for companies faced with burgeoning IT costs. Chapter seven introduces a survey on managing IT projects in three sectors. The survey looked at nearly 200 private and public sector organisations and was interdisciplinary. Chapters eight and nine continue our discussion of the survey. Other relevant literature is also introduced for comparative purposes.

Chapter eleven considers some cross-national comparative data on managing IT in British and Japanese companies. It focuses on the current problem facing Japanese companies which is the growth and under-performance of the white collar sector. Here it is argued that whereas many British academics have focused on the issue of transferring Japanese management techniques to western companies, Japan is likely to adopt HR strategies of job-reduction and rationalisation from the West in the light of economic downturn and bad debt.

Chapter twelve considers an important subject which is becoming more relevant to the field of managing technology. That is, organisational learning as a means of enhancing competitive advantage. Here it is argued that organisations need to re-evaluate their definitions of the skills needed to manage IT projects and IT specialists. In essence, managers need to place a higher premium on tacit skills if the ideal of the knowledge organisation is to become a reality.

Case study

Merging new technology with old technology: supporting a legacy system at a UK bank

A £25m computer project was recently begun at a UK bank. Its aim is to move all of the services which currently exist on the mainframe to personal computers (PCs). The mainframe will continue to store all the corporate data whilst the PC will present a graphical front end. As such the project can be viewed as a client-server development, but rather than a networked PC acting as the server, it will be the central mainframe. This overall layout is shown in Figure 1.7

The existing use of the data is typical of the mainframe dumb-terminal arrangement. All of the data is accessed by pre-defined programs written in COBOL (Common Business Oriented Language) and represent a legacy system. The database has been developed over the past decades and has become unstructured.

That is, data is repeated across different tables, rather than being defined only once. In an attempt to maximise this data, each branch across the country would have terminals to access the appropriate tables. By so doing, customers would be able to view their account details, set up standing orders, transfer funds, cancel cheques, order cheque books, and so forth. Any branch would be able to present this service to any bank customer, irrespective of where their account was held.

The project can be divided into three separate but interacting areas: mainframe, PC and middle-ware (which connects the first two). The mainframe side was responsible for writing the new data access required. PC developments were concerned with graphical user interface developments, screen flow and data input. The

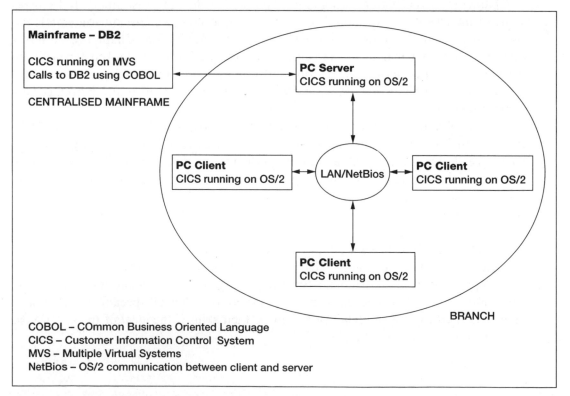

Figure 1.7 Structure of client-server and mainframe network

middle-ware provided the means whereby a client PC could send a request across a local network, through its server to the mainframe and return with the required data. This is the ability of two totally different systems to act seamlessly, and represents the latest step in computer developments.

This system followed a typical client-server cycle. Unlike the traditional linear development paths, Figure 1.8 shows the complicated cyclical process that was conducted before any code for the final system was written.

The total process can be divided into two parts: development of the GUI and system operation, and the structure of the code. The system was given a high profile by the bank. Over two man years of effort went into the design of the screens and their navigation. Involved in this process were over fifty end users, split into five groups. Each group met for a couple of hours each week and gave opinions on the development of the screens and how they could be improved.

Other groups of senior managers met weekly to assess the development. The project owners also liaised with the developers on an ongoing basis. Throughout this process, the various stakeholders analysed numerous developmental issues. A significant amount of brainstorming was apparent. This development cycle is depicted by the functional specification and demonstration stages. The whole purpose of the multi-stage development cycle is an attempt to align IT user needs with the business strategy.

The code development followed three distinguishable stages. They were, 'proof of concept', 'fast prototyping' and 'development of re-useable code'. The proof of concept occurred prior to any other development work being carried out to verify if it was possible.

The structure of the code can be seen to follow an object-oriented approach (OO). In an attempt to standardise the screen design, every screen object is derived from a single 'super class'. For example, all the datafields, lines and list boxes would use the same font, size and colour. For this inheritance approach to work, the defined classes had to be stable. It was there-fore essential that the structure of the scre[en] was achieved at an early date in the project li[fe] cycle. A different type of object property, namely encapsulation, was applied to the development of the business and customer classes. Encapsulation means that the class being addressed knows nothing about any other. This enables these classes to change without affecting any other part of the program. Thus, this is the opposite of the inheritance property. All the encapsulated classes (which represented over 70% of the final system code) were accessed by non-OO programmers. This had the advantage of using the benefits of OO without having to spend a lot of time and money bringing all of the programmers up to speed.

The development of this client-server mainframe system was an attempt to present a new structure to the existing legacy system. When first written, the mainframe system operated within a static business climate. Technology management was central to its operation. Today the system is operating within a very different business climate. For example, whereas the mainframe operated within a centralised environment, the concept of client-server technology is based upon a decentralised environment.

The primary goal was to create a new system, while at the same time to minimise the changes to the legacy system. This is a relatively low-cost option which supports twenty-year-old mainframe technology, but also offers new business systems to the user. Nevertheless, the standalone nature of the mainframe system meant that the original COBOL programs cannot be easily manipulated using the PC client-server technology.

A serious problem is in the retrieval of large amounts of data. Since there is a physical limit of 32k bytes to the string passes between the two, only a couple of hundred records can be retrieved. Rather than passing a request which returns all the data at once (a standard operation for PC client-servers) multiple calls had to be made. The associated complexity forced the operation to be very slow.

One of the most significant influences on the

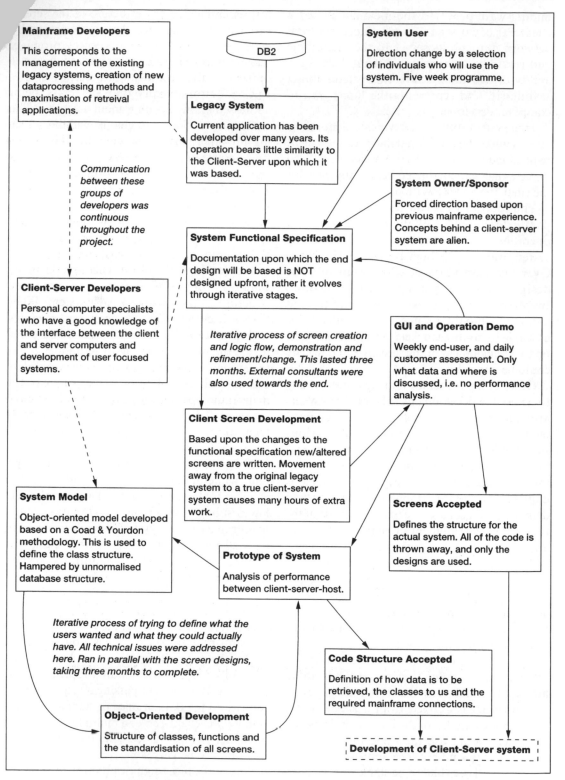

Mainframe Developers

This corresponds to the management of the existing legacy systems, creation of new dataprocessing methods and maximisation of retreival applications.

DB2

System User

Direction change by a selection of individuals who will use the system. Five week programme.

Legacy System

Current application has been developed over many years. Its operation bears little similarity to the Client-Server upon which it was based.

Communication between these groups of developers was continuous throughout the project.

System Owner/Sponsor

Forced direction based upon previous mainframe experience. Concepts behind a client-server system are alien.

System Functional Specification

Documentation upon which the end design will be based is NOT designed upfront, rather it evolves through iterative stages.

Client-Server Developers

Personal computer specialists who have a good knowledge of the interface between the client and server computers and development of user focused systems.

Iterative process of screen creation and logic flow, demonstration and refinement/change. This lasted three months. External consultants were also used towards the end.

GUI and Operation Demo

Weekly end-user, and daily customer assessment. Only what data and where is discussed, i.e. no performance analysis.

Client Screen Development

Based upon the changes to the functional specification new/altered screens are written. Movement away from the original legacy system to a true client-server system causes many hours of extra work.

System Model

Object-oriented model developed based on a Coad & Yourdon methodology. This is used to define the class structure. Hampered by unnormalised database structure.

Screens Accepted

Defines the structure for the actual system. All of the code is thrown away, and only the designs are used.

Prototype of System

Analysis of performance between client-server-host.

Iterative process of trying to define what the users wanted and what they could actually have. All technical issues were addressed here. Ran in parallel with the screen designs, taking three months to complete.

Code Structure Accepted

Definition of how data is to be retrieved, the classes to us and the required mainframe connections.

Object-Oriented Development

Structure of classes, functions and the standardisation of all screens.

Development of Client-Server system

Figure 1.8 The initial circular development cycle for the client-server development

speed of the project development was the input by senior managers (remembering that screen design directly affected the structure of classes). The project managers all had mainframe backgrounds. Thus their perception of screen design and usability was different from that of the PC development team. In contrast to the GUI, character user interfaces (CUI) were proposed, the latter being more easily understood by mainframe managers.

The development process was therefore influenced by mainframe managers. This was shown by the decision to develop screens on the basis of their experience of DOS-like systems. As a result, they were disinclined to fully exploit all the features of a windows system. The differences between DOS and windows is shown in Figure 1.9.

The proposals pushed by mainframe managers had serious implications on the operation of the screens. Since they had exerted a great deal of influence about the design of the screens, the information contained within them was not wholly appropriate for the business users' requirements. Essentially, the users wanted a top-down approach to screen development where they could define what information they

needed regarding, for example, a customer account. However, the mainframe managers preferred a bottom-up (technology driven) approach whereby the existing data contained within the mainframe dictated the information content of the screen.

Seemingly, a mismatch occurred between the information that could be supplied from the mainframe, and the information required by the users. Although the mainframe was the central repository of all customer data and information, new business developments created the need for new information.

After much deliberation between the mainframe and PC developers with the users, a decision was taken to rewrite some of the DB2 tables and COBOL functions on the mainframe.

After many months of development work, the new screens were finally accepted by the users. So far, the project has cost about £7 million. Phase 1 has now ended and most of the initial prototyping code will be scrapped. In phase 2, the complete system will be written. Using the screen designs and OO development from phase 1, the entire system will be coded.

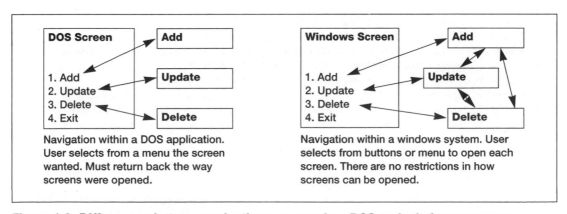

Navigation within a DOS application. User selects from a menu the screen wanted. Must return back the way screens were opened.

Navigation within a windows system. User selects from buttons or menu to open each screen. There are no restrictions in how screens can be opened.

Figure 1.9 Differences between selecting a screen in a DOS and windows program

Discussion questions

1 Do you believe that the decision to base the PC client-server system on the established mainframe-dumb terminals was the right choice?
2 Since the senior (mainframe) managers were responsible for the outcome of the project, should they have control over its design and development?
3 Given the high degree of uncertainty in the initial development stages, what is the most appropriate way to manage project costs?
4 What are the problems of legacy systems?
5 Do you think that much of the cyclical development process was the result of using the OO methodology against an unstructured database and programming language (COBOL)?

References 1

Adler, P.S., McDonald, D.W., MacDonald, F. (1992) 'Strategic management of technical functions'. *Sloan Management Review*, Winter.
Avison, D.E., Fitzgerald, G., Wood-Harper, A.T. (1988) 'Information systems development: a tool kit is not enough'. *The Computer Journal*, Vol, 3, No. 4, pp. 379–380.
Benbasat, I., Dexter, A.S., Mantha, R.W. (1980) 'Impact of organisational maturity on information system skill needs'. *MIS Quarterly*, Vol, 4, No. 1, pp. 21–34.
Benjamin, R.I. Rockart, J.F., Scott-Morton, M.S., Wyman, J. (1984) 'Information technology: a strategic opportunity'. *Sloan Management Review*, Spring, pp. 3–10.
Boynton, A.C., Jacobs, G.C., Zmud, R.W. (1992) 'Whose responsibility is IT management? *Sloan Management Review*, Summer, pp. 32–38.
Bryson, C., Currie, W. (1994) 'IT and organisation structure in the private and public sectors: some preliminary findings', working paper, Department of Management and Organisation, Stirling University.
Case, A. (1993) 'Building the next generation of legacy systems', *ADM research note*, October 4, SPA-210-928. Gartner Group.
CIMA (1993) *Performance measurement in the manufacturing sector*, CIMA.
Computer Weekly. (1988) 'Ambulance service switches off system', 19 October.
Computing (1994) 'IT managers face disruptive change', 13 October.
Currie, W. (1989) *Managerial strategies for new technology*. Gower.
Currie, W. (1994a) 'The strategic management of large scale IT projects in the financial services sector'. *New Technology, Work and Employment*, Vol, 9, No. 1. pp. 19–29.
Currie, W. (1994b) *The strategic management of AMT*. CIMA, London.
Currie, W., Bryson, C. (1995) Managing IT professionals: a crisis in management control? in Glover, I. and Hughes, M. (eds) *The professional-managerial class*, Avebury, Aldershot (forthcoming).
Currie, W., Bryson, C. (1995) 'Generalist managers, IT specialists and the process of software development: a crisis in management control?', paper to be presented at European Conference on Technological Innovation and Global Challenges, Aston, 5–7 July.
Davenport, T. H & Short, J. E (1990) 'The new industrial engineering: information technology and business process redesign.' *Sloan Management Review,* Vol, 31, No. 4, pp. 11–27.
Davenport, T.H. (1993) *Process Innovation: reengineering work through information technology*, Harvard Business School Press, Boston.
Davenport, T.H., Eccles, R.G., Prusak, L. (1992) 'Information politics'. *Sloan Management Review*, Fall, pp. 53–65.
Dec, K. (1993) 'Client/server key research findings during 3Q93' *Research note. K-900-151* published by the Gartner Group, Stamford, CT.
Dec, K., Miller, C. (1994) 'A guide for estimating client/server costs', *C/S research note*, April 18, R-810-105. Gartner Group.
Dopson, S., Stewart, R. (1993) 'Information technology, organisational restructuring and the future of middle management'. *New Technology, Work and Employment*, Vol, 8, No. 1, pp. 10–20.

Dugdale, D., Jones, C. (1991) 'Discordant voices: accountants' views of investment appraisal'. *Management Accounting*, November, pp. 54–59.

Earl, M. (1994) 'The new and the old of business process redesign'. *Journal of Information Systems*, Vol, 3, No. 1, pp. 5–22.

Earl, M. (1989) *Managerial strategies for IT*. Prentice Hall.

Ein-dor, P., Segev, E. (1982) Organisational context and MIS structure: some empirical evidence. *MIS Quarterly*.

Ewusi-Mensah, K., Przasnski, Z.H. (1994) 'Factors contributing to the abandonment of information systems development projects'. *Journal of Information Technology*, Vol, 9, pp. 185–201.

Farbey, B., Targett, D., Land, F. (1994) 'Matching an IT project with an appropriate method of evaluation: a research note on 'evaluating investments in IT'. *Journal of Information Technology*, Vol, 9, pp. 239–243.

Farbey, B., Land, F., Targett, D. (1993) *IT Investment: a study of methods and practice*. Butterworth-Heinemann.

Friedman, A. (1994) 'The stages model and the phases of the IS field', *Journal of Information Technology*, Vol, 9, pp. 137–148.

Frost, P.J., Egri, C.P. (1990) 'Influence of political action on innovation'. *Leadership & Organisation Development Journal*, Vol, 11, No. 1, pp. 17–25, Vol, 11, No, 2, pp. 4–12.

Fruin, W. M. (1993) *The Japanese Enterprise System*. Oxford: Clarendon Press.

Galliers, R.D., Merali, Y., Spearing, L. (1994) 'Coping with information technology? How British executives perceive the key information systems management issues in the mid-1990s'. *Journal of Information Technology*, Vol, 9, pp. 223–238.

Garrett, R. (1987) *The learning organisation*. Fontana Collins.

Garvin, D.A. (1993) 'Building a learning organisation'. *Harvard Business Review*, July/August, pp. 78–91.

Gibson, C. F., Nolan, R. L. (1974) 'Managing the four stages of EDP growth'. *Harvard Business Review*, January/February, pp. 76–88.

Gietz, W. (1993) *SQL Windows Programming*. Gupta Corporation.

Grindley, K. (1991) *Managing IT at board level*. Pitman.

Henderson, E. (1990) 'Admissions system seizes up'. *Times Higher Education Supplement'*, 27 July.

Henderson, J.C & Venkatraman, N (1994) Strategic alignment: a model for organisational transformation via information technology, in Allen, T.J. & Scott-Morton, M.S., *Information Technology and the Corporation of the 1990s*. Oxford University Press, pp. 202–220.

Hutchinson, C., Rosenberg, D. (1994) 'The organisation of organisations: issues for next generation office IT'. *Journal of Information Technology*, Vol, 9, pp. 99–117.

Jarvenpaa, S.L., Ives, B.I. (1993) 'Organising for global competition: the fit of information technology'. *Decision Sciences*, Vol, 24, No. 3, pp. 547–579.

Kaestle, P. (1990) 'A new rationale for organisational structure'. *Planning Review*, Vol, 18, No. 4. pp. 20–22.

Keen, P. G. W. (1981) 'Information systems and organisation change', *Communications of the ACM*, 24, No. 1, pp. 24–32.

Lacity, M. C., Hirschheim, R. (1993) *Information systems outsourcing*. Wiley.

Lincoln, T.J., Shorrock, D. (1990) 'Cost-justifying current use of information technology'. T. Lincoln (ed) *Managing information systems for profit*, Wiley.

Maccoby, M. (1993) 'Why should learning organisations learn?' *Research Technology Management*, May/June, pp. 49–52.

McFarlan, F. W. (1984) 'New electronics systems can add value to your product and throw your competition off balance'. *Harvard Business Review*, May/June, pp.98-103.

Meiklejohn, I. (1990) 'Whole role for hybrid'. *Management Today*, pp. 113–116.

Mintzberg, H. (1993) *The rise and fall of strategic planning*. Prentice Hall

Mitev, N.N. (1994) 'The business failure of knowledge-based systems: linking knowledge-based systems and information systems methodologies for strategic planning'. *Journal of Information Technology*, Vol, 9, pp. 173–184.

Morone, J.G. (1993) 'Technology and competitive advantage – the role of general management'. *Research Technology Management*, pp. 6–25.

Nolan, R.L. (1977) 'Controlling the costs of data services'. *Harvard Business Review,* July/August, pp. 114–124.

Nonaka, I. (1991) 'The knowledge-creating company'. *Harvard Business Review*, November/December, pp. 96–104.

Palmer, C., Ottley, S. (1990) *From potential to reality: hybrids – critical force in the application of information technology in the 1990s*. A report by the BCS Task Group in Hybrids, British Computer Society.

Parsons, G.L. (1983) 'Information technology: a strategic opportunity'. *Sloan Management Review*, Vol, 25, No. 1, Fall, pp. 3–14.

Porter, M., Millar, V. (1985) 'How information gives you a competitive advantage'. *Harvard Business Review*. July/August, pp. 149–160.

Porter, M. (1985) *Competitive Advantage: creating and sustaining superior performance*. Free Press: New York.

Pugh, D. S., Hickson, D. J., Hinings, C. R., & Turner, C. (1969a) 'The context of organisational structures'. *Administrative Science Quarterly*, Vol, 14, No. 1, pp. 91–114.

Pugh, D. S., Hickson, D. J. & Hinings, C. R. (1969b) 'An empirical taxonomy of structures of work organisation'. *Administrative Science Quarterly*, Vol, 14, pp. 115–126.

Rowe, C., Herbert, B. (1990) 'IT in the boardroom: the growth of computer awareness among chief executives'. *Journal of General Management*, Vol, 14, No. 4, pp. 32–44.

Sauer, C. (1993) *Why information systems fail: a case study approach*. Alfred Waller, Henley on Thames.

Senge, P.M. (1990) 'The leader's new work: building learning organisations'. *Sloan Management Review*, Vol, 32, pp. 7–23.

Shank, J.K., Govindarajan, V. (1992) 'Strategic cost analysis of technological investments'. *Sloan Management Review*, Fall, pp. 39–51.

Sinur, J. (1994) 'Questions and answers – legacy systems'. *Applications, Development and Management Strategies*, Research note. Published by the Gartner Group, Stamford, CT.

Stammers, T. (1994) 'DEC's Alpha chip for the future' *PC Week*, 20.9.94, pp. 16.

Stata, R (1989) 'Organisational learning – the key to management innovation'. *Sloan Management Review,* Spring, pp. 63–74.

Synot, W.R. (1987) *The information weapon: winning customers and markets with technology*. Wiley.

Thamhain, H.J. (1992) 'Developing the skills you need'. *Research Technology Management*, pp. 42–47.

Tricker, R. I. (1992) 'The management of organisational knowledge', in R. Galliers (ed) *Information Systems Research*. Alfred Waller, Henley on Thames, pp. 14-27.

Vedin, B. (ed) (1994) *Management of change and innovation*. Dartmouth, Aldershot.

Walsham, G. (1993) *Interpreting information systems*, Wiley.

Wijnhoven, A.B.J.M., Wassenaar, D.A. (1990) 'Impact of information technology on organisations: the state of the art'. *International Journal of Information Management'*, Vol, 10, pp. 35–53.

Willcocks, L., Griffiths, C. (1994) *Management and risk issues in large-scale IT projects: a comparative analysis*. Oxford Institute of Information Management, Templeton College, Oxford.

Wysocki, R.K., Young, J. (1990) *Information systems*. Wiley.

CHAPTER 2

Information Technology and Competitive Advantage

Introduction

In the last decade a wealth of academic and business literature has emerged on the relationship between IT and competitive advantage. Much of this literature is prescriptive since it advises managers about the competitive advantages to be gained by introducing the latest technology. Whilst the use of IT prior to the early 1980s was believed to offer competitive advantages through increased productivity and reduced costs, the current wave of technological change is seen to offer companies unprecedented benefits in the form of an information resource (Porter and Millar, 1985). Irrespective of the nature of the business, IT is perceived as a vital panacea to sustain and improve competitive position.

The success stories span a variety of industrial and commercial sectors. Key IT applications leading to competitive advantage include the much publicised American Airlines reservation system SABRE; Merrill Lynch's account management system; the use of IT at Otis Elevators; the on-line reservation system TOP at Thompson holidays and many more. Business advantages from IT are perceived to arise in the following interrelated fields. First, IT is seen as a vital tool to enhance a company's competitive position over its rivals. Second, the strategic use of IT will improve productivity and performance throughout the organisation. Third, IT will facilitate new ways of managing and organising work. Fourth, IT will generate new business since it provides faster and more timely information for decision making (Earl, 1989. Porter, 1985).

The interest in the link between IT and competitive advantage is fuelled by the need for companies to compete more effectively in the global marketplace. This concern is related to the wider debate about the industrial decline of Anglo/American economies in recent years (Porter, 1992. Thompson, 1989). Many studies show the progressive economic decline of Anglo/American businesses, particularly in manufacturing, and the loss of market position to overseas rivals, notably the Japanese (Williams, et al, 1991). Opinions differ on exactly when this decline began, although a consensus exists that many west European and North American companies have 'managed their way to economic decline' through poor process and product innovation strategies, an emphasis on short-termism and lack of training to name but a few (Hayes and Abernathy, 1980). This has not been helped by government industrial policy (or the lack of it) which dictates that companies either 'sink or swim' depending upon market forces and their ability to successfully manage innovation and change (HMSO, 1994).

Poor economic performance of many Anglo/American companies throughout the 1980s and 1990s has led to more serious problems of numerous company closures and high unemployment. Economic ills of this nature, coupled with intense overseas competition and the perception of a widening technology gap between Japan and the West, have encouraged business organisations to reconsider their IT strategies (assuming they have them). This is also fuelled by new entrants to the competitive arena in the form of the emerging markets of the Pacific rim and central and eastern Europe. Other competitive threats exist in the form of the recent deregulation of the financial services sector and new EC rules on competitive tendering for public sector contracts. Faced with these challenges it is little wonder that firms look towards IT as an effective solution to their problems.

The perception of IT as an effective panacea to enhance competitive position is greatly assisted by the slick marketing by management consultants and IT suppliers. Here IT is seen as a tool to enhance productivity and reduce headcount. Indeed, many IT vendors use the same list of benefits to justify the purchase of their product whether this is computer aided design (CAD) or office automation. Vendor 'hype' about technology is often expressed on the basis that, unless firms keep up to date with the latest state-of-the-art technology, they will be outstripped by their competitors. This argument assumes that firms have a simple choice. They either 'automate or liquidate' (Currie et al, 1993).

This chapter explores the popular link between competitive advantage and IT by reviewing influential contributions from British and North American sources. It is argued that one problem in forming a conceptual link between competitiveness and technology is the assumption that technical change alone is the panacea to cure industrial ills of low profitability and performance. The discussion draws from a number of relevant examples on the strategic choices facing companies in their pursuit to achieve competitive advantage through IT. It concludes by arguing that whilst IT may improve efficiency and performance, the more ambitious goal of competitive advantage from IT is attained only under certain conditions. This is dependent upon the ability of companies to nurture a culture of innovation which places a high premium on organisational learning, skills and training, and a better fit between IT, structure and strategy.

Competitive advantage, technology and the value chain

The popular literature on the link between IT and competitive advantage in the 1980s stressed the importance of using information as a resource. Some writers even went as far as to speak of 'an information revolution' and cautioned that all companies would be affected by it (Forester, 1980). The notion that IT would 'transform' administrative processes, products, company structures and hierarchies, the nature of work organisation and even the rules of competition urged many senior executives to start thinking about an IT strategy for their company. IT was no longer to be perceived in the narrow context of the responsibilities of the EDP or IS department (Tavakolian, 1991). Instead it had to be understood as a valuable resource which would be instrumental in creating and sustaining competitive advantage.

Porter and Millar's (1985) influential article on 'How information gives you competitive advantage' outlined three areas where 'the information revolution' was affecting the rules of competition. They said that:

- IT changes industry structure and, in so doing, alters the rules of competition
- IT creates competitive advantage by giving companies new ways to outperform their rivals
- IT spawns whole new businesses, often from within a company's existing operations

The authors assert that information technology 'is more than just computers'. They argue that an important concept linking IT and competition is the 'value chain' (Figure 2.1). The value chain

'divides a company's activities into the technologically and economically distinct activities it performs to do business. We call these value activities. The value a company creates is measured by the amount that buyers are willing to pay for a product or service. A business is profitable if the values it creates exceeds the cost of performing the value activities. To gain competitive advantage over its rivals, a company must either perform these activities at a lower cost or perform them in a way that leads to differentiation and a premium price (more value).... The value chain for a company in a particular industry is embedded in a larger stream of activities that we term the 'value system'.... Every value activity has both a physical and an information-processing component. The physical component includes all the physical tasks required to perform the activity. The information-processing component encompasses the steps required to capture, manipulate, and channel the data necessary to perform the activity' (Porter and Millar, p. 150–2).

Firm Infastructure	Planning models				
Human resource management	Automated personnel scheduling				
Technology development	Computer-aided design	Electronic market research			
Procurement	On-line procurement of parts				
	Automated warehouse	Flexible manufacturing	Automated order processing	Telemarketing Remote terminals for salespersons	Remote servicing of equipment Computer scheduling and routing of repair trucks
	Inbound logistics	Operations	Outbound logistics	Marketing and sales	Service
	Primary activities				**Margin**

Figure 2.1 Information technology permeates the value chain (adapted from Porter and Millar, 1985)

Key to the work of Porter and Millar is the notion that technology has a crucial role to play in improving efficiency levels, specifically in relation to information processing. These authors seemingly adopt a technological determinist position since they ascribe a critical role for IT in transforming businesses from non-profitable to profitable entities. IT is seen to play a crucial part in the attainment of competitive advantage since its organisational impact is all-pervasive. The authors develop a framework which shows that IT permeates the value chain. They divide a firm's activities into two broad categories – primary and support activities. Here technology development is classified as a support activity along with the firm infrastructure, human resources and procurement activities.

The framework outlines a variety of technologies from CAD to flexible manufacturing. The important message is that IT may be used in all the company's activities and different technologies may reflect key managerial strategies at a given point in time. For example, the introduction of a MIS for the on-line procurement of parts may be used alongside the JIT production management system (Currie and Seddon, 1992). This will alter a company's dealings with its suppliers and customers by driving down the costs of inventory, while at the same time improving its ability to deliver quality products on time. IT used in the marketing and sales areas may provide valuable information for managers which will, in turn, enable them to take more informed product strategy decisions. Similarly, IT used in management accounting in the form of relational databases may greatly improve a company's understanding of product costs and profitability (Wu, Seddon and Currie, 1992).

Porter and Millar (1985) stress the importance of linking technologies throughout the firm to improve overall efficiency and cost reduction. In spite of large capital expenditure on IT, the authors argue that the effective use of technology will produce a whole variety of business benefits such as improved productivity and efficiency, less bureaucracy, data/information for strategic decision making (e.g. for marketing, production, HRM, accounting, among others), cost reduction, and also the ability to 'spawn new businesses'.

The concept of the value chain is important since it illustrates the range of benefits available to companies which effectively manage the internal and external linkages relating to their key activities. Using IT strategically, a company may find that it is spending too much time and money on one particular area. A good example of this is found in Japan, where managers use IT to measure manufacturing performance in a variety of areas. For example, even though they measure direct and indirect labour and materials costs in line with Anglo/American companies, they go further than their competitors in their attempt to break-down overhead costs. Here they measure performance indicators on machine capacity and downtime, scrap and waste levels, space allocation and product quality and rework (Currie, 1991).

Japanese firms also place a high value on managing the activities of their suppliers, and this is a crucial element of the JIT philosophy. This enables them to focus on those areas where performance is poor so they can develop problem solving solutions. Interestingly, whereas the Japanese have ruthlessly pursued efficiency measures in the manufacturing arena, recent evidence suggests that their exploitation of IT in administrative/support areas has been poor (*Japan Times*, 1994). Many Japanese companies are therefore seeking solutions to improve their administrative operations, with the accent on job reduction through 're-engineering' and restructuring. Such a situation will inevitably lead to the end of the much prized life-time employment system (Hori, 1993). This is discussed more thoroughly in chapter eleven.

However, in accordance with Porter and Millar's recommendations, Japanese manufacturers seemingly show a greater propensity to measure cross-functional performance than their western counterparts. This is achieved by the development of management information systems (MISs) and decision support systems (DSSs) where relational databases can feed data on manufacturing performance to the accounting and HR departments for business analysis. The generation of data to expose poor performing areas is obviously useful for the purpose of identifying areas for performance improvements. The idea of the value chain is therefore important since it encourages managers to look beyond their narrow functional area. By doing so, they are able to adopt a company-wide approach to performance measurement.

Another area addressed by Porter and Millar is how IT can generate new business. This is seen to occur in three distinct ways. First, many ideas for new businesses can only be enacted if they are 'technologically feasible'. With the development of commercial ITs in recent years, many new process and product technologies have entered the market. The authors cite the example of modern imaging and telecommunications technology which support facsimile services such as Federal Express's Zapmail. Numerous other examples also exist.

Second, the authors demonstrate how IT can create a demand for new and improved products. They cite the example of Western Union's EasyLink service, which is a high-speed data communications network that allows PCs, wordprocessors and other electronic devices to communicate internationally.

Third, they show how new businesses may emerge from existing businesses. The financial services sector is a good example with the development of the First Direct bank (see below). In their article, Porter and Millar (1985, p.158) advocate five steps which senior executives may follow to 'take advantage of opportunities that the information revolution has created'. They are as follows:

- Assess information intensity
- Determine the role of information technology in industry structure
- Identify and rank the ways in which information technology might create competitive advantage
- Investigate how information technology might spawn new businesses
- Develop a plan for taking advantage of information technology

The authors assert that companies need to evaluate the information intensity in the value chain of their entire operations. Businesses with a vast number of suppliers and clients will obviously find this task quite daunting since the scope for information will be all-consuming. It is likely that a more manageable task will be to identify only a few areas for performance improvement, and seek to develop technical applications accordingly. The authors further advise managers to 'predict the likely impact of information technology on their industry's structure'. Whilst this is important, a common problem facing companies is their lack of internal expertise to make such predictions. This is not helped by the rapid pace of technical change, and the less than objective advice given to firms by IT suppliers regarding IT benefits. Similarly the task of identifying and ranking how IT leads to competitive advantage is equally challenging. It is argued that competitive advantage through IT demands high-level capital investment which only the large organisations can meet.

Whereas some technological developments in the form of the Automated Teller Machine (ATM), for example, have significantly changed the operations of banks, the outcome of the more esoteric applications development work undertaken by the same organisations may be difficult to predict. Large-scale IT development work is both high risk and expensive, and the outcome may be successful or unsuccessful (as in the case of TAURUS, see Currie, 1994).

The exploitation of technology to develop new businesses is often cited as indicative of the IT revolution. Again, IT has been used in a variety of companies for new business development, in addition to rationalising existing businesses in manufacturing and financial services. Yet given the range of technologies available, the vast majority of IT is used in a support capacity. This is particularly the case in administrative and clerical work.

Finally, Porter and Millar advise managers to develop an effective plan to exploit IT in their organisation, in other words an IT strategy. The main message of Porter and Millar's (1985) work is that IT can achieve competitive advantage in a variety of commercial settings. The conceptual framework is also useful since it highlights the links between business activities and the IT choices available to companies. This issue is addressed in more detail in the following section.

IT and competitive advantage

Another influential writer on IT and competitive advantage is McFarlan (1984, p.98) who cites three examples where business organisations have gained competitive advantage from IT. First, a major distributor offers its customers the opportunity to enter their orders direct by using an on-line network. The main advantage of the system is to reduce order-entry costs, while at the same time enhancing flexibility to customers in the time and processing of order submission. Further advantages accrue from the system in the form of 'adding value for customers and a substantial rise in their sales'.

Second, a regional airline seeks to testify to the US Congress that a national carrier has substantially reduced its competitive position. It asserts that the national carrier, 'through access to the reservation levels on every one of the smaller airline's flights, can pinpoint all mutually competitive routes where the regional is performing well and take competitive pricing and service action'. The fact that the regional airline is unable to gain access to the data held by the national carrier renders the former at a competitive disadvantage. Third, a major aerospace company has requested that all its key suppliers implement CAD to its own CAD installation. This would significantly reduce the time and cost of carrying out design changes, parts acquisition and inventory. Such a change would again lead to competitive advantage.

McFarlan (1984) urges companies to address five key questions in relation to the impact of technology. He asserts that if the answer is *yes* to one or more of the questions, then 'information technology represents a strategic resource that requires attention at the highest level'. The questions are as follows:

- Can IS technology build barriers to entry?
- Can IS technology build in switching costs?
- Can the technology change the basis of competition?
- Can IS change the balance of power in supplier relationships?
- Can IS technology generate new products?

In the case of barriers to entry, McFarlan argues that it is important for companies to 'hook' their customers into using their products and services. In the case of the distributor mentioned above, the company successfully opened up a new electronic channel to its customers which was unrivalled by its competitors. Customers were further reluctant to introduce technology into their companies from competing vendors (distributors). McFarlan (1984, p.99) argues that

'An example of such a defensible barrier is the development of a complex software package that adds value and is capable of evolution and refinement. A large financial service firm used this approach to launch a different and highly attractive financial product, depending on sophisticated software. Because of the complexity of the concept and its software, competitors lagged behind, giving the firm valuable time to establish market position. Further, the firm has been able to enhance its original product significantly, thus making itself a moving target'.

In another area, he asserts that customer reliance on the suppliers electronic support system coupled with increased operational dependence and 'normal human inertia' are likely to reduce the prospect of choosing another supplier. He uses the example of electronic home banking in that once a customer has learned to use the system, it is likely that the time and cost of selecting and learning another home banking system will be prohibitive. Thus, the customer is successfully 'hooked' by the supplier.

Reflecting on whether IT can change the basis of competition, McFarlan, along with others, argues that in industries dominated by 'cost-based competition', technology has 'permitted development of product features that are so different that they cause the basis of competition to change radically'. He cites an example of a major distributor of magazines to newstands and stores. This industry was considered to be dominated by *cost-based* competition. During the 1970s, the company used electronic technology for cost control in the sorting and distribution processes. Fewer staff were required and inventory levels were also kept to a minimum. The company therefore became a low-cost producer. This strategy was effective during this period but required radical rethinking later on.

This took place during the late 1970s when the company decided to capitalise on the knowledge that the majority of its customer were 'small' and 'unsophisticated', and not aware of their profit margins or cost-base. The company decided to utilise its records of weekly shipments and returns from a newstand to provide relevant information of what was being purchased on each newstand. Programs were developed to calculate profit per square foot for every magazine. This information was related to the magazine sales from each newstand taking into consideration the ethnic and economic composition of the particular locality.

The exercise enabled the distributor to forecast how each newstand could improve its product mix. McFarlan states that, 'Instead of just distributing magazines, the company has used technology to add a valuable inventory management feature that has permitted it to raise prices substantially and has changed the basis of competition from cost to product differentiation'.

The strategic use of IT has enhanced the competitive position of companies in a variety of sectors. In manufacturing industry for example, the effective use of AMT in the form of CAD/CAM, FMS, robotics, NC, etc, in conjunction with the adoption of new management practices such as JIT, TQM and TPM, among others, have significantly altered the rules of competition.

Similarly the financial services sector has witnessed vast changes brought about by new technologies such as the client-server architecture, multi-tasking (MS Windows) and 4GLs. New methodologies have further influenced the rules of competition in banking and insurance in the form of object-oriented programming (OOP). These technologies were discussed in more detail in the previous chapter.

Using a similar approach to Porter and Millar (1985) above, McFarlan (1984) provides a strategic grid in which to locate firms depending on their use of IT. The strategic grid offers a useful conceptual framework and reinforces the point that not all firms

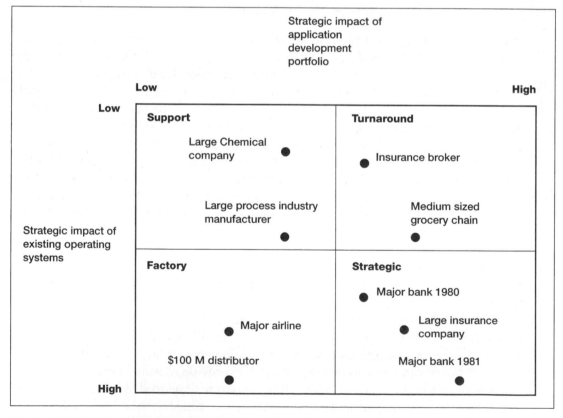

Figure 2.2 Position of information systems in various types of companies
(*Courtesy:* McFarlan, 1984)

necessarily use IT strategically. On the contrary, some may not need to employ IT as a strategic device.

In the case of the large chemical company and process industry manufacturer, IT is seen as a providing a *support* activity. These organisations are not characterised by their high investment in IT. Nor is it likely that senior executives will incorporate IT as part of their overall strategic business plan. This scenario adequately fits managements' perceptions of IT in what has been described as the DP or EDP era, when it was common for technology to be managed by IT professionals alone (Earl, 1989. Friedman, 1989. Gibson and Nolan, 1974. Nolan, 1977, 1979).

Earl (1989) also utilises this framework, but unlike McFarlan he contends that a cement company would adequately fit the *support* quadrant. He states that

> 'Perhaps a cement company would fit this quadrant where some administrative systems help improve internal efficiency and islands of specialist technology may be gradually introduced to innovate the manufacturing process'.

In the area of the *factory* quadrant, McFarlan places a $100 million distributor company and a major airline. This quadrant incorporates IT which is crucial to existing operations but is not critical to a company's overall strategic direction.

Earl (1989, p. 6) instead places a steel works in this quadrant. He contends that advanced on-line, real-time systems were a product of the DP era. These designated systems were designed for planning and controlling iron and steel production. They were an important part of running the business, although not crucial to the company's survival. Here it is important to run a tightly managed shop as far as technology is concerned, but the IT budget must not exceed agreed financial limits. In the factory quadrant, it is likely that IT budgets are significant, yet the key goals are reliability and efficiency. Large-scale, large-budget speculative IT systems development work is not usually undertaken by those firms in the factory quadrant.

The *strategic* quadrant is arguably one of the most important for assessing the degree to which companies deploy IT for competitive advantage. Here, McFarlan cites two financial service organisations – a major bank and a large insurance company. Without IT these organisations would not function. Similarly, Earl uses a credit card company as another example. In the *strategic* quadrant, IT has always been, and will continue to be, crucial to all aspects of the business, for IT is a major part of the corporate infrastructure. Here IT is an integral part of the business. Product-market strategies and IT are inextricably linked and IT is clearly more than a support function. As a result, the IT budget is likely to be huge, and an IT director is likely to sit on the main board. In addition, line managers receiving IT services ideally have a good understanding of the strategic uses of IT, and may even spearhead systems development work. The vast financial resources invested in IT in the financial services sector is further indicative of the strategic use of IT in core and service business processes. This is confirmed by comments from senior banking executives that, 'if we want a system, we develop it ourselves'. Large IT departments in banks therefore see themselves as not only following but leading in the area of systems development for large-scale IT projects (Currie, 1994b).

In the fourth quadrant, companies recognise the growing importance of IT as a means to improve competitive position, and are thus described as operating in a *turnaround* situation. McFarlan cites two examples – an insurance broker and a medium-sized grocery chain. Whilst IT may not have been important in the past, the current competitive economic climate has forced these firms to reassess their operations. This line of reasoning is indicative of the 'automate or liquidate' logic which challenges firms to improve their operations in order to stay in business. Earl (1989, p.7) says that, 'In such turnaround firms, IT budgets are jumping up step-curves, leadership is coming from the board, a top IT executive is being appointed, and education programmes on information management are being commissioned for senior executives. A variety chain store retailer exemplifies this quadrant'.

The strategic grid is a useful analytical tool to determine where firms are positioned in four distinct quadrants. It also represents whether a firm uses IT strategically or otherwise at a given point in time. As we can see from McFarlan's company examples, the strategic use of IT was enhanced at a major bank within the space of one year. This is demonstrated in practice in a number of ways. First, the increased sophistication of new technologies adopted by the bank. Banks have further improved their strategic use of technology since McFarlan's 1984 example as demonstrated by the current choice in technologies to include the new client-server environment, multi-tasking and OOPs.

But the recognition that competitors also deploy IT strategically means that competition becomes increasingly cut-throat, forcing businesses to look for cost savings elsewhere, i.e. staff reduction, productivity improvements, new business development, business process reengineering, among others.

Again, using the example of banking, IT has significantly improved information about customers and their behaviour, and also enabled the development of new services to be targeted to selected customers (both domestic and corporate).

Earl (1989) contends that three forces drive the strategic grid. They include:

- The relationship between the potential of IT and a firm's operations and strategy (e.g. selecting the most appropriate technology in the marketplace for the nature of the business)
- Executive strategic choices for IT (e.g. staff reduction, business development or productivity and quality enhancements)
- Competitive environment (e.g. an assessment of what competitors are doing and their exploitation of IT)

An appropriate example of a firm occupying the *strategic* grid is the First Direct bank. Peppard (1993, p. 62) claims that

'Technology now underpins most new services provided by financial institutions. In retail banking, it has become very expensive to have branch office presence in prime locations. IS/IT in the form of automated teller machines (ATMs) reduced significantly the costs associated with having a high street presence. The Midland Bank launched its First Direct banking initiative in 1989. This was the UK's first bank to open 24 hours, 7 days of the week. It has no branches or local staff as all its transactions are handled over the telephone. Customers can pay bills, arrange personal loans, order foreign exchange, etc. In order to make this service possible a sophisticated computer and communication system had to be designed to enable each First Direct bank clerk to have all information on every customer at his/her fingertips'.

In a changing business climate characterised by intense competition, Earl (1989) argues that firms occupying the *factory* or *support* quadrants are now realising that their survival depends upon an effective business strategy which takes into account the strategic use of IT. Many of these firms have now moved into the *turnaround* quadrant since they have embarked upon ambitious programmes to improve their competitive position using state-of-the-art technology. However, the realisation that IT is crucial in the pursuit of competitive advantage is not sufficient in itself. Firms originally occupying the *support* and *factory* quadrants are unlikely to change their perception of the role of IT overnight even though they may recognise that capital investment in the latest technology is a vital ingredient for survival.

Four interrelated reasons are paramount. First, it is likely that the DP legacy prevails in these firms where IT is perceived as a support function for other departments. Old habits die hard and such a perception will arguably influence management decisions on investment appraisal and implementation of IT. Many companies continue to be structured in the traditional functionally-based way. This contributes to the marginalisation of the IT department as it competes for resources like other departments.

Second, the perception that IT provides a service is somewhat incongruous with the notion that IT plays a strategic role in the organisation. In management accounting terms, the IT department or division is usually classified as a cost-centre and, like many other cost centres, is likely to be rationalised in periods of recession.

Third, *factory* or *support* firms attempting to maximise the use of IT are unlikely to have highly trained IT personnel at all levels. Again, the assumption that IT is a cost burden may actually inhibit the transition to a *turnaround* situation if adequate investment is not made in hardware and software, skills development and training. Employees may be reluctant to learn new skills and, in many cases, the firms wishing to upgrade their IT facility may not have the in-house expertise to provide training. External training for all is also likely to be perceived by managers as too expensive.

Fourth, it is unusual for firms without a history of strategically managing IT to have a mixture of technical and business skills at board level. Such an absence of *hybrid* skills may significantly reduce the opportunity to formulate and implement effective IT strategies (Earl and Skyme, 1992). Indeed, a shortfall in business-related IT skills at this level may lead to the development of poor IT strategies – resulting in a competitive disadvantage.

There are numerous examples where firms have squandered resources in the pursuit of strategic IT applications development. Yet the overriding message from the management literature on IT urges firms to learn from the IT success stories. Perhaps a more appropriate approach to IT strategy would be to consider the many pitfalls of introducing IT!

McFarlan (1984) finally considers the potential of IT to change the balance of power in supplier relationships to enable new product development. He cites the example where JIT control systems can significantly reduce inventory levels in the automobile industry among others. CAD systems also offer competitive advantages in the form of better quality design drawings, ease of modification, storage and retrieval. However, vendor 'hype' about the advantages of CAD must be treated with caution.

As Medland and Burnett (1986, p. 143) argue, the 'fallacy' of enhanced productivity from CAD is not a reliable justification in isolation even though it is by far the most common justification for CAD. Thus

'It is far from being the case that more drawings are equivalent to more, or better, design. On the contrary, more drawings may not only mean that unnecessary work is being done inefficiently; they may also result in unnecessary work being done, or necessary work being done inefficiently at the manufacturing stage. It would in many ways make far more sense to turn the argument on its head and justify CAD on the grounds that it allows designers to do more or better work while producing fewer drawings'.

In the case of new product generation, there are numerous examples in both the financial services sector and in manufacturing industry where information and advanced manufacturing technology have generated new services and products. New services may be internally and/or externally provided. For example, the ability to generate new data and transform it into vital information may improve the internal efficiency of a bank, for example, and generate new business externally.

The example of the First Direct bank given above is significant in the development of a new business opportunity. Similarly, in the case of IT, AMT, decision support systems (DSS), and management information systems (MIS), better quality data may be obtained in a number of performance areas. Improved information will benefit all aspects of the business from the personnel department through to production and marketing. In the case of CAD, the issue is not simply whether it will improve the efficiency or productivity of designers, but its capability to undertake work which could not be done using manual methods (the drawing board).

Medland and Burnett (1986, p.152) address this issue by stating that

'Although most CAD systems will obviously have to be justified on the grounds that they will allow a business to do the things it is already doing better, faster or more economically and efficiently, it is important not to forget that CAD may also allow a business to do things that it could not do before. In some instances this can be because the skills required were simply not available prior to the advent of CAD.... In others it is because CAD offers an opportunity for looking at a design problem from a new angle and thus leads to new solutions being found for old problems'.

Whilst these authors agree that CAD may achieve competitive advantage they advocate caution in the evaluation and investment appraisal of the technology. As we shall see in chapter four, some companies have simply adopted the vendor's list of justifications for CAD (not to mention other technologies) in spite of the obvious conflict of interests. This suggests that the customer's perception of CAD as a competitive weapon may be at odds with their practical experience, particularly when CAD fails to deliver vendor's promises. This may lead to the investment being perceived as a failure and possible under-investment in future IT projects. The solution to the problem of poor performance of technology is often perceived as poor strategy formulation, or no strategy whatsoever.

In this context, the next section considers some of the key issues relating to strategic planning for IT, as strategic planning is often seen as the route to achieving competitive success through IT.

Strategic information systems planning

Earl (1992) contends that strategic information systems planning (SISP) has become a key priority in many organisations in recent years. A study into SISP experiences in twenty seven companies, where IS managers were interviewed along with general and line managers, found that five different SISP approaches were being adopted. They are labelled as follows: Business-Led, Method-Driven, Administrative, Technological, and Organisational. The taxonomy of five areas is intended as a diagnostic tool for evaluating and analysing company SISP experience. Earl however recognises that whilst companies may produce formal documentation outlining their strategic and operational plans for technology, it is important to remember that informal, *ad hoc* sub-strategies also emerge. Indeed, the political dimension of SISP should not be overlooked (Markhus, 1983).

The study found that four companies and two case study firms (a more in-depth analysis of firms) adopted the business-led approach to managing IS. This figure is surprisingly low given the wave of literature throughout the late 1980s and 1990s on the importance of aligning business needs with IT. Indeed, much of this literature merely assumes a strong relationship between IT and business benefits. The business-led approach asserts that business planning should 'drive' SISP and not the other way around. In the majority of companies (particularly in the UK) business planning is an annual managerial exercise. In the context of business planning for IT, it is common for companies to pinpoint the business areas which require IT applications development, etc. The person responsible for this activity is usually the IT or IS director (but it is important to remember that these positions are not commonplace in all companies).

Once the IT director has determined the areas requiring IT investment, it is written into the business plan before it is put to the board of directors for approval. The board of directors in this capacity are likely to undertake a 'rubber-stamping' operation and assess the proposed expenditure on the basis of a 'sound financial case'. The business plan is likely to contain a detailed financial breakdown of proposed IT expenditure for the coming year. The plan will also contain a summary of expected benefits. They may be in the form of productivity and quality enhancements in specific business areas, labour reduction, and the use of new IT applications to generate new business (Currie, 1989. Farbey et al, 1993).

However the attainment of an itemised list of business benefits from IT or the more ambitious goal of competitive advantage is not clear cut. In many companies, the exercise of formulating a business plan for IT serves more as an outline of how resources will be spent and the expected business benefits. It is less common in Anglo/American companies for business plans to contain detailed accounts of how these benefits will be met in practice.

According to Earl (1992, p.8), 'General managers see this approach as simple, 'business-like', and a matter of common sense. IS executives often see this form of SISP as their most critical task and welcome the long overdue mandate from senior management.' Yet the formation and implementation of business strategies is not clear-cut. This creates problems for IS managers who have to interpret business strategies in accordance with their own IT strategy. In many organisations, business strategies are implicit rather than explicit, and IS managers have to embark upon lengthy processes of interviewing managers, convening meetings, analysing documents and assessing where the business is going, prior to formulating IT proposals. Power struggles may also occur when IS managers take the lead in proposing IT solutions to specific business problems, particularly where business managers feel threatened by IT. Similarly, IS managers may experience communication difficulties with general managers, as IT options tend to be shrouded in confusing terminology, not easily understood by the latter.

Earl further states that it is unlikely that users and line managers will be involved in the formulation of the IT business plan. This creates additional problems in the process of evaluating and implementing IT and ultimately in the achievement of any tangible benefits leading to competitive advantage. For even though it is important that IT directors or managers formulate an IT strategy for the business, the perception from users and other 'stakeholders' that IT strategy is a 'product' of the IT function further adds to the remoteness of IT within the organisation. This is witnessed by the comments from users that IT rarely meets their needs, which leads to a reluctance by top management to commit further resources to future IT projects.

Against a background of strategic planning problems for IT, Earl (1992) nonetheless claims that the general perception that IT is a strategic resource heightens the status of the IT department and gives 'greater legitimacy' to its activities. In turn, IT representation at board level, even without the support of line managers and users, also serves to increase the time spent by senior managers on IT-related matters.

A second approach adopted by companies for their SISP is called the method-driven approach (Earl, 1992). This approach was adopted in two companies and a further two case study firms. Advocates of the method-driven approach prefer formal methodologies and techniques for the planning and implementation of IT. Earl contends that some of the problems related to the business-led approach may drive IT directors to seek a method. This is also fuelled by the fashionable literature on strategic planning as a prerequisite to improving performance. The desire for a method may involve the use of external management consultants for IT strategy formulation (if not implementation), or simply to enhance the status of IT planning for the boardroom agenda. Earl is critical of this approach since he argues that formal methods for SISP seldom provide a remedy because they are unlikely to incorporate a 'strong enough business strategy technique'. Furthermore, those who advocate a formal method are unlikely to possess the relevant skills.

The method-driven approach is likely to be pursued in one or two forms. First a 'figurehead personality' (commonly labelled a technical champion) may drive IT strategy from within the company. This person is likely to strongly influence senior managers even though their knowledge and experience of business-related IT matters may be limited. As we shall see elsewhere in the book, there are numerous senior managers in charge of IT departments in Anglo/American companies who lack technical knowledge. Their entry into these positions is based on their knowledge of business administration or, alternatively, the length of time they have worked in the company rather than their technical expertise. One reason why people with business skills are preferred over technical professionals is the perception (usually by non-technical managers) that the former are 'better communicators'.

Here, technical people suffer what may be described as *professional stereotyping*. Because they are seen to possess technical skills, it follows (so the argument goes) that they prefer to work with computers as opposed to communicating with people at all levels of the organisation. This perception has led to the emergence of a dual career structure in many leading organisations where it is uncommon for technical professionals to enter management as the entry criteria for a managerial career path is evidence of 'business knowledge' coupled with good 'communication skills'. This subject is discussed at greater length in chapter five.

Where IT business-related skills are in short supply in organisations (whether this is merely the perception of senior managers or a practical reality) the search for a formal method may involve the use of external management consultants. Indeed, an absence of people with adequate technical skills at senior levels (whether this is based on prejudice or not) leaves little alternative but to use consultants – since the formulation of a method implies some knowledge of technical processes. Earl (1992, p.8) contends that

> 'Often a vendor or consultant plays a significant role. As the challenges unfold, stakeholders determine the 'best' method, often as a result of the qualities of the consultants as much as the techniques themselves. The consultants often become the drivers of the SISP exercise and therefore have substantial influence on the recommendations'.

One of the most formidable problems of using external consultants is the failure of their IT strategy or *method* to be adopted by the client company. As Earl points out, those who are intended to embrace such a strategy may simply label it as the 'xyz strategy'. In other words, it is the strategy of the consultancy firm and not that of the client. In spite of claims that the strategy is 'tailored' to the client's needs, the strategy is likely to contain all the prejudices of the consultant (or team of consultants) and/or, at worst, simply constitute an off-the-shelf, unworkable solution and be of no use to anybody. The consultant's recommendations may therefore be deemed inappropriate by senior managers for a variety of reasons.

First, top managers may be reluctant to accept the strategy if it advises high expenditure on IT. Such advice may contradict the business plan (which may not be related to the consultancy firm's report). Second, 'off-the-shelf' IT solutions proposed by the consultancy firm may not take into consideration many of the informal processes which operate within the client company. Third, IT strategies which involve *re-engineering* or *restructuring* may create internal conflicts and be counterproductive to achieving any tangible benefits from IT. A common example is where people interpret the presence of management consultants as a threat to their job security. Fourth, consultancy advice, as opposed to being radical in content and recommendations, may fail to address the key issues. In this context, senior managers may choose to ignore the advice even though it has consumed a significant amount of company resources.

In the light of the above point, Earl contends that formal methods are problematic although it should be recognised that they 'do not always fail completely'. Occasionally, unexpected benefits accrue from formal methods. Earl cites an example where managers in one company felt they had gained from the exercise since it had exposed the gaps in 'strategic thinking'. Perhaps this is the key benefit of a formal approach to SISP. Unlike the general business-led approach outlined above, the method-driven approach may encourage managers to analyse in greater depth their requirements for IT. Having said this, it is likely that any formal methodology for IT will only be effective if it is developed in accordance with the wider organisational climate in mind (e.g. the existing relationship between IT and other functions; management hierarchy; nature of the business; IT budget; skills profile, etc). This is because, all too often, a solution is put on the boardroom table which advocates an 'ideal-type' scenario with little or no analysis of how the company will achieve this state of affairs. This is particularly the case in some of the more optimistic literature advocating the competitive gains to be made from IT.

The third approach described by Earl is the administrative approach to SISP. This was found in five companies. Here the emphasis is upon resource planning. Earl (1992, p.9) contends that

> 'The wider management planning and control procedures were expected to achieve the aims of SISP through formal procedures for allocating IS resources'.

Different business units or departments submitted IT investment proposals to formal committees. These proposals were then examined on the basis of

> 'project viability, common system possibilities, and resource consequences. In some cases, resource planners did the staff work as proposals ascended the annual hierarchical approval procedure. The administrative approach was the parallel of, or could be attached to, the firm's normal financial planning or capital budgeting routine. The outcome of the approach was a one-year or multi-year development portfolio of approved projects'.

What sets this approach aside from the previous two approaches is the greater bureaucracy underpinning the process of SISP. Apparently, it is unlikely that any system will be developed unless it is written into the annual or 'multi-year development portfolio of approved projects'. Certain pitfalls are associated with this approach. First, the lengthy bureaucratic procedures in formulating an IT strategy may not keep pace with the rapid changes in IT hardware and software. Second, the committee structure, whilst appearing to be methodical and organised in its assessment of IT proposals, may lack a certain flair when it comes to prioritising IT projects for the business. Some committee members are unlikely to possess the relevant IT-related business skills for strategy formulation. This may lead to a tendency to judge individual proposals too simplistically and purely on the basis of their presentation and narrow financial justification for IT expenditure. Third, IT projects that are financed by the steering committee may be subject to alteration at a later date. Again, time delays may inhibit project progress as the owner of the project (the business unit or department) has to seek further committee approval before making any changes. An example is perhaps the decision by a project manager to use an alternative software package for applications development work. Authorisation will need to be obtained before the software package may be purchased and further delays may occur as analyst/programmers and managers require training. Earl cites a common problem with the administrative approach since it may lack a *strategic* dimension to IT planning.

As opposed to formulating strategies from the top, the administrative approach is likely to be 'bottom-up', where a variety of business units or departments compete for scarce resources. This approach is also unlikely to reward individual flair and creativity as project proposers must operate within the rules set out by the steering committee. Such a situation may result in managerial inertia and the emergence of political 'game-playing' as managers learn to manipulate the figures to shed a more optimistic light on their IT preferences (see also Currie, 1989).

A further problem with administratively dominated SISP is the likelihood of capital rationing throughout the organisation. Steering committee decisions to allocate resources in the fairest way may encourage business units to select the cheapest and not necessarily most appropriate IT for their purposes. Similarly, the fragmentation of this approach means that a number of disparate IT systems are likely to emerge, making future plans to integrate data between departments almost impossible.

Drawing on his research, Earl (1992, p.9) contends that, 'The emphasis on resource planning sometimes led to a resource-constrained outcome'. This was demonstrated by the application of spending limits on the IS budget by senior executives. This was done with the view that such cuts would not impose problems for the realisation of IT strategies. Here it is important to remember that whilst steering committees may centrally plan their IT strategies, the practice of administering resources throughout the organisation is determined by selecting from a diverse range of project proposals from business units, divisions or departments. It is therefore highly unlikely that senior managers from different areas have communicated their IT plans with each other. On the contrary, the competitive nature of applying for resources is likely to have the opposite effect where senior managers in the various business-units actively discourage their staff to engage in cross-departmental communication.

Against a background of increased bureaucracy, management and staff inertia, time-delays and the emergence of IT sub-strategies, Earl (1992) found that administratively driven SISP did, however, produce some positive benefits. For example, a clearly defined procedure for requesting resources for IT meant that managers and staff were aware of how the system operated. This clearly has some advantages over *ad hoc*, administratively deficient systems in other companies where resources for IT is given on the strength of a sound business case delivered by a forceful personality!

Another advantage of the administrative approach is that 'all users and units had the opportunity to submit proposals'. Users were therefore more involved and 'were encouraged to make application development requests'. According to Earl, this 'did produce some ideas for building competitive advantage'. On occasion, rules were broken as the CEO or finance director decided to honour a 'radical', off-beat investment proposal which later proved to be successful. This situation demonstrated that, from time to time, IT project proposals were honoured which emphasised wider benefits than ones based purely on financial criteria. For example, proposals may emphasise the need to improve customer service or quality – two important benefits which are difficult to quantify by traditional investment appraisal techniques. Finally, the administrative approach had the advantage of tightening up the resource allocation procedure. IT was managed in conjunction with other business activities which assisted in the objective of aligning IT to the needs of the business.

The fourth approach mentioned by Earl (1992) is the technological approach. This approach was adopted by four companies. This approach is technical in orientation and assumes that 'an information systems-orientated model of the business is a necessary outcome of SISP and, therefore, that analytical modelling methods are appropriate'. Whilst this approach may at first seem reminiscent of the methods-driven approach, it is different in two important respects. First, the final product is a business model or series of models. Second, the approach seeks to apply a formal method based upon 'mapping the activities, processes, and data flows of the business'. This approach is more ambitious than the methods-driven approach since it aims to determine 'blueprints' or 'architectures' for IT planning. These architectures may include 'data, computing, communications, and applications' and computer-aided software engineering (CASE) may be considered an appropriate tool. According to Earl, (1992, p. 10)

'A proprietary technology-orientated method might be used or adapted in-house. Both IS directors and general managers tend to emphasise the objectives of rigorous analysis and of building a robust infrastructure'.

There are at least five identifiable problems with the technical approach to SISP. First, it is particularly time-consuming in terms of individual effort and resources. A full appreciation is needed of how the business operates before any methodology or 'systems architecture' can be meaningful. Second, the emphasis upon building a business model may appear too technical thereupon 'displacing business priorities'. Third, top managers and users are unlikely to fully embrace or even understand the model, let alone be in a position to discern how it will be useful for running the business. Fourth, the failure to understand the model may result in its total rejection by non-technical and even technical personnel, or worse still, an adoption of only some aspects of the model. The case studies on TAURUS and a Scottish bank (featured at the end of the chapter) show that analyst/programmers and managers rarely fully embrace project methodologies in the writing of code even though they are expected to do so by project managers and team leaders. Fifth, a significant problem with formal technology-orientated methods arises because they impose certain rigidities on the business which may be highly inappropriate in a changing business climate. According to Earl (1992, p.10), one company aborted an 'enterprise modelling exercise' on the recommendation of the users and, in another, 'development of the blueprint applications was axed by top management three and a half years after initiation'.

The final approach described by Earl is the organisational approach which was followed in six companies and in one case study firm. This approach is characterised by two key factors. First, SISP is perceived as a process which involves the 'continuous integration' between the IT function and other business units. Second, organisational learning is crucial to the development of IT in three ways. According to Earl, IT development emphasised only one or two themes which would grow in scope over several years. These strategies were seemingly long term as firms planned the development of IT to achieve tangible business benefits over a significant period. Among the examples given by Earl, an insurance company was aiming to reduce administrative costs through IT over time.

In some cases, multi-disciplinary business teams were assigned to work on a particular business problem from which an IT strategy would emerge. The influence of an IT executive on the team was seen here as important because this individual would be able to advise the team on how and why IT would resolve their particular business problems. Also, themes were broken down into specific business-related problems. Occasionally, the failure to meet project deadlines at the agreed cost was acceptable only 'if they allowed evolving ideas to be incorporated'. Earl contends that in some companies, IT strategies were 'discovered through implementation'. This shows that, unlike the common call for companies to develop a strategic plan and then implement it, the organisational approach offers the advantage of organisational learning. Here, IT strategy is formed in an iterative fashion, possibly from a series of sub-strategies. This approach is described as organisational for six key reasons:

1. Collective learning across the organisation is evident.
2. Organisational devices or instruments (teams, task forces, workshops, etc) are used to tackle business problems or pursue initiatives.
3. The IS function works in close partnership with the rest of the organisation, especially through having IS managers on management teams or placing IS executives on task forces.
4. Devolution of some IS capability is common, not only to divisions, but also to functions, factories, and departments.
5. In some companies, SISP is neither special nor abnormal. It is part of the normal business planning of the organisation.
6. IS strategies often emerge from ongoing organisational activities, such as trial-and-error changes to business practices, continuous and incremental enhancement of existing applications, and occasional systems initiatives and experiments within the business.

Earl's (1992) research illustrates the differences in SISP which are adopted in a variety of organisations. This work contributes to our understanding of the management of technology and cautions that not all strategies for innovation are successful or indeed, designed to win competitive advantage. Whilst some companies emphasise financial planning in relation to IT investment, others encourage the pursuit of organisational learning and staff development.

However, a common tendency of most companies featured in Earl's work is the accent on tangible (financial) returns from IT. This is problematic because such a priority tends to favour short-term strategic planning processes over and above a longer-term approach. As the last example shows, many strategies are formed over the long term as a consequence of people learning about the opportunities and pitfalls of introducing technology. Whilst this study does not advocate any one particular approach as being 'ideal' for managerial or administrative purposes, it is useful in the sense that it illustrates a number of options open to decision-makers on how they might choose to introduce IT.

In the next section some recent literature is considered which supports the link between competitive advantage and IT, but advocates process innovation as the way forward for contemporary business organisations.

Gaining competitive advantage through process innovation and re-engineering

Whilst the concept of competitive advantage was popular throughout the 1980s, the 1990s saw the emergence of two other concepts – process innovation and re-engineering. According to Davenport (1993, p.1)

'process innovation combines the adoption of a process view of the business with the application of innovation to key processes. What is new and distinctive about this combination is its enormous potential for helping any organisation achieve major reductions in process cost or time, or major improvements in quality, flexibility, service levels, or other business objectives'.

The author cites a number of examples where firms have gained competitive advantage through process innovation. At IBM Credit, the preparation time for supplying potential customers with a quotation for either purchasing or leasing a computer was reduced from seven days to only one. The result was a tenfold increase in the number of quotes prepared for customers. Another example cited by the author is the insurance company, Mutual Benefit Life, which was trying to offset a declining real estate portfolio and, with the use of IT, actually halved the costs associated with its policy underwriting and insurance process. Similarly, the US Internal Revenue Service made significant gains through process innovation by collecting 33% more dollars from taxpayers with only half its former staff and as many as a third fewer branches.

Davenport claims that radical process change initiatives have been called various names, e.g. business process redesign and business re-engineering. However, he believes the term *process innovation* is more appropriate for a number of reasons. He claims that

'Re-engineering is only part of what is necessary in the radical change process; it refers specifically to the design of a new process. The term process innovation encompasses the envisioning of new work strategies, the actual process design activity, and the implementation of the change in all its complex technological, human, and organisational dimensions' (Davenport, 1993 p.2).

He asserts that process management was discovered and successfully implemented by Japanese companies. This he believes is an important factor in explaining the success of many Japanese manufacturing firms throughout the 1980s and 1990s. In particular, Japanese firms have improved the processes of product development, logistics and sales and marketing.

Davenport asserts that process innovation is invariably 'customer driven'. He cites the automobile and retail industries as two key examples. He contends that due to the intense global competition in the 1980s, automobile manufacturers forced their suppliers to improve the quality, speed and timeliness of their manufacturing and delivery processes. This was done in a number of ways through JIT control systems to MRP II initiatives. However, the result was a general improvement in operations between customer and supplier (if not business relations) as suppliers were invariably forced to accept lower profit margins than before. In the retail industry, Davenport shows how Wal-Mart has established practices of 'continuous replenishment, supplier shelf management, and simplified communications that have significantly influenced its suppliers, including such giants as General Electric' (p.3). IT has obviously been a crucial component in achieving benefits in both these industries, even though the author prefers to attribute these improvements to process innovation.

Unlike many of the above studies which allude to the advantages of perceiving IT in cross-functional terms, the concept of process innovation advocates that IT is unlikely to achieve competitive advantage unless managers adopt a company-wide perspective. Here, companies are seen as comprising a variety of important and not so important business processes. Davenport asserts that it is the task of business managers to identify the key processes and seek ways to improve them – through process innovation. He recognises that this may be difficult given the complexity of organisations, but argues that the efficient management of between 10 and 20 processes will greatly enhance performance and, in turn, the bottom line. The concept of viewing corporate activities as a series of interrelated processes is useful (if not new) and is assisted by the development of various forms of IT which have the capability to integrate data/information (e.g. client-server, multi-tasking, CAD/ CAM, etc). He advocates the development of 'cross-functional solutions' since he believes that traditional business approaches to meeting customer requirements are too 'functionally based'. He outlines the fundamentals of the process innovation approach:

> 'Adopting a process view of the business – a key aspect of process innovation – represents a revolutionary change in perspective: it amounts to turning the organisation on its head, or at least on its side. A process orientation to business involves elements of structure, focus, measurement, ownership, and customers. In definitional terms, a process is simply a structured, measured set of activities designed to produce a specified output for a particular customer or market. It implies a strong emphasis on how work is done within an organisation, in contrast to a product focus's emphasis on what. A process is thus a specific ordering of work activities across time and place, with a beginning, an end, and clearly identified inputs and outputs: a structure for action. This structural element of processes is key to achieving the benefits of process innovation. Unless designers or participants can agree on the way work is and should be structured, it will be very difficult to systematically improve, or effect innovation in, that work' (Davenport, 1993, p.5).

Writing recently on business process redesign (BPR), Earl (1994, p.7) differentiates between core and support business processes. He asserts that core processes are those which are 'central to business functioning, which relate directly to external customers. They are commonly the primary activities of the value chain'. Support processes, on the other hand, are those 'which have internal customers and are back-up (or 'back office') of core processes. They will commonly be more administrative secondary activities of the value chain'.

Davenport asserts that 'hundreds of firms' in the USA and Europe are currently introducing some form of process innovation. But it is important to remember that this form of innovation will only be successful if managers in these firms change the 'existing Western paradigm' which perceives performance improvement and innovation as two activities in isolation of traditional managerial work (p.23). He voices a common criticism about Western management that innovation and performance improvement is placed in the hands of '*ad hoc* cross-functional teams' or project teams, task forces, steering committees or even individuals rather than being managed and coordinated by senior executives.

Here innovation is treated as a 'one-off' activity which leads to the adoption of various 'off-the-shelf' initiatives which are rarely successful. This is also witnessed by the

Western managerial paradigm where management consultants are commonly brought in to manage innovation by developing IT strategies, JIT control systems, TQM and team-building, re-engineering programmes and a whole host of other initiatives designed to improve performance. However, according to Davenport, process innovation is only likely to be successful provided senior managers are fully involved. He outlines a framework for process innovation which consists of five steps (p.24):

1. Identifying processes for innovation
2. Identifying change levers
3. Developing process visions
4. Understanding existing processes
5. Designing and prototyping the new process

This framework shows many similarities to the work of Porter and Millar, McFarlan, and Earl (above) since it invites managers to carefully consider their innovation strategies. Along with the previous authors, Davenport's (1993) work is prescriptive in its approach and advocates the benefits of 'process orientated thinking'. But unlike the previous studies, the above framework for process innovation places a greater emphasis upon perceiving business activities as a series of interrelated processes, with the recommendation that firms should reduce their processes and eliminate or incorporate other processes.

One of the attractions of process innovation as a complement to existing frameworks (see above) arises because recent developments in IT have led to greater possibilities for functional integration between departments. In some respects, the notion of functions and departments is anathema to those who advocate process innovation, since much of this literature seems to suggest process integration. A second attraction is that managers are encouraged to think laterally about business processes and, by doing so, gain a greater understanding of how the various 'parts of the jigsaw fit together'.

Perhaps the real strength of process innovation is the realisation that effective organisational change will only occur provided managers think through the business processes for which they are responsible. However, a number of points are relevant in assessing the contribution of process innovation as a key concept in managing innovation. First, behaviour in organisations is inherently political, thus making objective evaluation of business processes highly problematic. Even where teams are involved, it is common for certain members to take decisions based upon self-interest rather than in the interests of the organisation as a whole. Second, it is very difficult to determine when a process begins and ends. In all organisations, a significant number of decisions are taken without referring to formal processes. This is commonly referred to as the 'informal' organisation. Clearly this contributes to the difficulty in identifying problematic processes for the purpose of performance improvement.

A relevant example is the strategic management of IT. In the 1980s, much of the literature on technical change provided an optimistic picture of the ease with which IT would transform businesses. Indeed, many studies in the late 1970s and early 1980s simply assumed that technology would revolutionise business processes. Two competing scenarios emerged with some advocating the optimistic consequences of IT (more interesting jobs, elimination of dull jobs, productivity and quality enhancement, the generation of new businesses, etc) and others cautioning against the pitfalls (less inter-esting jobs and unemployment). Whilst the 1980s saw a number of key competitive advantages from IT (see those mentioned above), more literature emerged on the diffi-culties facing companies to successfully exploit IT. Disaster stories were usually kept out of the press although many anecdotel accounts emerged which suggested that IT often failed to deliver what the business required and was 'too expensive'.

Concluding remarks

The purpose of this chapter was to consider some of the relevant literature in three areas – competitive advantage and IT, strategic information systems planning, process innovation and business process re-engineering. Whilst the literature on competitive advantage and IT from the 1980s tended to overstate the benefits from IT, more recent literature published from the 1990s onwards now considers the need to innovate and re-engineer business processes. Moreover, the role of IT in organisations is now seen to involve everyone, and not simply those working in the IT department. In the next chap-ter, we consider the subject of IT strategy formation as this is considered by many as a prerequisite to achieving competitive advantage.

Case study

BPR and outsourcing in Western Europe

In a recent survey on BPR and outsourcing by the London-based research company Input – Impact of re-engineering on outsourcing – Europe 1994, some 90 European IT users in the private sector were interviewed about the rela-tionship between BPR and outsourcing. About 30 of these organisations were already involved in outsourcing operations at varying degrees.

For UK outsourcing suppliers moving into the consultancy market, such as CSC and EDS, Input's findings demonstrate a shortage of large-scale outsourcing deals with major UK companies. UK executives are less willing than their continental European counterparts to believe that outsourcing suppliers have a rele-vant understanding of their business or are best placed to offer good advice on BPR. This clearly highlights a current tendency on the part of IT departments and senior executives not to embrace 'total outsourcing' as the way forward.

The survey found that only 45% of the conti-nental European users believed their IT supplier or in-house department had an in-depth under-standing of their business. Coupled with this,

only 15% believed their outsourcing partner would be able to fully contribute to their BPR strategy.

The survey also found that 55% of European executives said that IT should play a part in BPR. The remaining 45% on the other hand said that IT was not crucial in BPR initiatives. Some 60% of German and French executives said that IT was important in BPR. This com-pared with 70% of UK executives who said that IT serves only as a supporting factor in BPR.

The survey showed that a large number of continental European executives believed that BPR was synonymous with improved efficiency which would lead to competitive advantage. However, opinions differed with some perceiv-ing BPR as a cost-cutting exercise, while others saw it in terms of company-wide improvements to business processes.

The latter was evident in French companies, where executives perceived BPR as important in speeding up business processes. In Germany, the emphasis focused on restructuring to achieve greater flexibility in working practices.

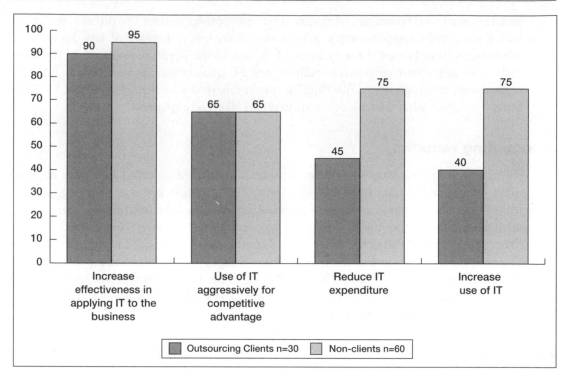

Figure 2.3 IT goals for outsourcing clients and non-clients

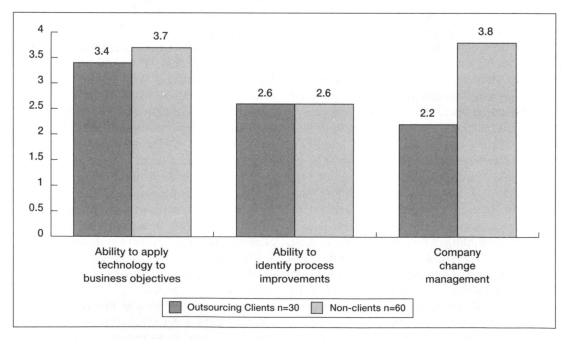

Figure 2.4 Comparative capabilities of IT departments and outsourcing vendors

UK executives cited the advantages of manufacturing improvements, lead time reductions and improved information processing and flows.

The majority of executives believed that in-house IT departments and outsourcing suppliers had similar capacities in terms of supporting BPR, although both parties needed to acquire more business awareness of core operating areas. One observation of the report says, 'If outsourcing vendors are to make a significant contribution to their clients' future use of IT, then they must improve their ability to identify process improvements'.

Only about 10% of UK respondents said that IT suppliers should offer or combine BPR with technical expertise. Conversely, in France and Germany, as many as 60% and 55% respectively said this combination was important.

The survey highlights a shortfall between executives' perceptions of the skills of in-house IT departments and their ability to plan, coordinate and manage BPR for performance improvement. French executives claimed their IT departments should become more commercially aware. In the UK, executives wanted faster decision making, the elimination of IT policy restraints, more technological progress (e.g. open-systems) and an ability to adapt to organisational and environmental change.

(Source: Linda Leung, 'Executive decisions', in *Computing* 25 August, 1994, p.39)

Discussion questions

1 How can BPR reduce company expenditure?
2 Who should manage the BPR strategy (general managers or IT managers)?
3 Why are UK executives threatened by outsourcing?
4 Why are people resistant to change?
5 How can IT play a significant role in BPR?

References 2

Armstrong, A. (1992) 'What is competitive advantage?'. *OMEGA: International Journal of Management Science*. Vol, 20. No. 3. pp. 281–282.

Currie, W. (1989) 'The art of justifying new technology to top management'. *OMEGA: International Journal of Management Science*. October, Vol, 17, No. 5. pp. 409–418.

Currie, W. (1991) 'Managing production technology in Japan'. *Management Accounting*, Vol, 69, No. 6, June, Part 1. Vol, 69. No. 7, July/August, Part 2.

Currie, W., Fincham, R., Hallier, J. (1993) 'Multi-disciplinary management of IT projects in the financial services sector, manufacturing industry and the public sector. Cost A3 Workshop publication, Glasgow Business School/Commission of European Communities.

Currie, W. (1994a) 'Outsourcing: friend or foe?' Paper presented at the Cost A4 International Research Workshop, Grenoble, France, 16–17 June.

Currie, W. (1994b) 'The management of large scale IT projects in the financial services sector'. *New Technology, Work and Employment*, Vol, 9, No. 1, March, pp. 19–29.

Currie, W., Seddon, J. (1992) 'Managing AMT in a JIT environment in the UK and Japan'. *British Journal of Management*, Vol, 3 No. 3, pp. 123–136.

Davenport, T. H. (1993) *Process Innovation: Reengineering work through information technology*. Harvard Business School Press: Boston.

Earl, M. (1989) *Management strategies for information technology*. Prentice Hall.

Earl, M. (1992) 'Experiences in strategic information systems planning'. *MIS Quarterly*. March. Vol, 17, pp. 1–21.

Earl, M. (1994) 'The new and the old of business process redesign'. *Journal of Information Systems*, Vol, 3, No. 1, pp. 5–22.

Earl, M., Skyme, D.J. (1992) 'Hybrid managers – what do we know about them?'. *Journal of Information Systems*, 2, pp. 169–187.

Edwards, C., Ward, J., Blytheway, A. (1991) *The essence of information systems*. Prentice Hall.

Farbey, B., Land, F., Targett, D. (1993) *IT investment: a study of methods and practice*. Butterworth Heinemann.

Forester, T. (1980) *The micro-electronics revolution*. Blackwell.

Forester, T. (1985) *The information technology revolution*. Oxford University Press.

Friedman, A.L. with Cornford, D. (1989) *Computer systems development: history, organisation and implementation*. Wiley.

Gibson, C. F., Nolan, R. L. (1974) 'Managing the four stages of EDP growth'. *Harvard Business Review*, January/February, pp. 76–88.

Hayes, R. H., Abernathy, W.J. (1980) 'Managing our way to economic decline'. *Harvard Business Review*, July/August, pp. 67–77.

HMSO (1994) *Competitiveness: Helping business to win*. HMSO, London.

Hori, S. (1993) 'Fixing Japan's white collar economy: a personal view'. *Harvard Business Review*, November/December, pp. 157–172.

Hopper, M.D. (1990) 'Rattling SABRE – New ways to compete on information'. *Harvard Business Review*, May/June, pp. 118–125.

Japan Times (1994) 'Reengineering revolution comes to Japan'. 7 February, p.7.

Kantrow, A. M. (1980) 'The strategy-technology connection'. *Harvard Business Review*, pp. 1–21.

McFarlan, F.W. (1984) 'New electronics systems can add value to your product and throw your competition off balance'. *Harvard Business Review*, May/June, pp. 98–103.

McKenney, J.L., McFarlan, F.W. (1982) 'The information archipelago – maps and bridges'. *Harvard Business Review*, September/October, pp. 109–119.

Markhus, M.L. (1983) 'Power, politics, and MIS implementation'. *Communications of the ACM*, Vol, 26, No. 6, pp. 430–445.

Medland, A., Burnett, P. (1986) *CAD/CAM in practice*. Kogan Page: London.

Morone, J. G. (1993) 'Technology and competitive advantage – the role of general management'. *Research Technology Management*, March/April, pp. 6–25.

Nolan, R.L. (1977) 'Controlling the costs of data services'. *Harvard Business Review*, July/August, pp. 114–124.

Nolan, R.L. (1979) 'Managing the crisis in data processing'. *Harvard Business Review*, March/April, pp. 115–179.

Peppard, J. (ed.) (1993) *IT strategy for business*. Pitman.

Porter, M. (1985) *Competitive Advantage: creating and sustaining superior performance*. Free Press: New York.

Porter, M. (1992) *The competitive advantage of nations*. McMillan.

Porter, M., Millar, V. (1985) 'How information gives you competitive advantage'. *Harvard Business Review*, July/August, pp. 149–160.

Tavakolian, H. (1991) 'The organisation of IT functions in the 1990s: a managerial perspective'. *Journal of Management Development*, Vol, 10, No. 2, pp. 31–37.

Thompson, G. (1989) The American industrial policy debate'. *Industrial Policy: USA and UK Debates*. G. Thompson (ed.), London: RKP.

Williams, K., Williams, J., and Thomas, D., (1983) *Why are the British bad at manufacturing?*, London: RKP.

Wu, B., Seddon, J., Currie, W. (1992) 'Computer-aided dynamic preventive maintenance within the manufacturing environment'. *International Journal of Production Research*, Vol, 30, No. 11. pp. 2683–2696.

CHAPTER 3

Strategic Planning and IT

Introduction

The prescriptive literature on competitive advantage and IT presupposes that organisations should develop and implement a clearly defined strategic plan to improve performance. This message has been repeated in the IT literature in the last decade, with many writers advocating an alignment of business and IT strategies. In many ways, an incontestable alliance has formed between strategy and IT which is supported by the popular precepts of 'the information resource' (Davenport, 1993), 'competing through technology' (Porter, 1985) and the 'strategy-technology connection' (Kantrow, 1980).

Irrespective of organisational setting and the uneven levels of diffusion across private and public sectors, IT continues to be perceived as a vital tool to enhance performance. Some of the literature adopts a cross-sectoral approach to the role of IT in contemporary organisations. For example, in financial services sector, IT is perceived to dramatically 'alter the rules of competition', spawn new businesses and achieve impressive economies of scale. Here, IT is embedded into the core business processes and therefore the infrastructure. Similarly in manufacturing, AMT in the form of CAD/CAM, FMS, robotics, and a host of other DSSs and MISs, is seen as vital to the pursuit of *world class* manufacturing. Indeed, there are many examples where manufacturers would not be able to compete, or even operate, without AMT.

In recent years, the interest in IT strategy formation has grown considerably. Contributions exist from a number of disciplinary sources, although it is argued that the topic is more appropriately researched from an inter-disciplinary perspective. This clearly imposes constraints on researchers (Mintzberg, 1993). But any discussion of strategy is meaningless if it only considers the influence and activities of a single department or function in isolation of the wider organisation. It is even more meaningless if it only concentrates on the influence of a 'figurehead' personality, like the CEO or *technical champion* who spearheads change. It is therefore important to analyse IT strategy formation in the wider organisational context, taking into account the conflicting interests of the various stakeholders. This introduces a socio-political dimension to our understanding of strategic processes which is often overlooked in the general and more specialist IT strategy literature.

The chapter is divided into five sections. First it considers an overview of the key debates within the strategy literature. Second, it focuses on the post-1950 conceptual developments in the generic strategy literature. Third, it looks at formal-rational frameworks for IT strategy formation. Fourth, the chapter considers contributions from the interpretative perspective which questions the use of formal-rational frameworks. Finally, the link between strategy and implementation is considered.

An overview of the strategy literature

Four broad areas of strategy formation are discussed in this overview. First it examines what we may describe as the generic strategy literature which tends to adopt 'a formal-rational view of organisations as systems with coherent purposes and shared goals' (Walsham, 1993, p. 143). Much of this literature has its roots in the fields of long-range planning, strategic planning and decision-making science, all of which preceded the current fixation on corporate strategy. Johnson and Scoles (1993, p. 22) point out that

> 'The traditional view of strategic management, common in books of the late 1960s and 1970s, was that strategy was, or should be, managed through planning processes, in the form of a neat sequence of steps building on objective setting and analysis, through the evaluation of different options, and ending with the careful planning of the strategy implementation'.

This approach became increasingly popular in the 1960s as companies sought to develop all-embracing strategic plans to guide decision making. In the more recent strategy literature, the formal-rational approach is still dominant, although it is often supplemented by a wider socio-political dimension which views strategy making 'as a process of crafting' (Johnson and Scoles, 1993, p. 22). Other work considers the wide gap which exists between strategic planning and reality. Mintzberg (1993, 1994) in particular, talks of the 'fundamental fallacies of strategic planning' and demonstrates, through careful examination of existing research and his own studies, that formal-rational frameworks are so divorced from reality, they neither explain nor influence corporate success or failure.

Two conceptual problems are evident in the generic strategy literature which inhibits a wider understanding of the strategy formation process. The first is the confusion in terminology. Little consensus exists between writers on strategy over what constitutes corporate strategy, strategic planning, decision making and strategy formation. It is not uncommon to find in some quarters of the literature that capital budgeting is presented as strategy formation. Some companies also treat strategy formation as synonymous with capital budgeting concerning the evaluation of IT projects (Currie, 1994b).

Whilst it is outside the scope of this book to enter into debate on terminology, it is important to recognise this confusion because it is reproduced in many contemporary studies on strategy making for IT. Second, IT strategy formation is seen as a sub-set of the wider strategic management process. Yet it is difficult to discern where this process fits into the wider strategic frameworks featured in many popular strategic management texts. Such frameworks encapsulate a wide array of variables which include the environment, culture and stakeholder expectations, resources and strategic capability, managing change, planning and allocating resources, and organisation structure and design, among other things. This is particularly problematic to our understanding of IT strategy formation. For if IT is perceived as a key strategic device to gain competitive advantage, IT strategy is perhaps more than simply a sub-set of the strategic management process.

Conversely, the prevailing situation where managers seek technical solutions to improve their competitiveness suggests that technology may drive strategy making. This is reflected in a recent comment made in the *FT* (26 April, 1994, p.4):

> 'As information technology becomes tightly integrated into the organisation's different business

units, it becomes difficult to separate the business processes from the technology itself ... as business processes become more automated, they become embedded in the information system. It becomes increasingly difficult to change one without changing the other'.

The second field of literature focuses entirely on IT strategy formation. Once again, the emphasis on rationality permeates this work. This is demonstrated by the recommendation that managers develop analytical strategic frameworks and models for IT (Wiseman, 1985. Wysoki, 1990. Earl, 1988. Grindley, 1991. Shank, 1985. Ward, et al, 1990). Here managers are advised to impose a framework on IT strategy formation. This is achieved under the auspices of the strategic planners or strategists, usually senior executives. This may be undertaken in a variety of ways. As with the generic strategy literature, these writers usually perceive IT strategy formation as a linear process based on a series of logical steps, delineated by checklists and supported by carefully selected techniques. These models and frameworks tend to present IT *strategy* as a series of articulated steps to be carried out in sequence. They are usually goal-orientated (see Figure 3.1). The logic underpinning the formal-rational approach is based on the six premises that decision makers:

1. can evaluate all the relevant information
2. can select the most appropriate course of action
3. can formulate a strategy
4. are able to implement the strategy
5. can improve performance
6. can enhance competitive position.

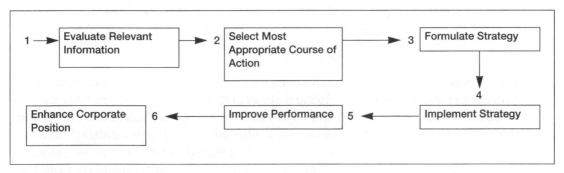

Figure 3.1 Formal-rational framework for managing IT

Many techniques have been designed for this purpose. For example, managers may do a SWOT analysis which identifies the strengths, weaknesses, opportunities and threats posed by IT. Or they may wish to identify the critical success factors (CSFs) which encapsulate those areas or activities which are vital in meeting a firm's objectives (Rockart, 1979. Boynton and Zmud, 1984. Shank, 1985. Shank et al, 1985). Other recommendations which advocate the formal-rational approach include the IBM systems planning model (IBM, 1984), and a five forces and value chain analysis (Cash and Konsynski, 1985. Porter, 1979, 1980).

The common thread which binds all this work is the view that strategy making should be a formal, controlled process steered by rational, analytical thought. Overall responsibility should also rest with senior executives since they are the 'architects' who craft and build the strategy. Fully developed strategies should typically be generic to facilitate implementation. They should be aligned to other strategic objectives such as budgetary parameters, change programmes, manpower planning, production management techniques (JIT, TQM, MRP), among others. Selected examples of formal-rational frameworks for IT strategy are discussed below. In particular, we consider Earl's (1989) framework which comprises strategies for information systems, information technology and information management.

The third area of literature relevant to strategy formation for IT concerns sociopolitical processes in organisations. This approach takes issue with the conventional contingency perspective (Child, 1972. Quinn, 1980. Mintzberg, 1978, 1979, 1993. Mintzberg and Waters, 1985). In the context of IT strategy making, Walsham (1993, p.149) advocates an 'interpretive' approach. He asserts that

> 'There is very little published work to date which attempts to describe interpretations of the way in which IS strategy forms in practice, or which discusses the discourse of IS strategy as a topic of importance itself'.

He is concerned that the vast majority of the IS strategy implicitly adopts a formal rational stance, even though the gap between planning and implementation is wide.

This concern is addressed by Mintzberg and McHugh (1985, p.160) who contend that

> 'Strategy making still tends to be equated with planning – with the systematic 'formulation' and articulation of deliberate, premeditated strategies, which are then 'implemented'. The traditional precepts of 'making strategy explicit', formulating before implementing, and designing a structure to 'follow' strategy remain intact in almost all of the literature. This view of strategy making, however, is unnecessarily restrictive; it is inconsistent with more contemporary forms of structure and sometimes with the conventional forms as well'.

The absence of interpretive contributions on IT strategy formation encourages many writers to re-examine earlier influential studies on decision making, notably those of Lindblom (1959), Simon (1960) and Cyert and March (1963). Much of this work is complementary to the 'interpretive' approach mentioned above since it highlights the *ad hoc* nature of decision making which arises from competing political motives, an inability to understand or assess information, budgetary constraints, confusion and trial and error among other things. These writers stress the limitations which hinder decision-making processes, and this has earned them the label of the 'debunkers of managerial decision making' based on their combined efforts to 'puncture managerial reason' (Hickson, 1987, p. 30). It is interesting to note that the early writers did not use the term strategy formation or strategic management. Instead, they adopted the term decision making. In this context, they were interested to examine the extent to which individuals could optimise the outcome of decision processes.

Incrementalism which is a term used by Lindblom (1959) provides numerous examples of how decision makers cope with handling limited and distorted information for decision making. Promoting the concept of the Successive Limited Comparison (SLC), he argues that the selection of value goals and empirical analysis of the required action are not distinct categories, but are closely related. The lack of distinction between means and ends supports the view that choices may be limited. This position leads Lindblom to argue that the simple choice between a range of decision criteria (exemplified in the formal-rational ideal approach, above) is problematic given that, in the real world, only a limited number of choices are available to decision makers.

Although the early decision making literature is not directly relevant to our discussion of IT strategy in contemporary organisations, it nonetheless provides some useful insights. Whereas Lindblom (1959) rejects all formal-rational positions on decision making by introducing the term 'the art of muddling through', Simon (1960) (although advocating a rational approach) is keen to draw a distinction between two types of decision making – programmed and unprogrammed. The former represents decisions which are routine and repetitive. They do not pose a problem to organisations as appropriate administrative procedures are in place for this type of decision process.

On the other hand, unprogrammed decisions are problematic to organisations since they represent *one-shot, ill-structured and novel* decision processes. A prime example is the introduction of a new computer system. Here, decision makers are likely to find there is no 'one best way' to guide their decision making.

It is interesting to note that the IT strategy formation literature is addressed from two distinct schools of thought. The first may be labelled the formal-rational approach, and the second, the interpretive approach. Whereas the formal-rational approach perceives IT strategy formation as a product of conceptual deliberation, the outcome of which is usually a framework or model which outlines a series of sequential steps which are delineated by checklists, the interpretive approach, on the other hand, views this process as highly problematic. Interpretive writers focus on the political processes which govern strategy formation and reject the simple logic that strategic models translate into IT success in the workplace. Concerns are also expressed about the gulf that exists between strategic planning and implementation.

The fourth area discussed in this overview is thus the emerging nature of strategy formation and implementation. Arguably, not enough research exists on the extent to which IT strategies actually achieve desired performance improvements. In many ways, there is an over-emphasis on the creation of strategy, yet insufficient attention on its results.

Mintzberg (1993, 1994) is particularly critical of the early empirical work on strategic planning which fails to address the issue of implementation. He gives numerous examples where companies have either succeeded or failed in spite of their strategic planning processes. He is also critical of the formal-rational approach which presents strategy as a framework which contains numerous boxes and lines, the linkages of which are rarely explained to decision makers. This work is particularly relevant to our understanding of IT strategy formation and implementation. However, a problem arises due to the dearth of empirical work which relates these two areas.

Whilst a plethora of studies exist which repeat the slogan that IT leads to competitive advantage, it seems that more work is needed which analyses the practical implications of strategic planning for IT. In recent years, the well-documented IT disaster stories have fuelled an interest in why so many strategic failures occur (Fichman and Kemerer, 1992.

Friedman, 1989. Currie, 1994b). The distinction between concept (strategy) and execution (implementation) is addressed by Mintzberg (1993, p. 282) who claims that

> 'Thinking and acting are most obviously separated in the dichotomy between formulation and implementation, central to all the prescriptive schools of strategy making – design and positioning as well as planning. In other words, the ultimate prescription is that organisations should complete their thinking before they begin to act'.

It is important to set the scene before examining the strategy literature in more detail in the following sections. In recommending more research work on the link between strategy and implementation, it is argued that IT failures are not simply the result of poorly defined or implemented strategic plans. Rather, they are largely to do with corporate managements' failure to recognise the key ingredients which lead to the successful implementation of IT. The traditional approach to strategy formation as an activity steered by senior executives, and implemented by middle managers, is one which, it is argued, is no longer an appropriate model for contemporary businesses. This is because IT now plays a central role in many private and public sector settings. It is also likely to be embedded into the infrastructure, and many of its core business and/or administrative processes.

Notwithstanding this, the notion that IT is merely a support function is generally accepted in many organisations. Consequently, senior managers often perceive the IT strategy as a *bolt on, optional extra* to the business strategy. In doing so, IT strategy becomes just another 'box' on the strategic framework. Implementation is therefore likely to be devolved to managers in the various divisions, departments or strategic business units (SBUs). This view of IT strategy is unnecessarily restrictive since it ignores the dynamic and creative process peculiar to managing technical change.

This brief overview of the strategy literature attempts to set the scene of how the IT strategy literature has developed over time. The following section looks more closely at the models and frameworks offered by the generic strategy literature.

Strategic management in organisations

In the generic literature on corporate strategy, the concept of strategy is defined as

> '*the direction and scope of an organisation over the long term: ideally, which matches its resources to its changing environment, and in particular its markets, customers or clients so as to meet stakeholder expectations*' (Johnson and Scholes, 1993, p.10).

These authors offer three elements of strategic management: *strategic analysis* – which is concerned with understanding the strategic position of the organisation in terms of the environment, and the likely effects on the organisation and its activities; *strategic choice* – which is to do with the formulation of possible courses of action, their evaluation and the choice between them; and *strategic implementation* – which is concerned with the translation of strategy into action (see Figure 3.2). They stress that the model is a useful device to enable individuals to 'think through complex strategic problems' and is not 'an attempt to describe how the processes of strategic management necessarily take place in the political and cultural arenas of an organisation' (Johnson and Scholes, 1993, p. 22).

What makes strategic decisions different from other types of decisions is their complexity (Johnson, 1987). The notion that planning is integrated decision making is found in the work of Ackoff (1970, p. 2,3) who writes

'Planning is required when the future state that we desire involves a set of interdependent decisions; that is, a system of decisions ... the principal complexity in planning derives from the interrelatedness of the decisions rather than from the decisions themselves'.

According to Johnson and Scholes (1993, p.10) there are three important elements of complexity. First, strategic decision making is essentially high risk since it is based on uncertainty of outcome. Second, strategic decisions demand an integrated approach since they span the entire organisation and the external environment. The authors claim that

'Unlike functional problems, there is no one area of expertise or one perspective that can define or resolve the problems. Managers, therefore, have cross-functional and operational boundaries to deal with strategic problems and come to agreements with other managers who, inevitably, have different interests and perhaps different priorities. This problem of integration exists in all management tasks but is particularly problematic for strategic decisions'.

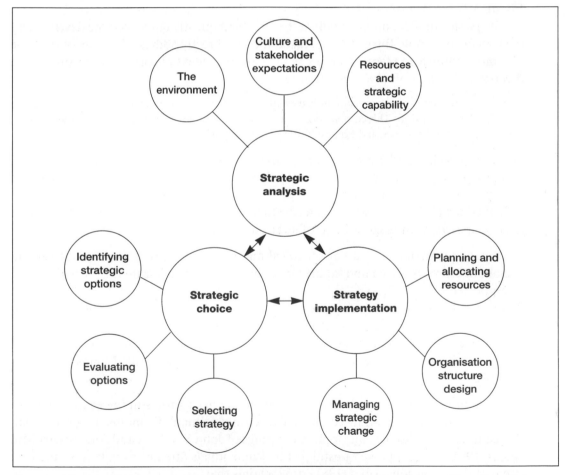

Figure 3.2 A summary model of the elements of strategic management (*Courtesy:* Johnson & Scholes, *Exploring Corporate Strategy*, Prentice Hall)

Third, the outcome of strategic decision making is likely to be *major* organisational change.

These authors are critical of the 'traditional view of strategy' common in books in the 1960s and 1970s, which advocates all-embracing strategic frameworks and models where

'strategy was, or should be, managed through planning processes, in the form of a neat sequence of steps building on objective setting and analysis, through the evaluation of different options, and ending with the careful planning of the strategy implementation' (Johnson and Scholes, 1993, p.22).

The formal-rational approach to strategic planning became increasingly popular in American companies from the 1960s onwards. Whereas it grew from being a 'budget exercise' during the 1950s, it emerged to become 'a virtual obsession among American corporations (and in American government, in the form of the Planning-Programming-Budgeting System, or PPBS)' (Mintzberg, 1993, p. 6). An emphasis on formal rationality permeated the early literature on strategic planning and this is demonstrated by Ansoff's (1965) elaborate fifty-seven box model which depicts strategy formation as a deliberate, cerebral process, decomposed into a series of steps to be followed in strict sequence (see Figure 3.3).

The publication of Ansoff's book in the mid-1960s greatly influenced the development of strategic planning. Interestingly, Ansoff did not directly address the issue of strategic planning but instead placed his work in the narrow context of corporate expansion and diversification. Ansoff (1965, p. 12) noted that

'The end product of strategic decisions is deceptively simple; a combination of products and markets is selected for the firm. This combination is arrived at by addition of new product-markets, divestment from some old ones, and expansion of the present position'.

He referred to his model as a 'cascade of decisions, starting with highly aggregated ones and proceeding toward the more specific' (1965, p. 205). Others writers who advocated this approach were Steiner (1969, 1979), and, more recently, Argenti (1980).

Mintzberg (1993, p. 42) asserts that the following three basic premises underpin what he describes as 'the Design School' of strategic planning:

1. Strategy formation should be controlled and conscious as well as a formalised and elaborate process, decomposed into distinct steps, each delineated by checklists and supported by techniques.
2. Responsibility for the overall process rests with the chief executive in principle; responsibility for its execution rests with the staff planners in practice.
3. Strategies come out of this process fully developed, typically as generic positions, to be explicated so that they can then be implemented through detailed plans of various kinds.

The formal-rational approach to strategic planning has its roots in the economic theories which promote the 'idealised rational or economic man'. Economic models of man can be traced back to the philosophical writings of John Bentham and John Stuart Mill (Jabes, 1981). This approach postulates that individuals attempt to maximise the outcome of their decisions. Jabes (1981, p. 57) claims that

'These ideas formed the basis for postulates in economics as well as learning theory in the behaviour

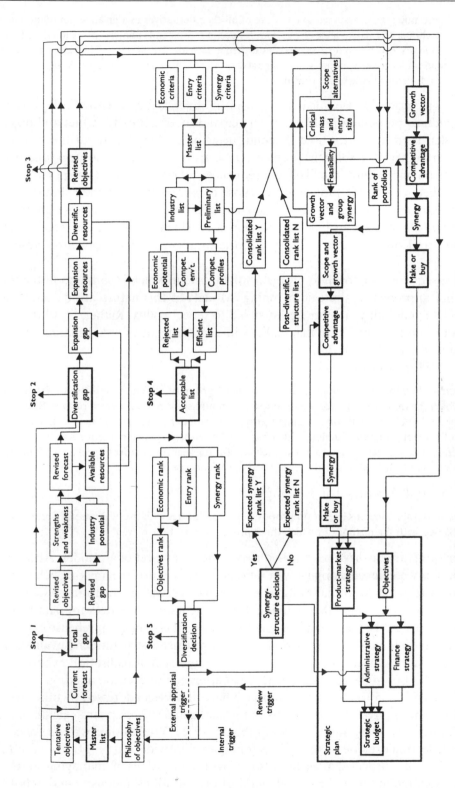

Figure 3.3 The Ansoff model of strategic planning (*Courtesy:* Ansoff, *Corporate Strategy*, McGraw Hill)

sciences. Economic man is assumed to be aware of all the alternatives in a given situation and acts rationally to choose the most viable one.... This reflects a means-ends analysis of rationality. If the appropriate means are chosen for specified ends, then a decision is rational.... The classic model of economic man is a normative model which suggests how decisions ought to be made. At best it would apply only to decisions made under certainty'.

The way in which rational decision making works in practice is defined by Carley (1981). First, individuals pinpoint a problem which demands action. Goals, values and objectives are identified and prioritised. Second, decision makers locate all the possible options open to them to resolve the problem which are translated into strategies, courses of action or policies. Third, the likely consequences following from strategies, etc, are predicted together with the probability of those consequences occurring. Fourth, the consequences of each strategy are then compared to the goals and objectives outlined in stage 1. Finally, a strategy or policy is developed in which consequences most closely match goals and objectives. In other words, the problem is either solved or close to being solved.

This five-sequence approach to problem solving is one which is common in the formal-rational approach to strategic planning. Models of this nature are described as 'abstractions from reality' and are not intended to reflect reality. Rather, 'it is intended to order and simplify our view of that reality while capturing its essential characteristics' (Forcese and Richer, 1973, p. 38).

Carley (1981, p.60) writes

'In economic thought, to be rational is to select from a group of alliterative courses of action that course which maximises output for a given input, or minimises input for a given output. Secondly, in systems analysis, decision theory, or game theory, to be rational is to select a course of action, from a group of possible courses of action, which has a given set of predicted consequences in terms of some welfare function which, in turn, ranks each set of consequences in order of preference. This second application of rationality can also be applied to the concept of 'planning'.'

Simon (1958, p. 423) writes that planning

'is that activity that concerns itself with proposals for the future, with the evaluation of alternative proposals, and with the methods by which those proposals may be achieved'.

A number of criticisms have been raised about the formal-rational model. Although these criticisms were directed originally at rational models of decision making behaviour, they are also relevant to formal-rational approaches to strategic planning. Gershuny (1978) argues that the notion that individuals must acquire all the relevant data before rational decisions can be taken assumes that to be rational is to be comprehensive. It also assumes that individuals have the mental ability to prioritise, structure and evaluate all decision alternatives. In reality, this is not possible and such a realisation exposes the inherent weaknesses in the economic or rational approach to decision making.

The pitfalls of the formal-rational approach have also been addressed by other writers, many of whom direct their criticisms to rational perspectives on strategic planning (Quinn, 1980. Gray 1986. Smircich and Stubbart, 1985). Whilst some writers concede that the intellectual exercise of strategic planning may provide a 'useful framework for strategic thinking' - provided managers also recognise the pitfalls of 'managing strategy within the social, cultural and political world of organisations' (Johnson and Scholes,

1993), others reject this approach by claiming it is unrealistic since it fails to consider competing values, objectives and power bases (Lindblom, 1959. Knights and Morgan, 1991. Mintzberg, 1993).

Criticisms have also been raised about the amount of detail contained in strategic frameworks, arguing that such a massive amount of information only serves to confuse rather than assist decision makers. Moreover, the strategic plan may not be communicated to all levels of the hierarchy and, as a result, become implemented only partially. Mintzberg and Waters (1985) draw a distinction between *intended* and *realised* strategies and stress that the latter is seldom a reflection of the former. Here they introduce the term *emergent strategies* to reflect the unexpected consequences of strategy formation which may or may not be beneficial to an organisation.

Strategic planning is also likely to be an annual senior executive responsibility which coincides with financial planning. Since the plan is the product of two or three weeks deliberation rather than an on-going, incremental process, it is likely that once the process has finished, the plan is simply typed and put into a filing cabinet. Indeed, in some organisations, strategic planning is inextricably linked to budgeting, where managers simply play the 'numbers game' without engaging in any real strategic thinking (Mintzberg, 1993). Mintzberg highlights the misconception where managers sometimes confuse objective setting with strategy making. He claims that it is 'wishful acting' to go through the process of strategic planning with a view that it represents strategy creation. He offers a diagram to illustrate the difference between performance control and action planning (Figure 3.4)

Here, the budgets hierarchy is linked to the objectives hierarchy, each being a top-down, bottom up or negotiated process, with the objectives at each level linked to one area of the budget. Mintzberg (1993, p. 85) asserts that

> 'This kind of performance control is certainly easier to understand and to do than the conventional strategic planning. Indeed, it is not uncommon for organisations to attempt the full process but end up with only this. In other words, what are called strategic planning exercises often reduce to the generation of numbers, not ideas – objectives and budgets, but not strategies. From the perspective of strategy formation, therefore, this constitutes a numbers game, a label that has had a certain currency in organisations themselves'.

The numbers game may actually impede strategic thinking since performance measurement and control tends to be geared to existing organisation structures and not future ones. Financial planning dressed up as strategic planning which is based on an extrapolation of past resource allocation processes is a poor foundation on which to build future success. This is reinforced in field research on managing technology in UK companies (Currie, 1994b). Here managers realising that first-time investment in IT imposes a new challenge to conventional capital budgeting activities seek to manage the strategic decision process through greater financial controls on decisions makers. Unfortunately, new technology in the form of CAD in the manufacturing environment, and client-server technology which is fast entering the financial services sector, are not amenable to old style financial measures of ROI and DCF (Currie, 1994b. Jones et al, 1993). This issue will be discussed in greater detail in chapter four.

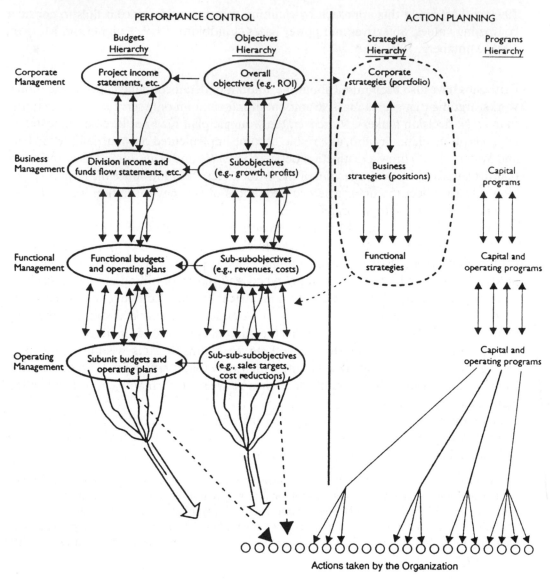

Figure 3.4 Planning as 'numbers game' (*Courtesy:* Mintzberg, *The Rise and Fall of Strategic Planning*, Prentice Hall)

Further problems with the formal-rational approach to strategic planning are, once again, related to the issue of financial control. Line managers responsible for implementing the strategic plan may find that normal day-to-day duties leave little time to concentrate on planned change. Nor may they have the resources to finance new initiatives. This is particularly the case in UK companies where senior executives espouse the benefits of conducting R & D projects, investing in new technology and training, yet suspend resources for these activities when the company enters a down-turn (Currie, 1989).

Much of the appeal of the generic strategy literature is its attempt to make sense of a disorderly and chaotic world. The advocates of formal-rational frameworks seemingly adopt the position that behaviour and decision making processes can be controlled in organisations for the purpose of achieving an optimal outcome. This view is also shared by many writers on managing technology. The next section therefore considers how the generic strategy literature has influenced the field of IT strategy.

Strategy levels and linkages

The view that managers should develop clearly defined strategies for IT is generally accepted in the IT literature. Numerous publications exist which advise managers how to craft strategies for their organisation. Problems arise, of course, because many of these strategies are generic and fail to differentiate between the needs of, say, the financial services sector as opposed to manufacturing industry or publicly owned corporations. This literature is fuelled by the current fixation on strategy in academic circles, and also by a consultancy industry which offers IT strategy formation as a key service to its clients. Whilst it is easy to criticise the development and application of IT strategic frameworks and models because of their poor success rate in delivering business benefits to organisations, some of these criticisms are unjust for two reasons. First, research has shown that managers in contemporary organisations are somewhat overwhelmed by constant technical change. They therefore view strategic frameworks as a useful intellectual tool to aid strategy formation and assist with resource allocation decisions.

Second, misunderstandings seem to exist about the purpose of strategic frameworks for IT. Or more importantly, how they should be interpreted and used by managers. Some companies use them to guide strategy formation and implementation. Others (arguably the majority) simply treat them as a conceptual tool to simplify complex phenomena. There are many examples of IT strategic frameworks in the literature. One such framework is developed by Earl (1989). In his popular book, *Management Strategies for Information Technology*, Earl (1989) develops a strategic framework which differentiates between three interrelated types of strategy formation – information systems (IS), information technology (IT) and information management (IM) strategies (Figure 3.5).

IS strategy

IS strategy is considered to be long term in orientation. Key questions relate to *what* a firm should plan to achieve by investing in IT. IS strategy is *business-led* and *demand-orientated* and is concerned with either supporting existing business strategies or developing new strategic IT choices. IS strategy falls within the range of responsibilities of senior management. These managers are unlikely to possess in-depth technical expertise, although they may understand the strategic possibilities of IT within their organisation. Earl (1989) asserts that 'most large organisations today are formulating IS strategies'. He cites a study where 84% of companies claim to be 'formulating IS plans of a long-term character'.

Irrespective of organisational structure, market and product grouping and nature of the business, an effective IS strategy may be formulated with the key objectives of utilising the information resource and, more ambitiously, spawning new businesses. The strength of this type of strategy rests on it being *demand-orientated* where the managers

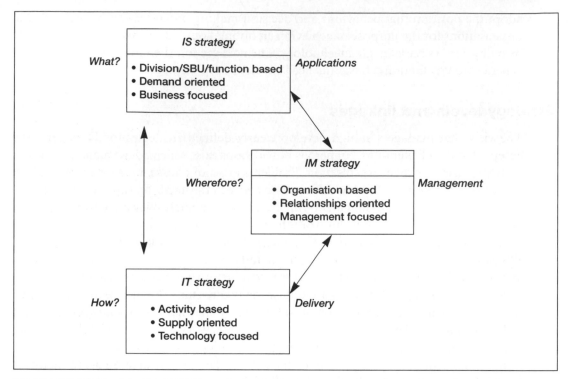

Figure 3.5 Three levels of strategy in IT *(Courtesy:* Earl, *Management Strategies for Information Technology,* Prentice Hall)

of the divisions, business units or departments communicate their IT needs to the wider organisation. IS strategies must therefore be business driven and capable of delivering tangible business benefits such as increased productivity, enhanced profits and possibly a reduction in headcount.

The reasons for embarking on an IS strategy are seen as fourfold. First, the 'sectoral threat' posed by IT is perceived as either an opportunity or a threat. Banks for example which develop new and successful IT services for customers obviously pose a threat to their competitors. Second, the importance of incorporating IT into the business strategy is now taken for granted in both the generic and IT strategy literature. The days when IT was simply the responsibility of the DP department are seen as a thing of the past. Nevertheless, the extent to which this has occurred in practice is not fully supported by empirical work which draws attention to the mismatch between IT strategy formation and practice (Currie, 1989a, 1994ab). Here it is shown that elaborate strategic plans seldom lead to all the objectives being met, as constraints in the form of financial resources, skills deficiencies, managerial incompetence and the development of *ad hoc*, emergent lower-level strategies threaten the grand plan. Third, the popular precept of 'competing through technology' which is commonly used by consultants, IT manufacturers and business schools provides an impetus for IS planning.

But the wide gap which continues to exist between strategic expectation and technical implementation reflects badly on the suppliers and consultancy services, not to mention the companies themselves. This is supported by recent research which shows that a significant number of companies have not achieved their expected business benefits from IT (Robson, 1993). Findings of this nature tend to fuel even more literature which advises managers to develop appropriate IT strategies.

However, many of these writers fail to address the issue that formal-rational strategic plans may actually contribute to technical failure. This is because strategic planning processes based on traditional performance measurement criteria (DCF, ROI, short-term returns and top-down management initiatives) may not be appropriate for the new technical climate of client-server, and the like. Fourth, the process of developing an IS strategy is likely to involve a thorough evaluation of the entire IT function by looking at the range of activities and services it provides to the company. This may help to lift IT to the top of the boardroom agenda and reaffirm that the old DP era has now been replaced by the new IT era (Earl, 1989).

IS strategies are intended to be directional and not detailed in scope and content. Earl (1989, p. 68) asserts that, 'Too much detail soon loses strategic intent and often gets bogged down in technical debate and short-term resource allocation arguments'. He is concerned to point out that a single IS strategy formulation methodology does not currently exist and attempts to impose one should be avoided. He recognises that all-embracing methodologies are unsuitable given the wide diversity of businesses and their associated requirements for IT.

Rather the *preferred mode* of IS strategy formulation is dependent upon the sector in which a firm operates. IS strategy formulation is also iterative since past experience is likely to influence current strategic goals and objectives. This may be highly dangerous if old-style performance criteria determines future investment. For example, performance indicators used in the mainframe environment may not be appropriate for client-server technology.

Earl (1989) advises that IS strategies are best 'managed as portfolios'. Thus

'At the level of the SBU, the applications strategic plan should consider the trade offs and balancing between risk and return – the financial portfolio model.... Not all the contents of the applications strategic plan have equal priority in timescale or for resources. Mandatory applications and maintenance enhancement are non-controversial. The other elements of the plan will have different pay-offs, risks and timescales.... The applications strategic plan therefore must be shaped into a portfolio which yields a smooth flow of deliverables year by year and hedges the many risks in IS development (Earl, 1989, p.86).

He cites six key problems with IS planning. First, he argues that many companies have failed to develop adequate business plans. This serves to confuse decision makers about the nature and scope of the IS plan. Second, many companies fail to agree on priorities. This introduces a socio-political dimension to IS planning since it implies that competing values and objectives inhibit rather than support technical change. Third, new technologies simply confuse managers since they demand new performance measurement criteria. In addition, new vocabularies for management philosophies such as JIT, MRP II, process improvement, process innovation and TQM, together with new technologies in the form of client-server, multi-tasking, multi-media, etc do not sit comfortably with traditional IS planning terminology. In other words, past IS plans are not appropriate to guide contemporary IS strategy making. Fourth, the rapid rate of technical change tends to overwhelm IS planners since it offers them new conceptual challenges. This is not helped by the IT skills shortages which exist in many companies, particularly in the PC related field where many businesses are finding that managers and staff with traditional IT skills experience must learn new skills and vocabularies. Fifth, traditional organisation structures which divide business functions are particularly unsuitable for the new 'process orientated' environment. This is creating problems in the areas of financial control and performance measurement as IT spans the entire organisation. For example, ITs which were traditionally used in functions such as marketing and human resources were not integrated. Nowadays, however, new client-server technologies have the capability to integrate business functions. This results in a blurring of the divisions in the old functionally based organisation structure and, in turn, demands a new way of conceptualising organisations and their associated business processes. Finally, IS strategies may help to locate how and where competitive advantage may be gained.

Given that corporate leaders in banking and manufacturing attempt to keep pace with the latest technologies, the attainment of competitive advantage is becoming increasingly difficult. In many respects, companies continue to invest in new technologies to stay in business, although the more successful ones exploit technology in new and untried ways. For example, a recent interview with a UK bank found that core business processes were being re-thought to determine how IT could be used to maximise customer information. This information may then be used to determine the products and services required by their customers. Using technology as an information resource to link business processes offers companies one example where they can gain internal competitive advantage. But this depends on managements' ability to pinpoint where process improvements and innovations can be made, and develop and apply technologies accordingly. This brings us to the second element of Earl's (1989) framework – the need to develop an IT strategy. Arguably, this is probably the most difficult part of the strategy formation process which is not helped by the rapid rate by which technologies are introduced in the marketplace.

IT strategy

IT strategy according to Earl (1989) is concerned with 'how' IS strategies will be implemented. IT strategy is described as *activity based, supply orientated* and *technology focused.* It is also about the delivery of workable IT solutions to business problems. The *technology-strategy connection* (Kantrow, 1980) is appropriate here since IT strategies are 'best seen as the technology framework or architecture which drives, shapes and controls the IT infrastructure' (Earl, 1989, p.95). IT strategy is not simply about the vision which senior managers adopt for their long-range IS planning, but instead the practical application of IT to the business. Four elements of the IT architecture are given by Earl which include computing, communications, data and applications. Computing refers to the information processing hardware and its associated operating system software. Communications refer to telecommunications networks and their associated mechanisms for interlinking and interworking. Data relates to the data assets of the organisation and the requirements of use, access, control and storage.

Finally, applications encapsulate the main application systems of the organisation, their functions and relationships, as well as the development methods.

The four elements of the IT architecture are interdependent. This means that each element influences and is influenced by the other elements. Ultimately, the IT architecture is designed to create an infrastructure which is more powerful than the sum of its parts. For example, the topology of a communications network is influenced by applications needs, data transmission requirements and information processing geography as well as by its own capabilities. Earl (1989, p. 95) contends that

> 'The technology framework can contain four levels of guidance. The four levels for each architecture element may be called frames'. The set of frames makes up the framework. The four levels consist of the following categories:

- *Parameters* – which are the major design parameters of each architecture element. They represent the essential needs, constraints and preferences that over time each element should attempt to satisfy.
- *Schemas* – logical, and perhaps physical, models of what is required of each architectural element and how they should work. Sometimes called models or blueprints they may either be the visual, logical state of the frame as it exists now or an agreed, detailed model of what is being pursued.
- *Policies* – concrete, practical statements of how each technological element is to be delivered. Included are technological policies, guidelines, procedures and standards.
- *Plans* – firm plans and goals for each element. These may include project plans or performance goals – plus time-phased actions which will move the framework to the next state of evolution. (p. 95)

According to Earl, the progression from the first frame (parameters) to the fourth (plans) indicates 'increasing degrees of business and technological certainty'. The ability of firms to tackle each element in the framework is dependent upon the 'business or technological imperative'. Moreover, each element should be tackled individually at first even though they are seen as interdependent.

Designing and building architectures was common in large organisations in the late 1980s. Earl asserts that the task of creating architectures is very difficult although four reasons for undertaking this activity dominate:

1. As technology becomes embedded in business operations and sector infrastructure, the need for systems and technology integration increases. Architecture provides a framework for, and a mechanism to, consider and design necessary interfaces, compatibilities and integration.
2. As technologies advance so rapidly, organisation structures evolve, and business needs change, the IS/IT function is concerned to establish the necessary amount of order in information processing. Architecture provides a framework for resolving and reviewing technology choices over time.
3. Once the information system (the what) is formulated, a set of policies and mechanics is required to ensure its effective and efficient delivery. Architecture provides a structure for implementing the IS needs of the business.

4. As the relationships between business strategy and capability and IT strategy and capability become closer, a technological model of the organisation is required. Architecture is already serving this need in companies in the delivery sector where IT infrastructure underpins business and sector activities. (p.97)

Earl contends that architecture is intended as a framework for 'analysis, design and construction of IT infrastructure' to steer an organisation over time. He asserts that the IT architecture is not 'set in concrete'. Nor is it likely to be fully worked through and detailed in every aspect. The time horizon of the IT architecture is likely to be five years. In this respect, it is evolutionary in nature, as each component of the architecture is subject to change.

Although this approach is useful in terms of breaking down the complexity of IT into conceptually manageable areas, it is not without problems. First, the technical focus depicted by an IT architecture may not be easily understood by non-technical senior managers. Here they may not be able to conceptualise how an IT architecture is related to the business strategy. It may also be perceived as 'too mechanistic' in orientation and, at the same time, impose constraints upon individual creativity. Earl (1989) contends that

'An appropriate horizon for architecture tends to be five years. Beyond that, business and technological uncertainty is too great and within five, short term needs can drive out longer term benefits' (p.113).

It is important to break down the architecture into modules, each of which includes a set of deliverables and short run performance targets. Companies which use this approach must develop their architectures over a three to five year period as they are unlikely to be effective under three years. According to Earl, the architecture is a framework for making technology decisions and therefore must help firms to determine how the various elements or 'pieces of the IT jigsaw' fit together. It is a framework for 'resolving conflicts' and is influenced by 'organisational mandates' and 'business imperatives', not forgetting technology. It is also a guiding framework and is only effective if it is used throughout the organisation.

IM strategy

The IM strategy, according to Earl, is distinguished from the IS and IT strategies because it is concerned with the 'wherefores'. In this context, IS and IT strategies can only be implemented if they are managed. IM strategy is described as *organisation based*, *relationships orientated* and *management focused*. Earl contends that the concept of an IM strategy began two decades ago when firms began to develop procedures for managing the DP function in the 'classic control stage manner'. Here, the IM strategy was likely to be found in the form of 'a management standards manual'. Earl claims that renewed management interest in IM strategy emerged towards the end of the 1980s, in part because of the growing managerial and user issues surrounding IT. The burgeoning financial investment in IT throughout the 1980s provided the impetus for firms to seek more effective management control over the range of IT activities. Earl gives six reasons which underpin the formulation of an IM strategy:

1. Information and IT are resources which need to be managed as efficiently and effectively as other resources.
2. The organisational, business and management impact of IT require IT/IS to be managed as an integral part of the business.
3. As business strategies increasingly are dependent upon, or created by, IT, the IT function is too important to be managed without some formalisation.
4. In the past lack of top management support and involvement has impeded the successful exploitation of IT.
5. As technologies advance and choices have to be made, technology matters do matter.
6. As IT becomes embedded in business and organisational life and pervasive in use, many stakeholders are involved, so that managements need to take strategic views.

Earl outlines the four tasks of information management – planning, organisation, control and technology. Planning involves the integration of IS and IT strategies with other decision-making processes. Organisation is often the most important task in the design and building of the architecture discussed above. It concerns issues of centralisation and decentralisation of the IT function, the formation of steering committees, management education and training, and reporting procedures of the IT function and the responsibilities of IT managers. Control issues invariably relate to the relationship between IT and finance. Key management activities are investment appraisal and performance measurement of IT. An important concern is the degree to which financial commitment to IT meets the IS and IT strategies outlined above. Finally, technology is related to priorities of the IT strategy, for example the design and development of methodologies for IT, security practices and data management techniques.

Earl's (1989) three categories of IS, IT and IM strategies provide a useful conceptual framework for discussing the inter-disciplinary nature of managing technical change. It is unlikely that the majority of organisations attempt to break down the strategic issues in relation to technology in this way. Nevertheless, the approach is an attempt to demonstrate that strategy formation for technology embraces a set of complex issues for management.

From rational to interpretive approaches of strategy formation and decision making

The popularity of the formal-rational approach to IT strategy formation is attractive to practitioners since it is both descriptive and prescriptive. As we saw above, this approach has its roots in economic theory and is largely concerned to optimise the outcome of decision making. Jabes (1981) differentiates between the traditional approach (the formal-rational approach) and the behavioural perspective (which is also called the interpretive approach). For whereas the former is based on the premise that individuals possess all the relevant information to maximise the results of their decisions, the latter perceives individuals to be only partially aware of 'all the options in the environment'.

In support of the behavioural position, Simon (1958, p.423) is critical of the definition of rationality used by economists. He argues that, for some people, rationality 'means the achievement of goals, some associate it with individuals maximising satisfaction, others conceive of it as a decision making process without regard to how successful a person is in achieving goals, and still others consider rationality to be broadly synonymous with intelligent purposeful behaviour'.

Simon's (1958) work is relevant to our discussion on strategy since he views decision making as one of the most important organisational activities. He believes it is 'synonymous with managing' (Jabes, 1981). He criticises economic perspectives which view decision making as a simple choice between alternative courses of action. He argues that it is also misleading to promote the view that decision makers are fully informed about all their options. Simon (1960, p.8) distinguishes between two types of decision: programmed and non-programmed. Programmed decisions, he argues, are routine and repetitive. Here, it is in fact possible to delineate a systematic, step-by-step process for decision making. This is facilitated by the development of administrative systems. He differentiates between two types of decision making techniques for handling programmed decisions. The traditional approach relies on habit or clerical routine. Simple and straightforward administrative systems are designed to process these decisions. The modern approach, on the other hand, uses the more sophisticated processing power of computers in the form of mathematical models, simulation techniques and electronic data processing.

The second type of decision according to Simon is more problematic. Non-programmed decisions are described as 'one shot' and 'ill-structured'. They are also likely to be 'novel, policy decisions'. Strategic decision making which is complex and uncertain also falls into this category. Simon claims that non-programmed decision making techniques are traditionally based upon judgement, intuition and creativity. Modern techniques, however, involve the use of 'heuristic problem solving' using computer technology. Although Simon was writing long before the development of the personal computer (PC), more up-to-date decision-enhancing technology is found in the form of Decision Support Systems (DSS), Management Information Systems (MIS), Knowledge Based Systems (KBS), Executive Information Systems (EIS) and Expert Systems (ES). Artificial Intelligence (AI) may also be added to the list, though few commercial packages currently exist in the business world.

Simon argues cogently that since individuals possess only limited cognitive information handling abilities, they are unable to predict the outcome of their decisions. Nor are they likely to be able to maximise the outcome of their decisions. He describes this situation as *bounded rationality*. So instead of using the term *economic man* (which sees decision makers as fully informed and rational), Simon proposes the term *administrative man* to describe behaviour which 'satisfices' rather than 'maximises' decision outcomes. Thus,

'Administrative man is unable to have complete and accurate information about the environment, so he searches through available choice alternatives until he hits upon the one that is 'good enough'. A choice is made when an alternative meets the minimum standard of satisfaction that the individual expects. The choice rarely coincides with an optimal decision, such as suggested by the model in economics. The interest is in feasible solutions that meet a minimal standard of satisfaction. Optimal solutions may not be feasible. During the search for a satisfactory alternative, the individual may realise that he is unable to find any alternative that meets his standards. He then lowers his level of aspiration, thereby lowering the minimum acceptable standard. If search shows that available alternatives are not satisfactory, the aspiration level may be raised. The whole process implies that the individual has a psychological set from which he determines subjective 'rationality' (Jabes, 1981, p. 58).

Simon argues that unlike the traditional economic model, administrative man operates from a simplified perspective of the real world. Whilst organisations may attempt to develop complex models to aid decision making, human limitations relating to 1) the ability to acquire all the relevant information, and 2) the ability to process the information, leads to the search for simplified models. In this respect, Simon's concept of 'satisficing' is useful in describing decision making behaviour which pursues sufficient, satisfactory goals rather than behaviour which seeks to optimise decision outcomes.

Types of decision	Decision-making techniques	
	Traditional	Modern
Programmed	1. Habit	1. Operations research; Mathematical analysis, models, computer simulation
Routine, repetitive decisions	2. Clerical routine; standard operating procedures	2. Electronic data processing
Organisation develops specific processes for handling them	3. Organisation structure, common expectations; a system of subgoals; well defined informational channels	
Non-programmed	1. Judgement, intuition and creativity	Heuristic problem solving techniques applied to: a) training human decision makers; b) constructing heuristic computer programs
One-shot, ill structured, novel policy decisions	2. Rules of thumb	
Handled by general problem solving processes	3. Selection and training of executives	

Table 3.1 Programmed and non-programmed decision-making (*Courtesy:* Simon, 1960, p.8)

The work of Simon (1958, 1960) has influenced many writers in the general business strategy literature. His work is also relevant to the IT strategy field. The significant contribution of Simon's work is that it focuses on the limitations of human brain processing capability (bounded rationality), although in common with the advocates of the formal-rational approach, he views decision making as a rationalistic, step-by-step process.

Other writers, notably Lindblom (1959), view decision making as a much more chaotic human activity. He proposes the concept of *incrementalism*, or the *science of muddling through*, to provide an alternative to *conventional* decision making theory. He believes that in complex decision making situations, it is not possible to identify all the objectives of the various stakeholders who would be affected by a policy. He argues that only a narrow range of possibilities is, in practice, likely to be considered by decision makers. The process of policy making is one of selecting between only a narrow range of alternatives. Decision makers are unlikely to dwell on values or goals given the narrow choice.

Unlike the rational approach to decision making, Lindblom (1959) argues that decision makers only select a manageable (rather than a comprehensive) range of alternatives. Summarising Lindblom's position, Richardson and Jordan (1982, p114) claim that

'In choosing which option to adopt, one has reference to values, but the choice of policy instrument is combined with the ranking of values. In this approach there is a tendency for policy innovations to be small-scale extensions of past efforts with an expectation that there will be a constant return to the problem to make further extensions and to reconsider the problem in the light of new data, etc. In other words, success limited comparisons (SLC) (Richardson and Jordan, 1982).

The above theories of decision making are relevant to our discussion of strategy formation for two reasons. First, the perspective one adopts as to whether strategies can be planned according to a formal-rational, menu-driven approach, or arise from a series of *ad hoc* decisions will determine managerial behaviour. On the one hand, organisations are likely to engage in formal, top-down, linear strategic planning if they believe that behaviour can be controlled. On the other hand, to accept the *ad hoc*, incremental perspective on decision making is to reject the notion that behaviour is amenable to managerial control strategies.

Lindblom's (1959) work on decision making influenced the later writings of Quinn (1980) who developed the concept of *logical incrementalism*. Quinn looked at nine multinational enterprises (MNEs) and concluded that senior executives attempt to achieve their objectives through an evolutionary approach to decision making. Logical incrementalism is a move away from perceiving strategy making as an all-encompassing activity, delineated by a neat sequence of steps. Instead, the logical incrementalist perspective demonstrates how strategies are formed from broad concepts which are ultimately translated into specific organisational commitments.

As Johnson and Scholes (1993, p. 44) point out

'Continual testing and gradual strategy implementation provide improved quality of information for decision making and enable the better sequencing of the elements of major decisions. There is also a stimulation of managerial flexibility and creativity, and, since change will be gradual, the possibility of creating and developing a commitment to change throughout the organisation is increased. Such processes also take into account the political nature of organisational life, since smaller changes are less likely to face the same resistance as major changes. It is also possible to accommodate the variety of resource demands and political ambitions of different groupings - or coalitions - in the organisation'.

This move away from rationalistic to interpretive approaches to strategy making is greatly advanced by the writings of Mintzberg (1978, 1979, 1993, 1994). Writing on the *pitfalls* of strategic planning, Mintzberg has, over the years, produced a wealth of material on the 'fallacies' of this activity. He argues that one of the problems with the traditional literature on strategic planning was an absence of empirical work on the consequences of strategy making. He claims that 'a kind of *normative naiveté* has pervaded the literature of planning – confident beliefs in what is best, grounded in an ignorance of what really does work' (1993, p. 226). He argues that just because an organisation claims to undertake strategic planning does not mean that it is effective, workable or desirable in the long or short term. Moreover, deliberate (intended) strategies may translate into emergent (unintended) consequences.

In his popular article of the late 1970s, Mintzberg (1978, p. 934) introduces the concept of 'strategy formation' and also identifies the 'emergent' nature of the strategy process. Thus,

> 'The usual definition of 'strategy' encourages the notion that strategies, as we recognise them *ex post facto*, are the deliberate plans conceived in advance of the making of specific decisions. By defining a strategy as 'a pattern in a stream of decisions', we are able to research strategy formation in a broad descriptive context. Specifically, we can study both strategies that were intended and those that were realised despite intentions'.

Similarly, Steiner (1979) identified ten key problems with the strategic planning process. They include:

Description

1. Top management's assumption that it can delegate the planning function to a planner
2. Top management becomes so engrossed in current problems that it spends insufficient time on long-range planning, and the process becomes discredited among other managers and staff
3. Failure to develop company goals suitable as a basis for formulating long-range plans
4. Failure to assume the necessary involvement in the planning process of major line personnel
5. Failing to use plans as standards for measuring managerial performance
6. Failure to create a climate in the company which is congenial and not resistant to planning
7. Assuming that corporate comprehensive planning is something separate from the entire management process
8. Injecting so much formality into the system that it lacks flexibility, looseness, and simplicity, and restrains creativity
9. Failure of top management to review with departmental and divisional heads the long-range plans which they have developed
10. Top management's consistently rejecting the formal planning mechanism by making intuitive decisions which conflict with the formal plans

The interesting point relating to Steiner's (1979) study on corporate planning was that human resource problems were far more important than technical impediments to the process. This point was also made by Abell and Hammond (1979) who said that 'the systems would have worked fine if it weren't for all those darn people'. In particular, top management were blamed for many of the pitfalls of planning. In Steiner's (1979) work, many of the failings of planning are attributable to top management failure, either through lack of support or through an inability to create the right organisational environment for corporate planning to succeed.

More recently, Mintzberg (1994, p. 15) outlines several pitfalls to strategic planning which comprise:

- the commitment pitfall
- the change pitfall
- the politics pitfall
- the fallacy of predetermination
- the fallacy of detachment
- the fallacy of formalisation

Mintzberg opines that

> 'Search all those strategic planning diagrams - all those interconnected boxes that supposedly give you strategies - and nowhere will you find a single one that explains the creative act of synthesising ideas into strategy. Everything can be formalised except the very essence of the process itself.'

This leads Mintzberg (1994) to conclude that the overriding fallacy is indeed the 'grand fallacy of strategic planning'.

Relating the above work of Simon, Lindblom, Quinn and Mintzberg to our interest in IT strategy formation suggests that all these approaches sit uncomfortably beside formal-rational explanations. With the exception of Simon, who adopts a linear approach to decision making (albeit one of 'bounded rationality'), the remaining writers perceive strategy formation as a complex and highly uncertain activity. This is well illustrated by Mintzberg, 1993, p.227, who claims that

> '... strategy making is an immensely complex process involving the most sophisticated, subtle, and at times subconscious of human cognitive and social processes. We know that it must draw on all kinds of informational inputs, many of them nonquantifiable and accessible only to strategists who are connected to the details rather than detached from them. We know that the dynamics of the context have repeatedly defied any efforts to force the process into a predetermined schedule or onto a predetermined track. Strategies inevitably exhibit some emergent qualities, and even when largely deliberate, often appear less formally planned than informally visionary. And learning, in the form of fits and starts as well as discoveries based on serendipitous events and the recognition of unexpected patterns, inevitably plays a key role, if not the key role, in the development of all strategies that are novel. Accordingly, we know that the process requires insight, creativity, and synthesis, the very things that formalisation discourages'.

Recent research by the author suggests that interpretive approaches to strategy formation best describe the behavioural processes, though a large number of organisations attempt to develop formal-rational, analytical models (Currie, 1994a). Field work conducted between 1990 and 1992 in Japan, the USA, UK and West Germany found that strategy making for AMT (CAD/CAM, robotics, FMS, etc) was not based upon the rigid adherence to a formal strategic planning process. Instead, it was *ad hoc* and incremental. In fact, financial decisions seemed to determine technology decisions, and not a thorough investigation of all the relevant information. Prior to strategies being formulated, senior managers from the SBUs, divisions or departments were allocated resources for the coming year. This determined the nature and scope of their investment in AMT. The process was also marked by political in-fighting as managers fought for scarce resources.

In Anglo/American companies, the annual budget varied only marginally. In times of recession, it was likely that the budget would be cut by, say, ten percent. This would obviously affect management choice about which systems to purchase and would inevitably lead to priority-setting decision-making designed to *satisfice* rather than *maximise* outcomes. When asked if it was possible to evaluate all possible alternatives before reaching a strategic decision, managers said this was impossible. Serious impediments to strategy formation for AMT were described as fourfold. First, budget uncertainty meant that managers could not develop strategies until they were aware of the financial parameters. Second, strategy formation for AMT was not an activity which consumed much attention from senior executives. These individuals were very concerned to ensure that 'technology delivers business benefits', but were not instrumental in achieving this objective. Their role was simply one of 'rubber stamping' budgets rather than developing strategy. The latter task was left to lower-level technical managers in many companies. Third, the speed with which technology changes continued to pose a threat to the strategy-formation process. In many companies, managers said they preferred to take strategic decisions for AMT 'in stages' (incrementally) rather than develop five-year plans. Fourth, managers argued that it was difficult to formulate AMT strategies because of the competing interests throughout the organisation and the communication gap between technical and non-technical managers. On this latter point, one manager argued that, 'Provided I talk in money terms, senior (non-technical) managers understand me. But the moment I become too technical, I lose them. The trouble is, a lot of the benefits from technology are about quality and not cost. But I can't seem to get this message across'.

In many of these organisations, strategy formation was described as '*ad hoc*' and 'an act of faith'. It was not based upon careful deliberation of all the relevant information and possible outcomes. Rather, it was often formulated by middle-level technical managers and, occasionally, IT contract staff. AMT strategies were also more modest in size and content. Indeed, they were usually planned over the short term (one year) and could be abandoned subject to a change of company policy (e.g. financial constraints). In addition, AMT strategies were rarely directly linked to business strategy. On the contrary, some AMT strategies were in open conflict with the business strategies in some companies. This was found in cases where the technology division planned to increase capital expenditure only to find that the business had frozen all financial support for the coming year. In some companies, technology projects had to be abandoned midway through completion (Currie, 1994a).

The significant finding from this research was that a wide gap exists between IT strategy formation and implementation. To use Mintzberg's terminology, *deliberate strategies* often gave way to *emergent strategies*, as the outcome of AMT varied considerably between organisations. Whilst it was easy to attain from organisations their strategic framework for technology, they were less prepared to discuss some of the poor results which arose post-implementation.

Strategy and implementation

The link between strategy and implementation is addressed here for two reasons. First it is argued that a vacuum exists between the normative literature on IT strategy and research on implementation. In the former, managers are advised to develop clearly defined, rational strategies for IT based upon a full assessment of all the relevant information. Yet the latter issue of implementation is rarely discussed.

Whilst formal-rational frameworks may be useful as heuristic devices to aid the IT strategy formation process, recent research on the problems of implementation suggests one of two things. First, that managers either develop a poorly constructed strategic plan for IT, or have no IT strategy whatsoever. Second, that implementation bears little relationship (if any) with the formal-rational strategy process.

Drawing again on research by the author (Currie, 1994a) into managing AMT in four countries, a tenuous relationship was found to exist between technology strategy and implementation. Implementation is a broad term. It refers to three areas. First, it refers to the implementation of IT strategies. Second it considers the technical consequences of introducing technology. Third, it covers the socio-political impact of technology on organisations. On the issue of strategy formation and implementation, it was found that strategies were introduced incrementally. But Anglo/American companies, unlike Japanese companies, rarely addressed the relationship between strategy (conceptual) formation and operational (practical) implementation. This suggested a separation between concept (thinking) and execution (doing).

In most cases, senior executives simply left the task of implementation to lower-level technical managers. This often meant that technical managers were responsible for interpreting the strategy, if not developing their own version. In fact, Anglo/American companies were very keen to promote the role of technical champion to describe an individual with the dual skills of strategic understanding and technical expertise. But problems arose when the so-called technical champion failed to deliver business benefits from technology. This situation often led to capital rationing for future technology projects.

Nevertheless, in the event that technology was seen to deliver business benefits, senior managers usually interpreted this as indicative of a successful IT strategy. But this view was not shared by technical managers who instead attributed the success to the experience and skills of the technical team. What characterised the strategy process in Anglo/American companies was its short-term, results-orientated (financial) focus. This translated into technology implementation which was geared to some form of return on investment (ROI). This could involve headcount reduction, productivity enhancement or, in the case of CAD, more drawings per draftsman (Currie, 1994a). These performance measures were usually crude and not subject to any detailed scrutiny by senior executives.

In Japanese companies, on the other hand, a closer relationship existed between technology strategy and implementation both in human and technical terms. Usually, companies developed three-year strategies for IT which were supported by detailed operational (implementation) plans. In fact, the strategy process was largely about implementation in many Japanese companies. And implementation was carefully linked to target setting. For example, strategic plans invariably contained an itemised list of expected financial and non-financial benefits from a range of technologies (CAD/FMS, robots, etc). Those responsible for implementing the AMT strategy were also expected to measure the extent to which technology could deliver tangible business benefits. What set Japanese companies apart from their Anglo/American and, to a lesser extent, West German counterparts was their relentless pursuit to operationalise their technology strategies.

Concluding remarks

The task of researching into strategy formation for IT is shown to be complex and challenging. Whilst formal-rational frameworks are useful for simplifying phenomena, operationalising them is fraught with difficulties. This leads the interpretive school to argue that behaviour is not easily controlled or even managed in organisations. Whilst the formal-rational approach to strategy formation and planning has come under severe attack, it is undoubtedly attractive to practitioners since it enables them to organise and prioritise strategic aims and objectives. But as Mintzberg (1993, 1994) points out, the *fallacy of predetermination* suggests a wide gap between documenting strategic aims and objectives and achieving them in practice (implementation). More research is clearly needed to discern the success rates of strategic planning, but differentiating between serendipity and best practice is not easy. Indeed, case study research shows that, although senior executives often claim to have an IT strategy, it is not always communicated to lower-level personnel. Nor is it adhered to when senior executives decide to make across-the-board financial cuts to departments (Currie, 1994a). Clearly, strategy formation is a dynamic and political process within organisations, the outcome of which is difficult to evaluate. Interpretive writers are keen to stress the socio-political interaction between various stakeholders in the strategy process (Walsham, 1993) especially insofar as political motives affect IT project outcomes (Currie, 1994b). This is discussed more closely in the next chapter on investment appraisal and evaluation of IT.

Case study

Small system development project

Whilst the popular IT literature encourages managers to develop clearly defined IT strategies to steer applications development work, there are occasions when technical and legal changes act as a catalyst for change.

Technology

There are many reasons why a functioning computer system is completely re-written. For example those systems which were written for DOS-based applications are replaced with others which are capable of maximising the benefits of new operating systems (such as OS/2). The full advantages associated with non-preemptive multi-tasking (e.g MS Windows) transform a stand-alone application into one capable of utilising information pertinent to other applications (i.e. wordprocessors, spreadsheets, databases, etc). The benefits of this approach are improved user friendly environments, faster data analysis, and numerous display formats. For example, the data contained within one application can be imported into Microsoft Graph and displayed as a three-dimensional graph, or incorporated into a document, or even used within a slide show.

Legal changes

Another reason why systems are written again is due to new legal requirements. In the example used in this case study the original system had been written using FoxBase. This was a DOS system which had been successfully running for several years. The program reported on the number of company shares which were held by the bank's customers. The new legal requirements are shown below.

If 2% or more of all the shares issued by a company are held (Material Interest)

If 10% or more of all the shares issued by a company are held by the bank and they belong to a third party (Non-Material Interest)

A material interest refers to a share which is owned by the bank. Thus all the associated share-holding benefits belong to the bank. As a result the shares represent a financial gain in the form of dividends and share price increases. A non-material interest is the holding of a share for a third party. Unlike a material holding, this does not represent a financial gain or loss to the bank.

Each day, all the share transactions of the previous day have to be recorded, and every Friday, all the Material and Non-Material holdings must be declared to the Bank of England. This is a legal requirement under which every UK bank must operate.

The project

The decision to write the replacement stand-alone application in a MS Windows based structure was based on a number of technical factors. First, the code which had been written for the original system was extremely complex in terms of how the system modules interfaced. From a month-long analysis of this code, it was decided that any attempt to rewrite the code would adversely effect the operational functioning of the program. Second, the support which had been available to this package from the manufacturer and internal help-desk had

ceased. The main reason was because it was considered obsolete. Finally, and most importantly, it was decided to migrate this application to Windows since it was the bank's policy to move in this direction.

The replacement system would thus be written in a new language and would be supported by the relevant development area. If the system was to be written in the old language, it would not receive adequate maintenance or support if errors occurred. However, the decision to use a new language would avoid this problem.

The budget was set at £30,000 and a 4 month time scale was agreed. This figure was arrived at by an analyst programmer rather than a project manager. Equally, the time scale was also set by the analyst/programmer. However, this individual had essentially based his calculations on an 'educated guess', since his knowledge of the technology was limited.

Initially, the analyst/programmer was given the responsibility to develop the software under the direction of a project manager. But it soon became clear that the projected delivery date had been underestimated by some thirty-five per cent. This was due to the complexity of the system and its specifications. The analyst/programmer, though competent in the language chosen (Visual Basic), was not familiar with applications development work in the financial services sector. Thus it was necessary to engage a second contract analyst/programmer who was able to help build the system and recover the lost analysis time. Also, the project manager was unfamiliar with the technology and the complexity of the intended system. As a result, he took a decision to hire additional staff.

As the system neared completion, two bank employees were hired to test the program. This work had not been initially budgeted for, but again provided an essential input into enabling a fully functional system to be released. In short, a project which was to be developed ostensibly by a single analyst/programmer ended up absorbing the time of the project manager, together with a second analyst/programmer and two system testers. Whilst the project was delivered on time, its final cost was almost £60,000.

Discussion questions

1 What was the strategy which initiated the development of the system?
2 Why do legal requirements underpin IS applications developments?
3 Why do IS projects go over-budget?
4 Do you think that new technologies determine management decisions to instigate IS projects?
5 Are IT contractors committed to doing a good job?

References 3

Abell, D.F., Hammond, J.S. (1979) *Strategic market planning*, Prentice Hall.

Ackoff, R.L. (1970) *A concept of corporate planning*. Wiley.

Ansoff, H.I. (1965) *Corporate Strategy*. McGraw Hill.

Argenti, J. (1980) *Practical corporate planning*. George Allen and Unwin.

Boynton, A.C., Zmud, R. W. (1984) 'An assessment of critical success factors'. *Sloan Management Review*. Summer.

Carley, M. (1981) 'Analytic rationality', in A. G. McGrew and M.J. Wilson, (eds) *Decision Making: approaches and analysis*. Manchester University Press.

Cash, J.I., Konsynski, B. R. (1985) 'IS redraws competitive boundaries'. *Harvard Business Review*. March/April.

Child, J. (1972) 'Organisational structure, environment and performance: the role of strategic choice'. *Sociology*, Vol, 6. No. 1. pp. 1–22.

Clark, K.B. (1989) 'What strategies can do for technology'. *Harvard Business Review,* Nov/Dec, pp. 94–98.

Cole, R.E. (1985) 'Target information for competitive performance'. *Harvard Business Review*, May/June, pp. 100–109.

Currie, W. (1989a) 'The art of justifying new technology to top management'. *OMEGA – The International Journal of Management Science*. October, Vol, 17, No. 5. pp. 409–418.

Currie, W. (1989b) 'Investing in CAD: a case of ad hoc decision making'. *Long Range Planning*, Vol, 22, No. 6, pp. 85–91.

Currie, W. (1994a) *The strategic management of AMT*. CIMA, London.

Currie, W. (1994b) 'The strategic management of large scale IT projects in the financial services sector'. *New Technology, Work and Employment*, Vol, 9. No. 1. March, pp. 19–29.

Cyert, R., March, J. (1963) *A behavioural theory of the firm*. Wiley.

Earl, M. (1988). *Information Management: The strategic dimension*. Oxford: Clarendon Press.

Earl, M. (1989) *Management strategies for information technology*. Prentice Hall.

Fichman, R.G., Keremer, C.F. (1992) 'Adoption of software engineering process innovation: the case of object orientation'. *Sloan Management Review*, Vol, 34. No, 2. pp. 7–22.

Financial Times (1994) A-Z of computing supplement, 26, April.

Forcese, D.P., Richer, S. (1973) *Social research methods*. Prentice Hall.

Friedman, A., Cornford, D. (1989) *Computer systems development*. Wiley.

Gershuny, J.I. (1978) 'Policy making rationality: a reformation'. *Policy Sciences*, 9, pp. 295–316.

Gray, D.H. (1986). 'Uses and misuses of strategic planning'. *Harvard Business Review*. January/February, pp. 89–97.

Grindley, K. (1991) *Managing IT at board level*. Pitman.

Hickson, D. (1987) 'Decision making at the top of organisations'. *Annual Review of Sociology*, Vol, 13, August.

Jabes, J. (1981) 'Individual decision making', in A. McGrew and M. Wilson, *Decision Making*. Manchester University Press.

Johnson, G. (1987) *Strategic change and the management process*. Basil Blackwell.

Johnson, G., Scholes, K. (1993) *Exploring corporate strategy.* Prentice Hall.

Jones, C., Currie, W., Dugdale, D. (1993) 'Accounting and technology in Britain and Japan: learning from field research'. *Management Accounting Research.* Vol, 4, pp. 109–137.

Kantrow, A.M. (1980) 'The strategy-technology connection'. *Harvard Business Review*, July/August. pp. 6–21.

Kharbanda, O., Stallworthy, E. (1991) Let's learn from Japan'. *Management Accounting*, Vol, 69, No. 3, pp. 26–33.

Knights, D., Morgan, G. (1991) 'Corporate strategy, organisations and subjectivity: a critique'. *Organisation Studies*, Vol, 12, No. 2. pp. 251–273.

Lindblom, C. (1959) 'The science of muddling through'. *Public Administration Review*, No, 19, pp. 79–88.

Mintzberg, H. (1978) 'Patterns of strategy formation'. *Management Science*, Vol, 24, No. 9. pp. 934–948.

Mintzberg, H. (1979) *The structuring of organisations: a synthesis of research.* Prentice Hall.

Mintzberg, H. (1993) *The rise and fall of strategic planning.* Prentice Hall.

Mintzberg, H. (1994) 'Rethinking strategic planning Part 1: pitfalls and fallacies'. *Long Range Planning*, Vol, 27, No, 3, pp. 12–21.

Mintzberg, H., McHugh, A. (1985) 'Strategy formulation in an adhocracy'. *Administrative Science Quarterly*, vol. 30, no. 2.

Mintzberg, H., Waters, J.A. (1985) 'Of strategies deliberate and emergent'. *Strategic Management Journal*, Vol, 6. No. 4. pp. 257–72.

Pascal, R., Athos, A. (1981) *The art of Japanese management.* Penguin.

Porter, M. (1979) 'How competitive forces shape strategy'. *Harvard Business Review*. March/April, pp. 137–145.

Porter, M. (1980) *Competitive strategy.* Free Press: USA.

Porter, M. (1985) *Competitive advantage.* Free Press: MacMillan.

Quinn, J. B. (1980) *Strategies for change: Logical incrementalism.* Irwin: Homewood, Ills.

Remenyi, D. (198). *Increase profits with strategic information systems.* NCC publications.

Richardson, J.J., Jordon, A.G. (1982) 'Policy-making models', in A, McGrew and M. Wilson, *Decision making*, Manchester University Press.

Robson, W. (1993) *Strategic management and information systems.* Pitman

Rockart, J. (1979) 'Chief executives define their own data needs'. *Harvard Business Review.*

Shank, M.E. (1985) Critical success factor analysis as a methodology for MIS planning'. *MIS Quarterly*, Vol, 9. No. 2. pp. 121–129.

Shank, M.E., Boynton, A.C., Zmud, R.W. (1985) 'Critical success factor analysis as a methodology for MIS planning'. *MIS Quarterly*, Vol, 9. No. 2.

Simon, H. (1958) *Administrative behaviour*, 2nd edition, Free Press of Glencoe: New York.

Simon, H. (1960) *The new science of management decisions.* Harper and Row.

Smircich, L., Stubbart, C. (1985) 'Strategic management in an enacted world'. *Academy of Management Review*, Vol, 10, No. 4, pp. 724–736.

S´acey, R.D. (1993) *Strategic management and organisational dynamics.* Pitman.

Steiner, G.A. (1969) *Top management planning.* MacMillan: New York.

Steiner, G.A. 91979) *What every manager must know.* Free Press: New York.

Walsham, G. (1993) *Interpreting information systems in organisations.* Wiley.

Ward, J., Griffiths, P., Whitmore, P. (1990) *Strategic planning for information systems.* Prentice Hall.

Wiseman, C. 91985) *Strategy and computers: Information systems as competitive weapons.* Dow Jones and Irwin.

Wysoki, R.K., Young, J. (1990) *Information systems: management principles in action.*

CHAPTER 4

Investment Appraisal and Evaluation of IT

Introduction

As we saw in the last chapter, the formal-rational approach to IT strategy formation is attractive to managers because it advocates the development of appropriate methodologies and techniques for introducing technology to achieve desired business benefits. This approach perceives IT strategy formation as a process of conceptual deliberation, the product of which is usually a framework or model which outlines a series of sequential steps, each of which are delineated by checklists. Such an approach is likely to be endorsed by senior executives since they seek to formalise the process by which technology is introduced into the organisation. Formal-rational frameworks are also widely advocated by management consultants and academics, many of whom seek to advise managers of the benefits of identifying the 'critical success factors' which lead to competitive advantage through technology.

In this chapter, we consider some of the theoretical and empirical literature on investment appraisal and evaluation of IT. The issue of evaluating IT is discussed in the context of the manufacturing industry and financial services sector. The discussion concludes by arguing that the task of evaluating IT continues to pose problems for managers, and this is shown by the ambitious attempts by some companies to revise their management accounting and control systems and procedures.

Achieving business benefits from IT

A common fallacy of some of the management literature on IT of the early 1980s was that introducing *new* technology would automatically produce business benefits such as cost reduction and the like. The somewhat misconceived alliance which emerged between IT and competitive advantage tended to engender a wave of optimistic literature about the impact of IT. Much of this literature was based around a scenario which advised managers to introduce state-of-the-art technology and, in doing so, increase productivity, reduce headcount and operating costs.

In fact, this scenario remains popular today, although it is not peddled with the same vigour. The caution against presenting IT as a panacea for business is partly due to the well-documented IT disaster stories featured in the popular press and academic literature, and also because managers in all sectors show a greater awareness of the likely pitfalls of IT. Most notably, the risks associated with the high cost of in-house and external IT development work, the poor diffusion of PCs and off-the-shelf software packages, skills shortages, implementation and maintenance problems and the financial, political and logistical difficulties of aligning IT with business strategy.

In many companies, the reputation of the IT function has been tarnished as senior executives complain that the annual IT spend consumes significant resources which seldom result in tangible business benefits. Common management complaints refer to the failure of IT projects to keep within time and budgetary constraints, the development of inappropriate IT systems, user problems, poor quality systems, difficulties in evaluating IT projects, poor project management and technical skills, implementation and maintenance problems, and a lack of business awareness among IT professionals. Faced with these problems, many senior executives, particularly in the US, now seek to 'outsource' their IT function and instead concentrate on 'core business' activities.

One reason for the lack of achievement of business benefits from IT, despite the large IT budget, is perceived by some as due to the failure of senior managers to align IT evaluation procedures and techniques with strategic thinking (Farbey et al, 1993). This problem is likely to arise from the rapid rate at which technology is introduced into the marketplace, leaving managers confused as to whether specific technologies will be appropriate for their organisation. The shortfall in knowledge and experience of these technologies is therefore likely to result in a desire on the part of senior managers to impose greater controls over the evaluation procedures for introducing and monitoring technology. Such controls are likely to be those found in traditional management accounting texts which emphasise the techniques of DCF and NPV for investment appraisal.

The issue of evaluating the business benefits from IT has been a concern for managers over the last three decades. According to Farbey et al (1993, p.3), when the House of Commons Select Committee on Trade and Industry asked in 1988 which was the most pressing issue relating to IT, the Chief Executive of IBM UK replied it was 'finding reliable ways of assessing investment in information systems'. This resulted in a government initiative to commission a report on IT evaluation for small and medium enterprises (SMEs).

The problem of identifying and measuring the business benefits from IT continues today, with many senior executives dismissing the IT function as a 'cost pit' (Lacity and Hirschheim, 1993). New technologies in the form of client-server, multi-tasking, multi-media, CAD and others, only serve to confuse managers and accountants in their pursuit to find the *one best way* to evaluate IT. The following sections examine research on the evaluation of CAD, yet the key issues relating to evaluation and investment appraisal are pertinent to all information technologies.

The evaluation of CAD since the 1980s

In a study of twenty large and medium sized UK manufacturers in the late 1980s, Currie (1989a) found that engineers became increasingly concerned that traditional management accounting techniques such as discounted cash flow (DCF) and net present value (NPV) were inappropriate since they failed to capture the *true essence* of CAD. In the majority of companies where engineers and accountants were interviewed, the former argued that senior managements' over-reliance on quantitative measures for evaluating CAD detracted from the real benefits behind its introduction. Many engineers argued that they were coerced by senior managers to adopt traditional management accounting practice for the formal evaluation of CAD such as DCF and NPV techniques. Important performance measures were nearly always financial and focused on productivity, direct labour and equipment costs. However, a large number of engineers disagreed with the quantitative evaluation procedure because they felt the real advantages of CAD were qualitative. This was demonstrated in practice by improved quality of design drawings, the ability to retrieve and modify design drawings, reduced lead times and the simple fact that complex design work could not be undertaken by traditional manual methods (e.g. the drawing board). In the mid-1980s, Medland and Burnett (1986, p. 143) recognised many of the difficulties facing managers in determining appropriate methods and techniques for evaluating CAD. However, they cautioned against overstating productivity as the key performance measure. They argued that many companies fail to analyse exactly what they mean by 'productivity' and, in the case of CAD, tend to use a simple measure of more drawings per draughtsman. They stressed that

> 'It is far from the case that more drawings are equivalent to more, or better, design.... It would make far more sense to turn the argument on its head and justify CAD on the grounds that it allows designers to do more or better work while producing fewer drawings'.

A study by Senker (1984) also found that CAD was justified on the basis that it would increase 'drawing office productivity' which would mean fewer draughtsmen in the medium to long term. Whilst the logic underpinning this assumption suggests that CAD allows the draughtsman to produce more drawings, it fails to address the issue of the quality of design work, both in terms of producing high quality drawings as well as using CAD to design new and more sophisticated products. Senker found that engineering managers admitted to providing 'spurious justifications' for CAD since the formal evaluation procedure which emphasised quantitative measures was at odds with their own perceptions of the benefits of CAD. Other writers on CAD during the 1980s similarly found that CAD was justified on the grounds that it would enhance drawing office productivity often by as much as 4-1 in the short term (Appleby and Twigg, 1987. Carnall and Medland, 1984. Senker, 1984).

Using the above studies as a background to research on CAD in the late 1980s, Currie (1989ab) was interested to examine the process by which CAD was introduced into large and medium sized UK manufacturing firms. Companies were selected on a random basis with the only requirement being that they had invested in CAD in the last eighteen months. Woodward's (1958) size classifications were used, with large companies having over 1000 employees and medium size firms between 200–999 employees. Size classifications are problematic to social scientists due to structural diversity. For example, large companies may be divided into several strategic business units (SBUs) or divisions, each of which may be responsible for its own capital equipment (IT) budget. Company size is also becoming more difficult to research in the light of continuous restructuring, rationalisation and downsizing, etc.

However, for the purposes of the CAD study (Currie, 1989ab), it was important to differentiate between single-site business entities (one-site companies) and companies which comprised several units. Many companies in the medium size category were in fact sites/divisions or units of large multi-nationals, although they appeared to operate as 'satellites' – that is, they were responsible for their own economic performance and survival in a fierce global business climate.

In dividing companies/units according to Woodward's (1958) size classifications, Table 4.1 gives the key decision maker in the evaluation of CAD in their organisation, together with the year when CAD was implemented and the financial investment at the time of interview (the mid to late 1980s). Whilst it was difficult to locate one individual as the key person responsible for the evaluation and implementation of CAD, an engineering manager (usually the head of the design function) was commonly charged with this duty. The managerial level of individuals responsible for this process varied between large and medium size companies. In large firms, it was common to find a senior engineering manager (occasionally at director level) responsible for CAD. In medium size firms, on the other hand, it was more common to find a middle-level manager in charge. Titles also varied among the managers interviewed ranging from CAD manager to chief designer. The level of financial responsibility also varied considerably, with one individual in a large manufacturing firm managing a £16 million investment and another, in a medium size company, responsible for only £50,000.

An interesting observation from the study was that large companies tended to invest in CAD much earlier than their medium sized counterparts. Interviewing engineering managers in the latter found that they were likely to 'wait and see' how CAD was 'working out' in the large companies before taking a decision to invest. Also, the late adoption in medium size firms was because suppliers concentrated on securing sales in large firms, particularly where the investment was likely to exceed £1 million over two to three years.

Unlike the popular perception that small companies are more 'go-ahead' and 'high-tech' than their larger rivals, it was in fact the large manufacturers who had the best CAD facilities. Large manufacturing firms also possessed the most technical expertise when it came to CAD, with one senior engineering manager (Case no. 1) running a government-sponsored company teaching programme for CAD users. This individual was aware of the many pitfalls of introducing CAD and argued that one of the key problems was 'a lack of senior management awareness about the potential of CAD'. Working in a global manufacturing company, he claimed that he and his team of 'technical experts' knew more about CAD than many of the vendor companies (suppliers). He reinforced this statement by saying that during his experience of advising CAD users from other firms, he had witnessed many 'technological disasters' where companies had followed the advice of 'untrained, non-technical senior managers' as well as that of 'spurious technical consultants'. He reasoned that where companies fail to train their managers or indeed promote technical people to higher-level managerial positions, the lack of technical knowledge in the higher managerial functions leads to the hire of external consultants 'who are even less likely to understand the nature of the business'. Whilst he felt there were 'some good technical consultants on the circuit' he was very critical of the situation where senior managers 'ignore the advice of their own people (employees)' and instead unquestioningly endorse the findings of external consultants.

The crux of the problem according to many engineering managers was an inability on

Large Sized Companies/Units				
	Title of key decision maker	*Management level*	*Unit*	*Estimated cost of CAD*
Case 1	Senior Engineering Manager	Senior	✓	£4.9m since 1980
Case 2	Head of CAD	Senior	✓	£16m since early 1980
Case 3	Corporate Engineering Exec.	Senior	✓	£12m since 1980
Case 4	Industrial Dev. Manager	Middle	✓	About £200k
Case 5	CAD Manager	Middle	✓	About £700k
Case 6	Chief Design Engineer	Middle	✓	About £2m
Case 7	Production Engineer	Middle	✓	About £10m since 1980*
Case 8	CAD Operations Manager	Middle	✓	$3–4 m
Case 9	CAD Manager	Senior		Not given
Case 10	CIM Manager	Senior	✓	£1.8m
Medium Sized Companies/Units				
Case 11	CAD Manager	Middle	✓	About £100k*
Case 12	Chief Designer	Middle	✓	About £100k*
Case 13	Design Draughtsman	Not a manager		£100k
Case 14	Contract Draughtsman	Not a manager	✓	£120k*
Case 15	DO Manager	Middle	✓	£120k since 1981
Case 16	Chief Mech. Design Engineer	Middle	✓	Awaiting decision
Case 17	CAD Manager	Middle	✓	£1m*
Case 18	Engineering Manager	Middle		£50k
Case 19	Engineering Director	Top Manager		£200k since 1984
Case 20	Technical Services Manager	Middle	✓	£300k

* Not total cost – excluding maintenance contract and/or training and/or software

✓ Represents sites/plants/divisions of companies. No asterisks represents single-site company

Table 4.1 Manager/person responsible for introducing CAD and level of investment
(Adapted from Currie 1989)

the part of senior non-technical managers to adequately evaluate the potential benefits (if any) from CAD. Commenting on the accounting techniques imposed by senior managers, many engineering managers said they were 'inappropriate' for evaluating CAD in contemporary highly complex manufacturing environments. One senior engineering manager (Case no. 1) argued that problems arose when senior non-technical managers demanded formal cost-benefit information to demonstrate the benefits and pitfalls of CAD. With over thirty years of engineering experience and responsible for a £4.9 million investment in CAD, one senior engineering manager said that he was 'constantly fighting a battle with accountants' to demonstrate the inadequacy of the present system of evaluating CAD and other technologies. He said that financial resources would only be released for CAD provided he could 'prove' to his superiors that it would result in a satisfactory return on investment (ROI).

He claimed that senior non-technical managers tended to impose management accounting controls on CAD investment in the form of DCF and ROI because 'they believe that by doing so, they can control the outcome of the investment'. It was found that engineering managers in as many as eighteen out of the twenty manufacturing companies were required to adopt a cost-benefit approach to CAD investment even though twelve were 'sceptical' about doing so.

The reason for the scepticism was based on the engineering managers' perceptions that traditional management accounting techniques could not capture the 'true potential of CAD'. Many engineers argued that their company's initial investment in CAD was simply 'an act of faith' even though it had been formally evaluated in cost-benefit terms. For example, one senior engineering manager (Case no. 2) claimed to adopt the vendor's evaluation documentation which promised that CAD would improve productivity by 4–1 within 18 months, reduce manpower by as much as 30 percent, and reduce drawing office lead times by a massive 50 percent.

At the time of interview, this individual remarked that, 'If I hadn't used this form of cost-benefit analysis, senior managers wouldn't have released the money for CAD. I know that these targets will not be reached, but I am hoping to make improvements on design work quality and through administrative cuts. If anything, we might need more people'.

One of the interesting findings of the CAD study (Currie, 1989ab) was that budgets for evaluating technology-associated costs were compartmentalised. Hardware, software, maintenance and training were each met by separate budgets, making it very difficult to locate the true costs relating to CAD. The formal-rational managerialist approach to capital budgeting and investment appraisal which is outlined in many accounting text-books was not found to exist in reality. Engineering managers with several years experience of 'playing the game' (of capital budgeting) claimed that 'budgets were manipulated to serve the interests of managers'. During one interview, the head of CAD operations (Case no. 2) said that he had been refused resources to upgrade the CAD facility to achieve greater integration between design and production. It was interesting to note that even though the company was claiming to pursue a policy of 'functional integration', each department had its own budget and competed for resources with all other departments (e.g. marketing and HRM, etc).

The reason why senior managers had refused resources was because the head of the production department's own request for additional resources had been honoured. However, the head of CAD operations pointed out that it since his request for additional funds was for a joint project with the production department, it was irrational of senior managers to evaluate individual budget requests in isolation of the wider manufacturing environment. This led him to believe that senior managers did not embrace a technology strategy as they tended to leave 'technical matters' to the engineers. This was met with some disdain by engineers who felt that senior managements' lack of knowledge about technology led them to impose tighter financial controls on capital expenditure as a 'substitute' for being 'misinformed'.

One of the problems with the existing procedure for resource allocation was that many engineering managers claimed they had to comply with a system which they believed was 'inappropriate' and 'misguided'. They understood the principle of why it was important to cost-justify CAD and other technologies, but they felt that a more 'holistic' and 'less adversarial' approach was preferable. They argued, for example, that the current emphasis on quantitative evaluation tended to detract from the important qualitative reasons for introducing CAD. Senior managers tended to 'overlook' the qualitative advantages of CAD and instead focused only on achieving an 'adequate ROI'. As a result, many engineering managers felt that since they had to evaluate CAD on the basis of 'spurious financial criteria', they were unhappy at being held responsible for the achievement of certain performance targets (i.e. productivity increases and head-count reduction).

Management responsibility for CAD

The allocation of responsibility for managing the change to CAD was given to a CAD manager (Case no. 17) in one organisation. This individual had little faith in the cost-benefit approach to evaluating CAD and was unwilling to accept any responsibility should CAD fail to meet the expected targets of increased drawing office productivity and head-count reduction. During the interview, he said that he was even asked by senior managers to predict how many customers the company would win as a result of CAD and also to quantify the increase in business. He dismissed this request as 'crystal ball gazing' and expressed the view that CAD 'was not a panacea to solve financial problems'.

It was interesting to note that CAD was seen by some managers as a 'glamorous technology' and was duly featured in company brochures. Some companies were required by their clients to implement CAD and nearly all the companies in the sample believed that 'CAD will dominate the drawing offices of the future'.

Some engineers claimed that the existing evaluation procedure for capital expenditure had two key advantages for senior managers. First, it encourages 'competition between budget-holders' (e.g. the heads of the business and administrative departments). This was evident in the above company where the design department was competing for resources with the production department – the latter being more successful on one occasion. Many engineers responsible for capital budgets and investment appraisal for CAD said that 'budgeting is a political process'. Indeed, many refused to divorce the formal-rational procedure from the 'politics of the organisation'. One manager said that, 'By whipping-up competition between budget-holders, senior managers believe they are keeping us on our toes. The trouble with the system, though, is that it encourages one to become single-minded and not company-minded'. In other words, individual managers wished to 'champion' their activities by winning resources and, in the process of doing so, impress their superiors.

Many stories were told of how managers 'championed the cause of CAD' to win promotion and/or a better position elsewhere. But the system of appraising individual performance did not always benefit the company as a whole. In the case of CAD, numerous managers said that budgets were 'manipulated to meet individual objectives'. This meant that budget-holders would engage in what is commonly described as 'creative accounting' to get round the rigidities of the system. For example, one CAD manager found that half way through a project, new software became available which was 'obviously more appropriate for the purposes of the project'. When he put in a request for additional funds to purchase the necessary up-grade, he was told by his superior that 'no more money is available this quarter'. This left the project manager (who was the budget-holder) with a serious dilemma and two possible options. First, he could use another budget (training) to meet the costs of the software and risk a reprimand if found out. Second, he could delay purchasing the software until next year and risk a serious over-run on the project. As it was, his designers and draughtsmen were complaining that using the old software was slowing them down considerably.

At the time of interview, the CAD manager decided to go ahead and purchase the software and try to 'disguise the costs'. His strategy was to send two of his designers on the vendor's software up-grade course and, in the event, purchase the software alongside the training. The total cost would be met by the training budget with the training being over-emphasised in comparison with the purchase of the software. This was felt to be a 'smart move' according to the two designers who went on the vendor's software up-grade course but one which 'should be unnecessary' in practice. These individuals believed that 'senior managers should think laterally about the business ... concentrate less on mea-suring costs and more on making sure a good job is done'. They were concerned that formal-rational capital budgets tended only to measure tangible items, such as the cost of hardware and software. Very few senior managers were able to evaluate the difference between the quality of various software packages and why an up-grade in software was important in the practical task of undertaking a CAD project.

Quantitative and qualitative benefits from technology

The CAD study (Currie 1989ab) highlighted the wide gap which existed between the evaluation of quantitative (financial) costs and benefits of CAD and the qualitative (non-financial) benefits. In eighteen of the twenty manufacturing companies visited, engineering managers had to provide a 'sound statistical (quantitative) case for evaluat-ing CAD'. Whilst they accepted the principle that managers should be accountable for the disposal of financial resources, they were unhappy that 'spurious cost-benefit' analy-sis is used to evaluate CAD. The concept of cost-benefit was attacked by one senior engineering manager (with thirty years experience of capital budgeting). He argued that, 'The logic that costs incurred should result in a benefit downstream is faulty. In the case of CAD, we comply with the accounting procedure which requests information on the likely cost-advantages of CAD. Recently, I justified a CAD proposal on the basis that it would increase drawing office productivity by 50%, reduce labour by 10% and reduce design lead times by 25%. I had to put a figure to these items to show how CAD would save money. I don't believe in these financial predictions. But I know that if I hadn't eval-uated CAD on the basis of a cost-benefit case, I wouldn't get the money. It's as simple as that'. He went on to say that, 'One advantage of the present system is that senior man-agers very rarely make me carry out a post-audit evaluation of CAD. This is too time consuming when I can demonstrate that my time is better used on day-to-day CAD pro-jects. They also work on the basis that once money has been released, it becomes a sunk cost. They are also too busy worrying about the next batch of capital budgets to be inter-ested in last year's ones'.

The vast majority of manufacturing firms carried out ex-ante as opposed to ex-post evaluations. Ex-ante evaluation involves managers assessing the likely costs of a project in conjunction with its expected benefits. In other words, managers may assume that if they spend £400,000 on a CAD system over three years, they may increase productivity by 80% and reduce drawing office staff by 30% during this time frame. Ex-post evaluation, on the other hand, is concerned with performance measurement and considers what costs have been incurred and if the expected benefits have been achieved in practice. Ex-post evaluation is much less common in organisations. In management accounting terminology it is usually called post-auditing.

In the CAD study, the problem of ex-ante and ex-post evaluation was compounded by the fact that engineers did not believe the performance criteria to be meaningful (e.g. the itemisation of benefits such as productivity and headcount). Nor did they think that enough attention was given to the 'soft' benefits such as quality of design work and the value of skilled as opposed to unskilled staff. One engineer said that, 'In this firm CAD is justified on the basis that all draughtsmen can work as equally productive. In my division, there are only two of us with experience of CAD. The remaining five draughtsmen are now expected to use CAD without any training or guidance from me or my colleague. But I can't afford to teach them because my own productivity will decrease resulting in a bad appraisal later this year. I don't think these issues have even been addressed by senior managers or the accountants'.

Only two medium size companies did not engage in a cost-benefit evaluation of CAD. One of the reasons was the relatively low capital investment in CAD compared with other company expenditure. Another reason was because senior management were perceived by engineers to be 'in touch' with the real strategic uses of CAD. One engineering manager argued that detailed cost-benefit information was usually required by those who perceive CAD as an 'investment'. His company, however, saw CAD as 'a necessary overhead'. He commented that, 'At our company, we see CAD as a vital tool to improve the quality of design work, and also because it impresses our customers. We didn't introduce it to reduce labour or increase productivity. Indeed, these things are inherently difficult to measure. We believe that benefits from CAD are qualitative and depend on the skill of the designer or draughtsman. Luckily, this is recognised by senior managers who are, themselves, engineers'.

This situation was unusual given that nearly all the manufacturing companies, irrespective of size, based their evaluation procedures on management accounting techniques such as DCF, NPV or 'payback'. In fact, a closer inspection of the techniques adopted showed that 'payback' was, by far, the most common method of investment appraisal. DCF was considered 'too complicated' by some managers. The significant reason for relying on cost-benefit evaluation was described by one corporate engineering executive as due to 'the British tendency to promote accountants rather than engineers to senior management or board level positions'.

Comments of this nature are not new and have been levelled at British industry for several decades. The Finniston Report published in 1978 addressed this very issue. The central argument was that too few opportunities existed for engineers to gain entry into senior level management positions. As a result, very few senior managers in leading British companies were technically aware. This meant that board level representation was dominated by senior personnel from finance and accounting, with little input from engineers and other technical specialists. In fact, the route to senior management was, in many British manufacturing companies, based on the attainment of 'business skills' which included an understanding of finance and budgeting as opposed to technical knowledge. Those who desired senior management positions were therefore encouraged to leave their technical specialisms and acquire business skills relating to the areas of finance, accounting, communication, managing people, marketing and forecasting, etc.

A study conducted by the Engineering Council (1988) (ten years after the Finniston Report) argued that, as opposed to perceiving engineers as too technical and specialised for general management positions, they are, instead, 'excellent raw material for management because, by virtue of their education, training and experience, they have the following:

1. an ability to quantify and to measure
2. appreciation of the significance of accurate and approximate information
3. recognition of importance of time scales
4. understanding of the importance of quality, reliability and safety
5. an ability to bring together theory and practice
6. an economic approach to decision making
7. a sound understanding of scientific concepts
8. a capability to optimise solutions from a range of options
9. an understanding of the use and management of technology
10. the capacity to make judgements based on inadequate information

Whilst many engineers in the CAD study were fully able to evaluate CAD and other technologies on financial grounds, their concern was based on the extent to which this information was reliable and appropriate. In this respect they were critical of reports which advocated training for engineers in the methods and techniques of finance and accounting because they urged that many of the benefits from new technology were qualitative and, hence, unmeasurable. This issue has been raised by many other writers (Barwise et al, 1989. Primrose, 1989. McNair et al, 1990. Nedo, 1989. Shank and Govindarajan, 1992).

Primrose (1989, p. 28) states that

'One of the consequences of this difficulty in justifying investment in AMT has been a tendency for engineers to allow themselves to be persuaded that levels of savings can be achieved which in practice turn out to be unrealistic and this in turn leads to the conclusion that AMT is a 'failure'. This problem can easily arise when a company is considering an area of technology with which it is completely unfamiliar and can be misled by untypical demonstrations or reports'.

Certainly manufacturing companies investing in CAD in the early 1980s were often confused about how best to cost-justify CAD. Engineers attempting to evaluate CAD for the first time were often persuaded by those wishing to sell their technology of the range of financial benefits stemming from CAD in the form of productivity enhancement and headcount reduction. In some cases, budget-holders would simply adopt the vendor's procedure for justification and present this information to senior managers.

However, towards the end of the 1980s the initial optimism about CAD was replaced by a greater caution as some companies' experiences of CAD reflected badly on the vendors' promises. In fact, some companies abandoned CAD altogether and returned to manual methods. In spite of the reluctance on the part of managers to embrace CAD as a panacea, the problem of finding appropriate methods and techniques to evaluate CAD continued. Engineering managers in the CAD study said that pressure to demonstrate the business benefits of CAD became more intense in times of recession and when previous investments in technology were perceived by senior managers to be unsuccessful. Engineers were also critical of the timescales imposed to realise the benefits from CAD.

In one company, the £12 million investment in CAD had led one Corporate Engineering Executive to attempt to quantify the qualitative benefits of CAD. He argued that whilst CAD had been 'a great success' the growing financial commitment to improving the CAD facility meant that he had to demonstrate to the board that it was a 'sound investment'. He therefore placed a value on each of the qualitative benefits which included

1. more detailed drawings
2. ease of modification
3. the ability to achieve right-first-time
4. better quality drawings
5. ability to win new customers
6. improved job satisfaction and motivation

As with the more traditional quantitative benefits of productivity and headcount reduction which are associated with CAD, he believed it was problematic to place a value on the above qualitative benefits. However, he saw this requirement as one which enabled him to 'play the game' (of capital budgeting). He described the activities of capital budgeting and investment appraisal and evaluation as 'rituals' which were essentially legitimation processes. He also believed that the common technique of evaluating 'payback' from CAD was 'flawed' for two reasons. First, he argued that since engineers and accountants did not understand their respective disciplines, it was essential to 'level down' and communicate in the 'common language of money'. This was not in itself a problem but the fact that it occurred meant that communication was, at best, 'superficial'. Second, the traditional method of evaluating capital projects using the management accounting techniques of DCF, NPV and 'simple payback' was not easily replaced even though they were 'generally accepted to be inappropriate for contemporary manufacturing environments' using CAD, CAM, robots and other advanced manufacturing technologies (AMTs). Senior management, however, were reluctant to abandon these techniques especially since they acted as a 'control mechanism' throughout the company. Moreover, some engineers argued that financial control was likely to become more intense as the level of expenditure in technology increased.

The findings of the CAD study (Currie, 1989ab) support other research which suggests that the dominant formal-rational approach to evaluating CAD is pursued in British companies primarily to realise short-term as opposed to long-term business benefits.

The study found that differences in the perception of CAD arose between those involved in its evaluation (senior managers and accountants) and those responsible for its implementation (engineers). Although the former usually carried out the cost-benefit evaluation of CAD, this information was essentially for the consumption of upper-level managers to satisfy internal and external financial reporting requirements. Whilst the study did not examine in detail such areas as the professional status of engineers and the dominant role of accountants in UK companies (Manpower Services Commission, 1987), these issues were raised by many of the respondents who believed that senior managers in UK companies were 'out of touch' with technology.

More specifically, they were uninformed about the strategic uses of CAD among other technologies. The study also highlighted a reluctance on the part of British manufacturing companies to invest in training; particularly technical training for engineers and senior managers. In fact, management training seemed to be equated with the development of 'business skills', based on the acquisition of finance, accounting, people skills and marketing. Indeed, those engineers wishing to 'become managers' would abandon their technical training and instead embark on management training in the form of the Master of Business Administration (MBA) and other 'business-related' courses. Training for technology was not seen as the route to senior management. On the contrary, many manufacturing companies possessed a dual career spine with technical careers occasionally reaching the level at which management training commences! Little wonder that many engineers came to view their discipline as 'a dead end career'.

The CAD study also found that an informal system operated alongside the formal-rational evaluation of CAD embraced by manufacturing companies. This was reflected in the tendency to 'manipulate' budgets to satisfy individual aims and objectives. If anything, those managers who 'played by the book' were unlikely to progress very far in the organisation because it was seen to be important to circumvent the rigidities of the capital budgeting system. This was achieved by allocating costs to other budgets with examples of engineering managers paying for software up-grades from the training budget. Many engineers commented that 'functional integration' or 'process innovation' was unlikely in the event of compartmentalising budgets and also by encouraging competition for resources between line managers.

Having completed the CAD study at the time at which CAD was being introduced in companies for the first time, a later study was carried out on the comparative management of AMT on Japanese, Anglo/American and West German manufacturing companies (Currie, 1994a). This study was interested to determine if evaluation methods and techniques had changed as a result of more experience using CAD and other manufacturing technologies. The study is discussed in some detail in the following section.

Evaluating the benefits from CAD in Japan, the United States, Britain and West Germany

The issue of determining the most appropriate methods for evaluating AMT continued to be just as important for global manufacturing companies during the early 1990s. Between 1990–2, a grant was obtained from CIMA to investigate the evaluation and implementation of AMT in Japanese, Anglo/American and Western German manufacturing companies (Currie, 1994a). Semi-structured interviews were conducted with engineers and management accountants and a link was found to exist between the level of expenditure and the extent to which senior managers sought to control IT investment.

As IT expenditure increased, so did senior managers' demands for a 'sound financial case' for evaluating proposed capital projects.

Whilst AMT was still justified by some engineers on the basis of 'an act of faith' judgement, this was not acceptable to senior managers, who instead imposed what they thought was a more formal-rational approach to evaluation in the form of DCF, NPV and 'payback'. This was more common in Anglo/American companies where short-term performance targets for AMT tended to be favoured over longer-term objectives. Japanese companies, on the other hand, differed from their Anglo/American counterparts because they tended to evaluate AMT according to longer time horizons (this is discussed at some length in chapter ten).

The realisation that successful evaluation and implementation was crucial to the survival of the company encouraged many manufacturers to align their technology strategies with the overall business strategy. However, this was more successful in some companies than in others, irrespective of markets and products. Interviews with engineering managers in Anglo/American companies found that evaluation procedures for AMT placed a high premium on financial information. As with the CAD study discussed above (Currie, 1989ab), it was stressed that whilst qualitative benefits were seen as important, particularly to engineers, senior (non-technical) managers were unhappy to incorporate this information into the formal-rational evaluation process.

Ex-ante evaluation continued to be more common than ex-post evaluation of technology. In the majority of Anglo/American companies, and to a lesser extent, in Japanese and Western German companies, the formal evaluation process for AMT was based on a financial assessment of the relationship between estimated costs and expected benefits. Occasionally, this process was described as 'guestimating' the benefits from technology and was criticised by many engineers as 'too mechanical' and 'narrow in orientation'. Very few manufacturing companies carried out detailed post-audits, although many senior managers expressed the view that past technical failures called for more post-implementation performance measurement.

Managers in some of the Anglo/American manufacturing companies also expressed concern that evaluation was 'piecemeal' and planned in accordance with an annual financial reporting structure rather than being linked to a manufacturing strategy (if indeed one was in place). Cross-national differences were found to exist between the more 'short-term' orientated western manufacturing companies and their longer-term eastern (Japanese) counterparts. There was some exception here because many Western German companies also adopted a longer-range plan for managing technology, which may be influenced by the predominance of engineers in senior level management positions.

Interviews with Japanese managers found little difference in the choice of management accounting techniques used to cost-justify AMT. DCF, NPV and simple 'payback' were commonly used. However, many Japanese managers said that AMT was planned 'over the long term', according to a three to five year plan. Also, the selection of performance indicators was wider than those used by Anglo/American and even some German companies. For example, Japanese managers were keen to point out that given the high cost of commercial property, particularly in Tokyo, and a population of some 120,000,000, it was important to utilise space efficiently. To this effect, Japanese managers quantified space saving from introducing new equipment. Many Japanese manufacturers were keen to introduce Flexible Manufacturing Systems (FMS) which could handle a wide range of production work. Other important qualitative benefits were aimed to:

- win market share
- reduce organisational functions/processes
- enhance machine capacity
- reduce floor space
- improve cross-functional/departmental communication
- align AMT with JIT/TQM philosophies
- improve quality

On the issue of managerial responsibility for evaluating AMT, many Japanese managers said that the role of the technical champion was not one which was encouraged by Japanese firms. The preferred approach was one of collective decision making, consensus and teamwork. The idea that one person could spearhead technological change was considered alien to some Japanese managers. Although suggestions from employees were encouraged, large-scale technology decisions were taken by 'expert teams' and not by individuals working alone. The evaluation process was described as 'top-down' at some leading Japanese companies because strategy was viewed as a corporate responsibility. Moreover, strategy and evaluation were perceived as two sides of the same coin.

Japanese managers said that specific technology proposals for CAD, FMS and robots, among others, were not usually discussed in isolation, but as part of an all-embracing manufacturing strategy. Technology was seen as 'the driving force' to gain competitive advantage and cost-reduction. Japanese firms were no less concerned to reduce costs than their European and North American rivals, but they also placed a high premium on the qualitative (intangible) benefits from AMT.

At several large manufacturing firms, it was stressed that 'no ceiling' was imposed by top managers on financial expenditure for strategic technologies. Instead, manufacturing strategies had to consider 'where the business was going' and develop enabling technologies to achieve their objectives. At the time of interview, Japanese manufacturers expressed concern that the 'bad debt' problem of the late 1980s had forced banks to rethink their strategies for issuing business loans, and this was likely to effect all sectors of the economy.

More recent evidence shows that the Japanese approach to evaluating AMT is likely to become increasingly short term as many Japanese firms feel the pressures of the economic recession (Hori, 1993. Currie, 1994a). Indeed, the traditional Japanese preserves of life-time employment, promotion according to seniority, teamworking and consensus decision making, are all likely to come under attack as leading Japanese firms begin to shed jobs and implement further capital rationing measures (*Financial Times*, 1993).

Evaluating IT in the UK financial services sector

The issue of identifying appropriate evaluation methods for IT is equally problematic for the UK financial services sector. In a recent study, Currie (1994b) found that banks and insurance companies in particular were keen to maximise their IT facility to achieve competitive advantage. This had led many financial services companies, with a growing annual IT spend, to appoint an IT Director to develop and implement an IT strategy. Some of the IT literature also supports the appointment of a senior executive to represent IT at board level (Earl, 1989. Rowe and Herbert, 1990). Farbey et al (1993, p.7) gives four key reasons why senior general managers today need to be more closely involved with IT:

- IT affects strategic issues
- IT is at the core of business processes
- IT accounts for large expenditures
- IT is complex

The notion that IT affects strategic issues is supported by many large financial institutions because IT is now integral to the core business. Decisions which affect the core business are likely to be taken by senior managers, thereby elevating the status of IT as a strategic issue. In addition, IT is now embedded into the core processes of banks, building societies and insurance firms. It is used to increase efficiencies, re-organise the business into more focused work groups, integrate different parts of the business which may operate in separate locations or functions, streamline business processes and, perhaps most significantly, improve customer service.

In the financial services sector, IT is currently re-engineering many of its key business processes by making a transition from proprietary mainframes to distributed computing based on a client-server approach (see chapter one). Only by adopting open, enterprise-wide computing can IT provide the increased flexibility and productivity demanded by contemporary networked, process-orientated enterprises.

In spite of the declining costs of PCs and the influx of software packages in the marketplace, many large financial services enterprises are spending more on their IT facility. Whilst hardware and software costs are tangible and easy to identify, escalating costs include software development work, networking, maintenance and the use of contractors and consultants. By all accounts, it seems that commercial IT is becoming more complex as users demand new and improved IT applications and equipment.

A recent survey into ten large financial services companies found that IT was treated as a cost centre as opposed to being a profit centre. Although eight organisations had a separate IT division, and another locating IT as subset of a larger division, IT was essentially seen as a 'service provider' or, in some cases, a 'support function'. This seemed to contradict some of the literature which suggests that IT should be a strategic function. This is because the notion that IT is merely a service provider suggests that customers (users or purchasers of the service) can choose from a range of suppliers – external as well as internal.

Table 4.2 shows that six of the ten financial services organisations employed an IT Director/Manager to manage IT projects. However, one bank and two insurance companies tried to forge a 'marriage of convenience' between the users and an IT manager. This was to ensure that IT projects were developed with the user's full commitment and involvement.

Managers in seven cases confirmed that a skills shortage affected the business. To remedy this, external consultants/contractors were brought in to undertake IT project

Nature Of Business	Where does IT fit in the organisation?	No. in IT?	Who is responsible for managing IT projects?	Who do you use to carry out IT project development	Do you outsource IT work?	What is your annual spend on IT?	How are the benefits of IT quantified?
Bank	Integrated into each business	700	Users/ IT Manager	Company employees and contractors	Yes	£70 Million	IRR
Bank	Separate IT division	51	IT Manager	Company employees and contractors	Yes	£5.2 Million	Payback
Bank	Separate IT division	50	IT Manager	Company employees and contractors	No	£3 Million	ARR
Bank	Separate IT division	10	IT Manager	Contractors	Yes	£0.3 Million	No Measure
Bank	Separate IT division	43	IT Manager	Company employees and contractors	Yes	£5 Million	Payback
Bank	Separate IT division	43	IT Director	Company employees and contractors	Yes	£6 Million	ARR
Information Provider	Separate IT division	168	IT Director	Company employees	No	£20 Million	Payback
Building Society	Separate IT division	100	Non Technical Manager	Company employees	No	£9 Million	Payback
Insurance	Separate IT division	785	Users/ IT Manager	Company employees	No	£15 Million	NPV
Insurance	Subsection of a division	625	Users/ IT Manager	Company employees and contractors	Yes	£40 Million	Payback

Table 4.2 The evaluation of IT in the financial services sector

development work. Some managers were concerned about this because they felt that some of their permanent employees (as well as themselves) were not keeping pace with some of the state-of-the-art technologies. Six financial services companies said they out-sourced IT work. Company No. 3 which claimed it did not outsource work seemed to contradict itself by admitting to using contractors. When this was put to the IT Manager, he said that, in his opinion, outsourcing was the hiring of an outside IT software house to carry out work off-sight. However, the use of contractors to undertake work internally is defined as 'body shop outsourcing' (see chapter six).

Nine of the ten companies confirmed that it was a requirement of senior executives to quantify the costs and benefits of IT. Payback was used in half the cases, and one bank claimed not to use any financial measures. The IT Manager concerned said that, 'Since it is difficult to quantify the benefits of any IT project, we don't bother. We feel that IT is a necessary expenditure and one we have to make to keep up to date'.

Clearly the evaluation of IT continued to pose a problem for managers in the financial services sector. Although banks and insurance firms tended to retain a separate IT division, they were also pushing responsibility for IT decisions to the users in the various business departments. In addition, many financial services companies were contracting in/out IT work, which is now commonly known as outsourcing. In this respect, responsibility for IT projects was likely to become diluted. Indeed, technical specialists often lamented that the users were given greater powers to commission IT systems, but without the technical knowledge to ensure their decisions were feasible. This meant that many systems were commissioned, only to find at a later stage they were untenable – financially, politically and technically.

Concluding remarks

This chapter has discussed a number of studies in the area of evaluating IT. A cross-sectoral comparison shows that evaluation problems are not confined to only one sector. Indeed, the problem of finding valid quantitative justifications continues today, and is arguably made more complex by the pursuit to link IT with strategic objectives around the company. Seemingly, traditional management accounting techniques continue to be used for evaluation purposes, although growing evidence demonstrates the problems associated with many of these techniques. For example, a negative DCF does not necessarily mean that an IT project should not go ahead. However, this argument is likely to be formally adhered to if a proposed IT project is politically undesirable. On the other hand, when projects are deemed *strategic*, they are usually resourced even though they cannot be justified in financial terms.

Two case studies follow the above discussion which exemplify some of the evaluation issues in both the manufacturing (below) and financial sectors (chapter 5). In conclusion, it is contended that IT evaluation is not simply a mechanical procedure where IT project proposals can undergo rigorous financial scrutiny. Rather, empirical evidence from case study and survey sources show the whole evaluation exercise to be a political process which does not always favour the most technologically or financially attractive outcome.

Case study

Managing CAD at a US manufacturing company

One of the most illuminating case studies was a North American paper-making and processing manufacturer, where the Treasurer (a management accountant) was responsible for evaluating investment in CAD technology. The firm had recently been taken over by a large company from Finland where senior executives had imposed new measures to obtain better cost control. Capital rationing was perceived by the Treasurer as a serious constraint which would threaten individual initiative and creativity. He said that, in the past, 'no clear strategy' had existed for technical change. But as investment now exceeded $1m it was important to 'manage the technology process' more effectively. He said that his company viewed the role of the 'technical champion' as an important one, although he was aware that relying on the judgement and advice of one person rather than a working party or steering committee was 'risky'.

The formal-rational method of obtaining funds for capital expenditure was described as 'simple and straightforward'. The Treasurer said that, 'senior managers like capital proposals to be on one page only'. To accommodate this, the form comprised a single side of A4 and requested a brief description of the proposed item/project; its justification and estimated costs and benefits. The form appeared to serve merely as a record of capital expenditure, although the Treasurer said that it was used irrespective of whether the proposed item/project was estimated to cost $1000 or $1 million!

The evaluation process for CAD and AMT in general was described as 'piecemeal'. The Treasurer commented that it was difficult to develop an AMT strategy for two reasons. First, the level of capital expenditure for the firm was determined by the parent in Finland on an annual basis. This made it difficult to assess the range of technologies available to the firm for purchase and implementation. Second, capital expenditure proposals were written by line managers who, between themselves, competed for scarce resources. It was pointed out that, instead of an all-embracing AMT strategy, the firm comprised a series of sub-strategies, each of which was 'championed' by one or two individuals (usually engineering managers).

Capital expenditure proposals exceeding $50k required the approval of the President (in Finland). Five years prior to the interview, the firm had invested in a CAD system for cost reduction in the drawing office. The initial investment in CAD was considered to be 'unsuccessful', according to the Treasurer, because the vendor had gone out of business. This had created a 'support nightmare' as the company were unable to obtain maintenance assistance, training and software up-grades.

This led the company to move away from what was described as 'an act of faith', 'gut reaction' approach to capital investment to one which was 'better organised' and 'more methodical'. The Treasurer pointed out that while ex ante (pre-implementation) capital investment appraisal had been difficult, so too was ex post (post-implementation) for CAD. Apparently, the company were unable to define appropriate performance criteria to be measured and monitored. Accordingly, the Treasurer said that, 'Our first experience with CAD was really an experiment. We knew there were benefits to be had, but we were not sure what they were; and even less sure about how to measure them'.

As a result, a more measured and structured approach was developed by the Treasurer for future investment in CAD. Unsurprisingly, the Treasurer had developed a method for assessing the costs and benefits of CAD purely from a financial perspective. The logic behind this system was described as follows:

'Specific estimates of savings are based upon a combination of practical experience, and on experience gained during the pilot project. This company generates approximately 2000 drawings per year. Estimated time to generate a new drawing varies from two hours to a maximum of about

80 hours, with an average of approximately 6 hours. Without the use of CAD, it is estimated that design modification of an existing drawing (when practical) results in a 50 percent saving (three hours based on the average drawing but higher for more complex design work). CAD has features which facilitate geometry modifications (i.e. stretching, re-positioning, and associated re-dimensioning). With the use of CAD, the estimated savings resulting from design modification increases to 85 percent (approximately five hours on average). It is estimated that successful retrievals will occur in approximately 15 percent without the use of CAD, and in about 50 percent with CAD'.

CAD was seen to benefit the areas of:

- design/drawings retrieval
- design standardisation
- standardisation of process planning
- enhanced production process (work cell formation)
- improved production scheduling

Whilst the Treasurer had faith in the above method of calculation, this was not shared by some engineers who used CAD. Criticisms about the Treasurer's approach ranged from mild irritation to outright rejection. Some engineers described it as 'spurious' and 'misguided'. Others believed it was 'too mechanical and 'overstated the quantitative case for CAD'.

Having calculated the amount of drawings produced in relation to their modification and retrieval rate, the Treasurer used this information to further calculate the costs and benefits of undertaking design work both manually and using CAD.

Manual and automated design work and the GT database

The Treasurer responding to pressure from above was adamant to explain that automated design work (CAD) using the Group Technology (GT) database was more cost-effective compared with manual design work. The Treasurer reproduced a document which outlined the 'philosophy' behind the GT database:

'The basic philosophy of group technology is to analyse a collection of manufactured items and classify them into subsets (families) based on common attributes. A single manufactured item is readily identified as a member of a given subset by a GT code. There is a wide base of knowledge regarding how to formulate a GT classification. Perhaps the foremost criterion for determining the structure of a GT code is its intended purpose'.

The figures given in Table 4.3 used to justify CAD using the GT database consisted of an ex ante evaluation process, since the Treasurer admitted that he had not, as yet, carried out a post audit (an ex post evaluation). The figures are based on the estimated time savings (man-hours) of undertaking both manual and automated (CAD) design work using the GT database. The time saving cost is deducted from the cost of using the GT database, the latter remaining the same in both examples. However, as the figures show, the estimated cost savings using CAD as opposed to manual methods are much greater. The cost of using the GT database was estimated at about $6,900. This figure was reached by calculating that it takes about ten minutes to search for a drawing on the database. Over a year the 2000 drawings which are produced would create a net saving of 330 man hours (2000 ÷ 6 = 333.3) but this is rounded down given that time saving is an approximation. An hourly rate of $21 thus generates a total cost of $6,930.

Similar calculations were made in connection with the time saving of using the GT database undertaking both manual and CAD work, and also the time savings in modifications of existing drawings stored on the GT database (e.g. stretching, re-positioning and associated re-dimensioning). Additional savings were calculated to demonstrate that CAD was a cost-effective investment. Thus:

'In either a CAD or non-CAD environment some additional benefits will also occur in the manufacturing area. Manufacturing Engineering and Pre-production Planning review engineering drawings and prepare Bills of Material (BOM) and Routings. At company X six people are involved with this process, approximately 30 percent of their time. The other 70 percent involves similar work on non-Company X designs, and on miscellaneous support activities. When an existing bill of material and associated routings can be retrieved and modified, a conservative estimate is that 60/70 percent savings can be achieved. With a 15 percent retrieval (non-CAD environment) the estimated savings are 390 man hours (approximately $8,500. With a 50 percent retrieval (CAD environment) the estimated savings are 1300 man hours (approximately $28,500)'.

Activity	Manual drawings using the GT database ($)	CAD drawings using the GT database ($)
Cost of GT database	(6,900)	(6,900)
Drawing savings	12,000	98,700
BOM/routing saving	8,500	28,500
Total	14,200	120,300

Table 4.3 Estimated savings from the Group Technology (GT) database

The Treasurer said that the above calculations were 'guestimates' and were necessary in the legitimation process to justify investment in CAD. He pointed out that senior executives were only interested in financial savings and were disinterested in arguments for quality and ease of modification of drawings. If anything, the Treasurer had quantified some of the qualitative aspects of CAD. For example, the notion that designers could retrieve and modify a greater proportion of drawings was based on an assumption that such drawings were of sufficient quality to validate this activity.

However, the qualitative aspects of either the GT database or CAD were not stated in the formal-rational capital investment appraisal process. The reason why retrieval time and ease of modification were instead given priority was because of their relevance to the 'right first time' manufacturing objective. Engineers at the company said that one of the significant advantages of CAD was its greater precision in the creative process of design work. CAD enabled designers to undertake complex and novel work. Using the GT database in a non-CAD (manual) environment, only 15 percent of drawings could be retrieved and modified (resulting in a 600 man-hour saving equalling $12,600). However,

using the GT database with CAD, 50 percent of drawings could be retrieved and modified with a saving totalling approximately 4700 man-hours and $98,700. This figure could increase in line with a further increase in the retrieval and modification rate of design drawings.

Table 4.3 is a comparison between manual and automated design and gives the estimated cost advantages of using CAD technology in terms of man-hours and the retrieval rate of design drawings. While the Treasurer was keen to formally evaluate CAD purely on a financial basis, engineering managers at the firm were sceptical of this approach. They argued that the real benefits of CAD were fivefold and led to improvements in the following areas:

- process innovation
- product innovation
- quality enhancement
- ability to undertake complex design work
- ease of modification

It was stressed that all of these benefits were very difficult to quantify using traditional management accounting techniques. Process innovation was perceived as an important benefit for two reasons. First, it was vital to 'give customers the right image' and this could be achieved by putting CAD in all the company brochures. Indeed, some customers requested that design work was undertaken using CAD to reduce design lead times. Second, engineers argued that CAD improved the manufacturing process and enabled them to compete more successfully in a competitive market. Manual design was seen as 'outdated and slow'.

Product innovation was linked to the ability to undertake complex design work. Many engineers said that, 'Whilst this firm attempts to quantify the costs and benefits of CAD in comparison with manual design, this is pointless where CAD is the only tool we can use to complete some categories of design work'. They were referring to the more complex and sophisticated products which would be too expensive to design (if at all possible) using manual methods.

Quality was a thorny issue because, once

again, it was difficult to quantify. Measures such as 'winning more customers' and 'improving customer relations' were not ones which senior executives considered in the formal-rational evaluation process. Nor were they particularly interested in other qualitative measures such as improved working conditions for designers, job satisfaction and better quality design drawings.

One engineer pointed out that, 'Although it is claimed that we generate 2000 drawings per annum, this is likely to decrease in time as we begin to re-use and modify existing design drawings. I think the current method of assessment is faulty for two reasons. One, it measures output (number of drawings) against retrieval and modification rates. But in time, we are likely to generate fewer drawings which will greatly reduce the percentage rates of retrieval and modification. This will make us look less efficient on paper, even though we are likely to be working harder and more efficiently. Two, there is no emphasis on quality issues under the present system. Some people argue that productivity and efficiency can be measured by the generation of fewer drawings. But if these drawings are of good quality and achieve 'right first time', this should not be an issue.'

Another issue which was raised concerned the development of skills. One engineer said that, 'CAD is sometimes seen as a panacea which will automatically improve the operation of the drawing office. In actual fact, it is just a tool. It can only be fully exploited by a skilful designer or draughtsperson'. Clearly, this case raises several issues about the formal-rational and informal approaches to evaluating CAD technology. The Treasurer who was responsible for evaluating capital equipment was, himself, a management accountant. Whilst he recognised some of the difficulties of relying solely on financial (quantitative) data, he nevertheless preferred this approach as the most appropriate legitimation process to justify CAD. The development of a 'sound financial case' for CAD was also demanded by senior executives since a more informal, 'act of faith' approach was unacceptable. However, ex ante evaluation took priority over ex post evaluation, since the firm did not actively engage in post-implementation evaluation. This was seen as 'time-consuming' and 'difficult to undertake'. Indeed, the Treasurer said that most of his time was taken up with the preparation of capital investment appraisal documents as opposed to 'wandering around the firm trying to evaluate the effectiveness of existing equipment'.

Whilst many engineers at the company were critical of the formal-rational approach, they recognised that 'money shouldn't just be thrown at technology without any recognition of the possible opportunities and threats'. In this capacity, engineers called for a more all-embracing and holistic approach to evaluating technology, taking into consideration some of the qualitative benefits.

Discussion questions

1 Do you think that the Treasurer should be responsible for evaluating CAD?
2 Was the evaluation process scientific?
3 Do you think the evaluation process was adequate?
4 Is it possible to financially evaluate CAD?
5 What are the managerial issues of the case study?
6 Are qualitative benefits just as important as qualitative ones?

References 4

Appleby, C., Twigg, D. (1987) *CAD diffusion in the West Midlands automotive components industry*, Wolverhampton Polytechnic: Centre for Industrial Studies.

Barwise, P., Marsh, P. R., Wensley, R. (1989) 'Must finance and strategy clash?'. *Harvard Business Review*, September/October, pp. 85–90.

Carnall, C., Medland, A. (1984) 'Computer aided design: social and technical choices for development', in M. Warner, (ed) *Micro-Processors, Manpower and Society*, Gower, Aldershot.

Clausen, C., Jensen, L. (1993) 'Action-orientated approaches to technology assessment and working life in Scandinavia'. *Technology Analysis & Strategic Management*, Vol, 5, No. 2, pp. 83–97.

Currie, W.L. (1989a) 'The art of justifying new technology to top management'. *OMEGA – The International Journal of Management Science*, October, Vol, 17, No. 5, pp. 409–418.

Currie, W.L. (1989b) 'Investing in CAD: a case of ad hoc decision making'. *Long Range Planning*, Vol, 22, No. 6, pp. 85–91.

Currie, W. (1994a) *The comparative management of AMT*. CIMA: London.

Currie, W. (1994b) 'New technologies, old management practices: an empirical study of evaluating IT projects in the UK financial services sector'. Working paper.

Currie, W.L., Seddon, J.J.M. (1991) 'Developing a MIS for a manufacturing environment'. Paper presented to the Northeast Manufacturing Technology Center at the Rensellaer Polytechnic Institute, Troy, New York State, USA, July.

Curtis, B., Krasner, H., Iscoe, N. (1988) 'A field study of the software design process for large systems'. *Communications of the ACM*. Vol, 31, No, 11. pp. 1268–1287.

Earl, M (1989) *Managerial strategies for information technology*. Prentice Hall.

Farbey, B., Land, F., Targett, D. (1993) *IT Investment: a study of methods and practice*. Butterworth-Heinemann.

Financial Times (1993) 'Japanese companies 'feel overstaffed', 12 January. 'Tough job for the job seekers', 15 December.

Hori, S. (1993) 'Fixing Japan's white collar economy: a personal view.' *Harvard Business Review*, November/December, pp. 157–172.

Jones, T.C., Currie, W.L., Dugdale, D. (1993) 'Accounting and technology in Britain and Japan: learning from field research'. *Management Accounting Research*, 4, pp. 109–137.

Lacity, M.C., Hirschheim, R. (1993) *Information Systems Outsourcing*. Wiley.

McNair, C.J., Lynch, R.L., Cross, K.F. (1990) 'Do financial and nonfinancial performance measures have to agree?'. *Management Accounting*, Vol, 72, No. 5, November, pp. 28–36.

Medland, A., Burnett, P. (1986) *CAD/CAM in practice*. Kogan Page: London.

NEDO (1989) *AMT: a strategy for success?* NEDO Technical Communications: London.

Nolan, R.L. (1977) 'Controlling the costs of data services'. *Harvard Business Review*, July/August, pp. 114–124.

Primrose, P. (1989) *The financial justification for AMT*. NEDO Technical Communications: London.

Robey, D., Markhus, M.L. (1984) 'Rituals in information system design'. *MIS Quarterly*, March, pp. 5–15.

Rowe, C., Herbert, B. (1990) 'IT in the boardroom: the growth of computer awareness among chief executives'. *Journal of General Management*, Vol, 15, No. 4. pp. 32–44.

Senker, P. (1984) 'Implications of CAD/CAM for management'. *OMEGA: The International Journal of Management Science*, Vol, 12, No. 3. pp. 225–231.

Shank, J.K., Govindarajan, V. (1992) 'Strategic cost analysis of technological investments'. *Sloan Management Review*, Fall, pp. 39–51.

Woodward, J. (1958) *Management and technology*. HMSO: London.

CHAPTER 5

Generalists, Specialists and Hybrids

Introduction

This chapter explores some of the key issues in managing innovation and technology in commercial and public sector settings. Perhaps the most topical issue concerns whether generalists or specialists should manage IT projects and technical staff. In recent years, fears about deskilling through IT have subsided as organisations seek more efficient ways to manage IT by attempting to develop the right skills mix.

This objective is fuelled, in part, due to the poor management practices which have led to IS failures. Whilst technology itself used to be the convenient scapegoat, there is growing evidence that most technology failures are indeed management failures. Some commentators argue that the solution is the hybrid manager. This individual possesses both business awareness and technical knowledge, and the dual skill set is perceived as a prerequisite for successfully managing IT.

The labour market and the IT professional

The last decade has witnessed a plethora of literature on the management of technology, with many studies aiming to locate *best practice* in private and public sector settings. Indeed the issue of managing technology has been addressed from a number of disciplines. For example, industrial relations contributions have focused primarily on the opportunities and threats from IT on the labour market, employment levels, working practices, job satisfaction and deskilling, among other things. Work published in the late 1970s and early 1980s tended to diverge into optimistic and pessimistic scenarios about the *impact* of new technology. On the one hand, some writers cautioned against the prospect of massive job losses as a result of automation, the 'degradation' of work, and the emergence of boring and alienating forms of work (Wood, 1982. Cooley, 1980. Jenkins and Sherman, 1979, 1981). On the other hand, the positive scenario highlighted the opportunities from technical change exemplified by job creation and the elimination of dirty, meaningless forms of work. These arguments are well documented in a range of academic contributions. To this day, the debate rages on and is made ever more complex by the rapid pace at which technology is introduced into the marketplace.

Other contributions from the human resources domain have considered wider managerial issues relating to the organisation and co-ordination of IT in the workplace (Allen and Scott Morton, 1994. Drucker, 1988, 1990). At the level of the labour market, some studies have considered the emerging opportunities for IT professionals in both the private and public sectors (Brittain, 1992. Willcocks, 1992). This phenomenon is brought about by the significant changes which have affected and continue to affect the labour market. For example, the severe global recession of the early 1990s has forced numerous companies to seek effective capital rationing of their operations.

In the private sector, delayering and downsizing have stripped out many middle management positions. Financial services companies and manufacturers alike have imposed severe job cuts to streamline their operations; and this has led to what is effectively the elimination of life-time employment in large UK companies. Even at managerial levels, short-term (three to five year) contracts have been imposed upon individuals – a phenomenon which up till now has been more commonplace at lower, non-managerial organisational levels (e.g. clerical, secretarial; production work, etc).

Similarly, in the public sector, the ubiquitous government policy of 'market testing' (defined by the UK government as 'an activity currently performed in-house which is subject to competition, the aim being to promote fair and open competition so that departments and agencies can achieve the best value for money for the customer and for the taxpayer') and the creation of the 'internal market', characterised by the purchaser-provider relationship, has led to changes in management styles and practices (Willcocks and Harrow, 1992).

Recent figures show that by the end of 1993, activities valued at £1.1bn had been market tested in 389 separate exercises covering 25,146 civil service jobs. The private sector was awarded work worth some £855m. By the end of 1994, new work worth £830m covering a further 35,000 jobs had been market tested. The government claims that it has so far saved more than £116m and, by the same token, cut the civil service payroll by 14,587 people. Market testing is supposed to mean that the in-house unit which currently performs the work enters a competitive relationship with the private sector for the right to retain that work (*Computing*, 30 June 1994). This has led to numerous in-house IT departments (in addition to other services such as catering, cleaning, refuse collection, etc) to prepare bids along with other IT vendors/consultancies. Failure to win the contract may mean redundancy for the original in-house employees or a new employment contract with the company who has won the contract.

However, there is an important 'escape clause' for government departments and agencies which do not welcome an in-house bid. Prior to market testing a particular service, an exercise known as the Prior Options Review (POR) occurs. POR can recommend that the department or agency bypasses the market test altogether, and either makes the unit/department (service) concerned into a semi-autonomous trading agency, or simply privatises it without consultation. The latter situation means that no allowance is made for an in-house bid.

Clearly, the changes brought about by 'market testing' have significant implications for the future of IT departments in both the private and public sectors. Part of the rationale for market testing is to encourage public sector managers and staff, in particular, to emulate the 'corporate' behaviour of managers in the private sector. This is achieved at least theoretically by a greater awareness of customer care. Key performance indicators consider: speed by which calls are dealt with; efficiency of providing the service; number of complaints; the achievement of cost cutting targets, etc. The public sector has witnessed vast changes in how it is administered, with the accent on tighter financial control and accountability. In local government, NHS trusts, police departments and education alike, public sector managerial work has become synonymous with managing budgets and performance measurement.

A common theme in both the private and public sectors is to align IT with the corporate strategy of the enterprise. Yet corporate strategy is likely to be interpreted differently by managers in the two sectors. In the private sector, the profit motive will obviously steer corporate decision making, and IT strategies are likely to be geared to cost cutting through headcount reduction and increased productivity. Conversely in the public sector, the term 'strategy' is relatively new, and is not necessarily compatible with the historical ethos of this sector as a service provider to the community. However, recent research applicable to both sectors shows that IT failures, in conjunction with a burgeoning IT budget, lead management to seek more effective ways to manage IT for business and administrative improvement (Sauer, 1993. Currie, 1994a). The notion that organisations should develop a clearly defined strategy for managing IT is therefore, once again, firmly on the agenda.

The core and periphery IT labour market

Labour market considerations are also pertinent to the issue of managing IT in the context of the organisational status and role of the IT professional. To the extent that social scientists have addressed the issue of the emergence of a core and periphery labour market differentiated by permanent, career-orientated positions forming the 'core', and less secure, part-time and temporary jobs represented by the 'periphery', it is interesting to consider the status of IT professionals within this scenario. Arguably, IT professionals are increasingly represented by employment contracts which are located in the periphery labour market. This is witnessed by two important factors. First, the vast changes which have occurred in public and private sector organisations such as the separation of 'core' and 'service' activities have arguably reduced the overall status of IT, despite contrary claims that it is a *strategic factor* in attaining competitive position.

This is borne out in a recent survey by Bryson and Currie (1994) who found that out of some 184 organisations, some ninety percent of them claimed that IT was a cost centre and service provider to the core business. In this respect service departments are likely to incur more severe cost cutting measures than their core business counterparts. This is significant for IT managers and staff, all of whom are likely to be threatened by cost cutting in the event of economic recession or any other across-the-board cost cutting exercise imposed by senior executives.

Second, the historical status and role of IT professionals as specialists serves as a major impediment to achieving upward mobility by way of promotion to managerial grades. This issue has been addressed from a number of quarters by academics, practitioners and successive British governments. The Finniston report of the late 1970s cautioned against the lack of technical specialists in senior management positions in British companies and stressed the absence of an 'engineering voice' in the upper echelons of management. Whilst very little has changed in the UK since the publication of the Finniston report, the difficulty facing those with a technical background in gaining entry to management careers is significant for two important reasons. One reason is that the lack of technical representation at senior level management is an important consideration for research into how British companies manage technology. A number of writers attribute the failure to exploit IT and AMT as a consequence of senior managements' lack of understanding of technical issues (Currie, 1994b).

In many organisations, access to senior management is through a general management route which emphasises the skills of organising, co-ordinating, budgeting and planning as opposed to technical specialism (Boynton et al, 1992. Morone, 1993. Rockart, 1988. Rockness and Zmud, 1989). Other studies have pointed to Britain having more accountants at senior managerial levels than other industrialised nations, most notably, West Germany, the United States and Japan (HMSO, 1987). Accountants are therefore better placed to impose their own views on important strategic decision making situations and, in this instance, are likely to evaluate issues from a financial standpoint than from another disciplinary perspective. A good example of this is in the area of evaluating IT (see chapter four) where financial considerations are given priority over other non-financial ones, namely quality, reliability, time to market and flexibility, etc.

The second reason is the solitary nature of IT work. This is particularly the case in analyst/programming, where IT specialists work in relative isolation whilst writing code to create software programs. Such isolation has helped to fuel the *myth* that 'IT people do not make good communicators' and are 'too introverted and narrow' for senior level managerial positions. Whilst this view is undoubtedly oversimplistic and not entirely supported by empirical research, it has nonetheless gained ground in management thinking and seemingly contributed to the reluctance on the part of companies to promote IT people. Some organisations go as far as to recruit graduates with non-technical backgrounds to work with IT, as they believe that such individuals will be better able to communicate across functions compared with their more technically literate (computer graduate) counterparts.

As a result of this state of affairs, those with good technical skills seek out other forms of employment to offset the prejudices and restrictions against IT staff in leading private and public sector organisations. One alternative is found in the thriving independent IT contracting marketplace, where IT professionals work on short-term contracts for a range of clients. Here, individuals with leading-edge IT skills sign up with an employment agency and become 'contractors'. The agency finds the client and employs the contractor on a short-term contract. This is a particularly lucrative set up for client, agency and contractor. The client can appoint an IT professional on a short-term contract to meet a particular IT project deadline, and therefore terminate the contract on completion of the work. The agency gains by taking a percentage of the rate earned by the contractor (usually 10 percent). The individual contractor also benefits by earning over and above the salary average for the work in addition to gaining experience from a number of industrial and/or commercial settings.

Whilst contract work is perceived by many writers on labour markets as commonly low paid and degrading, contracting work in the IT field is perhaps an anomaly since it offers high financial rewards, particularly to those with scarce IT skills. Indeed, the rapid rate at which technology changes seems to almost guarantee a permanent skills shortage, as IT professionals learn new languages and packages. This benefits those who keep pace with the latest technologies as employers are forced to pay high rates for premium IT skills. The further benefit to IT professionals is the ability to retain their technical skills and earn 'managerial salaries', as opposed to opting for a career in management where they are obliged to abandon their technical training in favour of 'managerial skills'.

The separation between managerial and technical skills in contemporary organisations has arguably led to severe problems in managing IT professionals and technology in general. Indeed, one of the important issues in the field of managing change and, more specifically, technical change is how best to control IT activities.

Managerial responsibility and IT

The growth in annual IT budgets throughout the last two decades, coupled with the popular precept that IT is a 'strategic device', serves to reinforce the view that IT should be managed at the apex of the organisation. Such a commonsense view however runs into difficulties insofar as technical skills are not seen as relevant to managerial work. This is reinforced by many business schools which include finance, human resources and marketing as core management subjects to the exclusion of managing technology.

Yet the boundaries which exist between managers and technologists are likely to impose severe difficulties for those involved in managing IT and those who are being managed (IT professionals) in contemporary private and public sector organisations. In this section, we consider some of the literature which addresses the issue of managerial responsibility for IT. Here, one of the key concerns is who should take control of IT – e.g. those with a non-technical (managers) or technical background?

Boynton et al (1992, p. 32) claim that 'over the last decade, general managers who report to functional areas other than information systems 'line managers' have increasingly gained information technology (IT) management responsibilities'. The authors stress that the most important factor which underlies this phenomenon is the growing requirement for line managers to 'manage interdependencies within and external to the firm in the light of

1. pressures to globalise operations
2. new competitive requirements (increasing product quality and decreasing time to market)

Whilst recognising the importance of IT as a means of solving 'business and strategic challenges', the authors argue that

> 'Although IT managers possess important technical and systems know-how, IT applications are best led by line managers who thoroughly understand the business situation' (Boynton et al, 1992, p. 32).

They further point out that in the past decade organisations are encountering greater technological and strategic complexities which, in turn, demands a re-evaluation of the 'IT management architecture'.

This is the 'locus of decision making for IT-related processes within a firm'. Similarly, Rockart (1988, p. 57–64) claims that

> 'In the 1980s, especially in the last five years, it seems that a quantum change has taken place. This

change can be summed up easily. Information technology has become inextricably intertwined with the business. It has, therefore, become the province not only of information systems professionals, but of every manager in the business no matter what his or her level'.

The issue of whether IT should be managed by general or technical managers is a critical one in the literature (Rockart, 1988. Zmud et al, 1987. Rockness and Zmud, 1989. Dixon and Darwin, 1989. Rowe and Herbert, 1990. Willcocks, 1992. Adler, et al, 1992. Smits et al, 1993. Morone, 1993). The issue has become more important as the strategy-technology connection (Kantrow, 1980) dictates that senior executives should align business strategy with IT strategies. Indeed, other writers caution against the lack of senior management involvement in the strategic management of technical functions as this leads to fragmented and piecemeal implementation of technology, where functional managers take decisions without adhering to the overall corporate strategy (Currie, 1994b). Adler et al, (1992, p. 19) claim that

'Too many businesses leave the technical functions – research and development (R&D), management information systems (MIS), manufacturing engineering, and so on – out of the business strategy process and exempt them from senior management's expectation that all the functions manage their internal operations strategically'.

A central theme relating to this debate is whether IT is managed centrally by a single IS department, unit or function or decentralised to the business units. Boynton et al (1992, p.33) claim that

'The best way to link IT consistently to a firm's day to day, core business processes is to centrally distribute IT management responsibilities to line managers. If the central IS function dominates IT management, this alignment will not occur for two reasons. First, in firms with dominant central IS functions, line managers have to place the fate of their operations and their careers in the hands of others. Thus they resist relying on IT resources that they neither control nor, most likely, fully understand. As the importance of IT resources increases, we believe that line managers will increasingly resist extreme dependence on a central IS function, even if the IS staff has been responsive to their needs in the past. With dispersed responsibility, line managers will use IT resources more effectively, learning to apply IT to business tasks just as they apply human, financial, and other key resources to business opportunities, problems, and threats'.

Complications arise, however, where IT is embedded into core business processes, and is therefore cross-functional in orientation. Here, it is likely that companies will retain a centralised IS function, although this scenario poses problems in terms of management responsibility and control. For example, a UK bank has addressed the issue of how best to manage IT by developing a strategic framework designed to fuse business understanding with IT knowledge. Whilst this organisation continues to operate a centralised IS division, it is forced to address the 'knowledge gap' which exists between business managers and technologists. The solution is seemingly to create a 'hybrid' manager – someone who possesses both managerial and technical skills. At the bank in question, relationship managers are senior managers with an understanding of the business, who liaise with line managers (from the business units) and project managers (technical specialists). This set-up is designed to ensure that managers from the business units will request the most appropriate technical solution from the IS division, since the relationship manager (theoretically) understands the business problem as well as the likely technical solution. The subject of hybrid managers is an important one in the literature and one that is addressed at some length below.

The hybrid manager

An accepted orthodoxy in the management literature on IT now presupposes that most of the evaluation and implementation problems relating to IT are managerial in nature (Earl and Skyme, 1992. Dixon and John, 1989. Edwards et al, 1989. Henderson, 1989. Keen, 1988. Miller, 1985. Sparrow et al, 1989). Indeed, 'technical problems' are often used to disguise poor managerial practice and guidance (Currie, 1994).

Yet the problems of managing IT become ever more complex and difficult to resolve in a climate of almost constant organisational change. New languages and packages are introduced into organisations at an alarming rate. At the leading edge of IT systems development, the rapid technological changes guarantee a continuing skills shortage. Those organisations with a large annual IT spend often resort to using external contractors and management consultancies to offset the skills shortage problem.

At the user end, staff often complain of the requirement to learn new packages such as word processing or spreadsheets. This often produces the inverse of what the packages are intended to achieve – productivity levels fall as new skills are being learned.

This scenario is a constant challenge to managers. Coupled with the human problems of introducing technical change, the growing financial costs impose greater burdens on managers to successfully manage the IT facility. Successful management of IT usually highlights some level of performance improvement, e.g. higher productivity; more efficient information generation; business process re-engineering (BPR) for improved operations and also headcount reduction.

However, skills shortages (of managers and staff) create an ongoing managerial dilemma. This is because managers and staff are trying to make sense of the technical changes, often from a skills base that is outdated and redundant. At senior levels, managers are expected to manage IT even though they may not possess any knowledge of what the systems can do or even if they are relevant to their own business requirements. Similarly, the in-house IS/IT department may comprise people with mainframe skills, even though many of the latest developments in technology are PC related.

The problem is compounded by managements' reluctance to train and retrain existing staff. At the user level, staff may find that technology is simply imposed upon them or, perhaps worse, individuals personally decide which system they wish to use. This produces the common problem of systems not being able to interface with one another, and is the result of an *ad hoc* approach to implementation where sub-strategies exist as opposed to a single IT strategy.

The lack of skills for managing and using IT, in turn, creates further confusion as traditional career paths tend to promote those with general management skills (budgeting, planning, co-ordinating, controlling, etc) even though the new technology seemingly demands some level of technical knowledge – particularly for those engaged in managing the evaluation, implementation and development of organisational technologies..

The common sense solution to this problem is thus presented in the literature as the 'hybrid manager' (Earl and Sykme, 1992. Kerr, 1989. Meiklejohn, 1990. Mercer, 1990.

Palmer and Ottey, 1990). Whilst this individual is likely to exist more as a figment of our imagination as opposed to a reality, the theory surrounding the 'hybrid manager' at least addresses the problem of fusing business skills with technical expertise. According to Earl and Skyme (1992, p. 172) the hybrid manager is a concept, 'a capacity for a role'. Indeed, it is a management development challenge and is not found in conventional organisational charts in most British companies.

In a report published by the British Computer Society, a recommendation was made for UK companies to train some 10,000 people to become 'hybrid managers' by 1995 (Palmer and Ottey, 1990). The report recommended that UK companies should develop people to 'conceive and implement' information systems in line organisations which would attract global customers and help the organisation to compete in the global marketplace. Key performance indicators were to improve time to market, cost, quality, service or any other factor relating to competitiveness.

Earl (1989) defines hybrid managers as

'people with strong technical skills and adequate business knowledge, or vice versa ... hybrids are people with technical skills able to work in user areas doing a line functional job, but adept at developing and implementing IT application ideas'.

Whilst there is not a wealth of literature on 'hybrid managers' Earl and Skyme (1992) inform us that the subject is discussed in other territories to include: information systems management (particularly project management); management of analogue functions (e.g. finance and R&D); studies of general management (e.g. the issue of generalists vs. specialists); and management roles and career development.

They point out that much of their literature search found that hybrids are commonly business managers with IT experience rather than the opposite scenario. This could mean that a general manager is put in charge of the IS/IT function, or that a technical specialist has moved into general management.

Whilst the idea of hybrid management is attractive, it none the less poses serious challenges to management in four key areas:

- Organisational career paths
- Managing technology
- Individual career strategies
- Education and training

Organisational career paths

The fact that a division exists in many organisations between managerial and technical career paths poses a fresh challenge to organisations wishing to develop hybrid managers. On the one hand, graduates are recruited on a management career path and work in the various business units. In this capacity, they acquire broad management skills which are likely to include finance, accounting, marketing, human resources and sales. On the other hand, technical career paths usually involve individuals learning basic programming. They may then embark on analysis work (analyst/programmer) before becoming a systems/project manager and then a DP manager (Keen, 1988).

Whilst graduates on management trainee courses are highly unlikely to move into programming as a strategy for career progression, the programmer wishing to gain promotion may move into management. Or more likely, this person may move out of programming into another disciplinary field, e.g. HRM. It has been pointed out that technical specialists abandoning their technical competences in favour of *managerial work* run the risk of losing their technical edge without being seen as 'real business people' (Earl and Skyme, 1992). Evidence also suggests that technical people are forced to confront a stigma which trivialises technical qualifications in favour of *managerial* qualifications such as the MBA and also undergraduate degrees in business administration.

Managing technology

One impediment to the development of the hybrid manager is the rapid pace at which technology is introduced into the marketplace. Skills shortages in management and technical fields are an impediment to organisational development, and to advocate the concept of 'hybrid management' as a solution to the management/technical gap seems only to compound the problem. Indeed, some writers have argued that hybrid management may not be possible where the demand for new skills is constantly changing. This includes management and technical skills (Carlyle, 1988, 1989).

Individual career strategies

Irrespective of the HR strategies developed by managers to promote the concept of the hybrid manager, a crucial factor will be the individual's perception of how a dual role will benefit his/her career. Whilst job-rotation is now common in Anglo/American companies, as well as being part of the traditional culture in many Japanese firms (Currie, 1994), career paths remain fairly rigid in the former countries. In this respect, those requiring a managerial career are likely to embark on the formal training offered by companies as opposed to opting for a less conventional career path. In the case of IT professionals, those wishing to embark on a managerial career are likely to abandon their technical training and 'repackage' themselves as business managers. This is also likely to be fuelled by the prejudices which afflict technical people which suggest they 'do not make good communicators'.

Education and training

Another challenge in the pursuit of hybrid managers is the training policies developed in organisations. Some writers suggest that many organisations do not have adequate training schemes for their IT staff and tend to label them as 'techies' (a term which reaffirms the prejudices mentioned above). Commonly, MIS managers only stay with a company for some 3/4 years and this is a further impediment to developing an *all rounder* with in-depth business and technical knowledge (Nolan, 1986. Carlyle, 1988). Arguably, the dynamic IT contract labour market is not conducive for developing 'hybrids', unless IT professionals confine their knowledge to one particular business arena, say the banking industry. Indeed, recent evidence suggests that IT management contract positions are on the increase as companies search for individuals with a track record of managing large-scale, complex IT projects (*Computer Contractor*, 1994).

However, in times of deep economic recession, IT professionals become less discriminating about the job market (permanent or contract/temporary), and this undoubtedly produces situations where individuals talk themselves into contracts which may not be wholly suitable for their particular skills set.

Management consultants, managers and IT staff

An important area relating to the management of innovation and technology is the role of management consultants. This topic has been somewhat overlooked by many academics, who instead focus on the roles and responsibilities of managers and staff permanently employed by organisations. In recent years, the growth of external management consultancy as a provider of 'off-the-shelf, packaged solutions' to common business problems has been enormous. Indeed, management consultancy is a vast industry. The big players in the IT field are companies like EDS, IBM, PA Consulting, Anderson, Coopers and Lybrand, Deloitte, Price Waterhouse, KPMG, Ernst and Young, SEMA, Hoskyns and Touche Ross.

There are numerous smaller IT consultancies, and many of these offer specialist services outside the terrain of the more generic solutions offered by the large consultancies. The smaller consultancies suffer from their size since they are often unable to provide adequate back-up services to their clients. As one manager in the financial services industry put it, 'Small consultancies do not have the 'comfort factor' which is present in the large firms. If something goes wrong with a contract with a small player, the manager who engaged the firm will be hammered. But if the same problem occurs with the big player, the retort is, "Well, I used the best there is, so it's not my fault!".'

In addition to the large and small IT management consultancies, agency contractors, working on a freelance basis, also comprise the IT labour market. As the discussion in the earlier part of the chapter shows, the IT contractor is becoming a more significant phenomenon in the labour market as a result of the expanding short-term/temporary employment contract. Large employers of IT staff, such as banks and local authorities, now seek to align their IT workforce to the fluctuating demands for IT projects. For example, it is now commonplace for banks to hire as many as 40 per cent of IT staff on a contract basis (which includes managers as well as technologists). Contractors, like management consultants, are expected to offer workable technical solutions to a particular business problem. In many cases, an effective solution is interpreted as a cost-cutting measure.

Large management consultancies have therefore been called in to rationalise business operations in a range of private and public sector entities. This has been a major phenomenon throughout the 1980s and 1990s. Information technology is often seen as a way to automate hitherto manual administrative practices. Examples of this are numerous. In the public sector, IT has automated administrative work in the Department of Social Security, the Inland Revenue and the NHS among others. Similarly, in the private sector, advanced manufacturing technology (AMT) has been critical in automotive production and a range of other manufacturing applications (Currie, 1994).

Recent reports, however, show that whereas the large consultancies have enjoyed unprecedented growth throughout the last decade, they are now facing more stringent performance tests from their clients (*Computing*, 4 August 1994). Interestingly, the large consultancies enjoyed operating in an almost 'blameless' business environment throughout the 1980s, when the economic upturn guaranteed them massive contracts from both the private and public sectors. On a number of occasions, the consultancy reports containing 'advice' were not put into practice by the client. This did not seem to reflect badly on the consultancy firm in question. On the contrary, the 'time and materials' (open ended) contracts, which were common throughout the 1980s, tended to produce a scenario where it was not in the interests of consultancies to see their recommendations put into practice! This is because more work was likely to arise as different 'solutions' were required by the client's ever-changing business strategy.

The cost-conscious 1990s, however, has produced a different set of circumstances to those of the previous decade. The performance of large management consultancies is now the focus of much attention, and this is likely to continue as private and public sector organisations try to obtain greater value for money from service providers.

In a recent article on the use of management consultancies in the IT field, it was pointed out that

'The truth is that fewer and fewer organisations are willing to accept the traditional prescriptive and report-based approach, long favoured by larger consultancies. Increasingly, they want to bring in consultants to implement strategies which have already been decided in-house.... More knowledgeable than the past, UK organisations are above all looking for value for money from consultancies. They have seen enough expensive disasters this decade, Wessex and Taurus fiascos, to make them think twice before embarking on an all-encompassing 'Big Project'.'

Whilst large-scale IT failures such as Taurus (see Case study below) are significant, empirical and anecdotal evidence of the success rate of both large and small scale IT projects produces a somewhat gloomy picture (Sauer, 1994). As we have seen elsewhere, so-called technical solutions for competitive advantage are less common than the IT vendors and some academics would have us believe. Many IT systems development projects are small scale, and do not produce alarming changes to business processes. Indeed, the 'hype' surrounding the concept of business process re-engineering (BPR) is akin to the same 'hype' which saw IT as a revolution in the commercial world in the first half of the 1980s (Forrester, 1980, 1985).

Massey (see *Computing*, 4 August 1994) points out that the consultancy Quidnunc attempted to interest the consultancy industry in a 'league table' of IT consultants based on 'customer feedback'. She claims that such an idea has been met by a 'distinct lack of interest'. Apparently, one major IT consultancy said that a league table would not be a good idea since 'the customer is not always the best person to judge whether a project is a success or not'.

The article reasons that a time will come when dissatisfaction with large consultancies will lead clients to seek out alternative solutions. First they may employ the services of smaller, specialist IT consultancies with whom they can develop a knowledge-sharing partnership. Second they may choose to develop more consultancy skills in-house. A recent survey by Business Intelligence, entitled *The Services Guide to IT Consultancies*, found that two thirds of respondents agreed that they would develop in-house consultancy, with only 1 percent strongly disagreeing with this strategy (survey discussed in *Computing*, 4 August 1994, p. 23).

In-house consultancy is a solution which is perhaps more common than the large management consultancies would like us to believe. For example, the IT labour market for contractors, discussed above, is a form of in-house consultancy, although the major pitfall is that once the contract period has finished, the contractor may leave to work for another client and take his/her knowledge away. It is unusual for IT contractors to terminate a contract mid-way through, as this reflects badly on the individual. However, a contractor who decides not to accept a subsequent contract from the client is not penalised. As a result, IT contractors, who live a somewhat 'nomadic lifestyle', are used to working in ever-changing environments (business and geographical) to gain a wide range of experience in different commercial and industrial settings.

The loss of knowledge to the client is an issue which is being addressed more and more by senior managers. At a UK bank, a policy of 'skills scraping' has been put in place. The idea is that IT contractors (on six month or 1 year contracts) will impart their knowledge of particular software languages, packages, techniques and methods to permanent IT staff. The concept of skills scraping is based upon two precepts. First it assumes that individuals who possess *the knowledge* wish to impart their expertise to permanent members of staff. Second, it assumes that knowledge is a commodity which can be transferred from one person to the next. Here, a parallel may be drawn between the concept of skills scraping and the role of the major IT consultancies, although some recent evidence shows that many of the major players now face more stringent tests to justify their services (and high fees).

Evaluating the large IT consultancies

In a recent study on managing IT projects in the private and public sectors, Currie and Bryson (1995) found that the following issues comprised the 'key problems' in using the large management consultancy firms:

- Too generalist in approach to business problems
- Provide 'off-the-shelf', packaged solutions
- Too expensive
- Do not understand the client's business
- Are not accountable
- Do not 'own the problem'
- May upset 'equilibrium' – e.g. create conflict with internal managers and staff
- Quality – do not always deliver a workable solution
- Fail to meet project deadlines
- They lack training/knowledge for some forms of complex IT development work

Managers in both the private and public sectors from banks, building societies, car makers, to NHS trusts and local authorities, all cautioned against the '1980s trend' of employing the services of management consultants. As the above itemised list shows, a range of concerns were mentioned. Large management consultancies were considered by some clients as 'too general' in their approach to specific business problems. One insurance company IT manager said that, 'To bring management consultants in really means that we have failed as professionals. I know this business inside-out – a consultant can't really provide a solution with four weeks exposure to our business'. Another manager in a local authority was 'dumbfounded' that, 'Vast sums of money are paid to management consultants, and our staff, in turn, receive a 2.9 percent pay increase'.

Other problems with large management consultancies were to do with cost in relation to value for money. Whilst managers in the manufacturing sector stressed that, 'The lack of funds for capital expenditure and R&D impose serious constraints for manufacturers trying to compete in world markets', similar capital rationing policies were also being imposed on the public sector and, perhaps to a lesser extent, the financial services industry.

The issue of value for money from large consultancies is one which has gained attention in the media. The Cabinet Office's Efficiency Unit report entitled *The Government's Use of External Consultants* claims that Whitehall could save £65 million a year if it made better use of consultants. Of the £508 million spent on consultants by central government in 1992 to 1993, savings of only £12.2 million were realised. In addition, some £201 million was spent using the services of just twenty firms. Of the top twenty, a dozen specialise in the 'black art of management consultancy'. The top twenty comprise many of the 'big names' in management consultancy.

The above figures reflect badly on the large management consultancies, and it is difficult to discern any adequate justification for such large amounts of public money invested when the returns are so small. Indeed, the whole notion of a 'partnership' between client and consultant becomes questionable when we consider other problems associated with this relationship.

Whilst the large consultancies may argue that their role is more than just seeking out 'cost cutting solutions' for their clients, the justification in using 'external advisers' must, none the less, include some notion of return on investment from the point of view of the client. This is common in all commercial service-provider relationships.

In conjunction with the ten problem areas itemised above, critics of large management consultancies raise three issues which need to be re-evaluated in terms of the client/consultant *partnership*. They are

- Strategy
- Skills transfer
- Implementation

Strategy

Whilst large management consultancies have worked for numerous clients in the area of IT strategy, there is some evidence to suggest that work of this nature has very few benefits for the client. Currie and Bryson (1995) found that many private and public sector organisations were critical of the use of external management consultancies for IT strategy because of a lack of understanding of the client's business requirements. Indeed, the whole concept of *strategy* was problematic to many IT departments largely because it was perceived in theoretical as opposed to practical terms. For example, strategy was interpreted very differently by IT managers in a range of private and public sector settings. Some IT managers perceived strategy in the context of purchasing decisions for hardware and software. Others looked upon an IT strategy in terms of how to cut costs using technology. For others, an IT strategy meant rationalisation and job reduction, and a whole host of other diverse interpretations.

Whilst the literature often advises companies to develop an IT strategy, the key question is 'Who should develop it?' Arguably, the large management consultancies have benefited from the lack of skilled IT staff in contemporary organisations. This is more pertinent to the public sector, where the 'civil service's in-house skill base has become so depleted that the use of outsiders is now unavoidable' (*Computing*, 11 August 1994, p. 13).

The issue of handing over the responsibility for IT strategy to consultants is also questionable in relation to the issue of skills transfer.

Skills transfer

Another problem associated with the large management consultancies is to do with skills transfer – or the lack of it. The traditional prescriptive and glossy report-based approach, practised by the large management consultancies, has arguably left a gap between theory and practice in the client organisation. The notion of skills transfer from consultant to client is not one which is commonly perceived as part of the former's remit. Whilst the notion of teaching *strategy* to senior managers was found by Currie and Bryson (1995) to be problematic for a range of reasons, skills transfer of specialist technical knowledge was also excluded from many IT consultancy contracts.

This is currently being addressed by a UK bank where skills shortages are having a serious effect on exploiting state-of-the-art technology. The bank recently offered employees the chance of earning a £1000 *bonus* if they could introduce an IT professional to the organisation who was suitable for a permanent contract in one of the IT units.

The bank is also reconsidering its use of large management consultants. One senior IT manager commented that, 'It is ridiculous how the consultancies have us (the bank) over the barrel on every contract. They come in, set up an office in the far corner, carve out a problem area which they can own, and recommend further work for them once their contract has finished. Nobody seems to know what we get in return'.

Implementation

The relationship between strategy and implementation is another area of concern. The subject of whether the consultancy firm should *implement* IT strategy is contentious. One IT manager argued that, 'It is not the job of the consultants to carry out the strategy. We use them to guide us on the way forward for systems development work'.

Whilst this view is popular in some IT departments, another way of looking at the problem is to turn it on its head. For example, where IT managers are powerless to accept that consultants are commissioned to develop *IT strategies* for the organisation, it is unlikely that they will want to see *implementation* removed from their domain.

However, another way of looking at the problem is for the organisation to devise its own strategy and ask the consultants to implement it!

In a recent article, Massey (1994, p.23) addressed this issue and found that many UK companies are questioning the traditional report-based approach and are, instead, asking the consultants to stay on and implement their solutions. Indeed, many of the large consultancies have

> 'embarked on their own change programmes during the past two to three years, becoming multi-skilled matrix organisations which can offer vertical market knowledge backed-up with technical knowledge.... Software companies have joined in the move to offer a one-stop shop, buying up management consultancies in order to broaden their services portfolio. The rise in specialist boutique consultancy seems to be at odds with this trend. If customers wish to buy everything from a single source, including business consultancy with IT implementation, then why are so many small consultancies doing so well?'

The rise of the small IT consultancy

On this last point, it seems that some of the reasons for the growth in the small IT consultancy are to do with quality, price and implementation. With the recent fiascos of Wessex, Taurus and the London Ambulance Service, companies are now loathe to hire in large management consultancies on the traditional 'cash cow of open-ended consultancy' which was popular during the 1980s and early 1990s. Interviews with a range of IT managers in both the private and public sectors has found some evidence that more stringent performance targets are being developed for management consultancies. One senior manager at a UK bank said that, 'The days of feeding a problem are slowly becoming a thing of the past. We are now looking towards hiring in consultants on fixed-term fixed-price contracts. The old daily rate system should be scrapped. It only encourages consultants to take longer to complete the job!'

Concluding remarks

This chapter has discussed some of the key issues relating to managing IT projects and specialists. The overwhelming conclusion is that no quick fix solutions are possible in the pursuit to gain greater efficiencies from IT by revising management methods and techniques. Field research questions the notion that generalists are better placed to manage IT since these individuals often lack both the knowledge and experience to critically assess IT project and staff performance. This was demonstrated in a number of cases where project managers without technical awareness were unable to pinpoint appropriate ways to measure and evaluate the performance of analyst/programmers by analysing their code. As a result, poor code translated into poorly constructed information systems which were unacceptable to the user. Arguably, the issue of how project managers evaluate the performance of their staff is one which has been hitherto overlooked in the management literature. Yet recent evidence of project failure calls into question the rhetoric that the generalist manager is better able to manage IS/IT.

Case study

The strategic management of large-scale IT projects in the financial services sector[1]

Introduction

A large body of literature on IT strategy formulation is concerned with a formal rational managerialist approach characterised by a coherent framework and shared goals (Walsham, 1993). The assumption behind much of this work is that clearly defined IT strategies will enhance business performance leading to competitive advantage (Earl, 1988, 1989. Kantrow, 1980. McFarlan, 1984. Porter and Millar, 1988). Some of this work offers prescriptions to IT strategists and managers on strategic planning (Ward et al, 1990. Feeny, 1988), managing change (McKersie and Walton, 1991), evaluating IT (Guba and Lincoln, 1981. Iivari, 1988. Kumar, 1990) and implementation (Willcocks and Mark, 1989).

Yet the notion that IT strategy formulation follows a rule-book and linear path is not supported by other writers who suggest an *ad hoc* dimension to the activity (Mintzberg and McHugh, 1985). According to Mintzberg and McHugh (1985:160):

> 'Strategy making still tends to be equated with planning – with the systematic 'formulation' and articulation of deliberate, premeditated strategies, which are then 'implemented...This view of strategy is unnecessarily restrictive; it is inconsistent with more contemporary forms of structure and sometimes the conventional forms as well'.

This article explores the key theme of strategy formulation in relation to primary and secondary data on the management of large-scale IT projects in the UK financial services sector. Two large-expenditure IT projects are examined. The first is the TAURUS project (Transfer and Automated Registration of Uncertificated Stock). This project collapsed in March 1993 and was the City's most expensive and ambitious IT project at an estimated overall cost of £400 million. Exploring secondary case study data on TAURUS, it is argued that the strategy formulation process was marred by short-term financial pressures and political conflicts which ultimately led to its failure. Published articles on TAURUS from 1991 to early 1993 highlight growing concerns about the nature and scope of the project and call into question its overall strategic direction. Whilst TAURUS may be described as a failure in strategic management, it is argued that the factors contributing to its demise are common to other large-scale IT projects.

The second case study is concerned with IT strategy formulation at a UK bank. Field research is currently being undertaken by the author to discern the development and implementation of IT strategies. The project currently under observation is a management information system (MIS) for the financial control and performance measurement of all IT expenditure. Using a semi-structured questionnaire, interviews are conducted with senior IT managers, IT professionals (systems analysts, programmers and database administrators) and the clients for whom IT systems are developed (project sponsors). Linking the secondary data on TAURUS with the field research at the UK bank, it is contended that a deeper understanding of IT strategy formulation in contemporary organisations is achieved through a multidisciplinary analysis. Important managerial functions along with technical services which interpret corporate IT objectives include finance/accounting and human resources. Key tasks relating to IT project management include planning, budgeting, co-ordination, implementation, maintenance and customer support. In this context strategy is an ongoing and haphazard process. This wider

[1]This article is reproduced with kind permission of Blackwell Publishers. It appears in *New Technology, Work and Employment*, Vol. 9, No. 1, 'The strategic management of large-scale IT projects in the financial sector', W. Currie.

disciplinary approach to IT strategy formulation is not yet echoed in the popular literature which instead perceives strategy as a 'stand-alone' corporate activity (Currie, 1994).

Theoretical approaches to strategy formulation and decision-making

The subject of strategy formulation has gained considerable attention in academic circles for several decades (Quinn, 1980. Mintzberg and McHugh, 1985. Child, 1984. Mintzberg and Waters, 1985. Waema and Walsham, 1990. Zuboff, 1980). The term 'strategy formation' was coined by Mintzberg (1978: p.934) who claimed that

> 'the usual definition of strategy encourages the notion that strategies, as we recognise them *ex post facto*, are deliberate plans conceived in advance of the making of specific decisions. By defining a strategy as 'a pattern in a stream of decisions', we are able to research strategy formation in a broad descriptive context. Specifically, we can study both strategies that were intended and those that were realised despite intentions'.

The view that strategy formulation comprises a clearly defined plan of action based upon a textbook model is popular in much of the IT strategy literature. Managers are urged to link their IT strategies with corporate and operational strategies to enhance overall performance and achieve competitive advantage (Earl, 1988. McFarlan, 1984. Feeny, 1988. Cole, 1985. Clark, 1989). Once a corporate/IT strategy is devised, it is assumed to filter down to the managerial and operational levels of the organisation where it will be implemented.

The conceptual approach underpinning much of this literature has its roots in an 'economic model of man'. Economic man is portrayed as operating within a framework of a 'closed decision model' (McGrew and Wilson, 1982). The model postulates that decision-makers seek an 'optimal outcome' to their decisions, facilitated by a process where consideration is given to all the *relevant information*. Taylor (1965) argues that

> 'Most individuals in making a decision believe that

their behaviour is completely *rational* or logical at the moment. There is an objective and several choices from which a choice is made (consciously or subconsciously) to achieve the objective'.

He asserts that individuals can separate 'emotional impulses' from 'rational responses' to enable decision-making 'under certainty'.
Harrison (1981, p.59) contends that

> 'The term rational decision-making epitomises the general confusion and widely varying interpretations surrounding this most important activity of managers in formal organisations'.

Rational decision-making in the context of economic theory is largely concerned with quantitative models of decision making. However, questions arise about the extent to which managers use such models for strategic decision-making in contemporary business organisations. The normative stance of the rational approach to decision making encourages individuals to have:

- a fixed objective
- unlimited time and money to spend in search and evaluation of decision criteria
- virtually perfect information regarding the probability of alternative outcomes
- inexhaustible cognitive power for comprehending, assimilating and retaining an infinite number of variables (Harrison, 1981, p.59)

Whilst we may concede that explanatory models of decision making serve a purpose in simplifying complex phenomena through 'an attempt to render subject matter intelligible by constructing its rationality' (Weber, 1947, p. 207), they are not meant to describe aspects of reality. Nor are they hypotheses. Rather they represent ideal typical models developed as an aid to interpretation and explanation. Lee and Newby (1983, p.176) maintain that

> 'An ideal type is, of course, not ideal in a normative or moral sense – that is, it is not a one-sided accentuation of those traits which are regarded as most desirable; it is *ideal* only in the sense that it is a mental construct which may exist nowhere in reality, although it helps to illuminate that reality'.

Since propositions in economic theory are ideal-typical reconstructions of how individuals behave, economic theory is rigorously concerned to develop a model to capture the essence of economic behaviour.

Strategy and IT

In the context of strategy formulation for IT, a rational framework is advocated for managers based upon an assumed relationship between the implementation of IT and competitive advantage (Earl, 1989. Morton, 1988. Porter and Millar, 1984. McFarlan, 1984). The normative approach adopted by many writers on IT strategy assumes that managers have at their disposal a rational framework for strategy formulation to enhance IT project performance leading to competitive advantage (Kantrow, 1980. Booz-Allen and Hamilton, 1981. Adler et al, 1992). One problem of constructing an ideal-typical presentation of a strategic framework is the extent to which it matches reality.

Although such ideal-typical constructions of social phenomena do not exist in pure form, they are nonetheless presented in the IT literature as offering a conceptual advantage to those concerned with strategy formulation. In contemporary business organisations, managers are urged to maximise the potential of IT by developing strategies to gain competitive advantage, improve productivity and performance, facilitate new ways of managing and organising and to develop new business (Peppard, 1993).

A competing analysis of IT strategy formulation takes issue with the rational text-book model mentioned above. The thrust of this literature questions the extent to which a formal strategic plan may be attained in practice. These writers highlight the political, organisational and human tensions inherent in strategic managerial activities (Wilcocks and Mark, 1989. Murray, 1989. Drucker, 1990. Scarborough, 1992). This alternative view emphasises the *ad hoc* nature of strategy formulation (Mintzberg, 1978. Mintzberg and McHugh, 1985. Mintzberg and Waters, 1985) and the emergence of substrategies which may detract from formal corporate objectives (McLoughlin and Clark,

1988. Currie, 1989ab, 1992ab. Currie and Seddon, 1992). Mintzberg and Waters (1985. p.271) maintain that '... strategy formation walks on two feet, one deliberate, the other emergent .... managing requires a light deft touch – to direct in order to realise intentions while at the same time responding to an unfolding pattern of action'. Examples of adhocracy in IT strategy formulation are best exemplified by case study research in a variety of organisational contexts. For the purpose of this case study, the following discussion considers secondary data on the recent collapse of the city-wide TAURUS IT project. This example of IT strategy formulation and implementation offers numerous examples of adhocracy in practice. To the extent that TAURUS was launched as a city-wide IT project to revolutionise the operations of the London International Stock Exchange (ISE), the original 'deliberate' strategic plan gave way to a series of *ad hoc* and conflicting substrategies which ultimately led to its demise.

The TAURUS IT Project: a failure in strategic management?

TAURUS (Transfer and Automated Registration of Uncertificated Stock) was a major IT project at the ISE for the 'dematerialisation' of share certificates to create paperless trading and computerised shareholdings. TAURUS was intended as a computerised database of investors and their holdings maintained by the ISE in its role as central operator. It would lead to paperless trading in the securities industry with the associated benefits of reduced costs for the share registrars (who maintain the list of holders of a company's shares) and the institutions and brokers for future account controllers of share transactions. Total dematerialisation would mean that share ownership would be stored electronically and investors would not receive share certificates. TAURUS would be linked to some 280 financial institutions, serving a range of stakeholders from registrars, brokers, market-makers, custodians to large investors (*Financial Times*, 1993).

TAURUS was planned in three phases. In the first phase, software would be designed and developed for the basic Settlement function involving the exchange of stock for cash. Settlement is the completion of a transaction after the delivery of securities to the buyer and the delivery of payment to the seller has been achieved, along with the transfer of title of the securities. Currently in Britain, there is a fourteen-day period for Settlement – longer than that of other markets (Cohen, 1993). The ISE imposed a twelve-month deadline in 1990 for development work yet acknowledged the 'demanding timetable' accompanying the first phase of the project. A target date for 'total dematerialisation' was set for the end of 1993.

The second stage of TAURUS was labelled 'participant testing', where the ISE's own system would interact electronically with the systems of other participants. Yet participants expressed the concern that 'it was not enough to interact individually with the Exchange through their own electronic link, but wanted to make sure that all the pieces of the jigsaw fitted into place ... e.g. if one broker instructed the central computer to send shares to another, would the second broker actually receive them on time? (*Financial Times*, 1993).

The rationale for TAURUS was fourfold. First the ISE believed that computerisation was necessary to remain competitive in a global market. Second, dematerialisation was perceived as synonymous with greater efficiency and reduced bureaucracy. Third, the financial benefits of TAURUS were believed to be immense and in accordance with the 'downsizing' and job rationalisation of the ISE.

A report by Coopers and Lybrand, Deloitte advised the ISE that TAURUS would achieve 'staff cost savings in the offices of participants and at the ISE of approximately £54m per year on a conservative basis... Assuming a discount rate of 12 per cent, and a steady build-up of TAURUS over three years, these annual staff cost savings represent a net present value, over ten years, of about £230m. Any further cost savings of accommodation costs or other overheads will increase this sum' (Tilley, 1990).

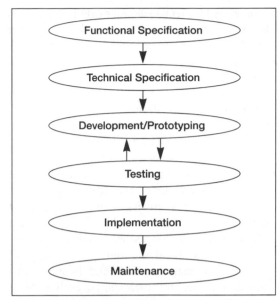

Figure 5.1 Stages in IT project development

Whilst these estimated savings were impressive, it was further recognised that any gains needed to be offset against the costs of development and implementation (and other hidden costs). Coopers and Lybrand, Deloitte estimated that such costs would be between $45m and £50m (at then current prices) over a period of four years to spring 1993 (Tilley, 1990). A fourth benefit of TAURUS was believed to be better service to customers through reduced risk and speed of processing.

At the end of the first phase of TAURUS in October 1991, lack of progress towards the dematerialisation of share certificates forced a revised deadline of April 1993 (eighteen months after the original plan). Writing in 1991, Whybrow argues that reasons for the delay were twofold – regulatory and technical. He argues that the ISE placed more emphasis upon the former. Whybrow (1991, p.15) claims that the ISE 'originally envisaged straightforward regulations for issuing and cancelling certificates'. Yet discussions with the DTI proved lengthy and resulted in a 150 page legal document containing complex regulations. 'Certificates were previously part of company law. They had been that way for the past 150 years and the whole structure reflected the use of paper. Customer protection had to be satisfactorily worked out; delivery against payment had to be guaranteed in both directions; when was the settlement irreversible? These questions all had to be resolved'.

On the technical side the communications server was incomplete at the end of 1991. Again, 'complexity' was used as the key reason. Whilst the delay was described as 'technical', many of the problems were believed to be managerial in nature. A senior business development manager described the problems as 'planning and project control' concerns (Whybrow, 1991, p.15). TAURUS was being designed and developed in a context of far-reaching hierarchical and managerial change at the ISE. Yet designing TAURUS in such a climate culminated in the decision in early 1993 to abandon the project.

The demise of TAURUS

Early in 1993 a decision was taken to terminate the TAURUS project. This decision followed months of confusion, delay and diffusion of responsibility and control over the desired end result. Reasons for the abandonment of TAURUS were threefold and to do with technical, managerial and quality control issues (Waters and Cane, 1993). First, software development work on TAURUS was conducted on an *ad hoc*, incremental basis. The ISE did not complete a full design for its computer system even though industry-wide testing was conducted in early 1993. Driven by pressure from the Securities industry to create the system, a firm foundation in the design, functionality and detailed explanation of how the various elements fit together was never undertaken. There was 'no architecture' to TAURUS.

The selected software package also required 70% rewriting. This work was conducted by separate teams working at the ISE and in the United States. Such diffusion of effort detracted from 'teamworking' and contributed to the fragmentation of the project. As Waters and Cane (1991, p.11) state, 'The problems were compounded by the constant redefining of the project requirements. The exchange paid £1m

for the x package. Revisions to it were projected to cost a further £4m, but by the end the software had cost £14m, and had still not been completed. (The software company) was hired on a 'time and materials' contract rather than a 'fixed-price basis – an arrangement now attacked by several exchange board members'.

Second, TAURUS was beset throughout by inadequate project management. Whilst a government rule-book or methodology called SSADM specified a linear and 'logical' (rule-book) approach to large-scale computer projects, it was not adhered to by project managers and staff, although important questions arise about the suitability of text-book methodologies given the complexity of the proposed system coupled with the wide array of stakeholders with competing interests.

Third, an absence of stringent quality control contributed to further delays and setbacks to TAURUS. Waters and Cane (1993) argue that computer systems engineers did not have their work checked by 'independent consultants' (assuming the latter were more knowledgeable about software languages, packages, etc). In turn, the diffusion of software development activities led to a 'quality control nightmare'. In particular, software development was a diffused and *ad hoc* activity where the end-result was something of a surprise. This resulted in an ongoing process of testing, rewriting and re-testing (a common activity in large-scale software development, albeit overlooked in the strategy formulation process).

In March 1993, after much deliberation, the TAURUS project was abandoned. Despite Settlements being one of the London Stock Exchange's core activities, providing some £47.5m of its £194m income, TAURUS was considered too complex and problematic to continue (Water, 1993). High-profile, large-scale IT project failure of this kind calls into question the nature of IT strategic planning. An interesting facet of TAURUS highlights a failure, at least in the early stages, to conceptualise the project in technical, political, organisational and managerial terms. Even the legal aspects relating to TAURUS were inadequately thought through. Clearly the original strategic plan would mean a 'whole new philosophy of working' and not simply an understanding of hardware and software (Walsham, 1992, 1993). The adhocracy associated with TAURUS seemed to emerge from an inadequate strategic planning process.

Secondary data on TAURUS suggests a narrow approach to strategy formulation where the 'system architecture' was conceptualised as an ideal-type which bore little relation to reality. Whilst the collapse of TAURUS has been hailed as a failure in strategic management (*Financial Times*, 1993) this case study is interested to discern whether such problems are common to other large-scale IT projects in the financial services sector. This has motivated further enquiry into IT strategy formulation at a UK bank.

Empirical research on managing large-scale IT projects at a UK Bank

Field work is currently being undertaken on IT strategy formulation at a UK Bank. Using Mintzberg and Waters (1985) terminology of 'deliberate' and 'emergent' strategies, field research compares the formal strategic plan for IT with the outcome, intended or otherwise. Interviews with senior managers and IT staff at the Bank suggest that a formal strategic framework is in place for managing IT projects, although the 'informal' organisation highlights several instances of adhocracy. Formal documentation from the Bank (Table 5.1) outlines the objectives and overall structure of the strategic planning process.

Technology and the business

Interviews with senior Bank personnel suggested that a key problem in developing IT strategies was in the relationship between 'technology and the business'. Many senior managers had acquired in-depth knowledge of banking but were unaware of the potential and scope of 'state of the art' technology. This had resulted in a range of IT projects which had 'failed to deliver what the business requires'. According to one IT project manager, 'The technology division responds to client demands. The trouble is, we give our clients what they ask for and not necessarily what they want'. Comments of this nature pointed to the difficulty of fusing business awareness with technical specialism, although part of the problem was in the Bank's interpretation of what constitutes business skills as differentiated from technical skills. Interviews with senior bank executives suggested some confusion regarding the appropriate skills for a 'changing business climate'.

Executive Management Guidance and Control	Sound planning and control of systems development must be ensured for the entire organisation. This requires that the department have a formal direct reporting relationship with executive management.
Organisational Commitment	Without a clear demonstration of the organisation's commitment, proper resources may never be allocated to the project.
Business Management Direction	Primary responsibility for the functional success of a new system should be placed with its major beneficiaries. Business management should therefore be in a position to provide clear guidance on project scope and direction to the project team.
Accountability of IT Project Management	The IT team must be clearly accountable for delivery of the agreed functionality. The organisation structure must allow the team to involve business management in all key decisions affecting a project, to resolve conflicts within the team and gain access to computing resources.

Table 5.1 Formal objectives and overall structure for IT

One line of enquiry regarding the career progression of individuals into senior management found little evidence of a technical background. This had created a 'shortfall' in business-related technical skills which the Director of Technology recognised as a key reason to 'restructure' the Technology Division. One formal document outlined the rationale for the restructuring. It emphasised the importance of technology as 'crucial' to the survival of the Bank and stressed that 'there is now a need for people to be able to manage complex projects and that the restructuring had created new, more demanding roles and jobs and therefore up-skilling of the workforce was required. Through the assessment process some staff have been judged to have skills which are not interchangeable with the new skills the new jobs require'.

The objective of the Technology Division to respond to business requirements was formalised in the above document (Table 5.1). 'Sound planning and control of systems development' is perceived as an important objective for executive management. According to the document the overall structure 'covers all projects initiated on behalf of business divisions and also projects initiated by technology in order to improve service levels or quality of the IT service'. Yet the document stresses that the 'primary responsibility for the functional success of a new system should be placed with its major beneficiaries' and not the Technology Division. Whilst this means that responsibility for the system is with the client (Project Sponsor), interviews with IT project managers indicated that 'failure to deliver' appropriate systems reflected badly on the Technology Division and was behind the decision to restructure and ensure that in future Technology provided a cost-effective service.

The structure of IT project management

Field research at the UK Bank indicated that greater financial control was seen as the key goal for the Technology Division. The formal structure underpinning all IT development work was headed by a Technology Steering Committee. This committee was responsible for the development of organisation policies for IT, the approval of all IT projects above £1m budgeted expenditure and £0.2m unbudgeted expenditure. IT projects over £5m required approval from the Board of Directors.

The Divisional Steering Committee acted within the policies and architectures set by the Technology Steering Committee. Its key responsibilities included: the agreement of annual technology budgets and quarterly revisions; approval of all significant projects (or budget allocations in the case of smaller grouped activities such as support/maintenance); ensuring that the business is adequately supported by production systems (this includes new business areas or products); prioritising of technology budgeted resources available to the division; regular review and monitoring of all major activities; submissions to the Technology Steering Committee as required, the resolution of conflicts, issues and problems raised by the Project Control Committees (PCCs); justification of material variances from Group strategic aims; establishing the PCC to execute and control specific division projects or portions of the budget and, finally, to ensure adequate business staff are made available to support technology projects.

The primary responsibility of the Technology Steering Committee and Divisional Steering Committee was in financial control and performance measurement of all IT work undertaken by the Technology Division. At a lower operational level, the PCC was primarily concerned with the approval, review, monitoring and control of project scope, plans and budgets; the submission of proposals and progress reports to the Divisional Steering Committee; the overall management of the progress of IT projects to ensure that problems do not amplify; to sign off and approve all agreed milestones throughout the life of the project; to ensure the commitment of qualified business personnel; to ensure that work is constrained while continuing to meet the original business objectives; to deliver the project or system, including the co-ordination of all related activities outside Technology;

the control and testing, conversion and installation tasks, to 'sign off' the system before 'going live'; and to establish project working groups to execute and control specific segments of the project as required.

The four key players in IT project development work were divided between the business groups and the Technology Division. The Project Sponsors' remit was to identify a particular business problem requiring an IT solution. This individual liaised with the Senior Business Analyst from the Technology Division to determine the financial cost of the proposed IT system and whether it was technically feasible. The Senior Business Analyst was supposed to offer dual skills in business awareness and technical expertise, although interviews with project managers at the sharp end of technology suggested an absence of up-to-date technical skills. One project manager said, 'The real innovation crisis at the bank is that most people have mainframe skills in an environment which is increasingly moving towards the PC (personal computer). New languages such as 4GLs also confuse senior managers because they have no experience of them'. Having agreed to develop a system the Project Sponsor delegated its 'ownership' to the Project Owner from the relevant business group who then coordinated its day-to-day management with the Project Manager from the Technology Division.

The rationale underpinning this structure was to develop closer links between the business groups and technology. One project manager said that lack of technical awareness was even more acute outside the Technology Division. He claimed that, 'There are very few people in senior management in the business groups who understand what IT can do for their business. This means that we are asked to provide a system which we know will not work in practice. A common problem is that we're asked to develop a highly complex system in six months which should really take two years. Another problem we face is trying to work towards a tight budget. We often tell the business that capital rationing at the outset will result in further costs down the line as poorly constructed software requires extensive rewriting'.

The Project Manager was central to the range of IT activities conducted at the Bank. It was described as a 'troubleshooting' role. Project managers interpret the functional and technical specifications and deliver a system in accordance with agreed functionality, time scales and budget. According to one project manager working on a management information system for cost control of IT expenditure, 'The roles of project sponsor, project owner, senior business analyst and project manager become blurred once a project is up and running. Part of this problem is due to political game-playing and personality clashes. If a project is going well, everyone wants the credit for it. If its going badly, I usually get the blame as project manager!'.

Developing a management information system

Part of the research agenda was to compare the Bank's formal strategic planning process with a current IT project. At the time of interview a management information system (MIS) was being developed to monitor and control bank-wide IT expenditure. This project was currently in its second year of development and showed many similarities with the TAURUS project discussed above. The client for the project was the Financial Control Unit, who were acting on senior executive pressure to improve financial control of IT expenditure. The notion that IT had not delivered appropriate systems by way of functionality and value for money to the various business groups was perceived as adequate justification to embark on the MIS project. In the first year of the project, a team of external management consultants had been brought in to identify 'business needs' and to develop a functional specification, e.g. a document outlining the range of information required by the Financial Control Unit. Once the functional specification was agreed by senior managers, the consultancy was hired to do the technical specification, e.g. how the system would be developed. At this point the Bank ran into serious skills-shortage problems. IT professionals with mainframe experience did not have the relevant programming experience in the languages/packages outlined in the technical specification. Consequently, the consultancy was hired once again to develop the system. At the end of the first year, a prototype system had been developed predominantly by the consultancy with some help from managers and IT staff at the Bank. During the testing stage (see Figure 5.1), the prototype system was found to have serious malfunctions which required further software development and rewriting. It emerged that the consultancy did not have experienced analyst/programmers in the 4GL used to design the system. Inexperienced staff were therefore assigned to the MIS project. At the technical level, the prototype system contained thousands of lines of repeated code compounded by vast repetition of software faults. No system architecture was present in the prototype system and the various modules failed to interface.

Given that the prototype system required major rewriting, the consultancy firm was dismissed and a decision was taken to hire a freelance expert in the 4GL programming. According to this individual, 'I have seen this problem time and time again. Consultancy firms win contracts on the basis that they have skilled people. In my experience, it's often the opposite. Another problem is that they are often paid on a time and materials basis rather than a fixed price, fixed term contract. The former means they guarantee future work at the vast expense of the client'.

At the time of writing, the freelance expert who was contracted by the bank for six months had undertaken major revisions to the MIS project. An in-depth interview exploring the various stages in IT project development (Figure 5.1) pointed to problems with the linear approach. It was stressed that the current managerial priority for cost-control often fuelled the development of poorly constructed IT work. This was because project managers were keen to 'sign off' work without ensuring it met quality standards. External consultancy firms on the Bank's 'approved list of companies' were hired to undertake complex IT development work but were not subject to stringent performance measures during the project. 'Emergent' strategies were therefore implemented as 'fire-fighting' measures to retain 'credibility' for the project. Comparing the 'deliberate' strategic planning process with the 'emerging' situation highlighted many contradictions.

Discussion and conclusion

A comparison with the TAURUS project and the MIS project at the Bank highlights three similarities in the strategy formulation process. First, financial considerations seemed to determine the development of both systems. In the case of TAURUS, estimated cost savings to the ISE seemed to outweigh considerations of technical feasibility, legal constraints and project management co-ordination and control. This was also the case in the MIS project where senior management demands for greater financial control of IT expenditure overshadowed important considerations regarding planning, skills resourcing and technical capability. Second, there was no 'systems architecture' outlining how the pieces of the IT development jigsaw would fit together. Software development on the TAURUS project was badly co-ordinated and managed, encouraged by a blurring of responsibility over task allocation. Similarly, the MIS project was assumed to follow a linear path to completion, although interview data instead suggested an iterative route. Third, the rationale for the use of management consultants was believed to be their greater knowledge and understanding over 'inhouse' managers and IT staff. Yet the reality indicated that the consultants also underwent a sharp learning curve in their attempt to develop a fully functional IT system. Fourth, senior managers in both projects seemed to underestimate the technical complexity. Implicit in this perception is that once an IT strategy is in place, the managers and technologists simply provide a technical service which is divorced from the wider business arena.

In conclusion it is argued that secondary data on TAURUS and empirical work at a UK bank demonstrate that managing IT projects is fraught with difficulties. This is supported in the literature on IT (Murray, 1989. Jones et al, 1993. Currie, 1994). Yet the priorities relating to the array of problems varies between the clients for whom the systems are developed, financial controllers, project managers and IT professionals. Whilst the common goal of adding value through technical development is shared by most, senior management emphasis upon short-term financial rewards through technology often detracts from other strategic considerations such

as skills development, organisational learning, technical capability and project management methods and techniques. Terms such as the 'software crisis' and the 'software bottleneck' used to describe the gap between technical ambitions and actual achievements (Friedman, 1989) are relevant to our analysis of managing large-scale IT projects in the financial services sector. Yet in the context of this research, they adequately describe the outcome of poor managerial strategies relating to IT systems development.

Discussion questions

1 Describe the events leading up to the failure of TAURUS?
2 Who was responsible for the failure of TAURUS?
3 Was TAURUS attributable to a managerial or technical failure?
4 Could the TAURUS disaster have been avoided?
5 What lessons can be learned from the TAURUS fiasco?

References 5

Adler, P.S., McDonald, D.W., MacDonald, F (1992) 'Strategic management of technical functions'. *Sloan Management Review*, winter.

Bilderbeek, R., Buitelaar, W. (1992) 'Bank computerisation and organisational innovations', *New Technology, Work And Employment*, vol. 7, no. 1.

Blaazer, C., Molyneux, E. (1984) *Supervising the electronic office*. Gower.

Boynton, A.C., Jacobs, G.C., Zmud, R.W. (1992) 'Whose responsibility is IT management?' *Sloan Management Review*, Summer, pp. 32–38.

Booz-Allen and Hamilton (1981) *The strategic management of technology*. Booz-Allen and Hamilton: Outlook, Fall-Winter.

Brittain, J.M. (1992) 'The emerging market for information professionals in the UK National Health Service'. *International Journal of Information Management*, Vol 12, pp. 261–271.

Carlyle, R.E. (1988) 'CIO – Misfit or Misnomer.' *Datamation*, 34, pp. 50–56

Carlyle, R.E. (1989) 'Careers in crisis.' *Datamation*, 35, pp. 12–15.

Child, J (1994) *Organisation*. Harper and Row.

Clark, K. B (1989) 'What strategy can do for technology'. *Harvard Business Review*. November/December. pp. 94–98.

Cohen, N. (1993) 'Settlement time to decrease'. *Financial Times*. 2 July, p. 10.

Cole, R.E (1985) 'Target information for competitive performance'. *Harvard Business Review*. May/June. pp 100–109.

Computer Contractor (1994) 'Contract managers', 30 September, p. 35.

Cooley, M. (1980) Architect or bee? Langley Technical Services, Slough, UK.

Currie, W. (1994) T*he strategic management of advanced manufacturing technology*. London: CIMA.

Currie, W., Seddon, J (1992) 'Managing AMT in a JIT Environment in the UK and Japan'. *British Journal Of Management*, vol 3, no. 3.

Currie, W (1992a) 'Managing AMT in a UK automotive plant: the cost of machine downtime', *Management Accounting*, vol, 70, no. 11, December.

Currie, W (1992b) 'Developing a performance measurement system for CAD in a US manufacturing company', *Management Accounting*, vol, 70, no. 10, November.

Currie, W (1989a) 'The art of justifying new technology to top management', in *OMEGA – International Journal of Management Science*, October, vol. 17, no. 5, pp. 409–418.

Currie, W (1989b) 'Investing In CAD: a case of ad hoc decision making', *Long Range Planning*, vol, 22, no. 6, pp. 85–91.

Currie, W., Bryson, C. (1995) 'Generalist managers, IT specialists and the process of software development: a crisis in management control?', paper to be presented at European Conference on Technological Innovation and Global Challenges, Aston, 5–7 July.

Dixon, P., Darwin, J. (1989) 'Technology issues facing corporate management in the 1990s'. *MIS Quarterly*, September, pp. 247–255.

Dixon, P.J., John, D.A. (1989) 'Technology issues facing corporate management in the 1990s'. *MIS Quarterly*, 13, pp. 247–256.

Donaldson, H. (1978) *A guide to the successful management of computer projects*. London: Associated Business Press.

Drucker, P (1988) 'The coming of the new organisation'. *Harvard Business Review.* January/February.

Drucker, P. (1990) 'The emerging theory of manufacturing'. *Harvard Business Review.* May/June.

Earl, M.J., Skyrme, D.J. (1992) 'Hybrid managers – what do we know about them?' *Journal of Information Systems*, Vol. 2, pp. 169–187.

Earl, M. (1989) *Managerial Strategies for Information Technology.* Prentice Hall.

Earl, M. (ed.) (1988). *Information Management: The strategic dimension.* Oxford: Clarendon Press.

Economist (1993) Banking: New tricks to learn. Survey. 10–16 April.

Feeny, D (1988) 'Creating and sustaining competitive advantage with IT', in M. Earl (ed) *Information Management*, Prentice Hall.

Edwards, B., Earl, M., Feeny, D. (1989) '*Any way out of the labyrinth for managing IS?*' Research & Discussion papers, RDP 89/3, Oxford Institute of Information Management, Templeton College.

Financial Times (1993) 'Taurus the octopus'. Article by Richard Waters, 22 January.

Forester, T. (1980) *The micro-electronics revolution.* Blackwell.

Forester, T. (1985) *The information technology revolution.* Oxford University Press.

Friedman, A (1989) *Computer Systems Development.* Wiley.

Guba, E.G., Lincoln, Y.S (1981) *Effective Evaluation.* Jossey-Bass, San Francisco.

Harrison, E. (1981) *The managerial decision-making process.* Boston: Houghton Mifflin Co.

HMSO (1987) *The making of managers*, HMSO: London.

Ivari, J (1988) 'Assessing IS design methodologies as methods of IS assessment'. in *IS Assessment: Issues and Challenges* (eds N. Bjorn-Andersen and G. B. Davis), North Holland, Amsterdam.

Jenkins, C., Sherman, B. (1979) *The collapse of work.* Methuen.

Jenkins, C., Sherman, B. (1981) *The leisure shock.* Longman.

Jones, C., Currie, W., Dugdale, D (1993) 'Uses and limitations of management accounting: Western problems and Japanese solutions'. *Management Accounting Research Journal*, September.

Kantrow, A.M. (1980) 'The strategy-technology connection'. *Harvard Business Review*, July-August.

Kerr, S. (1989) 'The new IS force'. *Datamation*, 35, pp. 18–22.

Kumar, K (1990) 'Post-implementation evaluation of computer-based IS: current practices'. *Communications of the ACM*, 33, No. 2. 203–212.

Lee , D., Newby, H. (1983) *The problem with sociology; an introduction to the discipline.* Unwin-Hyman.

Massey, J. (1994) 'Consulting boom', *Computing*, 4 August, pp. 22–23.

McFarlan, F.W. (1984) 'Information technology changes the way you compete'. *Harvard Business Review.* May–June.

McGrew, A., Wilson, M (eds) (1982) *Decision Making Approaches.* Manchester: MUP.

McKersie, R.B. Walton, R.E (1991) Organisational Change. In Scott-Morton (ed.) *The corporation of the 1990s: Information technology and organisational transformation*, OUP.

McLoughlin, I., Clark, J. (1988) *Technical Change at Work.* OUP.

Meiklejohn, I. (1990) 'Whole role for hybrid'. *Management Today*, March, pp. 113–116.

Mercer, C. (1990) *Hybrid managers: a role analysis*, MSc thesis, Social & Applied Psychology Unit, Sheffield University.

Mintzberg, H (1978) 'Patterns of strategy formulation', *Management Science*, 24, No. 9, pp. 934–948.

Mintzberg, H., McHugh, A. (1985) 'Strategy formulation in an adhocracy'. *Administrative Science Quarterly*, vol. 30, no. 2.

Mintzberg, H., Waters, J.A (1985) 'Of strategies, deliberate and emergent'. *Strategic Management Journal*, 6. No. 3, pp. 257–272.

Morone, J.G. (1993) 'Technology and competitive advantage – the role of general management. *Research-Technology Management*, pp. 6–25.

Morton, M.S. (1988) 'Strategy formulation methodologies and IT' in M. Earl (ed.) *Information Management: The strategic dimension*. Oxford: Clarendon Press.

Murray, F. (1989) 'The organisational politics of information technology: Studies from the UK financial services industry'. *Technology Analysis & Strategic Management*. vol. 1, no. 3.

Nolan, R. (1986) 'Business needs a new kind of DP manager', *Harvard Business Review*, No. 54, pp. 40–45.

Palmer, C., Ottley, S. (1990) *From potential to reality: hybrids – critical force in the application of information technology in the 1990s*. A report by the BCS Task Group in Hybrids, BCS.

Peppard, J (1993) *IT Strategy For Business*. Pitman.

Porter, M.E., Millar, V.E. (1984) 'How information gives you competitive advantage'. *Harvard Business Review*. July–August.

Quinn, J. B (1990) *Strategies for Change: Logical Incrementalism*. Irwin: Homewood.

Rockart, J.F. (1988) 'The line takes the leadership – IS management in a wired society'. *Sloan Management Review*, Summer 1988, pp. 57–64.

Rockness, H., Zmud, R.W. (1989) *Information Technology Management: Evolving Managerial Roles*. Morristown, New Jersey: Financial Executives Research Foundation.

Rowe, C., Herbert, B. (1990) 'IT in the boardroom: the growth of computer awareness among chief executives'. *Journal of General Management*, Vol. 15, No. 4, pp. 32–44.

Scarborough, H. (1992) *The IT Challenge: IT and Strategy in Financial Services*, Prentice Hall.

Scarborough, H,. Lannon, R. (1988) 'The successful exploitation of new technology in banking', *Journal of General Management*, vol. 13, no, 3.

Smits, S.J., McLean, E.R., Tanner, J.R. (1993) 'Managing high-achieving information systems professionals'. *Journal of Management Information Systems*, Vol. 9, No. 4, pp. 103–120, Spring.

Sparrow, P., Gratton, L., McMullan, J. (1989) *Human resource issues in information technology*, Survey. P.A. Consulting Group.

Taylor, D. (1965) 'Decision-making and problem solving', in J. March (ed.) *Handbook of Organisations*. New York: Rank McNally and Co.

Tilley, L. (1990) 'A revolution in share registration'. *Banking Technology*. November.

Waema, T.M., Walsham, G. (1990) 'Information systems strategy formation in a developing country bank'. *Technological Forecasting and Social Change*, 38, No. 4. pp. 393–407.

Walsham, G. (1992) 'Management science and organisational change: a framework for analysis'. *OMEGA: International Journal of Management Science*. vol. 20, no. 1, pp. 1–9.

Walsham, G. (1993) *Interpreting information systems*, Wiley.

Waters, R. (1993) 'The plan that fell to earth'. *Financial Times*, 12 March, p. 19.

Waters, R., Cane, A. 91993) 'Sudden death of a runaway bull'. *Financial Times*. 19 March, p. 11.

Ward, D.J., Griffiths, P., Whitmore, P. 91990) *Strategic Planning for Information Systems*. Prentice-Hall.

Weber, M. 91947) *The theory of social and economic organisation*. New York: MacMillan.

Whybrow, M. (1991) 'The sign of the raging bull'. *Banking Technology*. November.

Willcocks, L. (1992) 'The manager as technologist', pp. 170–196; in L. Willcocks and J. Harrow (eds.), *Rediscovering public services management*. McGraw Hill.

Willcocks, L., Harrow, J. (1992) *Rediscovering public services management*. McGraw Hill.

Willcocks, L.P., Mark, A.L. (1989) 'IT systems implementation: Research findings from the public sector'. *Journal of Information Technology*. vol. 2, pt. 2. pp. 92–103.

Wood, S. (1982) *The degradation of work*. Hutchinson.

Zmud, R.W., Boynton, A.C., Jacobs, G.C. (1987) 'An examination of managerial strategies for increasing information technology'. *Proceedings of the Eighth Int. Conf. on Information Systems*.

Zuboff, S. (1988) *In the age of the smart machine*. Basic Books: New York.

CHAPTER 6

Outsourcing: the New IT Strategy

Introduction

The IT outsourcing bandwagon has grown considerably in recent years (Lacity and Hirschheim, 1993a), particularly in British and North American private and public sector organisations. Three reasons are paramount. First, the global economic recession has forced many senior executives to search for cost savings, particularly in overhead areas such as IT divisions/departments. Second, the rhetoric behind market testing, compulsory competitive tendering (CCT), process innovation (Davenport, 1993) and business process re-engineering (BPR) (Swatman et al, 1994) has led many senior executives to reassess their company-wide performance. Third, the *supplier hype* about IT outsourcing, coupled with unacceptable IT failure rates (Currie, 1994a. Sauer, 1993), encourages private and public sector organisations to view outsourcing as the cost effective alternative to in-house systems and applications development (Snell, 1994). In this chapter, we review some of the academic and trade literature on IT outsourcing and analyse the advantages and pitfalls of this alternative IT strategy.

The outsourcing market

Any discussion of the strategic management of IT should not ignore the growth in outsourcing. The outsourcing phenomenon is a major development in recent years with potential revolutionary changes in the management, evaluation, implementation and maintenance of corporate IT services. It is also offering fresh challenges to IT professionals in the form of new career opportunities in the emerging market for contract programming, project management and corporate management paths in the expanding IT outsourcing sector.

The growth in the outsourcing market has been considerable particularly in the US and to a lesser extent in the UK. In 1989 US literature on outsourcing estimated the market to be worth $12.8 billion with an annual expected growth of 20 percent (Krass, 1990. McCormick, 1991. McMullen, 1990). The Yankee Group believed that all Fortune 500 companies will consider outsourcing with 20 percent signing a contract by 1994 (Eckerson, 1990). A recent report from the US Forrester Research Inc. estimates that data centre outsourcing was a $10 billion business in 1993, with an annual growth rate of 10 percent. Client-server outsourcing, on the other hand, is currently only a $2–3 billion business, although it is growing at a rapid rate of 40–50 percent per annum (*Datamation*, 1994). Oltman (*Computerworld*, 1990a, p.77) claims that

'Outsourcing is here to stay; it's not just a flash in the pan or a temporary solution. Information content – the value of bundled hardware, software, communications, services and so on – distributed through outsourcing contracts could total more than $100 billion by 1995'.

Although outsourcing is sometimes viewed as a narrow activity, it may span a wide number of organisational activities. For example, outsourcing may involve simply hiring a few contract IT professionals for systems development work or a much more ambitious contract involving technology-based business operations, software re-engineering, maintenance, systems operations, network services, systems building and integration, education and training and many others. Arthur Anderson have identified four key trends which are driving outsourcing. They include: the shortage of information technology specialists and business systems professionals, deregulation of capital markets, globalisation which is intensifying international competition, and the high volume and velocity of financial transactions which require a flexible and rapid response. They also claim that outsourcing is concerned with business and systems integration, systems management and facilities management (quoted in *Computerworld*, 1990a).

Outsourcing as a managerial strategy and practice is not new. Outsourcing is often confused with the term Facilities Management (FM). FM is also a misunderstood term and there are many diverse definitions in the IS trade literature. The Central Computer and Telecommunications Agency (CCTA) states that

'The term FM is defined as the management and operation of part or all of an organisation's IT services by an external source: a) at an agreed service level, b) to an agreed cost formula and c) over an agreed time period. The FM contract may further include IT consultancy, the management of IT services, the provision of new services and ownership of hardware and software' (CCTA, 1990).

Whilst this definition appears synonymous with outsourcing, Hoskyns (1991) perceive outsourcing as an umbrella term which incorporates many FM activities:

'IT outsourcing is a broader definition of FM to cover the contracting out of specified services to a third party within a controlled, flexible relationship. Outsourcing therefore covers FM type services and a range of contracts with more intangible benefits. It includes not only such services as computer centre operations, network operations and applications management, but also systems integration'.

The current interest in outsourcing is due, in part, to the publicity surrounding high expenditure and ambitious outsourcing contracts of the last few years. One of the problems facing companies which are currently considering outsourcing is the vast amount of hype which surrounds recent outsourcing contracts.

Table 6.1 gives the top nine outsourcing contracts to be signed in recent years.

As we can see from Table 6.1, these contracts have been negotiated with large organisations who specialise in this type of service. Electronic Data Systems (EDS) the computer services company, which is owned by General Motors, has won a $3.2 billion contract to take operation of Xerox's computer and telecommunications network. This outsourcing contract is believed to be the largest of its kind, according to present estimates. It is also the first to encompass the world-wide information management operations of any company. For example, EDS will assume responsibility for Xerox data-processing, telecommunications and computer network services in nineteen countries, and provide and maintain the computer applications that support Xerox's internal business processes.

Company	Vendor	
Xerox	EDS	$3.2 billion
System One	EDS	$2 billion
Inland Revenue	EDS	$1.5 billion
Enron	EDS	$750 million
First City	EDS	$600 million
Eastman Kodak	IBM	$500 million
National Car Rental	EDS	$500 million
First Fidelity	EDS	$450 million
American Bankshares	Perot Systems	$400 million

Source: Adapted from *Computerworld*, 8 April 1991; *Financial Times*, 16 June 1994

Table 6.1   Top nine outsourcing contracts

In addition, it will assume responsibility of data centre operations, including the main ones in the US and Brazil; world-wide voice and data communications; desktop systems support; and existing business-support applications. In contrast, Xerox will retain control of the architecture of its computer systems, strategy and new programme development. It will also continue to service and supports its customers.

As with many large-scale outsourcing contracts, 1,700 Xerox employees (which includes 1,400 in the US and 750 in the UK) will transfer to EDS over the next 18 months. Such a large-scale outsourcing contract is still relatively rare, as Xerox has taken the unprecedented step of outsourcing almost all of its information management operations in order to 'focus resources on our core business of document processing, which is critical to ensure our continued success in a fiercely competitive industry', according to the chairman of Xerox. In addition, the Xerox contract, like many others, was initiated to cut costs. The chairman of EDS said of the Xerox contract, 'This is the first truly global commercial information management outsourcing arrangement and provides an opportunity for EDS to showcase its proven capabilities'.

One of the most significant reasons underpinning outsourcing is the desire on the part of the outsourcer to select an outsourcing vendor who has access to state-of-the art technology coupled with the skill and expertise of managing IT to maximise efficiency at reduced cost. Table 6.2 lists the seven major IT outsourcing vendors.

Survey research on outsourcing

The outsourcing phenomenon is relatively new and has not yet been widely discussed in academic circles (with the exception of a book by Lacity and Hirschheim, 1993b). However, the subject has received much attention in the IS trade literature and also from management consultants, many of whom already have outsourcing contracts with large companies. A survey was published by PA Consulting (1993) who examined the UK IT Outsourcing market. The survey was based on 230 responses to a questionnaire sent to a selection of readers of *Financial Director* and *Informatics* magazines in addition to the clients and contacts of PA Consulting. Respondents fell into the following groups: IT Directors 49 percent, Finance Directors 36%, other business roles 13 percent and other

Company	Revenues ($ millions)	Percentage of Market
EDS	5470	40.1%
IBM	3250	23.4%
Anderson Consulting	1440	10.5%
Computer Science Corp.	1440	10.5%
DEC	1000	7.3%
KPMG	600	4.4%
AT & T	500	3.7%

Source: Yankee Group as reported in CIO, June 1990, p.34

Table 6.2 Top seven outsourcing vendors

IT roles 2 percent. It is interesting to note here the prevalence of financial management in IT outsourcing decisions.

The survey (PA Consulting Survey 1993) found that:

- There is widespread and growing use of outsourcing in all aspects of IT, from strategy through delivery.
- This use is chiefly tactical, with short-term contracts covering only a few parts of an organisation's IT rather than the large, long-term, strategic contracts for many aspects of IT service provision which is currently much talked about.
- The benefits of outsourcing are not just in cost cutting; it can deliver business and IT service improvements as well.
- Getting the benefits is by no means straightforward – most organisations lack the critical skills needed to embark on a new sourcing strategy and to manage their outsourced contracts.
- There are high levels of concern about IT outsourcing, with significant numbers of organisations reporting problems of cost escalation, over-dependence and lack of flexibility from their suppliers.

Whilst there are a number of definitions of IT outsourcing, PA Consulting inform us that it refers to 'the delegation to an external third party of the continuous management responsibility for the provision of IT services under a contract that includes a service level agreement'. They state that, 'Commonly considered to have originated in the USA, IT outsourcing is now a boardroom topic in the UK and Europe. Interest is spreading to other countries as more and more businesses concentrate on what they do well and, in turn, rely on others to provide supporting services'. Oltman (*Computerworld*, 1990a, p.77) defines outsourcing as, 'turning over, or sharing, responsibility for all or part of an organisation's information technology function with a third party'. The notion of outsourcing as a partnership between client and vendor is not shared by all, although it is certainly encouraged by vendor organisations and other interested parties.

The annual IT spend – a runaway train?

The PA Consulting Survey shows that some 30 percent of the respondents represent organisations with an annual IT expenditure of more than £5m. The large proportion of respondents who individually spend less than £5m is consistent with the trend to devolve budgets to divisions or departments within a large organisation. Over 70 percent of the contracts already let for IT outsourcing are for less than £1m in value, with 78 percent of all contracts lasting for three years or less. These relatively low contract values and short terms imply a certain caution and possibly a tactical rather than a strategic approach to outsourcing. It may also reflect a move to 'smart sourcing', where organisations have let a number of contracts with selected suppliers for different components of their IT needs.

The Survey found that whilst a wide range of IT services have been outsourced from 'strategic planning to operational running', only a minority of companies 'go as far as relying almost totally on their suppliers'. Technical support is the most common service outsourced, 'reflecting increased specialisation and the difficulty most organisations have in justifying, recruiting, retaining and managing these specialists as well as the risks associated with the concentration of key skills in one or two individuals'. Other areas where outsourcing is popular is applications maintenance and development. According to PA Consulting, this correlates 'with the increasing demand for new systems using new technologies and the need to maintain 'legacy' systems, perhaps spurred on by dissatisfaction with in-house performance'.

However, the Survey shows a reluctance to outsource systems and technical strategy and business analysis. 'This is particularly pronounced for private sector IT directors'. PA Consulting argue that, 'In our view it is unwise to outsource strategy and delivery functions to a single supplier: there is an inevitable conflict of interest which undermines confidence in the supplier's advice. Of course some business directors see their in-house IT function in a similar vein and are separating the roles of 'corporate adviser' and IT supplier'.

The Survey shows a move away from traditional facilities management (data operations). While 25 percent of respondents claim to have rejected the idea of outsourcing this service, the possible decline in this market will be replaced by a growth in outsourcing other services. Nearly half of the respondents (48 percent of the sample) said they were exploring outsourcing arrangements for a much broader range of IT services. This move was often led by IT directors whom, the Survey found, were more likely to consider outsourcing than their business colleagues.

The Survey found similarities in IT management in the private and public sectors. In spite of the focus on 'market testing' in the public sector which emphasises high value, low cost services, this sector was only 'marginally more likely to outsource the business facing activities (systems and technical strategy and business analysis) than the private sector'.

The perceived organisational benefits of outsourcing

Unsurprisingly, cost savings were the most important perceived benefit from IT outsourcing, although financial benefits did not always accrue. Thirty per cent of respondents reported no savings from outsourcing, with some claiming that costs had increased. Other important benefits from outsourcing were access to IT skills, improved quality, headcount reduction, flexible resourcing and the release of managers to concentrate on other activities.

Interestingly, the Survey shows that 44 percent of IT directors expected a reduction in headcount compared with only 32 percent of business (non-IT) directors. Conversely, over 42 percent of business directors expected better access to improved technology compared with only 24 percent of IT directors. PA Consulting conclude that 'this could reflect the continuing concern of some business directors that in-house IT organisations cannot keep pace with technology development. These findings also reflect a tendency of IT directors to overstate the potential of in-house technology'.

The tendency to assume an ease with which benefits from outsourcing will accrue to companies is overstated in the IS trade literature. The decision whether or not to choose outsourcing is linked by some to the survival of the business (*Computerworld*, 1990a. Huber, 1993). Some advocates of outsourcing place it in the wider context of key strategic business benefits. Oltman (*Computerworld*, 1990a, p.77) claims that outsourcing will enable firms to 'respond to the rapid internationalisation of business when the rules change every week; improve return on equity; keep up with dramatic technological change and differentiate their company from the competition; answer the growing shortage of information technology and business systems professionals'. Moreover, 'In the short term, outsourcing will cut costs and help manage the business better. In the long term, outsourcing can add value'.

Glib statements of this kind may be dangerous and lull potential outsourcing customers into a false sense of security. Whilst outsourcing is perceived by many as a panacea to cure organisational ills of low profits and productivity, skills shortages and obsolete technologies, the 'hype' surrounding outsourcing is akin to the 'automate or liquidate' arguments for IT investment in the early 1980s. Lessons learned in hindsight, however, show that IT investment has not always delivered the business advantages suggested by the vendor trade literature and continues to pose problems to managers in the form of evaluation, implementation, maintenance, skills development and payback. Some of these issues are considered in the next section.

The perceived organisational pitfalls of outsourcing

In conjunction with the realisation of benefits from outsourcing, respondents in the PA Consulting Survey (1993) pointed to a number of problem areas. Forty six per cent reported problems of over-dependence on their supplier, whilst 40 percent reported cost escalation and a lack of flexibility of suppliers. Comparing the perceived pitfalls of outsourcing with the results found that 26 percent of respondents expected a loss of control of IT but only 7 percent reported that this had created a problem. This implies that relinquishing control of IT had not posed serious problems for the majority of outsourcers. Similarly, damage to staff morale was expected by 31 percent of respondents and reported as a problem by only 21 percent.

The problems of outsourcing contracts were described as fivefold. They included: cost escalation, maintaining quality, over-dependence on suppliers, lack of supplier flexibility and lack of management skills to manage the supplier (this was reported by 67 percent of public sector companies).

The issue of cost escalation and over-dependence on suppliers was a crucial concern of respondents. PA Consulting point out that, 'This may be an inherent consequence of the formality of contracting with a third party or it may reflect greater uncertainty about future needs for IT'.

Skills shortages were also seen as an impediment to outsourcing. This was reported by both private and public sector organisations irrespective of size. Seven areas were highlighted to include: sourcing strategy, selecting services to outsource, market analysis, selecting suppliers, preparing service level agreements (SLAs), negotiating contracts and managing suppliers.

The outsourcing phenomenon

According to Lacity and Hirschheim (1993a) the 1980s were characterised by a wealth of literature advising companies of the strategic advantages of information systems. Success stories at American Airlines, Merrill Lynch and American Hospital Supply demonstrated how IS could return qualitative and quantitative benefits to the business. Strategic IS plans were developed and implemented in many organisations, but the results were often disappointing. Yet in spite of these disappointments, companies were continuously advised to invest greater sums in IS in conjunction with their re-engineering and rationalisation strategies.

Following the initial optimism about the strategic advantages of IS/IT, the 1990s saw greater caution following the realisation that technology does not always deliver expected results. Whilst technology was often made the scapegoat of failure, a closer examination usually highlighted managerial failure. Companies realised that rapidly changing technologies and methodologies outpaced the learning curve of managers and IT professionals. Skills shortages became (and remain) a serious impediment to the implementation of technical strategies. Thus managers increasingly looked outside their organisations for technical and decision-making support. This fuelled the outsourcing phenomenon where executives were 'promised savings of between 10 percent and 50 percent off IS expenditures. Prudent companies are advised to follow suit behind Eastman Kodak, American Bankshares, Enron, Continental, and others'.

The desire to cut IS costs through outsourcing proved very attractive to companies. As Lacity and Hirschheim (1993b) point out, this led to a number of hastily put together outsourcing deals which were seemingly justified by vendor hype rather than a full assessment of all the facts. In spite of well documented outsourcing failures, these authors argue for 'smart sourcing' where companies retain strategic applications and outsource all those IS/IT services where they have little or no expertise.

Types of outsourcing

Lacity and Hirschheim (1993b) provide a taxonomy of outsourcing options. They are divided into body shop, project management and total outsourcing options. Body shop outsourcing refers to a situation where management use outsourcing as a means of meeting short-term IS/IT demands. The use of contract IT programmers and associated personnel fall within this category. For example, the common problem of in-house skills shortages is a key impetus behind body shop outsourcing contracts. Project management outsourcing is employed for all or part of a particular IS project. Outsourcing suppliers will develop a new system and/or support an existing application. Disaster recovery, network management and training also come under this category. Total outsourcing is even more ambitious. As the name suggests, the outsourcing supplier (vendor) is given full responsibility of selected areas. Common areas include hardware (data centres and telecommunications) and software support (applications development and maintenance). This type of outsourcing is sometimes described as the transfer of 'the keys to the kingdom' or 'the crown jewels' to the outsourcing supplier.

Total outsourcing is described by the authors (p.3) as

'The vendor typically charges a fixed fee for a pre-specified number of services, known as the 'baseline'. The customer is guaranteed that their IS costs for this baseline will be fixed over the contract duration, typically five to ten years. During the contract period, services not included in the baseline may be purchased from the vendor for an access fee. Deals are often sweetened with financial incentives, such as stock purchases, loans at low interest rates and postponed payments. At the outset, these deals are extremely attractive, especially to an organisation that suffers financially. But the implications in the long term are unclear'.

Many organisations use body shop (contract IT staff) in conjunction with project management forms of outsourcing. Grindley (1991) claims that, in 1980, only 6 percent of the average systems development budget was spent on outside contractors compared with 32 percent by 1990. He says that about 9 percent of IT directors currently outsource all their systems development work. The growth in contract IT staff has been remarkable. Whilst about 70 percent of all contract work is provided by agencies who liaise with the client (*Computer Contractor*, 1994) recent evidence suggests that 36 percent of existing in-house programmers also have ambitions to become contractors. In addition, some 58 percent of existing contractors intend to remain contractors either working for a consultancy or software house. This survey found that only 16 percent of in-house programmers felt that their company offered a lucrative career path (Grindley, 1991). Whilst contracting work is commonly associated with poor working conditions, instability and low pay, IT contracting, particularly for those with scarce skills, offers excellent renumeration and opportunities to develop a wide range of experience in different professional settings. The decision to use contractors, however, often creates tensions within organisations. This conflict often results from permanent staff feeling threatened and envious of IT contractors, especially since the latter are well renumerated and possess state-of-the-art skills.

Lacity and Hirschheim (1993b) claim the optimism underpinning outsourcing is found in the IS trade journals, outsourcing seminars and vendor solicitations. First, these reports are made during the 'honeymoon' period, before purchasers of outsourcing services have been able to evaluate the contract. Second, financial savings are usually estimated with little evidence of actual savings following an outsourcing contract. Third, the failures of outsourcing are under-represented. At the contracts stage, many companies are encouraged by the seemingly wide array of benefits from outsourcing in the form of technical expertise, applications development and maintenance, cost reduction (headcount, etc) and increased quality and efficiency of IS services. Fuelled by the fact that IS is categorised as an overhead, arguments in favour of cost reduction are attractive to senior executives. Contracts are drawn up on the basis of a range of expected benefits, with cost control being a top priority. Indeed the decision as to whether companies choose to outsource or retain an in-house IS department/division is invariably determined by cost evaluation. Having selected the outsourcing option, the ability to achieve cost reduction is often indicative of the success or failure of the outsourcing contract, even though other benefits (access to scarce skills) may be of crucial importance. IS contracts are also shrouded in secrecy and may cover a period of between five and ten years. At the present time therefore, the long-term impact of large-scale, high expenditure outsourcing contracts is difficult to evaluate.

The outsourcing contract

An investigation of the IS trade literature tends to give an over-optimistic picture of the possible benefits of outsourcing. One reason is that outsourcing vendors understandably promote the success stories of their clients with a view to winning new business. In particular, outsourcing is presented as an effective corporate strategy to reduce the size of the IS department, save money, tap into 'expert skills' located at the outsourcing vendor and improve the quality of IS services. Whilst these attractive benefits have convinced some senior executives that outsourcing is the right strategy for their companies, others (usually in hindsight) have become increasingly wary of the 'hype' surrounding this issue. Lacity and Hirschheim (1993ab) give many examples of senior managers reassessing their company's outsourcing deals. Some companies report bitter disappointment with their outsourcing vendor, especially in the area of contracts.

The authors state that contrary to the 'hype', outsourcing vendors may not be more efficient than the in-house IS department. The latter may be able to deliver effective results irrespective of external support. Also, companies which have already embarked on outsourcing realise the importance of negotiating a tight contract. The authors state that there are various 'myths' associated with outsourcing which they divide into two categories. First, the 'mass production efficiency myth' relates to cost per mips (million instructions per second), hardware costs and software costs. In one firm, the IS department operated a 28 mips shop. When this firm sought outsourcing evaluations, the five vendors were unable to match the performance of the in-house IS function.

In the case of hardware, the authors argue that

'Economic theory purports that large companies have lower average costs than small companies partly because they receive volume discounts on inputs. The volume discount theory presumes that large companies buy in bulk and therefore receive quantity discounts. This argument extends to the outsourcing arena by assuming that outsourcing vendors buy hardware for less' (Lacity and Hirschheim, 1993b, p.235).

Two reasons are given why this argument is flawed. First, large internal IS departments receive comparable discounts to outsourcing vendors. Second, smaller companies may pursue 'hardware strategies' to reduce costs which are similar to those adopted by outsourcing vendors. Software costs are a further area where myths have been generated to support outsourcing. The notion that cost reduction is obtained when fixed costs are spread over additional units of output (many clients) is misleading. In the past software companies based their charges on site licenses. This was a fixed fee to enable a company to use one software package at a single data centre site. This arrangement obviously benefited outsourcing vendors and supported their arguments for mass production software efficiency. However, the software companies subsequently changed their charging structures to reflect the growing trend in outsourcing. Customers are now charged according to the size of the hardware. The so-called 'group licenses' are particularly punitive to outsourcing vendors and other users of large machines, thus making outsourcing more expensive to potential customers.

According to the authors, a further myth relating to outsourcing contracts is the ease of access to 'expert' talent. In a number of companies, the outsourcing vendor recruited the majority of the client's in-house IS staff which meant that existing skills were utilised rather than new skills. This talent was in both technical and business related skills. New recruits with scarce skills could therefore be assigned to work for their previous employer and be charged out at a high rate by the vendor organisation. Outsourcing vendors also headhunted the best talent from their client organisations. This situation was particularly ironic since the latter had actually paid for the development and training of these individuals. Client companies realising the problems associated with poaching often resorted to bribing individuals to remain at the company with financial incentives and other perks. This situation made companies realise the problems of not documenting important information and relying instead on knowledge which was contained in the heads of certain individuals. This was common in the case of applications development projects, where highly trained knowledge workers (analyst programmers/developers/maintenance personnel) were likely to be the only people who understood how the system worked.

The most crucial element to the success of outsourcing was the contract negotiated between client and vendor organisations. Many instances now exist where client organisations, in hindsight, wish they had considered important factors before signing the (often a 10 year) contract. The notion of working in 'partnership' which is encouraged by outsourcing vendors is problematic. First, it should be remembered that client organisations and outsourcing vendors are usually both commercial organisations with separate profit and loss statements. Whilst each organisation may wish to pursue an effective and successful partnership, problems arise when the outsourcing company fails to realise the expectations of its client. For example, many outsourcing 'partnerships' have suffered when the vendor imposes additional fees for work which is not in the original contract. Whilst the client organisation may assume the vendor will offer certain services and support as part of the contract, outsourcing vendors are usually quick to explain that these are 'extras' and will be charged for accordingly.

In many respects the notion of partnership gives a false sense of security to the client organisation. In turn, the promises which are made by the sales staff of the outsourcing vendor are meaningless if they are not included in the legally binding contract. As Lacity and Hirschheim (1993b, 243) explain, 'the contract is the only mechanism that establishes a balance of power in the outsourcing relationship'.

Many early outsourcing contracts were signed in haste and justified largely on the grounds of cost savings. Usually the client organisation simply signed a vendor's standard contract which was biased towards the vendor, particularly in the area of changes in IS activities and technology. Many client organisations also signed incomplete contracts. Again, this favoured the outsourcing vendor since additional services were chargeable. Client organisations also suffered because they rarely hired the services of legal experts with outsourcing knowledge. This failing has led many client organisations to repent at leisure since outsourcing vendors cannot be tied to loose contracts. Performance measurement of vendors has also been haphazard in a number of cases. Some companies have failed to adequately assess the service levels of vendor companies. Others have found that penalty clauses for failure on the part of the vendor to deliver satisfactory service is excluded from the outsourcing contract. The lack of termination clauses has also posed problems to clients wishing to relinquish ties with the vendor.

An important area of concern for clients negotiating an outsourcing contract is the 'change of character' clause. On a number of occasions, clients have found that vendor companies impose charges on their customers when new technologies are introduced which change the nature of work organisation. For example, the move to local area network (LAN) technology and the implementation of new software packages is viewed by some vendors as a change of character and by others (the client) as a change of technology. In the case of a change of character, the vendor may argue that it is fair to impose additional costs on the client. However, the rapid pace at which technology changes does not necessarily mean that new software packages change the character of work. In addition, the growth in LAN technology creates problems for clients with service level agreements for PCs. Some vendors argue that maintenance for each PC should be charged at the same unit of cost even though volume increases do not equal costs.

The above examples relate to contractual problems rather than to technical concerns. What is clear is that companies wishing to pursue outsourcing arrangements need to consider the wide array of potential problems before signing a legally binding contract. In particular, they need to detail all the areas they wish to outsource and agree with the vendor the parameters of each specific IS service. Whilst the problems facing client organisations are often interpreted as a failure on the part of the vendor to provide adequate service levels unless additional fees are charged, the perception in client organisations that outsourcing contracts are partnerships rather than business contracts may be described as a managerial oversight. This brings us on to the next section which considers the role of senior managers in negotiating, co-ordinating and controlling outsourcing.

Senior management and outsourcing

Lacity and Hirschheim (1993b) found that only two of the thirteen companies surveyed believed that IS departments were 'critical to corporate success'. The majority of companies were deeply concerned about the 'cost burden' of IS. In particular, many companies were concerned that IS often failed to deliver tangible business advantages. Two reasons were identified by the authors to demonstrate corporate concerns about the 'burdensome, costs-pits' associated with IS. First, senior managers usually lacked a working knowledge of how IS could be managed to achieve strategic business benefits. This lack of understanding led to scepticism and caution on the part of senior non-IS managers and to under-investment. Second, the traditional accounting system which categorised IS expenditure as overhead led senior managers to impose cost controls on IS expenditure. The authors show that in one company, overhead functions such as IS were not seen as strategic. Thus

'The accounting structure of an overhead account only allows management to focus on costs rather than benefits. When senior managers focus on rising IS costs, they seem less likely to hold a favourable view of the IS department. Now, the question remains whether senior managements' view of IS determines the accounting structure or vice versa. Either way, a relationship is apparent' (Lacity and Hirschheim, 1993b, p.193–4).

Clearly, managers who viewed IS as a value-consuming, cost-centre part of the organisation were unsympathetic to the demands of IS managers for increased resources to enhance the internal IS function. This is because the key objective for managing overhead-designated functions is cost minimisation and control (Quinn, Doorley and Paquette, 1990). In the last decade the tendency to rationalise overhead functions has been stepped up, with managers pinpointing areas for outsourcing. As Lacity and Hirschheim (1993b, p.193) state, 'The theory of outsourcing overhead accounts is that a vendor, through economies of scale, can produce a service cheaper. This also allegedly frees management from focusing on tedious overhead activities so they can expend their energies on more strategic issues'. The authors (1993b, p.198) identified six common reasons for initiating outsourcing evaluations.

	Participant's reasons for initiating outsourcing evaluations
1	Reaction to the efficiency imperative
2	The need to acquire resources
3	Reaction to the bandwagon
4	Reduction of uncertainty
5	Elimination of a troublesome function
6	Enhancement of credibility

Table 6.3 IS outsourcing framework

Since the authors found that eleven out of thirteen companies accounted for IS as an overhead function, the efficiency imperative was a key reason for initiating outsourcing evaluations. However, the authors state that

'Since no concrete measure of actual efficiency exists, senior managers formulate only a perception of efficiency. When senior managers perceive that IS is inefficient, they initiate outsourcing evaluations to improve efficiency. In a similar vein, IS managers themselves initiate outsourcing evaluations. This way, IS managers 'prove' that the IS department is already efficient or is making strides to become efficient' (Lacity and Hirschheim, 1993b, p.199).

Resource acquisition was another important reason for investigating outsourcing. Some companies undergoing financial difficulties saw outsourcing as a way to acquire resources such as managerial and technical skills, IT upgrades and even cash. Indeed, outsourcing suppliers encouraged business by offering potential customers various 'sweeteners' in the form of the latest PCs and access to scarce skills (the latter often exaggerated by the outsourcing sales team).

The outsourcing 'bandwagon' was fuelled by the IS trade journals and associated literature where IT vendors advertise the success stories of their clients. Much of this literature overstates the financial benefits to companies with the explicit message that outsourcing success stories can be copied. The rhetoric surrounding outsourcing is also helped by the poor opinion of in-house IS departments (as cost-pits) held by senior executives as well as users of IS services (see also Snell, 1994).

The desire to reduce risk and uncertainty by employing the services of an external outsourcing agent was the preferred option at some companies, according to Lacity and Hirschheim (1993b). Part of this preference is due to a conceptual link between IS and the theory of economies of scale. For if one accepts that outsourcing companies possess 'state-of-the-art' technologies which may be unaffordable to the client company, the latter will benefit from the dual advantages of 1) keeping costs to a minimum through scale economies and 2) the ability to maximise 'expert knowledge and skills' which are employed by the outsourcing company.

A further benefit to the client from outsourcing is the ability to plan for fluctuations on IS project work which is not easily achieved with an in-house IS department. For example, applications development projects could be planned according to customer convenience with issues such as over-manning and poor productivity becoming the problem of the outsourcing company. Management considerations would therefore come under the remit of the outsourcing company, as the client would simply worry about receiving a product on time, within budget and to the exact technical and operational specifications.

Another significant reason for outsourcing is the 'elimination of a troublesome function'. The financial categorisation of IS as an overhead as opposed to a value-added function continuously imposes pressure on IS managers to demonstrate value for money. This is becoming ever more present in the public sector where, in the UK, compulsory competitive tendering (CCT) will come into force within the next few years. Service providers such as the IS/IT department will therefore tender for contracts like any other service such as catering, cleaning and gardening, to name but a few.

A final reason for outsourcing is to enhance the credibility of managers responsible for negotiating the contract. From a political perspective, the low status of IS within many organisations tends to pave the way for senior executives to demonstrate their business acumen by outsourcing IS as a cost effective alternative to running an in-house department. Political decisions of this nature are usually taken by non-IS senior executives, or sometimes by IS managers who wish to manage the outsourcing contract. In the event of the outsourcing contract being perceived as a success, those responsible are likely to increase their own standing within the organisation. However, too many outsourcing contracts tend to be evaluated in the 'honeymoon period' before a sufficient amount of time has passed to evaluate the contract more thoroughly.

Outsourcing the 'Crown Jewels' or 'Keys to the Kingdom'

In support of IS outsourcing, Huber (1993) claims that the crisis affecting the Continental Bank during the 1980s led to its search for

> 'ways to cut costs in order to devote relatively limited resources to the bank's strength: establishing and maintaining secure business-customer relationships. The search ended in Continental's now celebrated passion for 'outsourcing' – hiring vendors to do the work of many of the bank's in-house service departments'.

He associates the decision to outsource IS with other outsourcing contracts such as catering, legal service and 'peripheral' services, although he claims that the decision to outsource IS was something of a 'revolution', since Continental was the first 'money-centre bank' to take such a decision. He asserts that, 'Eyebrows rose, heads shook, and tongues wagged when Continental, in December 1991, signed a ten-year, multi-million dollar contract to buy information technology services from an IBM subsidiary' (Huber, 1993, p. 121).

The decision to outsource IS at Continental was based on the rationale that the bank should concentrate on its core business and not channel large resources into simply running a support function such as IS. Senior managers apparently were convinced that serving customers was a key element to banking and crucial to the survival of the business. Huber (1993) argues that since banking was becoming increasingly competitive, Continental had to develop new ways to support 'business customers and wealthy individuals' through personal banking services. The two sides of the business, originating loans and selling banking services, demanded cross-functional teamwork and departmental co-operation. 'What we didn't need was any function that distracted the team from its main job as financial intermediary'.

In addition, the success of other outsourcing contracts such as legal work led senior executives to pursue IS outsourcing more rigorously. From late 1990 a number of outsourcing proposals were being considered. The author (Huber) was responsible for the bank's back office and data-processing operations. These operations were considered highly problematic. The IS function was considered inefficient since budgets and projects often over-ran. Huber (1993) claims that, in effect, the bank was outsourcing technology services to bank employees, but not receiving a satisfactory service. Four problems were apparent:

1. The existing mainframe technology was outdated and unable to provide the flexibility to meet stringent lead times.
2. The lack of flexibility of mainframe technology encouraged the development of a plethora of small desk-top systems and databases which served the needs of individual business units. Whilst a 'systems architecture' was later initiated to integrate this technology, this work was taken over by the outsourcing vendor.
3. Staff problems severely inhibited the in-house IS function. Some 500 people were employed by the bank's original in-house IS department, 'about half the number needed for major systems upgrades or large conversion projects and about twice the number needed for day-to-day maintenance ... top technical people didn't want to work at a bank, where IT assignments paled in comparison with the opportunities at companies that focused on technology'.
4. Financial constraints posed another serious problem to the internal IS function at the bank. Keeping up-to-date with technology required huge investments in cash and skills development. Over time, the bank found it increasingly difficult to find the resources for the IS function: a key factor in leading to the decision to outsource.

Huber (1993) argues that whilst it is important for banks to manipulate data, the 'conventional wisdom' which dictates that banks should retain complete internal control of IS is questionable. So is the notion that to relinquish control of IT is to endanger a 'core competency'. He asserts that the real core competencies of the banking business are twofold: an intimate knowledge of customer requirements and relationships with customers. Continental aims to implement a strategy of serving as 'a financial intermediary between clients and markets'. Thus

> 'We provide tailor-made products to satisfy an individual customer's requirements and strive to provide new, integrated services to help clients manage their money and their risks. The raw materials that make up these products are information and technology, commodities that change almost every day. And access to them is what is important. What is not important is owning the computers, employing the technical staffers, and managing the operation' (Huber, 1993, p.124).

Another issue which fuelled the outsourcing decision at Continental was the change in the technological marketplace. In decades past, 'proprietary technology' which was built up over time could enhance profitability. Today, the speed with which technologies are cloned and lose value means that few competitive advantages can be gained by retaining an in-house IS function. Advocates of IS outsourcing therefore point to the advantages of being able to 'tap into' the latest 'cutting-edge' technologies and up-to-date skills available at leading outsourcing vendors. IT costs would also move from fixed to variable with greater flexibility and decision making power to determine future IS investment.

A firm of consultants was hired by Continental to conduct 'reality testing' among 100 business and IT managers. The results found 'little resistance' which was thought to be due to the 'success' of other outsourcing projects such as legal services and catering. However, as the outsourcing evaluation process gathered momentum, staff anxieties grew, with many becoming concerned over their job security. A significant human relations problem was the knowledge that change was about to take place coupled with a lack of detailed plans regarding the consequences of outsourcing.

A decision was taken that once an outsourcing vendor had been selected, the bank would retain a number of 'technically literate business people' to liaise with the outsourcing vendor. The bank's range of in-house IS activities was broken down into component parts to assist the evaluation process. The two most sensitive areas were maintenance of existing systems software and applications development. After much deliberation, a lot of the resistance to outsourcing evaporated. Ultimately, a decision was reached to follow an ambitious outsourcing route with the expectation that benefits would accrue in four key areas:

1. Technology improvements. Outsourcing was perceived to offer huge benefits in technology acquisition as the vendor would use only the most up-to-date systems.
2. Strategic enhancements. Additional resources would accrue to the business-banking franchise; improved business unit involvement in and control over software; better use of internal resources and an ability to manage fluctuations in the requirement for IS services.
3. Financial gains. Since the IT payroll would be cut and costs would move from fixed to variable, considerable cost savings would accrue. The bank's technology resources would also be sold.
4. Management and IT budgeting improvements. By retaining legal and financial consultants and specialists in outsourcing transactions, the activities of bidding, evaluation, selection and contracting reflected the interests of the business.

Continental requested vendors to offer proposals which assumed responsibility for the great majority of the internal IS function. First, the vendor would be expected to purchase from Continental all existing equipment and network hardware. Second, the vendor would assume financial, legal and administrative responsibility for all hardware leased by Continental. Third, offer other outsourcing customers the use of Continental's data centre and charge for the service. Fourth, hire all staff originally employed by Continental who perform tasks which would become the responsibility of the vendor. These staff would also be offered comparable salaries and corporate benefits.

The three outsourcing vendors were evaluated on three important criteria. The first concerned the vendor's technical experience and knowledge of Continental. The second related to the plans for Continental's existing IT staff. In particular, the bank was concerned that many IT staff understood the existing systems. Much of this knowledge, however, was not well documented and was lodged 'in the heads' of key employees. The third area concerned legal issues in the form of the nature and scope of the ten-year contract between Continental and the vendor company.

Whilst Continental's experience of outsourcing is hitherto optimistic, practitioners remain divided about its potential benefits and pitfalls. A *Computerworld* (1989) article outlines the pros and cons of outsourcing with Stephan Gladyszewski from the General Signal Corporation cautioning against outsourcing 'the life blood of the business'. He asserts that outsourcing vendors 'sell their services to companies by focusing on two very emotional and extensively documented issues' – cost reduction and operational control. The continuing executive focus upon cost reduction coupled with a desire to improve control over the IS function are two important areas used by vendors to justify outsourcing. Benefits accruing to these areas are simply assumed by vendors and often supported by spurious statistical data which can only be proved or disproved once an outsourcing contract has been signed.

According to Gladyszewski, if a company wishes to reduce IS costs, it can apply the same cost reduction strategies to all IS activities and therefore achieve comparable cost savings with a vendor. He claims that his organisation has already achieved 10–20 percent cost savings along the same lines as those discussed by outsourcing vendors. On the issue of control, Gladyszewski claims that 'IS is perceived as out of control, not able to deliver to the business what it needs, when it needs it, for the economies that make sense'. He attributes this problem to a lack of senior management understanding and support for IS in addition to poor communication between management and IS staff. He says that

> 'Senior management makes the decision to outsource because they can cut the costs and eliminate all the problems at the same time. This is a rather easy decision' (*Computerworld*, 11 December 1989, p. 74).

However, the notion that senior managers can simply pass on their IS problems to an outside agency and acquire immediate 'quick fix' solutions is over-optimistic. According to Gladyszewski, IS is the single most important competitive weapon in the 'arsenal of US companies'. In turn, information systems are the 'infrastructure of the business'. Senior executives should therefore determine exactly what their information requirements are and search for improvements accordingly.

A common misconception about outsourcing is the notion that control is enhanced by placing IS responsibilities in the hands of an outside agency. Gradyszewski argues that if senior executives cease to control the infrastructure (the information resources and staff) their power is undermined in the change and improvement process. He asserts that

'I would not want to manage projects where I do not control the infrastructure and, most importantly, the people that manage the infrastructure. If management is concerned about costs, then challenge your IS operation to reduce its expenses. General Signal's IS organisation went to management with a plan to reduce costs, and we delivered on it' (*Computerworld*, 1989, p.74).

The decision to outsource or retain an in-house IS capability seems to be based upon whether IS is seen as a commodity (Kass and Caldwell, 1990) or an integral part of a company's competitive strength. The IS trade literature is divided on the issue and offers many examples both for and against outsourcing. Those who perceive IS as a commodity usually offer glib justifications for outsourcing such as 'Why manage commodities such as DP and telecommunications?' (Kass and Caldwell, 1990) or 'Our business is running assistance programs, not owning and operating computer systems.... People should do what they're good at' (*Computerworld*, 1990b). Advocates of outsourcing therefore welcome the opportunity to pass on IS responsibilities to 'expert' vendors to enable their staff to concentrate on core activities. Having opted for outsourcing, the key question is selecting a suitable vendor.

Selecting outsourcing partners

In a recent study on managing large-scale IT projects in the financial services sector, conflicting accounts were given by managers and IT professionals about the benefits of outsourcing (Currie, 1994ab). Interviews with one large Scottish insurance firm found that IT outsourcing was discouraged on the basis that, 'If we need a system, we design it ourselves'. A senior IT manager said that information technology was the major part of the insurance business and to outsource would mean a serious loss of control and decision-making authority. He also believed that outsourcing vendors did not understand the nature of the insurance business and were therefore unable to embark upon applications development projects. At this company, the 625 people working in IT were mostly graduates who had undergone further IT training in FORTRAN and COBOL. Like many other companies in the financial services sector, this firm was suffering from the rapid pace at which technology changes. The new client-server environment was posing problems since very few permanent employees understood this area. The IT manager said that, contrary to worrying about the skills shortage, he would be worried if his firm did not have a problem in this area. He reasoned that to progress in IT was to constantly train and retrain individuals. Skills shortages were thus an inevitable part of managing the IT function. Yet further interviewing suggested an absence of training, particularly in the new languages and packages. This firm also discouraged the use of contract IT staff, believing instead that in-house staff should develop systems. Only about 7 contract IT staff were hired by the company: a reduction from 30 people. Whilst body-shop outsourcing was not favoured (i.e. the hire of individuals to work on projects), the company did in fact outsource small systems development project work to a local software house.

Like many other companies, the selection process for outsourcing work was described as 'rigorous', although further examination suggested it was based upon 'the devil you know'. The IT manager said that small software houses (a few people) posed a problem since they could go out of business and leave a support nightmare. On the other hand, larger software houses with 'a track record' were favoured. Selection was based upon the portfolio of work undertaken by the software house, not necessarily at the client site. References from other clients were sought to support the selection process. The IT manager said that in the past, outsourcing project work had failed for four key reasons outlined below:

1. Failure to meet client requirements
2. Poor quality
3. Failure to deliver on time
4. Logistical reasons (geographical and support problems)

For logistical purposes, this company (like many others) set up work space for the software house in the IS department. Cross-fertilisation between software house staff and internal IT staff was encouraged, although not always achieved. The IT manager said that outsourcing arrangements were made specifically for work which the company did not wish to undertake. This work was described as 'drudgery work'. However, further examination suggested that external software houses were brought in for PC integration and network contracts, areas where existing staff were unskilled.

A discussion with a senior manager at a Scottish bank with about 100 contractors and many other outsourced systems development projects elicited some interesting comments on outsourcing. It was pointed out that selection criteria for outsourcing vendors was based largely on size of company and reputation. The large management consultancies were therefore better placed to tender for outsourcing contracts. However, in recent years, the burgeoning fees of large consultancy firms in conjunction with their failure to deliver on occasion had led senior managers to re-evaluate their outsourcing strategies. The senior manager commented that, 'Large consultancy firms charge an enormous amount but there is a comfort factor involved. If an outsourcing contract goes belly-up, a manager will not get his fingers burned for hiring such a firm. However, he may get into trouble if a small firm was given the job and messed up. His boss will say, 'wasn't it obvious that deal would go sour? Why did you go with such a small firm?'

Whilst the large consultancy may boost the support and back-up often absent in a small software house, the senior manager said that it was not unusual for agency contract IT staff to have better skills than IT staff at the large firm. Recognising this, he was currently considering an outsourcing tender from three agency contract IT staff, all of whom had worked at the bank in excess of one year. He reasoned that, 'When you find people who are capable of doing a job well in a climate of severe skills shortages in the UK, you should hang on to them'. Similar to the IT manager at the insurance company, the senior manager at the bank felt that the large consultancy bubble was likely to burst 'given time'. The bank had experienced IT 'disasters', albeit not on the same level as the TAU-RUS fiasco mentioned elsewhere in the book, but similar project development failures at the hands of external management consultants. Like all outsourcing partnerships, the senior manager was adamant that, 'Consultancies like us are commercial enterprises.

They will tell you they have the skills even if you know they are exaggerating. They simply want the business. But things are tightening up here and we don't want to pour money down the drain for IT applications development work that fails'.

Concluding remarks

Clearly the issue of IT outsourcing is one which is likely to become even more topical in the next five years, as many companies and government departments choose outsourcing as a viable option. Although it is difficult to offer formal conclusions on the likely outcome of outsourcing as a form of IT strategy, the decision to outsource raises a number of critical and complex issues for management. These issues are concerned with the strategic planning of IT, evaluation and performance measurement of the outsourcing supplier, the development and implementation of IT, training and organisational learning, the development of service level agreements (SLAs) and the maintenance of legacy and new information systems, among other issues.

At the present time it seems that many companies perceive outsourcing as a cost effective and workable solution to the problems associated with a burgeoning annual IT budget. But the degree of cost saving and potential benefits to companies who choose outsourcing as the way forward remains open to debate. From our discussion on outsourcing above, it is apparent that some caution is advised with respect to the notion that outsourcing automatically equates with better service at a reduced cost. Indeed, as Lacity and Hirschheim (1993ab) demonstrate in their case study research, a number of companies who have chosen the outsourcing route are not wholly satisfied with their decision.

A closer examination of many outsourcing deals suggests that once the initial 'honeymoon period' is over, the client is faced with a number of fresh challenges which amount to new problems for management. As we saw above, one important problem was where the outsourcing vendor increased their charges for new services which were assumed (by the client) to be already included in the standard contract (Deutsch, 1994).

This suggests that the euphemistic notion of a 'partnership' between client and vendor is somewhat misguided, since it is not altogether the case that the two parties share the same aims and objectives. In conclusion, it is argued that whilst outsourcing may be a workable strategy for IT for both private and public sector organisations, it should not be entered into simply as a cost reduction exercise or to simply relinquish management responsibility of a problematic function. Having said that, current trends suggest that, with the advent of unprecedented changes in the public sector such as Compulsory Competitive Tendering (CCT), together with further capital rationing in the private sector, it is likely that outsourcing will increase. Yet it remains to be seen whether the outsourcing bandwagon will begin to slow down as companies realise that new skills are required to manage the outsourcing contract.

Case study

Outsourcing in South Australia: a high risk strategy?

Background

Perhaps more than other states in Australia, South Australia (SA) was hit very hard by the recent economic recession. In February 1991, the government-backed State Bank had accumulated debts of more than $3 billion in only a few years. Apparently, the debt was the equivalent of $2000 for every man, woman and child living in SA. Following the success of the Liberal Party's election campaign in December 1993, the new Government embarked on an ambitious scheme to transform the publicly owned computer infrastructure of the state. An Office of Information Technology was set up that embraced all six of the government mainframe MVS processing computer sites, and a detailed audit of public sector computer infrastructure and assets followed.

A few months later, two multinational computer companies, IBM and EDS, were invited to bid for the multi-million dollar outsourcing contract. This would be the single largest public sector outsourcing contract in Australia. The contract covers the outsourcing of mainframe and midrange computer processing, local area and wide area networks and network management (Harris, 1994).

The outsourcing contract

'At 4.30am on 13 September 1994, the Premier, Mr. Brown, finally grasped his equivalent of the Holy Grail. After years of letters, telephone calls, meetings and top level negotiations, Mr. Brown secured the first stage of what he sees as the future of South Australia. Information technology is the new buzzword in State Government circles. For Mr. Brown, the move to have a huge new computer industry here is the equivalent of the commencement of a new motor car industry.

That 4.30am conference resulted in the United States computer giant Electronic Data Systems (EDS) winning the right to be the preferred bidder for a multimillion-dollar contract

to take over the State Government's computing operations.

Locked in battle with EDS had been IBM, the company which had teamed with Mr. Brown before the election to trumpet an agreement in principle about future computing operations in SA.

Some of the world's best legal brains have been involved in the negotiations over the computing contract – one expert being flown in from the US to take part in the exhaustive process which, at one stage, had EDS close to walking out and looking at offers from New Zealand and Queensland.

Make no mistake, this contract has the ability to be 'bigger than Ben Hur', as the Premier said at a recent press conference.

It will mean a huge investment in the State in terms of dollars and manpower. Spin-offs in areas such as computer and software manufacturer and the construction industry will put the State at the forefront of the information technology movement.

As the Premier claimed at the first of two press conferences he held, all the while smiling like a proud father after the birth of twins, to announce the details of the birth of the IT era, no one should underestimate the value of the project to SA. He said the IT industry had the potential to create tens of thousands of jobs and boost SA's economy. 'It will bring tremendous benefits to many people', he said. 'Not in the year 2000, but immediately. IT is a high technology industry which feeds on itself – growing dramatically in the process'.

The immediate benefits of the IT era for the State include:

- A $40 million capital works program at Technology Park, north of Adelaide, including a $13 million building for EDS and an $11 million centre of computing excellence.
- An urban housing development around Technology Park on 500 ha of land,

constructed by a private developer.

- As many as 3500 construction site and off-site jobs expected to flow from the residential estate.
- The government predicts at least 1500 new jobs will be created directly from the capital works program at Technology Park.
- These jobs are expected to be created over a 10 year period and will lead to an expected improvement in the State's economy of more than $500 million. The Government expects to save at least $100 million a year through outsourcing its computer processing with EDS.
- During the Estimates Committee hearings last week, this figure was revised to about $200 million.

This move to IT, the industry of the future, goes back to 1992 when Mr. Brown, as opposition leader, was approached by a number of technology companies about the potential for an IT industry in SA. He was told of the significant expansion of the electronics industries, particularly in software development. Mr. Brown told the Estimates Committees these approaches followed IT companies' frustration at the indecision and failure of the then labour government'.

At one stage, a group of companies asked him to attend a private meeting and, for two hours, highlighted what they described as 'the absolute bungle' by the Labour government. According to Mr. Brown, the government of the day 'had lost its nerve'.

These meetings with IT companies continued throughout 1993 and culminated in a strategy to attract the industry to SA. As Mr. Brown has made clear throughout his statements on IT, SA had to be the first State into the field. It had to take 'the bold step' of outsourcing on a grand scale. It was at this stage that Mr. Brown pulled his rabbit out of the hat. He produced an in-principle agreement with IBM, aimed at creating a 600 job, $150 million investment in SA.

'Immediately after the election, I was determined that we grasp the nettle, go through a due process and bring about my vision', Mr. Brown said. As a result, earlier this year he held a series of 90 minute meetings with each of the major international IT companies including EDS, IBM, Digital, DEC and Fujitsu – about 10 of them – at which they made major presentations.

This process eventually led to senior management from a number of the companies flying to Adelaide from the US for further talks. One of the executives, a man described by the Premier as 'one of the fathers of the modern computer industry', told the Government: 'You are making some very bold moves but you are taking the right moves and what you are trying to achieve here will be a quantum leap for SA'.

As a result of these meetings, the Government decided to make that quantum leap and, in March, a Cabinet subcommittee began conducting parallel competitive negotiations with EDS and IBM for outsourcing large-scale processing, local processing and data network services.

Both companies submitted what became known as Best and Final Offers (BAFOs) by the end of June and the subcommittee set out on an eight-week evaluation process of them. This included sending a top-level team overseas to see the competitors in operation.

At the end of August, EDS was considered to have made the superior offer but not a sufficiently attractive one to submit to Cabinet for final approval. Further negotiations with EDS began in early September with teams of up to 20 a side involved.

At one stage, the SA Government had six lawyers on the team negotiating with EDS. The negotiations became, according to one Government source, 'very intense' between 2 September and the early hours of 13 September. And through all of this, hanging over the head of EDS like the Sword of Damocles, was the threat of IBM stepping into the breach.

The Cabinet's subcommittee met on the morning of Sunday 11 September and still regarded the EDS offer on outsourcing as unsatisfactory and sought further negotiations. These continued throughout that day, and the day after, and into the early hours of 13 September.

It was at 1.30am, when things got really sticky, that the Premier joined the negotiations and spoke to EDS Asian general manager Mr. Ed Yang, in New Zealand. EDS had almost walked out twice and the Premier could see his IT vision on the brink of vanishing in a puff of silicon smoke.

There were two sticking points which needed to be cleared up to have the IT industry headed for SA's version of Silicon Valley on the dusty northern Adelaide Plains. The Premier and Mr. Yang cleared them up, resulting in the final identification of parameters upon which the agreement would be reached.

The lawyers ended their week at 4.30am on 13 September 1994 and, less than four hours later, Cabinet was called in to seal the deal. Mr. Brown had triumphed and could hardly contain himself four hours later when he announced a 'historic decision' which would see SA make a giant leap forward. The following day, Mr. Yang paid tribute to the Premier and the SA Government's negotiating team. He said Australia and NZ had a culture which was in tune with the Asian region. He saw Adelaide as 'kind of like a space station serving the area'.

'We are very excited about this opportunity', Mr. Yang said. 'We were attracted by the Premier's IT vision. I guarantee it will be successful'. Mr. Yang said SA and EDS would be involved in what was undoubtedly the largest technology infrastructure partnership awarded in Australia.

One of the first benefits will be that EDS, which is owned by General Motors, will transfer all of GMH's data processing to Adelaide. This will mean that up to 60 highly skilled technicians will be required to support both the new information processing centre at Technology Park and GMH's requirements.

The benefits continued to flow this week when the Premier announced phase three of his plan. He released letters from four companies –

Amdahl Australia, Silicon Graphics, Digital Equipment Corporation and GEC Alsthom – confirming their intentions to invest in SA as a result of the EDS contract.

Mr. Brown said Silicon Graphics in particular (the company which developed the graphics for Jurassic Park and The Flintstones) was interested in relocating its Australian headquarters to Technology Park.

Mr. Brown said it had been a huge success in only nine months for SA. Other government negotiations had been going on for up to 18 months. In Victoria, for example, outsourcing work has been negotiated for only one department.

The Premier has accused the Opposition of, at times, acting like vandals trying to sabotage the computer deal. But the Opposition's infrastructure spokesman, Mr. Kevin Foley, says, 'The jury is still out and will be for the best part of three or four years. That's when the decisions can be made whether this is a good or a bad thing'.

Mr. Foley told the Estimates Committees that the computer contract was an area of risk that involved $1 billion of Government expenditure. It was appropriate and incumbent on the Opposition to scrutinise it. The ALP would not be spoilers but constructive and provide that scrutiny not in a mischievous way or a way to score cheap political points. The Opposition, quite rightly, is worried whether EDS can deliver what it promises. The Premier says the Government is paying EDS so much per year and, in return, it must provide a complete service. He says it is like buying cars. 'The Government says it will buy 100 vehicles. You are contracted to supply those vehicles to this specification and at this price', he says. 'Whether the car company, ultimately makes a profit or a loss is its own concern. I stress the fact that the Government will pay EDS only so much and it must deliver'.[1]

[1]Source: Greg Kelton, SA in the high-tech big league, in *The Advertiser*, 21 September, 1994, Adelaide, SA.

Discussion questions

1 What does the SA Government hope to achieve through large scale outsourcing?
2 Assess the opportunities and threats of the outsourcing contract.
3 What are the political and economic consequences if the outsourcing contract fails?
4 What are the employee relations issues of the outsourcing contract?
5 Do you think the SA Government was right to opt for outsourcing IT?
6 What skills are needed to maximise the outsourcing arrangement?

References 6

Buck-Lew, M. (1992) 'To outsource or not?'. *International Journal of Information Management*, Vol, 12, pp. 3–20.
CCTA (1990) *Managing Facilities Management*, IT Infrastructure Library, Central Computer and Telecommunications.
Computer Contractor (1994) 'Opening doors', 4 March, pp. 43–45.
Computerworld (1989) 'Outsourcing: the great debate'. Vol, 23, 11 December, pp. 69–74.
Computerworld (1990a) '21st century outsourcing', J.R. Oltman. Vol, 24, 16 April, pp. 77–79.
Computerworld (1990b) 'HUD set to outsource', G. H. Anthes. Vol, 24, 3 December, pp. 1 and 119.
Computerworld (1991) 'Outsourcing at Southland: best of times, worst of times'. Vol, 25, 25 March, p. 61.
Currie, W. L. (1994a) The strategic management of large scale IT projects in the financial services sector'. *New Technology, Work and Employment*, Vol, 9, No. 1. March, pp. 19–29.
Currie, W.L. (1994b) 'The emerging market for IS Outsourcing in the financial services sector', discussion paper, Department of Management and Organisation, Stirling University.
Datamation (1994) 'Outsourcing as a survival tactic'. April 15, pp. 48–52.
Davenport, T. H. (1993) *Process Innovation: reengineering work through information technology*, Harvard Business School Press, Boston.
Deutsch, S. (1994) 'Outsourcing part three: transfer and copyright obligations'. *Computing*, 2 June, p.40.
Eckerson, W. (1990) 'Changing user needs drives outsourcing'. *Network World*, Vol, 7, No, 27, 2 July, p. 1 and 47.
Grindley, K. (1991) *Managing IT At Board Level: The Hidden Agenda Exposed*. Pitman.
Harris, J. (1994) Southern discomfort: SA Government outsourcing. *MIS*, Australia.
Hoskyns Group plc (1991) *Annual Report and Accounts*.
Huber, R. L. (1993) 'How Continental Bank outsourced its crown jewels'. *Harvard Business Review*, January/February, pp. 121–129.
Kass, E. and Caldwell, B (1990) 'Outsource, Ins, Outs'. *Information Week*, Vol, 260, 5 March, p.14.
Lacity, M.C., Hirschheim, R. (1993a) 'The information systems outsourcing bandwagon'. *Sloan Management Review*, Vol, 35, No, 1, Fall, pp. 73–86.
Lacity, M. C. and Hirschheim, R. (1993b) *Information Systems Outsourcing: Myths, Metaphors And Realities*. Wiley.
Loh, L., Venkatraman, N. (1992) 'Determinants of information technology outsourcing: a cross-sectoral analysis'. *Journal of Management Information Systems*, Vol, 9, No, 1, pp. 7–24.
Krass, P. (1990) 'The dollars and sense of outsourcing'. *Information Week*, Vol. 259, 26 February, pp. 26–31.
McCormick, J. (1991) 'Outsourcing action', *Information Week*, No. 337, September 10, pp. 84–92.
McMullen, J. (1990) 'New allies: IS and service suppliers'. *Datamation*, Vol, 36, No. 5, 1 March, pp. 42–51.
Owen, M. and Aitchison, D (1988) 'Facilities management: the alternative information technology revolution'. *Industrial Management and Data Systems*, May/June. pp. 15–17.

P. A. Consulting Survey (1993) *UK IT Outsourcing Survey*. PA Consulting Group: London.

Quinn, J., Doorley, T. and Paquette, P. (1990) 'Technology in services: rethinking strategic focus'. *Sloan Management Review*, Vol, 31, No. 2. Winter, pp. 79–87.

Sauer, C. 91993) *Why information systems fail: a case study approach*. Alfred Waller: Henley on Thames, UK.

Singer, C. (1990) 'Life after facilities management'. *Computers In Healthcare*, June, pp. 29–33.

Snell, T. (1994) 'Report reveals user discontent with in-house IT.' *Computing*, 9 June, p. 14.

CHAPTER 7

Managing IT in the Private and Public Sectors: Organisation Structure

Introduction

This chapter considers the results from an interdisciplinary questionnaire survey on the management of IT in UK private and public sector organisations. The theme of organisation structure and IT covered in this chapter is part of a wider interdisciplinary project on the management of IT, funded by the Scottish Higher Education Funding Council (SHEFC). The selected research method combines quantitative and qualitative approaches, as both methods are relevant to the primary research questions (Bryman, 1988. Gable, 1994).

A significant part of the research agenda examined possible links between survey and case study data. The research objective was not intended to be prescriptive or deterministic. Instead, it was designed to highlight possible linkages relating to the key themes of structure, strategy, evaluation, implementation, and the management of IT professionals. Organisations were selected from the financial services, manufacturing industry and the public sector. Cause and effect explanations of a deterministic nature were avoided given the subtle and complex nature of the relationships under scrutiny.

A survey questionnaire was designed to elicit data on the above themes from a wide trawl of UK organisations. Complex statistical methods such as multiple regression or analysis of variance were not applied as this was inappropriate. Instead, simple cross-tabulation was sufficient for the purpose of establishing relationships between certain phenomena. Where possible, the data is presented in diagrams and tables.

To supplement the questionnaire survey, in-depth case study interviews were conducted with IT managers in the three sectors. These organisations were selected largely from the survey organisations. In a number of cases, IT managers were interested to participate in the research since they were keen to have sight of the results. Whilst it is recognised that methodological problems afflict all research studies into IT/IS (Galliers, 1992), the dual approach of using survey and case study approaches was intended to reduce the margin of error for interpreting the results. For example, where respondents had appeared to interpret certain questions on the questionnaire survey differently from other respondents, they were likely to be contacted for a follow-up case study interview. Hopefully, this would iron out some of the anomalies of how certain questions were interpreted by respondents.

The case studies also proved to be interesting since they added a richness to the research study which is impossible in snap-shot survey research (Easton, 1982). The following section begins with a discussion on the key reasons for adopting a cross-sectoral approach to research on managing IT.

Managing IT in three sectors – the research study

The decision to look at three specific sectors on managing IT was taken on the assumption that cross-sectoral variations may occur in the key areas of structuring IT activities, strategy formation, evaluating IT and managing IT professionals and projects. It was felt that these areas needed to broken down into themes for the purpose of simplifying the many complex issues. The themes were originally developed from an in-depth literature review where key topics and questions emerged (see chapter one).

In this chapter, we consider the theme of organisation structure in relation to IT. This research topic was made popular some decades ago by the Aston researchers (Pugh et al, 1969ab) and Joan Woodward (1958). In recent years, however, the popularity of the topic has been eclipsed by the current wave of interest in corporate strategy and, one of its derivatives – strategy and IT.

But the relationship between organisation structure and IT is an important one, particularly where IT alters the structural nature of competition and the way in which firms do business (Porter and Millar, 1985). Other writers place IT at centre stage in organisational restructuring decisions (Davenport, 1993) given that specific IT applications can significantly alter information flows. More important, where IT becomes embedded into core and service business processes, it will undoubtedly help to shape the organisation structure. This is evident in organisations which have been 'downsized' using the latest technology to reduce information flows between the various functions (Currie, 1994b).

Since the range of information technologies used by the sample organisations was seen as important, the questionnaire survey presented respondents with a list of technologies to include CAD/CAM, communications technology, robotics, databases, networks and CAL/CBT.

It was recognised that not all types of technology were likely to be used by every organisation in the sample, for example the use of CAD/CAM in many public sector organisations. Whilst the selection of new technology was by no means exhaustive, respondents were asked to add any other forms of technology which they were currently using or which they were planning to use in the future. By requesting information on the type of IT or AMT used by the organisation, it was possible to cross-reference this data with the data on organisation structure. For example, links could be made between the size of the organisation and the level and scope of the technology they adopt. It was expected that large organisations in the high technology business sectors would be more likely to use state-of-the-art technology than, say, public sector organisations (e.g. education institutions, local authorities, etc). Banks were expected to have a large annual IT spend, and use the latest technologies in complex systems development work.

A second theme of the questionnaire was to elicit information on strategic issues. The nature and scope of the questions were developed from the debates found in the current academic and business literature on strategy (Johnson and Scholes, 1993. Mintzberg, 1994. Walsham, 1993. Currie, 1994b). Whilst the normative IT strategy literature assumes a strong relationship between IT and corporate strategy, the questionnaire was designed to show the extent to which respondents perceived their organisations to embrace an IT strategy. They were also asked who (if anyone) was responsible for developing an IT strategy, or if it was developed by steering committees or expert teams, etc.

They were also asked about the time span of their IT strategies (e.g. whether it was long term – up to five years; medium term – up to three years, or short term – up to one year). Part of the remit to include a section on strategy was to identify the key stakeholders in the IT strategy formation process and whether it was part of an overall business strategy or merely an adjunct to it. The issue of whether IT is aligned to the business strategy is an important topic in the IT literature (Henderson and Venkatraman, 1994).

The role of external management consultants was also considered in the strategy section, particularly as outsourcing becomes an 'alternative IT strategy' to some UK organisations. Indeed, outsourcing IT to a third party is becoming a major phenomenon, as numerous organisations reassess the effectiveness of their IT departments. Outsourcing is likely to affect public sector organisations more acutely in the next five years, particularly with the advent of market testing, Compulsory Competitive Tendering (CCT) and the close of the Regional Health Authorities. It is suggested that the latter will be replaced by local offices of the NHS executive (described as 'outposts of the Department of Health' – *Computing* 25 August, 1994, p.10). This will lead to an explosion of business in the health market, and the sweeping privatisation will significantly effect NHS computer operations.

It is unlikely that the new offices will be able to run IT departments. Since the traditional suppliers of these services are likely to be 'axed', the private sector will step in as the only alternative. Staff working in the traditional computer operations fields of the NHS will either be made redundant, or will find themselves working for a new employer, as the services not central to the administration of the new NHS will be sold off to private buyers. This *revolutionary* change in the public sector will completely alter the structure and configuration of IT services in the NHS. Other areas of the public sector are also likely to undergo vast changes, as non-core administrative service areas are put out to tender.

A third theme of the questionnaire survey was concerned with the financial evaluation of IT in the three sectors. Questions were based on current debates within the academic and trade literature about the difficulty of finding appropriate performance indicators for IT (Currie, 1989ab, 1994a. Jones et al, 1993. Farbey et al, 1993. Primrose, 1989. Shank and Govindarajan, 1992). In particular, the questionnaire survey was designed to gather data on the level of expenditure on IT per annum; the personnel responsible for preparing the IT budget; the choice of management accounting techniques used in the appraisal process (e.g. NPV, ARR, IRR, payback); and the use of qualitative data in the IT evaluation process.

Whilst the majority of the academic literature on IT evaluation confirms the use of financial measures over non-financial (intangible) ones, respondents were asked to provide information on these topics to enable a cross-sectoral comparison between the financial services, manufacturing and public sector organisations. It was also interesting to gather data on IT evaluation given the growing publicity surrounding commercial and public sector IT failures, a more recent failure being the city-based TAURUS disaster (Currie, 1994b).

A fourth theme examined human resource issues relating to managing IT projects. This area focused on the roles and responsibilities of IT professionals in relation to other managerial and non-managerial IT 'stakeholders'. A particular area of interest was to find out the extent to which organisations with a large annual IT spend had an IT director/manager, or instead managed IT at lower levels using non-IT managers or staff. Respondents were also asked to give their views on three important skills required for IT project management. In addition, questions were included about the level and range of training for IT at the organisation, an area which has been given attention by the two Government White Papers on science and technology (HMSO, 1993) and competitiveness (HMSO, 1994).

It was recognised that survey research, like any other research method, is not without problems. Whilst the questions were written in concise English in an attempt to avoid misunderstanding, it was inevitable that some confusion would arise over certain topics and/or terminology. Mintzberg (1993, p.97) also cautions us about some of the pitfalls of conducting survey research. Thus

'As good scientists, we are all expected to rely on hard data systematically collected. Anecdotal evidence is supposed to be soft, biased, and superficial. Yet we have just seen exactly the same about hard data – that these have a decidedly soft underbelly. The systematic collection of data about ill-specified processes does not provide much insight into what is going on out there'.

Accepting the premise that 'hard data', like so-called 'soft data', may be equally flawed and imperfect, the questionnaire survey was supported by follow-up field visits, equally divided between the three sectors. Access to these organisations was relatively easy since many of the IT Managers who had responded to the questionnaire were interested in the outcome of the project. A sizable number of them had requested a summary of the findings.

During the first year of the project, some thirty field visits were undertaken using the questionnaire as the framework for the extended interview. This enabled the clarification of many of the terms used in the questionnaire to avoid misunderstanding over the recording and interpretation of the results. The field research also served as a useful addition to the survey since it invited a more candid response from the interviewee, usually an IT Manager. This provided a richer source of information than would have been the case by simply relying on the survey data.

Survey

The questionnaire survey on managing IT projects in the UK originated for two reasons. First, it was intended to elicit up-to-date information on the management of IT projects in three different UK sectors: financial services, manufacturing and public sector organisations. The cross-sectoral perspective was intended to provide a deeper understanding of some of the societal, organisational and managerial differences relating to IT which affect both private and public sector organisations. Second, an interdisciplinary approach was preferred to examine the cross-functional linkages relating to managing IT projects in the three sectors. The questionnaire survey was designed to blur the demarcation boundaries which exist in organisations by adopting an interdisciplinary perspective. Key themes covered in the survey were those belonging to the disciplinary fields of strategic management, human resources, management accounting and management science. It is contended that interdisciplinary approaches in managing IT are more valid than narrow, single disciplinary studies.

Examples of such themes are: the corporate level at which IT strategies are developed (Adler et al, 1992. Boynton et al, 1992. Schein, 1994); the nature of the strategic planning process (Ciborra and Jelassi, 1994); the key 'stakeholders' or personnel responsible for implementing the IT strategy (Rowe and Herbert, 1990. Earl, 1993); the political processes and emerging nature of strategies (Markus, 1983. Robey and Markus, 1984. Davenport et al, 1992. Currie et al, 1993); the role of the technical champion (if applicable) and external agents (management consultants) in the strategy process; and any other current developments in the IT industry which are likely to influence IT strategy formation and implementation, such as outsourcing (Currie, 1994c).

A preliminary telephone inquiry was undertaken, but this proved unsatisfactory as respondents requested a hard copy of the questionnaire. Some aspects of IT were also considered 'too sensitive' to discuss on the telephone, e.g. the annual IT spend. A mail questionnaire was instead selected. This proved more appropriate and offered the advantage that respondents were more likely to have the added advantage of being able to complete it in their own time. The researchers were hoping for a twenty-five percent response rate. This would give a total of 250 completed questionnaires.

The questionnaire was six pages and covered a broad topic area. In particular, it comprised thirty seven questions relating to the key themes of IT structure, strategy, evaluation, implementation and behavioral/managerial issues. The questions were designed to elicit a mixture of quantitative and qualitative data. Hard data was requested on, for example, company size; turnover; job title of person responsible for managing IT; annual IT spend; number of people who work in IT; and financial structure (e.g. profit and cost centres).

Many open-ended type questions were also incorporated into the questionnaire. Rather than always offering a checklist of alternatives to elicit a straightforward affirmative or negative response, respondents were asked to give their views on certain topics relating to the key themes above. Whilst open-ended questions pose difficulties at the later stage of interpretation, the richness of qualitative data was believed to outweigh some of these pitfalls. We also welcomed the respondent's own choice of vocabulary in the interpretation of some of the open-ended questions. Organisations and individuals were promised anonymity and data was to be treated as strictly confidential.

Sample

The sample for the mail questionnaire was selected from a large commercial database which contained over 8000 UK and Eire organisations who subscribed to the *Computer User's Handbook* (CUH, 1994). The CUH was up to date and represented a significant number of organisations with a large annual IT spend. Organisations were selected randomly, although one criteria was that they possessed at least 150 personal computers (PCs). The organisations were categorized as follows: Public (UK SICC codes 91–95), Financial/Services (UK SICC codes 81–83, 96), Manufacturing (UK SICC codes 21–26, 30–49). This produced a list of some 904 organisations, all of whom were sent a questionnaire.

The addressee for the questionnaire was the contact name provided in the database. This was predominantly the most senior manager of information technology in the organisation. In about 20% of responses, the questionnaire was completed by a manager other than the addressee. This person was usually the addressee's deputy, or an IT manager in cases where the addressee was a non-IT manager, e.g. Managing Director. The response rate was between twenty and thirty-five percent. A number of questionnaires were returned incomplete as the individual no longer worked for the organisation. Other questionnaires were not fully completed.

Organisation structure and IT

In this section, we concentrate on the results from one theme of the questionnaire survey. It considers the relationship between organisation structure and IT. Over the past few decades a number of researchers have placed organisation structure at centre stage of their analysis of organisation behavior (Pugh et al, 1969a, 1969b. Mintzberg, 1979. Child, 1984). One view has been that certain types of structure enable the organisation to adapt more favorably to environmental uncertainty in the form of economic turbulence (Blanton et al, 1992). Some commentators have argued that an optimum model of organisation structure exists which allows for the maximum utilisation of IT (Davenport and Short, 1990. Jarvenpaa and Ives, 1993. Kaestle, 1990). This model is in the form of a decentralised, fairly flat structure based on products or services rather than on functions. The overriding rationale for a decentralised structure for IT is that users are now in a position to select the technologies most appropriate for their business requirements instead of having technical solutions imposed upon them from a centralised IT division/department (Tavakolian, 1991).

However, the simple centralisation versus decentralisation debate about IT structures has seemingly given way to a more complex analysis which emphasises the variety of structural forms that currently exist between organisations which share many similarities by way of product range, business area and management style, among others. In this context, some writers argue that organisations should develop an appropriate structure where state-of-the-art IT is fully utilised (Davenport, 1993).

Seemingly, one way to improve the level of utilisation would be through organisational restructuring using IT to re-engineer business processes (Davenport and Short, 1990). It has been pointed out that large IT investment alone does not bring instant rewards, rather it needs to be supported by strategic initiatives and organisational restructuring (Schnitt, 1993). Business process re-engineering (BPR) is the term applied to the process of restructuring in order to achieve the 'knowledge based', integrated and flexible structure (Davenport, 1993). Here, the role of IT is seen as vital in the attainment of competitive and information leverage (Callahan et al, 1993. Kelleher, 1993. Stainton,

1993. Tapscott and Caston, 1993. Vincent, 1993). The degree of decentralisation within the organisation is another aspect of structure (and culture) where IT is significant. Heap (1989) argues that IT enables organisations to re-centralise whilst supporting decentralised, dispersed and participative structures. But this requires the full commitment of senior management, a flexible work force and a primary support role for information provision. This introduces the perception that IT-based decentralisation may not be synonymous with devolution of power. Rather, it may enhance the power of management at the centre (Ashburner, 1990).

Kaestle (1990) examined the balance between forces promoting centralisation (to maximise low-cost, shared resources) and those which promote decentralisation (to improve market responsiveness). It is suggested that successful firms balance these forces by adopting an optimum centralised or decentralised solution at any point in time. Tavakolian (1991) supports the view that organisational context is critical to the level of decentralisation.

It is suggested that the emphasis on strategy and IT has created a dearth of theoretical and empirical research on the role and impact of IT on organisation structure and vice versa. Many surveys on IT tend to perceive structure as a subset of wider organisational and managerial issues. Similarly, case study research often treats organisation structure as being less important than other factors, e.g. management style, size, strategy, evaluation and implementation. Whilst case study research is often based on a relatively small sample of only a few cases, it none the less has the major advantages of eliciting in-depth data on an organisation.

One pitfall of this approach is that individual case studies may not be very representative of a specific commercial or public sector setting. This may result in over-generalisation and the emergence of a one-dimensional view. For example, the narrow and prescriptive classifications of service-based organisations which are characterised by one approach to IT, or process-based organisations by a different approach, seemingly provide an over-generalisation of IT management. Empirical research studies based on much larger samples in terms of number of organisations are few and far between, and there is a shortfall of surveys on organisation structure and IT which has been apparent for over a decade (Ein-dor and Segev, 1982). In fact, it seems that the research topic of organisation structure and IT has declined in popularity since the influential studies of Pugh et al (1969ab) and those of Woodward (1958). The literature on IT is now dominated by strategic approaches to technology, with some commentators seemingly ignoring the structural imperatives which constrain or support organisational behaviour.

It is suggested that research into the management of technology is more appropriate through an interdisciplinary approach which incorporates key variables of structure, size, evaluation, implementation and maintenance of technology. Indeed, it is argued that narrow, single disciplinary approaches often exclude important considerations discussed in other research territories. This leads to distortions in research design, and the likelihood that some topics are overstated, whilst others are treated with lip-service or even ignored.

An interdisciplinary approach is also reinforced through comparative work in different organisational settings. This chapter considers the relationship between organisation structure and IT in conjunction with a number of contextual variables including the physical attributes of the organisation, the sector to which it belongs (private or public), its primary business or service role (e.g. manufacturer, NHS trust, local authority, etc) and the scope of its IT facility. The intention is not to be prescriptive or deterministic; so the crafting of a tightly parametered research model is avoided.

Preliminary findings and analysis of survey data

It is argued that any discussion of the relationship between organisation structure and IT should consider both the external and internal environments. This is in addition to how IT activities are managed and coordinated within the organisation. The key parameters are therefore:

- External environment
- Internal environment
- Managing and coordinating IT

The external environment represents important considerations which influence the internal organisational structure which supports the IT facility. It is therefore suggested that the relationship between organisation structure and IT will be sector specific. For example, private and public sector organisations operating in different external environments will adapt their organisation structure and IT accordingly. External constraints are those in which the organisation has little or even no control. The external environment also encapsulates labour market conditions, government influences, legal considerations and many other factors.

Conversely, the internal environment allows for greater control in the areas of organisation structure and how the various managerial functions coordinate and control their activities. For example, organisations structured according to functional, product or matrix functions are crucial in terms of understanding the relationship between organisation structure and IT (Child, 1984). The nature of the core business will undoubtedly influence the relationship between organisation structure and IT. Whilst IT in some firms may be embedded into the core business processes, it may simply serve as a support function in others. In this capacity, the drive to 're-engineer' the firm will depend on the degree to which IT is utilised and exploited.

The third area which refers to managing and coordinating IT is important, albeit not easy to research through quantitative or qualitative research methods. This is because the political nature of management serves as an impediment to simple classification (Robey and Markus, 1984. Davenport et al, 1992). In recent years, a wealth of literature has been generated on the political nature of management and organisation. Whilst this literature has made a significant contribution to management theory, it detracts from some of the harder issues such as organisation structure. We will now discuss the three themes in more depth, and specify how they are relevant to the survey questionnaire.

External environment – Sector

It is generally accepted that the sector in which the organisation operates is significant in terms of influencing the structure of IT activities. This view is supported by Johnston and Carrico (1988) who claim that industry-related considerations are a key variable in understanding an organisation's use of IT. Many authors have sought to show differences in the role of IT between service-oriented industries and process-oriented industries (Cash et al, 1988. Premkumar, 1992). Premkumar (1992) stated, 'Service-orientated industries such as insurance, financial services and banking can be expected to have a greater stake in IS operations'.

Raghunathan and Raghunathan (1990) caution against such a stereotypical approach by stating that differences in managing IT exist between organisations in the same industrial sector. This is because the utilisation and integration of IT into the organisational structure varies between IT departments at any given point in time (Raghunathan and Raghunathan, 1990).

Industries are often classified as belonging to different sectors and we can incorporate another division into this classification by distinguishing between the public and private sectors. Clearly, organisations operating in one or the other sector are likely to embrace a specific 'mission statement' and therefore a different managerial approach to IT (Willcocks and Harrow, 1992)

But it is also important to sub-divide the public sector into sub-sectors given the wide variations which exist between service provider organisations. Indeed, the structure of some public sector organisations may be more similar to some private sector structures than to other public sector structures (even within the same setting). Thus the sub-sectors used are Civil Service/Government Agencies, NHS (all but one were NHS trusts), Public Administration (80% responses were from local government), and Education (88% of responses were from Further and Higher Education institutions).

Recognising the variations between organisations in the public sector, the private sector was also heterogeneous. For the purposes of simplicity, we confined our sample to two important private sector categories, and a distinction can be postulated between the financial services and manufacturing sectors. Financial service organisations are noted for their wide exploitation of new technology and significant annual IT spend. Here, IT is often a large division/department or unit, with large in-house systems development work being undertaken. We divided the financial services sector into three sub-sectors: banking services, insurance and business services.

Our questionnaire survey found the manufacturing sector to be more diverse in terms of its core business activities. Companies that produce IT and electrical goods can be expected to extensively use a range of technologies from CAD/CAM to robots, although IT may not be embedded into the management/businesses processes of marketing, finance and human resources, among others. A recent study found that IT was not fully exploited in the administrative areas of Japanese and British manufacturing companies (Currie, 1994b), unlike the extensive use of IT in the financial services sector.

The final category used in the survey was 'other'. This represented a 'catch-all', to cover some of the *ad hoc* responses from charities and research or conservation organisations which do not fall easily into a private or public sector category. The sectors and sub-sectors are summarised in Table 7.1.

Sector	Category	Number	% Total
Public	Public Administration	25	14
	Education	30	16
	NHS	11	6
	Civil Service/Govt. Agencies	7	4
Finance	Banking services	17	9
	Insurance	12	7
	Business services	15	8
Manufacturing	IT/Electrical	9	5
	Engineering	14	8
	Other	35	18
Other		9	5
Total		**184**	**100**

Table 7.1 Sectors and sub-sectors

Physical attributes

The size of the organisation may influence many other aspects. Large size may have some advantages which allow for economies of scale and the ability to generate in-house specialisms. It is likely that large organisations such as banks and local authorities will have a high annual IT spend, and many staff assigned to IT projects. Conversely, large IT divisions may be characterised by a degree of inertia, and they may experience communication difficulties with the business departments they serve.

Organisation size is commonly measured in terms of the number of employees (Woodward, 1958). Ein-dor and Segev (1982) found no significant relationship between number of employees and degree of centralisation of IT activities. Other measures relating to size such as annual turnover are inappropriate, as are measures of profitability and number of orders generated. In some organisations, turnover has no practical meaning, whereas in others the turnover figure itself is misleading since it reflects the nature of the main commodity of the organisation (e.g. companies operating in the money markets may have daily turnovers of billions of pounds).

The breakdown of the survey showed that 15% of organisations had less than 500 employees; 45% between 500 and 1999; 24% between 2000 and 4999; 7% between 5000 and 14999; and 15 had over 15000 employees. The largest organisations were regional or major city councils and big manufacturing conglomerates.

There were more minor physical considerations. The number of sites is a physical aspect which may create problems of logistics and communication in the coordination and management of IT. Organisations were categorised into single-site entities (11% of the sample), 2-5 sites (31%), 6-20 sites (24%), 21-99 sites (21%) and 100 or more sites

(13%). Clearly, the number of sites and their geographical location will have a significant impact on the structuring of IT activities. This is even more likely where IT is embedded into core and service business processes.

The spread of sites can influence the scale of the problems mentioned above. Nearly 46% of organisations located their sites within a short distance from one another (i.e. within a city or region). About a third had sites spread throughout the British Isles and 21% had a transnational spread of sites.

The number of sites was unsurprisingly correlated with the size of the organisation, although some organisations in the smaller size categories did have numerous sites. The correlation of size and spread of sites was less frequent, with nearly a quarter of those in each of the two smallest size categories having a transnational spread. But to reiterate the above point, the main summary measure used was the size of the organisation measured by employee numbers.

Internal considerations – organisation structure

McFarlan and McKenney (1983) and Cash et al (1988) support the view that the form of organisation adopted has an influence on the locus of responsibility for IT functions. There are two main forms of structuring an organisation. The first is into divisions (for example, through function, product or market stream) and the second is by a matrix. The most popular form is to create divisions. This was found in 69% of organisations. Some 13% claimed to operate within a matrix structure, whilst 19% said they used a mixture of the two.

The survey also requested data on how service functions like IT, personnel, accounts and stock control were centralised or decentralised. This provides an insight into the prevailing philosophy within organisations on how these activities should fit within the overall structure (Ein-dor and Segev, 1982. Wheelock, 1982). The results showed that some 69% of organisations claimed that IT was a centralised activity, with a further 18% claiming that it was devolved to the business units. In the remaining organisations, only some services or parts thereof were devolved.

One interesting facet from the responses to the questionnaire survey was the linkages which existed in organisations between structure, IT and financial arrangements.

Financial structure

The financial structure of organisations tended to be divided into two principal forms, profit and cost centres. In the public sector, the notion of a profit centre was not always applicable given that departments were not necessarily intended to make a profit but, instead, simply to provide a service. One IT manager at a government agency said that it was not within his remit to make a profit for his IT division. Yet if he operated on a commercial basis, he would carefully select his clients within the business units and possibly not serve those whom he felt were 'too much trouble'.

Whilst some 48% of the sample claimed their organisations were structured into cost centres, only 15% said they were divided into profit centres. In addition, some 37% said they comprised both profit and cost centres. Qualitative data from the survey and follow-up interviews, however, suggested that with the advent of Compulsory Competitive Tendering (CCT), more service departments, like IT, would adopt a profit centre status, or even become totally independent (Currie and Bryson, 1994)

Although cost and profit centres are simplistic definitions of how organisations perceive their financial arrangements, they are important insofar as recent organisational restructuring in both the private and public sectors has arguably been influenced by the finance function (at the company or government level). Manufacturing industry has undergone significant restructuring, largely as a consequence of economic downturn, capital rationing, severe global competition and the need to seek out new performance indicators for measuring quality and customer service, among other things (Currie, 1994b). Similarly, the new CCT and market testing initiatives in the public sector have led to a revision in the financial structure to facilitate the provider-purchaser relationship (*Computing*, 30 June 1994). In this respect, even cost centres are encouraged to behave as profit centres.

IT spend

The survey also requested data on the annual IT spend from the sample organisations. Such data was difficult to acquire since IT budgets may be interpreted in narrow terms, e.g. the cost of hardware or software, or more comprehensively, and thus measure the cost of IT associated activities such as training and software license fees.

The response to this question was interesting. Some organisations claimed to spend only a few thousand pounds on IT, whereas others claimed to spend as much as £300 million. Over half said they spend less than £2.5 million annually with one sixth spending £10 million or over. Clearly, the size of the organisation is a significant factor in the annual IT spend. Taking this into consideration, a measure was derived to calculate annual IT spend per employee. Some 35% of organisations appeared to spend less than £1k per employee, 53% between £1k and £10k, and 12% £10k or more on IT per employee. It seems that the number of employees within an organisation correlates with the annual IT spend per person, since it decreases directly in line with the increase in the size of the organisation.

Staffing

There were a total of some 18,100 IT staff working within the 184 UK organisations represented by the survey questionnaire. The average figure would appear to be about 100 IT staff per organisation, but over one third of organisations had 20 or fewer IT staff; 28% had 21 to 50 IT staff, and 18% had between 51 and 100 IT staff. Whilst only one fifth had over 100 IT staff, a quarter of them had large complements of more than 500 IT staff. This contributed to the high average figure. Interviews with IT managers across a range of organisations suggested a continuing trend to reduce the numbers of permanent IT staff, and instead hire more freelance contractors.

A measure of IT staff as a proportion of total staff was also derived. In 35% of organisations this proportion was less than 1% and in 41% it was between 1 and 5% with 5% of organisations having one quarter or more of their staff being in IT. However this ratio only rarely exceeded 5% in organisations with less than 2000 employees. There were rare exceptions such as in the insurance and aerospace industries.

The composition of the IT staff was difficult to determine with complete accuracy because there were different interpretations of job titles and common usage of hybrid jobs such as analyst/programmer. In fact, many organisations had ceased to separate the analyst from the programmer. Some IT groups could be readily identified. There were seven distinct categories: IT managers (7% of total IT staff); project managers (5%); relationship managers (27%); analysts and programmers including all hybrids (38%); database administrators (2%); hardware engineers (4%); and 'other IT staff' (17%) which consisted mainly of support staff and operational staff. The ratio of IT managers to total IT staff was also calculated. In 46% of organisations this ratio was 1:10 or less, 45% had a ratio of more than 1:10 up to 1:25, and 9% had a ratio of more than 1:25. A further observation was that over a quarter of organisations had only one individual categorised as their IT manager. Obviously job titles vary between organisations. For example, it was common for banks to have an IT Director (a senior manager) controlling IT, whereas firms with a low IT spend, or where IT was not seen as vital, may put a junior manager in charge of IT.

Role of IT in the organisation

The role of IT in the organisation was difficult to determine. Whilst the 'hype' which surrounds IT advises organisations to keep pace with latest developments, the complexity, deployment and utilisation of IT varied considerably both between and within private and public sector organisations. In the financial services industry, the annual IT spend was often very large. IT was also embedded into the core business processes of banks and insurance companies, and was crucial to the smooth execution of these businesses. Conversely, manufacturers tended to invest heavily in advanced manufacturing technologies such as CAD/CAM, FMS and robots, etc. But administrative services within manufacturing companies appeared to be less sophisticated than in financial services companies.

Public sector organisations appeared to invest heavily in IT, although appeared not to exploit IT resources like the financial services industry. Public sector firms tended not to perceive IT as a 'strategic device'. Nor did they appear to possess the same high-level skills base as their financial service or manufacturing counterparts. Pay rates for IT staff were also much lower in this sector.

The survey data suggested that IT was critical to the survival of some organisations, but was only peripheral to the core activities in others. This is important in relation to the perceived effectiveness of IT and IT management. But simple stereotypical classifications are problematic given the diversity within sectors. For example, if we adopt the view that service industries tend to place a higher premium on their IT function than, say, public sector organisations, the evidence suggests the need to sub-divide sectors. This is because, even in a high technology company which manufactures computer equipment, the use of IT by the administrative functions may not be perceived as crucial to the survival of the business. Moreover, the role of IT management may also be less significant compared with other groups, e.g. marketing and finance.

We therefore contend that it is important to consider two important factors. They are – the relationship between IT and the core business and the use and diversity of IT within the organisation.

Nature of core business

The relationship between IT and the core business has been well documented in the literature for over a decade. McFarlan (1984) produced a quadrant comprising four *ideal types* of the position of IT in various types of organisation. They were strategic, support, turnaround and factory. Whilst we have raised some concern about the adoption of rigid classifications and stereotypes, we none the less believe they are useful in terms of simplifying our data.

The survey data suggested that in 10% of organisations, IT was integral to the core business, and could therefore be perceived as a strategic device according to McFarlan's (1984) interpretation. Some 44% of organisations said that IT was used for some business applications, but was not vital (e.g. a support function). Some 26% of organisations said that IT was being used in some core business functions, but used as a support device in others (possibly a turnaround situation). Finally, 20% said that IT was only a peripheral factor in the organisation.

Use and diversity of IT

The use and diversity of IT applications within the sample organisations was difficult to ascertain. Since all the organisations were selected from the *Computer User's Handbook*, they all contained a minimum of 150 PCs. The numbers of IT staff employed and IT spend have already been considered. Whilst the number of PCs used by the organisation is not a satisfactory measure in itself, we devised a measure of the ratio of the number of staff to the number of PCs. Some 11% of all organisations said they had one or more PCs per staff member; 26% had a ratio of more than one to three staff per PC; 40% had a ratio of more than three to ten staff per PC; 19% had a ratio of more than ten to fifty staff per PC; and 4% had more than fifty staff per PC. (This of course takes no account of the use of mainframes or of the degree to which the PCs are networked.)

Questions were also asked about the range of IT applications used by organisations. As many as 97% said they used IT networks and databases; 93% used communications and information applications; 57% used Computer Assisted Design/Machinery; 36% used Computer Assisted Learning/Teaching; 17% used Automated Manufacturing Techniques; and 11% used robotics (the latter applying almost solely to the manufacturing sector).

Analysis of main parameters – IT structure

Three main categories were used to reflect how IT was structured within the sample organisations. They comprised 1) a separate IT division/department or unit; 2) IT as partially or totally integrated into other functions or structures; and 3) IT outsourced to a third party. Categories 1 and 2 can be further sub-divided. Table 7.2 gives a breakdown of how IT was structured in the sample organisations using the three categories.

		Single IT Unit		IT Partially/Totally Integrated into Other Units			Third Party
		Separate dept.	Sub-set of dept.	Multiple IT depts.	Decentralised & integrated	Mix of single single and decent.	Totally out-sourced
Structure of IT Activities (% of Sample Size)		69	17	1	7	7	1
Internal Structure of Organisation	Divisions	70	18	1	6	4	1
	Matrix	45	23	0	18	14	0
	Mixed	79	9	0	0	12	0
Service structure	Central	73	14	0	6	6	1
	Devolved	53	28	0	9	9	0
	Mixture	67	17	4	4	8	0

Table 7.2 Organisational structure and IT fit within this structure (as a percentage of sample size)

The Table shows that divisional organisational structures with centralised services were more likely to have a separate IT division/department or unit (these terms can sometimes be used interchangeably). We expected that organisations with matrix structures, characterised by decentralisation, would be more likely to have integrated IT units which served the various business units. But there were many exceptions to this set-up. The findings show that in matrix organisations, only a quarter of organisations had decentralised their core services (slightly more of those with a mixed structure had done so), and they were less likely to decentralise and integrate their IT. We may now examine the possible influence of the other considerations under each type of IT structure. Only those factors where differences occur are discussed.

Separate IT division, department or unit

Nearly all the banks and building societies had separate IT divisions/departments or units. This was repeated in the civil service and manufacturing sectors. Some 69% of all organisations in the sample claimed to have a separate IT division/department. The business services sector and the NHS were less likely than other organisations to have a separate IT function, although it was still over half. Unsurprisingly, very large organisations were unlikely to have a separate IT function, as the logistics of this were difficult to manage.

Multiple IT departments

Insurance companies tended to have many IT departments attached to the various business operations. Indeed, IT managers working in this sector often said that their business was in IT, since it was embedded into all of the core activities. This was more pronounced than in banking or building societies. Insurance companies also had a very high staff-to-PC ratio, which again reflects the pervasive use of IT in this sector.

IT unit as sub-section of another department

This form was most common in the NHS and in the general manufacturing sector (about a third of organisations in each sector). It was rare in the education field and virtually non-existent in the banking sector. It was also less common in organisations with a large annual IT spend; a high proportion of IT staff; greater diversity of IT applications; multiple sites; IT as a profit centre status; and also in transnational organisations. Organisations where IT was a sub-section of another department tended to be influenced by the relationship between IT and the nature of the core business. For example, where IT was not seen as a strategic device, or embedded into the core business, it was likely to be managed as a sub-section of another department, e.g. finance. This may or may not be the most appropriate way to locate IT within the organisation structure.

IT integrated and decentralised

Total integration of IT into the other areas was most prevalent (more than twice any other sector) in business services. It had not occurred in IT/electrical manufacturing and the civil service (although case study evidence showed that integration was occurring in the civil service). No organisations in banking or public administration had moved to total integration, although a few had partially integrated IT. A quarter of the largest organisations had partially integrated IT and a higher-than-average proportion of integration had occurred in organisations with a high annual IT spend; those where IT was more essential to core business; those with a high proportion of IT staff to other staff; and those which used many types of IT.

IT outsourced to a third party

There was only one example of this in the survey. The organisation had outsourced its IT to a facilities management company. Whilst many organisations outsource software development to a third party or even hire contract IT staff, the outsourcing of the majority of IT services is defined by Lacity and Hirschheim (1993) as 'total outsourcing'.

Financial status of IT

There were four categories which represented the financial status of IT. They were 1) profit centre, 2) cost centre, 3) a mixture of 1 and 2, and 4) facilities management. Although the latter is unconventional, the act of total outsourcing transfers the financial management of IT to a third party, although the client continues to monitor IT expenditure. Table 7.3 gives a breakdown of the four categories in relation to the survey findings.

The Table shows that IT was perceived as a cost centre in the majority of organisations, irrespective of whether the organisation claimed to be divided into profit, cost or a mixture of the two. IT was more likely to be a profit centre in organisations which were structured into profit centres, than those which were cost centres.

As for the other characteristics we find no IT profit centres in the insurance sector, engineering and general manufacturing and the civil service. The greatest concentration

		Profit Centre	Cost Centre	Mix of Profit and Cost Centres	Facilities Management
Financial Status of IT in the Organisation (% of Sample Size)		7	90	1	3
Financial Status of the Organisation	Profit centres	17	78	4	0
	Cost centres	3	95	1	1
	Mixture	8	89	0	3

Table 7.3 Organisational financial structure and IT (as a percentage of sample size)

of IT profit centres is in business services, public administration (although some of these may be 'budget centres') and IT/electrical manufacturing. Profit centre status is also linked to:

- higher spending on IT
- IT linked to core business
- higher proportion of IT staff to all staff
- higher provision of IT
- more types of IT present
- higher number of sites
- transnational organisations
- mixed structure (matrix and divisions)
- mix of integrated and separate IT unit.

Managerial responsibility for IT

In about 91% of organisations, an individual was specifically in charge of IT. Whilst this is unsurprising, an examination of the job titles of these individuals gave some idea of status within the overall managerial hierarchy. Examination of the titles of managers who head up the IT function found that 4% did not have an IT-related title, e.g. Operations Manager. IT was possibly not their principal domain of management. Organisations which were less likely to have an IT director (usually a senior manager) or manager were associated with:

- business service sector and NHS
- IT more essential to core business
- having only 2-5 sites
- mixed organisational financial structure
- IT integrated to other functions.

A very strong likelihood of having an overall IT manager is associated with:

- organisations with over 15000 employees
- transnationals
- mixed structure (matrix and divisions)
- profit centres.

Restructuring and IT

Over 70% of the organisations had been restructured within the last five years. Some organisations claimed that restructuring was continuous and reflected the evolutionary nature of organisations. The forms of restructuring were diverse. It seemed that some organisations opted for centralisation or decentralisation for no apparent reason (one organisation was centralised then decentralised within a short time period). The extent of restructuring ranged from minor (reorganising only a few divisions) to fundamental restructuring. In some cases, changes took place because of corporate moves such as take-overs, mergers or acquisitions. Expansion and globalisation also necessitated restructuring in some firms. The impetus to rationalise took the form of downsizing (e.g. by delayering the management structure), business process re-engineering (BPR) and streamlining down to core activities.

The greatest propensity for restructuring in the private sector had occurred in general manufacturing and business services. Interestingly, the insurance sector had not restructured its activities as much as the previous two. The economic downturn coupled with greater competitive pressures had forced many commercial organisations to opt for capital rationing and restructuring. In the public sector, much of the change was driven by legislative policy or privatisation, e.g. the creation of NHS trusts.

IT was seen to play a part in the restructuring process in about half of the sample organisations. IT had helped to restructure every civil service organisation and three quarters of the banks and building societies had been restructured. Only a third of IT/electrical manufacturers said that IT was linked to the restructuring process. How organisations are structured (e.g. functional, matrix, etc) appeared to make little difference to the role played by IT in the restructuring process, although IT is possibly more likely to have an impact on matrix structure reorganizations. This is because it is possibly easier to introduce IT in smaller segments of the organisation than as a widespread, all-pervasive IT strategy.

Whilst IT is perceived by many writers as a strategic device which may have a revolutionary impact on the business (McFarlan, 1984) our survey data showed that IT was not perceived as a major factor in organisational restructuring initiatives. Rather, it seemed that economic and financial imperatives, such as recession, poor profitability, capital rationing, intensifying global competition and reduced orders, were more significant in the restructuring process.

Instead IT was commonly perceived by respondents as a facilitator of change. It could generate new businesses, improve information flows, generate information (on customers, financial accounts, personnel and sales records, etc), reduce administrative lead times, and enable organisations to process large amounts of paperwork, among other things.

Concluding remarks

The questionnaire survey generated some useful data on the relationship between organisation structure and IT in contemporary private and public sector organisations. In summary, it seems that the majority of organisations continue to retain a separate IT division, department or unit. This would suggest that moves to create a dynamic and decentralised structure to encourage greater user involvement are, as yet, fairly uncommon.

Whilst respondents in the two sectors reiterated the goal to give users more powers to select and control IT, senior managers were equally keen to retain control over IT resources, particularly IT expenditure. This was seemingly achieved more effectively by having a centralised IT division or department where the annual IT spend could be monitored more closely.

Whilst the centralised IT facility was common across sectors, however, many public sector organisations faced an uncertain future. Indeed, some public sector IT departments were unsure if they would exist in the next few years. In this context, decisions to restructure IT appeared to be taken largely from political imperatives, and not necessarily on the grounds of efficiency gains. Few organisations appeared to integrate IT with other business or administrative functions. This was the case even in matrix organisations with decentralised, core services. Indeed, the ambitious goal of business process re-engineering to improve information flows across the organisation appeared to be hampered by functional boundaries, professional divisions and political infighting. Few organisations therefore reported that IT was effective in breaking down these barriers, although some claimed this would occur in time.

The survey also found that IT was, by and large, perceived as a cost centre. It was therefore threatened by rationalisation policies like any other cost centre. Some evidence from the public sector suggested that IT could become a profit centre, or even an independent entity, as a result of CCT and privatisation. This would produce opportunities and threats to existing purchasers of IT services, as independent IT departments would enjoy more freedom to select, *and reject*, their customers.

The structuring of IT activities into large IT divisions was similar in both the private and public sectors. However, the survey data suggests that market testing and CCT would revolutionise IT services in the public sector in the coming years. Whilst this would create market opportunities for IT professionals (Brittain, 1992) it would also have a major impact on the IT labour market in terms of job security. One significant change would be a rise in IT contract labour – not only in specialist analyst/programming work, but also in contract IT management positions, such as project management (*Computer Contractor*, 1994).

The survey found that an 'ideal' organisation structure for IT was difficult to identify. Organisations were not simply restructuring to align IT to the business strategy (Henderson and Venkatraman, 1994). Nor was technical change solely responsible for organisational restructuring. On the contrary, it seemed that most restructuring decisions were initiated for cost-cutting purposes. This finding is supported in a paper by Conti and Warner (1994) who claim that the most likely outcome of restructuring and re-engineering will be 'downsizing and cost reduction'.

Business process re-engineering using IT often amounted to little more than a distant goal rather than a practical reality. Some notable exceptions were in the financial services industry such as banking and insurance. Yet the continuing status of IT as a cost centre and service provider implies that IT departments are, at the present time at least, more likely to be a victim of restructuring rather than a catalyst for organisational change. The following chapter continues our discussion of the questionnaire survey by examining the relationships between structure, strategy and IT outsourcing.

Case study

Project management styles in information systems development

Background

Theoretically, an information systems project may be managed according to four distinctive types of project management: structured, dynamic, stable/controlled or *ad hoc*. This is shown in Figure 7.1.

Structured project management. IS work in this category reflects a formal-rational approach to project management. The type of work commissioned may be broken down into its various constituent parts, and follow a linear developmental path. Analyst/programmers may be brought in to work on various modules of the project, thus reducing the requirement for teamworking. The goal is to encourage knowledge creation using tried and tested structured project management methods and practices. The theory behind this is that creativity is enhanced when IS projects are carefully managed, controlled and organised.

The project management style is likely to be in the form of *direct management control*. Each module of the project has its own functional specification, technical specification, budget allocation, time scale and set of business deliverables. Planning and co-ordination become all important as project managers impose tight deadlines on the technical team. Structured project management is perceived as an appropriate

style for IS development work which is clearly specified by managers, IT professionals and the users. Structured project management styles are appropriate for IS work designed to improve performance in targeted business areas. The desire to adopt a formal-rational methodology is intended to prevent IS projects exceeding budgetary and time constraints.

Dynamic project management. This approach to project management encapsulates IS development which is undertaken in a dynamic and high-risk environment. IT professionals are likely to be highly qualified technically, although the developmental parameters of the project are new and untested. A good example is where an organisation embarks upon an ambitious business processing re-engineering (BPR) project. It is also likely that the project will impose a heavy burden on financial resources by way of staffing and equipment. Since the project may be justified on strategic grounds, it is also likely that formal evaluation methods will not be appropriate for cost analysis.

Teamworking is essential in the dynamic project management environment as all members are expected to apply their technical skills and organisational knowledge in the design process. In many ways, knowledge creation is

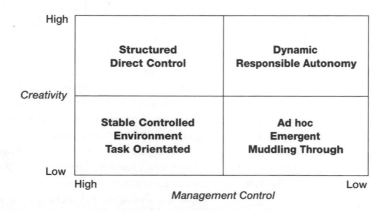

Figure 7.1   A matrix of IS project management styles

an important part of undertaking dynamic one-off IS projects. This type of project poses a serious management control problem given that the outcome is high-risk and uncertain. As a result, project managers are more likely to select IT professionals whom they feel they can trust. In this context, *responsible autonomy* is appropriate as team members are likely to work with little supervision throughout the duration of the project. This is also expected to unleash individual creativity and encourage organisational learning.

Stable, controlled project management. This form of project management is a deviant form of the structured approach mentioned above. When IS projects are perceived not to be progressing satisfactorily, management impose tighter controls on the technical team. For example, a project may exceed its budgetary limits, or may not deliver the appropriate business solution to the users. As a result, management impose even tighter financial and human constraints. Additional performance targets are imposed which are indicative of stringent management control. This stifles creativity among the project team, and further reduces the likelihood of a successful outcome.

Ad hoc project management. This approach to project management may be described as a deviant of the dynamic approach mentioned above. *Ad hoc* project management usually emerges through a breakdown of teamworking, and is further affected by the lack of direct management control. For example, political difficulties within the project team may result in dispersed creativity. This is likely to occur when team members become confused about the desired end goal of the project. In high-risk uncertain IS projects, the technical team may experience constant redefinitions from the client about what is required. This is likely to be met by devising quick-fix solutions, which may also be rejected by the client. The project therefore becomes ill-defined, over budget and fails to meet deadlines.

Politically, this situation is explosive, since the technical team is likely to complain that the objectives of the project keep changing. This problem is perhaps more common as business strategies are constantly revised in a severely competitive economic climate. For example, a bank may decide to change the original objectives of an information system on the basis of new legislation. On other occasions, project managers may decide to halt a project midway through and ask the technical team to use another programming language. This is because the initial assumption that one language is superior over another may turn out to be incorrect at the prototyping stage.

What is important in the emergent *ad hoc* approach is that creativity is reduced in conjunction with a lack of management control. This fuels a serious problem where motivation among individual team members is weakened. The project may also develop a life of its own as managers assume that team members are working responsibly and autonomously.

From the matrix of project management styles given in Figure 7.1 we can see that structured and dynamic project management styles are perceived to encourage creativity. However, management control is expected to be high in the structured approach, yet low in the dynamic approach. Alternatively, projects which are undertaken in a stable, controlled environment or an *ad hoc* one tend to stifle individual creativity. In the case of the *ad hoc* approach, creativity is reduced because management have allowed the technical team to work independently. On the flip side, creativity is also lost when projects become over controlled and managed. In this respect, projects which are carried out in stable, controlled and *ad hoc* environments respectively may be seen as the deviant outcomes of their structured and dynamic opposites. For example, effective project management styles exercised in a structured environment may encourage creativity and knowledge creation. However, an over-emphasis on management control may stifle creativity. Equally, dynamic projects which encourage responsible autonomy may become *ad hoc* and unstable, a situation which may also adversely affect creativity.

An IS development project

The example below discusses the development of an information system which was based upon the dynamic project management approach, but became *ad hoc* and unstructured over time. Figure 7.2 shows the original project development team. This team was constructed on the grounds that all these skills would be required for the successful outcome of the project. Their brief was to discover whether it was possible to interact with the existing mainframe via a PC. The project was divided into five separate but related areas: the PC, the server, the mainframe, communication between the PC and server, and communication between the server and the mainframe. It was recognised at the outset that this project was both complex and high risk. Given this, a consultant was assigned to each of these areas, with the purpose of working together as a team.

Each consultant had a detailed knowledge of their own specialist area and some knowledge of the related areas, i.e. the network specialist understood LAN and WAN technology, and the communication links between the PC, server and mainframe, but little of how the programs were to be written. After five days, the consultants had achieved their end objective (with the PC displaying data from the mainframe via existing legacy systems). Having achieved this objective, they did not set out to document how this was achieved. Interestingly, the project did not have an identifiable project manager, as politically its high-risk uncertain status created a hands-off approach by the management team. In other words, no project manager wished to be associated with an unsatisfactory outcome.

Fortunately, the outcome was a success, at least technically. But the lack of management produced a situation where the technical team were not given instructions to fully document all stages of the project. Instead, they simply copied the code which was used to act as a template for all future development. This meant, for example, that new code written to interact with the server was not documented. The next phase in the project development was to provide the users with a prototype of the desired system. This can be seen as a rapid application development phase. Figure 7.3 shows how the technology was organised to achieve this objective. It should be noted that not only was the operational environment totally different, but the number of people actually involved was reduced from five to two.

Two of the original consultants returned to their company. A third consultant was assigned to another project within the company. This left the PC and mainframe consultants working

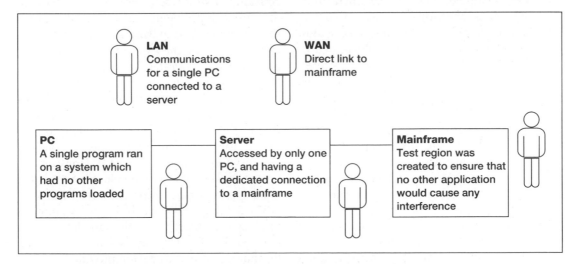

Figure 7.2 Original structure of development environment

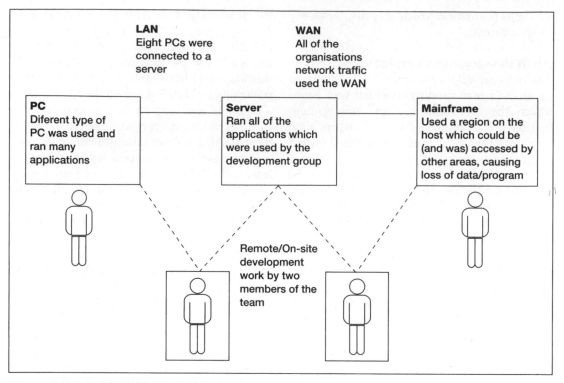

Figure 7.3 Later stages of the development environment

together. Unsurprisingly, the 'new' environment was far from stable. On the PC side the environmental settings which had been copied from the test cell were totally inappropriate. Rather than running one software package, several were now installed. This caused operational conflicts which had not previously occurred. The mainframe was no longer insulated against other development work. This is illustrated by the removal/deletion of data, other users interacting with the mainframe, and slowing response times or blocking requests. What was far more serious however was the absence of any real knowledge of how the server operated and connected to the mainframe and PC.

What made this situation worse was the remote development work which was undertaken by the two other consultants who were involved with the operation of the server. Although given no terms of reference for what they did, they wrote programs which were to run on the client and the server PCs. These programs were undocumented and contained numerous 'bugs'. The lack of documentation meant that many hours were spent trying to understand how the programs worked. When these programs caused a serious system failure, the consultants who wrote the programs tried to diagnose the problems and resolve them over the telephone. This produced a series of logistical problems for the two consultants working on site, as the programs were not supported by the two consultants who had returned to their company. Yet any criticism about the quality of the programs were countered by the consultants who had written them, since they claimed they were still at the developmental stage (i.e. ß-code) and therefore should not be used. However, the on-site consultants were unable to progress the rapid application development work without it.

The development stage took over two months to meet the objectives, although the original timescale was fixed at only two weeks. However, the more lengthy time period provided:

- A clear understanding of the technical environment
- Full documentation of the system modules
- External technical support from the consultants
- A requirement to clearly define project tasks and deliverables

- Tighter project management and control

The total cost of the second phase was £25k, about £18k more than the original financial allocation. The total cost of the project was estimated to be £25 million.

Discussion questions

1 Explain the matrix given above. Why are stable, controlled and *ad hoc* project management approaches deviant forms of structured and dynamic approaches respectively?
2 What is the most appropriate project management style for information systems development?
3 How would you assess the project management approach in the case study
4 What are the advantages and disadvantages of the structured, dynamic, stable, controlled and *ad hoc* approaches to IS project management?
5 What is meant by direct control and responsible autonomy? (Friedman, 1989)

References 7

Adler, P.S., McDonald, D.W. & MacDonald, F (1992) 'Strategic management of technical functions', *Sloan Management Review*, winter, 19–37

Allen, T. J. & Scott-Morton, M. S (1994) *Information Technology and the Corporation of the 1990s*. Oxford University Press.

Ashburner, L (1990) 'Impact of technological and organisational change'. *Personnel Review*. Vol, 19, No, 2, pp. 16–20.

Blanton, J. E., Watson, H. J & Moody, J (1992) 'Towards a better understanding of information technology organisation: a comparative case study'. *MIS Quarterly*, Vol, 16, No, 4, pp. 531–555.

Boynton, A. C., Jacobs, G. C., Zmud, R. W. (1992) 'Whose responsibility is IT management?' *Sloan Management Review*, Summer, pp. 32–38.

Brittain, J. M (1992) 'The emerging market for information professionals in the UK National Health Service'. *International Journal for Information Management*, Vol, 12, pp. 261–271.

Bryman, A (1988) *Quantity and Quality in Social Research*. Routledge.

Burrows, B (1994) 'The power of information: developing the knowledge based organisation'. *Long Range Planning*, Vol, 27, No, 1, pp. 142–153.

Callahan, C.V., Quarls, H.F & Treat, J. E (1993) 'Restructuring opportunities: new rules and new tools for today's oil-company managers'. *Oil & Gas Investor*, 4–6.

Cash, J.I., McFarlan, W., McKenney, J.L. & Vitale, M.R (1988) *Corporate Information Systems Management: The Issues Facing Senior Executives*. Irwin, Homewood, Illinois.

Child, J. (1984) *Organisation*. Harper and Row.

Ciborra. C., Jelassi. T. (1994) *Strategic information systems*. Wiley.

Computer User's Handbook (1994) VNU Publications, London.

Computing (1994) 'Sweeping privatisation clouds the future of NHS computer operations', 25 August.

Conti, M., Warner, M. (1994) 'Taylorism, teams and technology in 'reengineering work-organisation'. *New Technology, Work and Employment*, Vol, 9, No. 2, pp. 93–102.

Currie, W. (1989a) 'The art of justifying new technology to top management'. *OMEGA*. October, Vol, 17, No. 5. pp. 409–418.

Currie, W. (1989b) 'Investing in CAD: a case of ad hoc decision making'. *Long Range Planning*, Vol, 22, No. 6, pp. 85–91.

Currie, W., Fincham, R., Hallier, J. (1993) 'Multi-disciplinary management of IT projects in the financial services sector, manufacturing industry and the public sector'. Cost A3 Workshop publication, Glasgow Business School/Commission of European Communities.

Currie, W. (1994a) 'The strategic management of large scale IT projects in the financial services sector'. *New Technology, Work and Employment*, Vol, 9, No. 1. pp. 19–29.

Currie, W. (1994b) *The strategic management of AMT*. CIMA, London.

Currie, W. (1994c) 'Outsourcing: friend or foe?' *Research Workshop – Management and New Technology*, 16-17, Universite Pierre Mendes-France, Grenoble.

Currie, W.L. & Bryson, C (1994) A survey on IT management at 184 private and public sector UK organisations: some observations on structure and strategy. Working Paper, Department of Management and Organisation, Stirling University.

Davenport, T. H. (1993) *Process Innovation: reengineering work through information technology*. Harvard Business School Press.

Davenport, T.H., Eccles, R.G. & Prusak, L (1992) 'Information politics'. *Sloan Management Review*, Fall, 53–65.

Davenport, T.H & Short, J.E (1990) 'The new industrial engineering: information technology and business process redesign'. *Sloan Management Review*, Vol, 31, No. 4, pp. 11–27.

Earl, M. (1993) 'Experiences in strategic information systems planning'. *MIS Quarterly*, Vol, 17, March, pp. 1–21.

Easton, G. (1982) *Learning from case studies*. Prentice Hall.

Ein-dor, P., Segev, E. (1982) 'Organisational context and MIS structure: some empirical evidence'. *MIS Quarterly*.

Farbey, B., Land, F., Targett, D. (1993) *IT Investment: a study of methods and practice*. Butterworth-Heinemann.

Gable, G.G. (1994) 'Integrating case study and survey research methods: an example in information systems'. *European Journal of Information Systems*, Vol, 3, No. 2, pp. 112–126.

Galliers, R. (ed) (1992) *Information systems research*. Alfred Waller.

Halachimi, A. (1991) 'Productivity and information technology: emerging issues and considerations'. *Public Productivity and Management Review*, Vol. 14, No. 4, 327–350.

Heap, J (1989) 'Information systems and organisational engineering'. *Management Services*. Vol, 33, No. 11, pp. 6–10.

Henderson, J.C & Venkatraman, N (1994) 'Strategic alignment: a model for organisational transformation via information technology', in Allen, T.J & Scott-Morton, M.S, *Information Technology and the Corporation of the 1990s*. Oxford University Press.

HMSO (1993) *Realising our potential: a strategy for science, engineering and technology*. HMSO, London.

HMSO (1994) *Competitiveness: Helping business to win*. HMSO, London.

Jarvenpaa, S.L., Ives, B. (1993) 'Organising for global competition: the fit of information technology'. *Decision Sciences*, Vol, 24, No. 3, pp. 547–580.

Johnson, G., Scholes, K. (1993) *Exploring corporate strategy*. Prentice Hall.

Johnston, R and Carrico, S (1988) 'Developing capabilities to use information strategically.' *MIS Quarterly*, Vol, 12, No. 1, pp. 37–48.

Jones, C., Currie, W. Dugdale, D. (1993) 'Accounting and technology in Britain and Japan: learning from field research'. *Management Accounting Research*. Vol 4, pp.109–137.

Kaestle, P. (1990) 'A new rationale for organisation structure'. *Planning Review*, Vol, 18, Pt 4, August.

Kelleher, J (1993) 'The reincarnated organisation'. *Computerworld*, September 13, 2–25.

Lacity, C & Hirschheim, R (1993) *Outsourcing*, Wiley.

Markus, M. L. (1983) Power, politics, and MIS implementation'. *Communications of the ACM*. Vol, 26, No. 6. June, pp. 430–444.

McFarlan, W (1984) 'Information technology changes the way you compete'. *Harvard Business Review*, May/June, 98–103.

McFarlan, W & McKenney, J.L (1983) *Corporate information systems management: the issues facing senior executives*, Irwin, Homewood, Illinois.

Mintzberg, H. (1994) 'Rethinking strategic planning Part 1: pitfalls and fallacies'. *Long Range Planning*, Vol, 27, No. 3, pp. 12–21.

Mintzberg, H. (1979) *The structuring of organisations*. Prentice Hall.

Mintzberg, H. (1993) *The rise and fall of strategic planning*. Prentice Hall.

Porter, M. (1985) *Competitive Advantage: Creating and Sustaining Superior Performance*. Harvard Business Review.

Porter, M. (1992) *The Competitive Advantage of Nations*. McMillan, London.

Porter, M & Miller, V. (1985) 'How information gives you competitive advantage'. *Harvard Business Review*, July/August, 149–160.

Premkumar, G (1992) 'An empirical study of IS planning characteristics at Amon Industries'. *OMEGA*, Vol, 20, No. 5/6, pp. 611–629.

Primrose, P. (1989) *The financial justification for AMT*. NEDO Technical Communications: London.

Pugh, D.S., Hickson, D. J. , Hinings, C.R., & Turner, C. (1969a) 'The context of organisational structures'. *Administrative Science Quarterly*, Vol, 14, No. 1, pp. 91–114.

Pugh, D.S., Hickson, D.J. & Hinings, C.R. (1969b) 'An empirical taxonomy of structures of work organisation'. *Administrative Science Quarterly*, Vol, 14, pp. 115–126.

Raghunathan, B., Raghunathan, T. S. (1990) 'Planning implications of the information systems strategic grid: an empirical investigation'. *Decision Sciences*. Vol, 21, Part 2, pp. 287–300.

Robey, D., Markus, M. L. (1984) 'Rituals in information systems design'. *MIS Quarterly*, March, pp. 5–15.

Ross, D.F. (1991) 'Aligning the organisation for world class manufacturing'. *Production and Inventory Management Journal*, Vol, 32, No. 2, pp. 22–26.

Rowe, C & Herbert, B. (1990) 'IT in the boardroom: the growth of computer awareness among chief executives'. *Journal of General Management*, Vol, 15, No. 4, pp. 32–44.

Schein, E. (1994) 'The role of the CEO in the management of change: The case of information technology', pp. 325–345, in T. J. Allen and M. S. Scott-Morton (eds) *Information Technology and the Corporation of the 1990s*, OUP.

Schnitt, D.L. (1993) 'Reengineering the organisation using information technology'. *Journal of System Management*, Vol, 44, No, 1. pp 14–20.

Shank, J. K., Govindarajan, V. (1992) 'Strategic cost analysis of technological investments'. *Sloan Management Review,* Fall, pp. 39–51.

Stainton, J (1993) 'How information technology contributed to business process redesign in the UK's third largest health insurer'. *Document Image Automation*, Vol, 13, No. 3, pp. 4–6.

Tapscott, D & Caston, A (1993) 'The demise of the IT strategic plan'. *IT Magazine*. Vol, 25, No. 1.

Tavakolian, H (1991) 'The organisation of IT functions in the 1990s: a managerial perspective'. *Journal of Management Development*, Vol, 10, No. 2, pp. 31–37.

Vincent, D.R. (1993) 'How eight firms transformed with technology'. *Financial Executive*, Vol, 9, No. 2, pp. 2–58.

Walsham, G. (1993) *Interpreting information systems*. Wiley,.

Wheelock, (1982) 'Service center or profit center?' *Datamation*, May, 1982, p. 167.

Willcocks, L., Harrow, J. (1992) *Rediscovering public services management*. McGraw Hill.

Woodward, J. (1958) *Management and Technology*, HMSO, London.

CHAPTER 8

Managing IT in the Private and Public Sectors: Strategy and Outsourcing

Introduction

This chapter continues our discussion of the questionnaire survey on managing IT in three sectors (Currie and Bryson, 1994). The survey was divided into four key themes covering organisation structure, IT strategy formation, IT evaluation and human resource strategies for managing IT projects and professionals. Whilst these themes are not mutually exclusive, the questionnaire survey was designed to separate complex issues for the purpose of clarity. In this chapter, we consider the results of the questionnaire survey on the themes of organisation structure and IT strategy. Chapter nine continues the discussion by examining the data on IT evaluation, performance measurement and some of the key human resource issues.

Organisation structure and IT strategy

One of the salient findings from the 184 usable questionnaires was the extent to which both private and public sector organisations had been, or were still being, restructured. Restructuring was largely the result of economic recession; new product/service development; legislative changes; government policy changes; and the introduction of new working practices such as just-in-time (JIT), etc. As we saw in the previous chapter, IT played a part in the restructuring process, although it was not the driving factor behind wholesale organisational change.

Many respondents perceived organisational restructuring to be an ongoing rather than revolutionary phenomenon. It was largely brought about by corporate concerns about products, markets, strategic mission and competitive position. The majority of public and private sector organisations said they had been restructured in the past five years. It was interesting to note that manufacturing companies had experienced greater restructuring than their financial services and public sector counterparts, though major changes were planned for the public sector which would come into force over the next five years. These changes, by and large, would be revolutionary in nature, as some IT departments could not even guarantee they would exist after 1997.

Some 50 manufacturing companies said they had been restructured compared with approximately 43 in the public sector and 30 in the financial services. Only about 7 of the manufacturing companies in the sample said they had not been restructured in the past five years compared with about 23 of the public sector organisations and about 18 of the financial services companies. For the most part, manufacturing companies had suffered considerably from the economic downturn, and many were keen to follow the Japanese model of extra lean production (Hayes and Pisano, 1994).

Follow-up interviews with IT managers suggested that definitions of restructuring varied both within and between the three sectors. For example, in the manufacturing sector, restructuring was brought about largely by capital rationing and the introduction of new working practices like JIT, TQM and TPM, among others. In the public sector, however, sweeping privatisation and outsourcing were completely changing the historical (public centred) nature of service provision. As a result of these changes, the shape and structure of public sector entities was also changing beyond recognition. The abolition of, for example, the Regional Health Authorities would mean that IT services would no longer be provided from publicly owned resources through central IT departments or units. Instead they would be sold off to private buyers, and thus become private companies. This would give them new decision making powers to choose with whom and when they do business. Unprofitable clients would undoubtedly be rejected in this scenario.

Whilst the issue of restructuring continues to receive wide publicity in the media, the survey was intended to discover the extent to which IT played a part in this process. In almost equal response rates of just under 25 organisations, each of the three sectors confirmed that IT was significant in the restructuring process. However, as many public sector organisations (about 23 in total) said that IT had not been a major factor in the restructuring process. This compared with about 28 in manufacturing and approximately only 7 responses from the financial services sector.

The comments on many of the questionnaires suggested that companies in the financial services sector perceived their IT facility to be an ongoing, evolutionary and inevitable financial commitment, and not simply a 'one off', occasional cost. As a result the majority of financial services companies perceived IT to play a major part in any recent restructuring process. One reason for this was because IT was now embedded into the core business processes of banks and insurance companies. Here it was vital in the areas of new business development; data storage, retrieval and handling; customer service; supplier relations; and business reorganisation and even re-engineering.

It was interesting to note that a greater number of manufacturing companies (about 28) said that IT had not played a vital role in restructuring. A closer examination confirmed that, in the past five years, restructuring had been brought about almost entirely through economic recession and low profitability. In this context, corporate restructuring was perceived by manufacturing managers as synonymous with 'downsizing' and 'rationalisation'. In this context, restructuring was almost entirely economically driven.

Many manufacturing companies confirmed that IT was introduced to achieve headcount reduction. Many managers complained that investment in IT and R&D had not been sufficient to improve profitability, let alone competitiveness. But like the responses obtained from the financial services sector, manufacturing companies said that investment in IT should be an ongoing financial investment which is crucial for growth and product development. Manufacturers were concerned to increase their annual IT spend, particularly in the areas of CAD/CAM, and other advanced manufacturing technologies (AMTs). Unfortunately, economic recession and severe global competition had reduced the resources available to manufacturers for investment in new technology and other change management programmes.

Comments elicited from public sector organisations were quite different from financial services and manufacturing companies. Perhaps for different reasons than manufacturing companies, many public sector organisations (about 23) said that IT had not played a part in the restructuring process. Many public sector respondents, notably from local authorities, NHS trusts and hospitals, said that IT management was in an 'embryonic form'. Many IT managers recognised the potential of IT to restructure the entire operation through the new client-server environment (among other technologies). None the less, they expressed two key concerns relating to their ability to use IT to effect organisational change. First, many public sector organisations did not have a history of in-house IT applications development work. This was unlike the financial services sector. As a result, many relied on the advice and guidance of external management consultants. But this strategy was proving 'too expensive' and 'high risk', as the consultants did not always give value for money (HMSO, 1994).

Second, the cost-cutting policies adopted in recent years in many public sector settings had not paved the way for ambitious in-house applications development work using state-of-the-art technology. Also wage levels between private and public sector organisations were rarely equal, even where people were apparently doing the same job. This meant that some public sector organisations could not attract highly skilled IS developers to their IT department as better rates could be earned in the private sector.

This was in spite of the fact that in-house demand for complex information systems was becoming even greater, particularly in areas such as medicine and local government. Consequently, the lack of skills afflicting many public sector organisations tended to add weight to management decisions to appoint external management consultants at *commercial rates*. Such a state of affairs was described by one public sector IT Manager as 'ludicrous'.

Interviews with IT Managers in a Scottish health board, an NHS trust and a government department showed that IT, like any other cost centre service providers, was now being *market tested*. Theoretically, this meant that in-house IT staff were encouraged to adopt a *commercial approach* to their customers (the departments they serve). In doing so, this might halt or eliminate the outsourcing threat. One IT Manager at a government department said his strategy was to 'retain a core of 50 IT staff and lose the remaining staff to other departments'. This, he hoped, would show the IT department in a favourable light because it would be able to compete with external vendors on both quality and price.

One of the difficulties facing IT Managers was the poor perception of senior executives that IT was a cost centre which was 'run by boffins'. In fact, as many as 135 organisations, out of a sample of 184, said that IT was a cost centre. This compared with only 10 organisations claiming that IT was a profit centre.

Since IT was seen by senior managers in all sectors as a 'service provider', it too would undergo the same cost-cutting measures as any other service, namely catering, cleaning and recruitment consultancy, among others. However, a large proportion of the sample

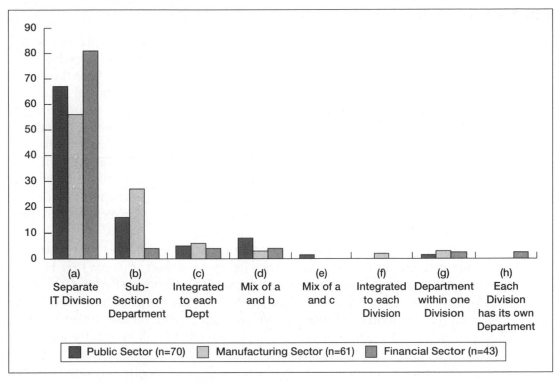

Figure 8.1 IT fit within the organisational structure

said that IT should not be perceived simply as a service department since it is integral to the core activities of organisations. Moreover, the choices surrounding IT such as whether to adopt client-server technology, CAD/CAM, robotics, etc, were described as 'more complex' compared with those relating to catering or cleaning services. Some respondents even mentioned business process re-engineering and argued that any re-engineering policies would involve IT.

The status of IT as a cost centre was also reflected in the career structure of IT professionals, many of whom complained that entry to senior level managerial positions was hindered by their IT specialism. As many as 118 organisations said that IT formed a separate division, with a further 30 claiming that IT was a sub-section of a department (e.g. finance, administrative services, communications or operations).

Whilst this would suggest that IT was an important entity within an organisation, a closer examination showed that IT managers were unlikely to occupy board level managerial positions, or even be able to represent IT at board level meetings. An interview with one public sector IT Manager found that, in spite of the organisation having appointed an IT Director with overall responsibility for some 280 IT personnel, this individual was not a member of the Management Group. He was not able to present his vision of IT strategy, but could only recommend his views to others who sat on the board. Thus the potential for distortion was high. This led him to argue that, although the title of IT Director existed, it was not a position which had 'much clout' compared with other senior level management roles.

Strategic planning for IT

Much of the academic literature on IT strategy which has emerged over the last decade adopts a normative approach and advises practitioners about the need to develop an IT strategy which is linked to an overall business strategy. The logic which fuels this debate seems to fall into four areas: financial, managerial, business and technical. First, it is argued that since corporate IT spend is large, and continues to grow, senior managers should develop an IT strategy to ensure the maximum value from resources. Second, IT is seen by many as too important a resource to be managed at lower levels of the hierarchy. Empirical research also suggests that many of the industrial relations and organisational problems resulting from technical change have stemmed from poor management practice, and are not the result of technical deficiencies or failure. Technology is often the convenient scapegoat to cover poor management decisions, however (Sauer, 1993).

Third, growing competition and the need to improve core business processes and even create new business opportunities have led many writers to argue that IT is an important factor in sustaining or winning competitive advantage (Porter, 1985. Allen and Scott-Morton, 1994. Earl, 1989). The logic of this argument dictates that if managers develop an appropriate IT strategy which is linked to their business objectives, their chances of achieving a competitive advantage through IT will be greatly improved. Fourth, the growing complexity and range of choice relating to IT suggests that managers should adopt an IT strategy, if only to make sense of their technology priorities. The recent stories of technical disasters such as the TAURUS fiasco suggest that technical change should be carefully planned and not implemented, *ad hoc*, or seen simply as a 'corporate panacea' (Currie, 1994b).

Recognising that strategic issues are important in the management of IT, albeit very difficult to research given the dynamic nature of the process, the questionnaire survey nevertheless included a number of questions relating to IT strategy formation and implementation. Respondents were asked first of all if they managed IT according to a strategic plan. Whilst many of the textbooks assume that IT is managed strategically – or at least advise that it should be – the questionnaire survey found that 88 percent of organisations claimed to have an IT strategy with some 12 percent claiming they did not.

A closer examination of the questionnaire data found that management perceptions of an IT strategy differed widely both between and within the three sectors. Some organisations where IT was managed by non-technical managers confused IT strategy with IT procurement. In this respect, the mere purchase of hardware and software was, according to these individuals, indicative of an IT strategy! At the other end of the spectrum, some organisations with an IT Director saw IT strategy as a vital part of the overall strategic planning process. This was common in banks and insurance companies where the annual IT spend exceeded several millions of pounds.

Those who claimed not to have a strategic plan for IT were unlikely to have a large annual IT spend. For example, some public sector organisations such as universities and government agencies did not perceive IT strategy formation in the same light as IT Managers operating in the private sector. On the contrary, follow-up interviews with some public sector IT Managers suggested that IT was becoming more integral to their organisation – a factor which implied that an IT strategy should be developed. Others who claimed not to have an IT strategy perceived the reason to be due to lack of senior management commitment to IT. Some IT Managers were critical that IT was managed in their organisation by middle level managers. They saw this a problem because it meant that IT tended to be introduced *ad hoc*, based on user choice rather than advice from technical experts. Still others in the sample claimed that management consultants were responsible for their IT strategies.

Whilst some IT Managers saw this as inevitable, given the lack of specialist skills relating to state-of-the-art technologies, others saw this as 'transferring the responsibility to outsiders'. Comments from some IT Managers suggested that whilst the consultants were able to 'dream up' IT strategies, their remit did not include implementation. The latter was, of course, the difficult part according to the IT Managers in question.

The eighty-eight percent of organisations which claimed to possess a strategic plan for IT were asked to specify the timescale according to long term (up to five years); medium term (up to three years); and short term (up to one year) plans. Figure 8.2 gives a breakdown of the responses received.

As we can see from Figure 8.2, some 52% of organisations (both private and public) said they followed a strategic plan for IT up to three years duration. Perhaps even more surprising was the figure of 42% who claimed to have a five year strategic plan for IT. Linking this finding with a number of other studies on strategic IT planning suggests that whereas many writers have claimed that strategies for IT are short term, piecemeal and *ad hoc*, with often disappointing results (Currie, 1994a. Jones et al, 1993), the findings from this survey seemed to suggest the opposite. However, the fact that some 94%

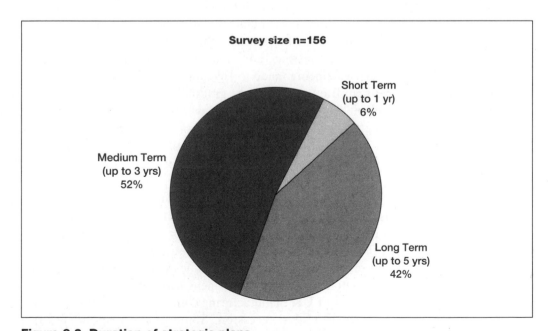

Figure 8.2 Duration of strategic plans

of organisations claimed to adopt a strategic plan from three to five years stops short of saying anything about the results of the strategic planning process.

A deeper analysis of strategic planning therefore suggests that a wide gulf exists between policy and practice. This is discussed at some length by Mintzberg (1993, p. 92) who is very critical of survey research in this area. He asserts that from the late 1960s a number of academics 'set out to prove' the advantages of strategic planning to companies.

> 'The approach was simple. You measured performance, which was easy enough, at least if you restricted yourself to conventional short-term measures of economic performance in business (or better still, the respondent's subjective ranking of their firm's performance, as some studies did). And you measured planning, which also seemed easy enough: you simply mailed a questionnaire to the head of planning (or to the chief executive, who was most likely to give it to the planners anyway, unless he or she threw it away instead), asking the respondent to tell you on seven-point scales or the like how much planning took place in the firm. Then you dumped all the responses into a computer and sat back and read correlation coefficients. You never even had to leave your office at the university. And that meant you never had to face all the distortions inherent in such research'.

Similarly, writing as recently as the mid-1980s, Starbuck (1985, p.371) was unable to locate any study which 'assessed the consequences of adhering to or deviating from long-range plans'. Comments taken from some of the questionnaires suggested that even where a strategic plan was in place for IT, some IT Managers were unaware of its exact content and scope. This would suggest that the strategic planning process was simply a ritual and part of the duties of board members, as opposed to being an important policy statement with practical implications.

Of the organisations who claimed to possess a strategic plan for IT, the sector breakdown is shown in Figure 8.3.

Whilst the three-year strategic plan was followed by just over half of all the organisations, many others, most notably in the public sector, also followed a five-year strategic plan for IT. When asked about the key facets of the IT strategic plan, each of the three sectors produced quite similar answers. For example, many public sector organisations said that major changes were being made to key administrative processes. At one government agency, the mainframe system was gradually being decommissioned to be replaced in 1997 by client-server technology. This was part of a five-year strategic plan for IT to ensure that better value would be attained from the IT spend. Other public sector organisations confirmed that, historically, strategic planning and resource allocation was planned over a five-year period. The key features of the strategic plan for IT in a selection of public sector organisations considered corporate business development; training and security arrangements; approved supplier policies; systems priorities; internal communications; the development of the infrastructure; the development of LAN technology; government legislation; cost reduction; replacement of mainframe; agreed corporate IT standards; business support and the utilisation of new technology.

A small proportion of the manufacturing companies said that strategic planning for IT followed a one-year plan. Perhaps the most salient reason for this was because of the uncertainty facing the future of UK manufacturing companies as a consequence of economic downturn and severe global recession. Some of the respondents from the manufacturing sector said that uncertainty about future profitability meant that strategic

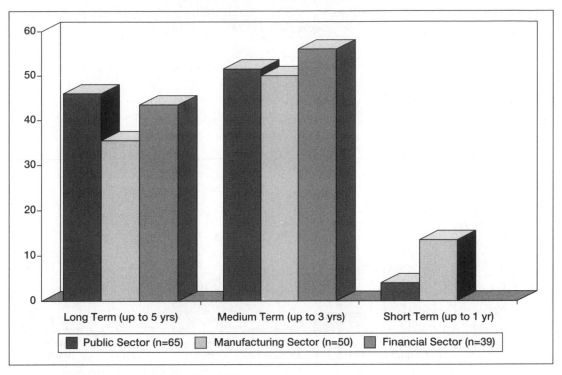

Figure 8.3 Duration of IT plan by sector

planning was becoming 'ever more short term'. Some IT Managers complained that it was impossible to plan beyond one year because of resource uncertainty. For example, money which was allocated for future investment in technology could be reallocated at any time depending on a variety of factors from reduced orders, poor profitability, production restructuring and relocation, among others.

Management and IT strategy

Given that eighty-eight percent of organisations claimed to have an IT strategy, it was interesting to determine who was responsible for its development. The normative management literature on this topic usually suggests that IT strategies are best developed by senior managers (Grindley, 1991). The questionnaire survey found that more than half of the respondents claimed that IT strategy was developed by senior level managers, and not always by senior IT managers.

However, to reiterate a point made above, the definition of an IT strategy was not always the same, irrespective of business sector. Figure 8.4 gives a breakdown of the seven categories with responsibility for developing an IT strategy. It is important here to differentiate between the development and implementation of the IT strategy. For although the majority of the respondents said that senior or board level managers were responsible for the IT strategy, in practice it was usually the middle-level managers who were charged with its implementation.

The level of responsibility for the IT strategy generally corresponded to the annual IT

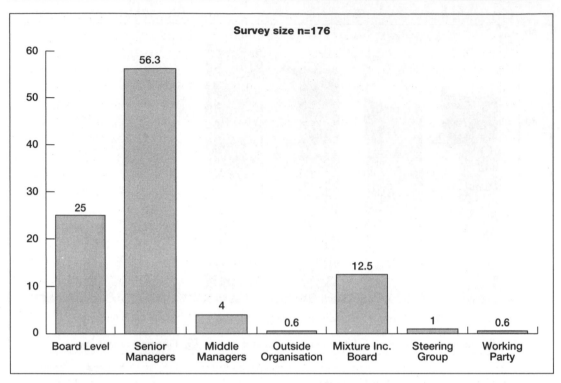

Figure 8.4 Who is responsible for IT strategy?

spend. As the annual IT spend increased, so too did the responsibility level for IT within the organisation. For example, one major Scottish bank claimed that IT strategy was developed by 'a team of experts' from each section of the business. Interviews with a senior IT manager at the bank found that part of the strategy process was to 'balance expertise' by utilising the skills and experience of both the IT professionals (managerial and non-managerial) and the business managers. The bank also employed the help of external management consultants for strategy formulation, particularly in the design of methodologies for planning, co-ordination and control. It was pointed out that IT strategy development was becoming ever more complex as a result of the plethora of new technologies available in the marketplace; the need to develop new state-of-the-art skills; deregulation in the financial services sector; rationalisation and cost cutting; and the reassessment of 'every key business process'. At the time of interview, senior managers stressed that every business process was being 'reconceptualised' with the ultimate aim of transforming the bank into 'the best bank in Britain'. About one hundred people were involved in the IT strategy development process, each of whom had to demonstrate how their ideas would benefit three key groups: customers, shareholders and staff. Cynics at the bank said that staff 'came a poor third' in the strategy process; and this view was reinforced by the recent round of managerial and staff redundancies (44 in all).

In the manufacturing sector, IT strategy was synonymous with survival. A number of manufacturers stressed that unless they were able to invest in AMT (CAD/CAM, FMS, robots, etc) and in ambitious R & D programmes, they would not survive. Whilst AMT strategies in the manufacturing sector were likely to be developed by senior-level managers, their implementation was often the responsibility of lower-level managers. A number of manufacturing managers also expressed concern that technology strategies were 'too piecemeal and *ad hoc*'; and this was seen as the consequence of capital rationing.

Public sector organisations seemed to perceive IT strategy development somewhat differently from their financial service and manufacturing industry counterparts. Many senior IT managers in the public sector stressed that it was important for them to become 'more business like' than had hitherto been the case. The reason for this was largely because of the new 'market testing' philosophy imposed upon the public sector by the government. Given the tighter reigns on resource allocation coupled with increased management accountability, many senior public sector managers were renegotiating their supplier and procurement arrangements. Embarrassing strategic IT failures in the form of the poor utilisation of information systems; staff rejection of specific IT applications; low staff morale and industrial relations problems brought about by technical change; the purchase of unsuitable IT and the rejection of expensive external consultancy advice, all reflected badly on the management within public sector IT divisions/departments. It was therefore important for public sector organisations such as government departments and agencies, the NHS and local authorities to become more efficient in both developing and implementing IT strategies.

The government recently specified two ways in which public sector organisations could improve their efficiency through market testing and procurement. The White Paper on Competitiveness stipulates that, '... the importance of the public sector as a purchaser is fundamental'. Many sectors of the UK industry (such as defence equipment and construction) are heavily dependent on its decisions. Good purchasing can have a profound effect on the competitiveness of firms. It can improve quality, assist innovation, reduce costs, set standards, and provide a shop window for world sales. In exercising its purchasing power, the Government has two fundamental aims:

- value for money
- improving the competitiveness of its suppliers (HMSO, 1994, p. 154)

IT managers operating in the public sector claimed that their own role, and the organisational position of IT, had fundamentally changed. IT was more than ever seen by the customers (users throughout the organisation) as a service, which could undergo 'market testing' like any other service. This led some public sector managers to become concerned about their own future, not to mention the future of IT. Consequently, any IT strategy had to be formulated within a customer-supplier framework.

Several IT managers stressed that, as a service provider, it was important for the internal IT division/department to compete for business like any external IT vendor. IT managers in many public sector entities from NHS trusts to government departments were now carrying out internal performance measurement (benchmarking) initiatives to determine their own competitiveness. One IT manager on a five-year contract supporting six NHS trusts said that it was part of his long-term IT strategy to purchase his unit (currently a computer services unit) and compete for business with other IT vendors. He saw his major competitive strength as 'expert knowledge' of the NHS, particularly the technologies utilised by hospitals.

The current wave of market testing was also felt by IT managers in the financial services sector and in manufacturing industry. In the case of banks and insurance companies, the increased efforts on the part of corporate executives to improve financial control meant that 'no service was immune from outsourcing'.

Outsourcing as the new IT strategy

Academic interest in IT outsourcing has grown in recent years as many commercial and public sector organisations consider outsourcing as a possible option for IT (Lacity and Hirschheim, 1993). Paradoxically, the plethora of academic and trade literature which advised senior executives throughout the 1980s to develop an IT strategy appears, in the present climate at least, to be in direct conflict with the current rhetoric in favour of IT outsourcing. For whilst a small proportion of companies in the questionnaire survey claimed to use external consultants to help define an IT strategy the vast majority used their own senior managers for this activity.

Management perceptions of the meaning of IT outsourcing differ between organisations, irrespective of business sector. In a recent publication on the subject, Lacity and Hirschheim (1993, p.2-3) give three definitions of IT outsourcing:

- Body shop outsourcing
- Project management outsourcing
- Total outsourcing

As we saw in chapter six, body shop outsourcing is where management uses outsourcing as a way to meet short-term demand. The most common type of body shop outsourcing is arguably in the use of contract programmers/personnel whose activities are managed by the client. Project management outsourcing is where management outsources a specific project or portion of IS work. Examples of project management outsourcing include the use of vendors to develop a new system, support an existing application, handle disaster recovery, provide training, or manage a network. In these cases the vendor is responsible for managing and completing the work. Finally, total outsourcing is where the vendor has sole responsibility for a significant piece of IS work. The most common type is total outsourcing of the hardware (e.g. data centre and/or telecommunications) operations. The newest outsourcing strategy is to turn over the entire hardware and software support to an outside vendor. Some have gone so far as to euphemistically term this type of outsourcing, turning over the 'keys to the kingdom'.

The authors state that body shop outsourcing is by far the most common, although some companies would not think that hiring contract IT professionals (programmers/analysts/project managers, etc) necessarily constitutes IT outsourcing. In the questionnaire survey, some 71 percent of organisations said they did not outsource their IT facility. This was against 29 percent who claimed they did employ the services of an IT outsourcing vendor.

It is assumed that, in the light of the above three categories, many of the organisations who claimed they did not outsource IT were in fact engaging in body shop outsourcing. That is, they employed contract IT staff on either a long-term or temporary basis. Obviously, categories of the above kind are problematic since many organisations may

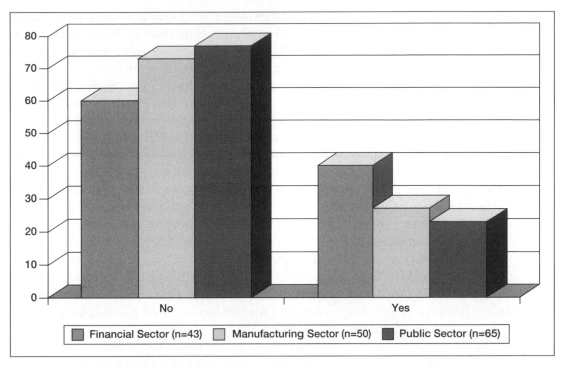

Figure 8.5 Proportion of companies who outsource

engage in all three forms at any particular point in time. For example, a bank may hire contract programmers on a short-term basis to meet a project deadline on an information systems project. These individuals are likely to be part of a team and will work closely with the bank's permanent staff.

Project management IT outsourcing may also take place when senior managers at the bank decide to hire an outside software house to design and develop a particular information system. This is likely to occur where the bank does not have the specialist IT skills in-house. Total outsourcing may also occur where senior managers decide that a particular business process is more efficiently undertaken by a facilities management/outsourcing company. An example is the outsourcing of database administration (DBA). This could be the management of the millions of customer transactions which are stored within hundreds of tables on a database. These DBA duties will involve both day-to-day data management, complete data back-up and failure recovery (e.g. if there is a power failure or some other problem which causes the mainframe to cease operating, then a second mainframe should be in place to ensure the continuation of services).

A cross-sectoral analysis of IT outsourcing from the questionnaire survey data found that companies in the public sector were more likely to pursue this strategy than their manufacturing or financial sector counterparts (see Figure 8.5). This was likely to reflect the shortage of skills in this sector, particularly in relation to project management and specialist IT skills. Many respondents from the public sector said that the introduction of compulsory competitive tendering (CCT) would increase IT outsourcing as IT divisions would be market tested like any other service provider.

The prospect of IT outsourcing was of great concern to many IT managers, simply because it could threaten the survival of their division/department. This perception was more evident in the financial services and public sector organisation than in manufacturing firms. IT managers interviewed in banks and insurance companies said they were 'constantly inundated' by external management consultants who claimed they could provide IT services cheaper than the in-house IT facility. One senior IT manager at a Scottish bank said that, 'Consultants target senior executives who have little understanding of IT. They come up with attractive proposals that will save money so it is not surprising that they are listened to. We are then asked if we can compete on price and quality. The trouble is trying to convince senior executives that many of these proposed cost savings are merely pie-in-the-sky and would never be achieved in practice'.

Manufacturing managers were also sceptical of IT outsourcing on a large scale because they felt that technology was better managed in-house and by managers with experience of manufacturing issues specific to the business. However, several manufacturing managers said that economic decline and capital rationing had led them to reassess their suppliers. More stringent performance measurement tests (benchmarking) on suppliers were now carried out with the objective of reducing costs and improving quality. This is of course in line with the aims and objectives set out in the recent government report on competitiveness (HMSO, 1994).

In public sector organisations, IT outsourcing was likely to be a direct consequence of government policy on compulsory competitive tendering (CCT) which was planned to take effect from October 1997. One IT manager with twenty five years experience of local government said that he was uncertain whether his IT division would be around in the next five years. He said that from 1 April 1996, the council would no longer exist since it would be merged with another council. This would affect all central services including IT. He saw three possible scenarios for the future of his own IT division.

First it could receive residual backing from the new council structure and provide IT services in a similar way to its current method of operating (e.g. developing, implementing and maintaining IT throughout the region). Second it could become absorbed by the leading council where its activities would be merged with other existing IT service providers. This would no doubt lead to job cuts in spite of the present council policy of no compulsory redundancies. Third the IT division could become a separate independent entity which operated as a business in its own right. This could emerge from a management buy-out where the new company could provide services to clients within the new council structure as well as others in the private sector. Should this scenario be followed, the new business would adopt commercial rates with the objective of profit maximisation rather than the present situation where any financial surplus was redistributed to the council departments.

At the time of interview the IT manager said that so much uncertainty surrounded the future provision of IT services that he was unable to plan ahead any longer than a year. This situation was not helping staff morale as many people were fearful of losing their jobs. It was also pointed out that cross-communication with managers from other district councils was 'totally forbidden'. Such a situation was akin to 'managing in the dark'.

On the subject of outsourcing the IT manager said that it was now official policy that some 80 percent of the total IT spend would be subject to CCT from October 1997. When asked exactly what he meant by 'total IT spend', he was unable to clarify this point. He said that because of the 'total confusion' about the future, the 80 percent could refer to software applications development, implementation and maintenance services and other support services. Whilst he saw this as a possible threat, he felt that his current team of 80 people in development, together with a further 100 in operations, communications and client consultancy (comprising the IT division), were more than able to provide cost effective and efficient IT services to a range of clients.

Whilst he felt his team could compete with any outside IT vendor, he was concerned that senior managers engaged in market testing activities may be impressed by the slick approach adopted by external management consultants. He saw this as a problem because although the existing IT division could not compete with external management consultants on image and presentation, they had experience and informal knowledge of the IT needs of a variety of public sector departments. Alas many of these qualitative advantages could be overlooked by senior managers who were likely to concentrate only on the financial forecasts presented in competitive tenders for IT work (Figure 8.6).

To support his belief in retaining a strong in-house IT division, the IT manager said that two important points should be noted. The first concerned loyalty of service where internal IT staff were keen to do a good job even if it meant working at home, unpaid. The prospect of IT outsourcing, according to the IT manager, would not necessarily equate with better service or reduced cost. The second was about providing IT services

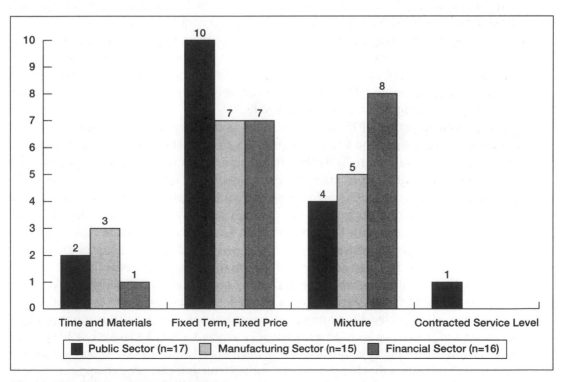

Figure 8.6 Outsourcing contract terms

across the board. He pointed out that, 'In my opinion, senior managers forget that at the moment we are unable to turn work down even if we want to. In a situation of CCT, and more so if we became an independent company, we would be very selective about the work we do. A lot of my staff offer help and advice to their clients even in their own time. If I was a director of an independent IT company, I would not allow my staff to do work unpaid. Outsourcing could therefore be more expensive for the client'.

In his opinion the IT manager argued that IT outsourcing was a symptom of the 1980s fixation on competition, performance measurement, value for money and market testing. But the notion that outsiders provide a better service simply because the client can play one supplier off against another was not an adequate reason in itself for outsourcing IT or any other service for that matter.

IT outsourcing contracts

The questionnaire survey was interested to examine some of the contractual issues in IT outsourcing, particularly in the light of recent evidence which points to some of the pitfalls in IT outsourcing (Currie, 1994b. Deutsch, 1994. Lacity and Hirschheim, 1993. Yazel, 1994). One of the more significant problems of any IT outsourcing deal is defining the legal contract which underpins the client-supplier relationship. Recent examples show that many companies that have signed an IT outsourcing contract have not paid enough attention to the small print (Currie, 1994c). This has often resulted in the situation where the client realises that many peripheral IT services are not included in the original contract and are subject to additional costs at full commercial rates. Deutsch (1994) says that IT outsourcing contracts are 'complex' and should be negotiated over a long period of time. He also stresses that no outsourcing service or activity should be undertaken without the contract being signed – nor even under an initial client-supplier agreement or letter of intent. He also advises that IT outsourcing contracts should 'build in' adequate terms which ensure that the business is not 'dislocated' in the event of the contract being terminated on either side.

Investigating the type of IT outsourcing contracts between client and supplier found that all sectors preferred the fixed term, fixed price contract (see Figure 8.6). Public sector organisations were more likely than manufacturing or financial services companies to negotiate fixed term, fixed price contracts; which was unsurprising given the likelihood of more stringent public accounting and auditing procedures. This reflected the different procurement arrangements under which public sector organisations operated.

Follow-up interviews with IT managers in all sectors confirmed that time and materials contracts where suppliers were given an open-ended financial contract and were expected to invoice the client at the end of the job were becoming fewer in number. This was fuelled by the situation where resources were harder to obtain leading IT managers and their clients to face more difficult IT choices. Market testing and competitive tendering were also forcing IT managers to provide their clients with a more detailed breakdown of their costs for a whole range of IT services. One IT manager at a UK bank said that it was now policy not to embark on open-ended contracts for IT services as past experience had shown that loose contracts simply 'run and run'. For example, the client is promised the delivery of an information system, although is unsure as to how much it will cost. This was one of the criticisms directed at the recent city-based TAURUS disaster, where software development work was seldom completed on time or to budget.

Interviewing an IT manager working for an NHS trust similarly found that time and materials contracts were discouraged in favour of the fixed term, fixed price arrangement. This manager said that, 'If the outside company fails to deliver the system by the due date, it is their problem not ours. Whilst late delivery may pose some problems for us, the cost is met by the supplier. Penalty clauses may also be built into the contract. Fortunately, our suppliers have so far delivered on time since they want to ensure that we use them in the future'.

Selection criteria for IT outsourcing vendors was interesting with competitive tendering being the most common. Many potential clients in all three sectors were reassessing their selection criteria, with many developing Service Level Agreements (SLAs) for the first time. One government agency had set up a 'framework agreement' for consultancy services to ensure that value for money was attained as well as quality of service. The framework agreement comprised five areas for assessing consultants. They included:

- Expertise relating to three areas: Scoping/strategy work
                                          Implementation work
                                          Operations
- History
- Cost
- Management organisation
- Control

The production services manager said it was now policy to advertise for consultancy services to tender for work throughout the European Union (EU). One consequence of this was that small consultancy services were unlikely to meet the above criteria. For example, a small software house with only five people in business for only two years could not demonstrate a 'history' of successful projects, nor a well supported management organisation. This meant that only large management consultancy firms were likely to tender for government contracts.

The three main areas of work where consultants were used were scoping/strategy activities where IT needs were assessed in conjunction with the overall business strategy; implementation work which comprised designing and developing information systems; and operations work where consultants were brought in to handle mainframe operations.

In a similar vein with other public sector organisations, the production services manager realised that his own IT division would also be subject to market testing like any other service provider. His strategy was therefore to retain some 50 'expert IT professionals' from a total of some 230 staff and 'lose the remaining people around the organisation'. He recognised that some IT services could eventually be outsourced, but it was likely that a smaller, leaner IT division would remain provided it could compete with other IT providers.

Another line of enquiry in the questionnaire survey was concerned with the preferences for IT solutions among the three sectors. Figure 8.7 gives a breakdown of six options open to organisations from acquiring IT 'off the shelf' to using the software provided by the parent company.

Figure 8.7 shows that a mixture of IT options was undertaken by organisations in the three sectors which included the decision to buy 'off the shelf' IT products; the in-house development of IT systems; and the modification of a commercial product to tailor it to the specific business requirement (e.g. a personnel or payroll system). Follow-up interviews with IT managers suggested that buying off-the-shelf IT products was the preferred choice, although one which was not always possible. A breakdown of these options by sector showed that buying off-the-shelf was favoured mostly by public sector organisations, followed by manufacturing and financial services companies. The manufacturing and financial services sectors, on the other hand, were more likely to develop their own IT solutions compared with the public sector; and the former was more likely to modify a commercial product than the other two sectors.

IT managers in all sectors said that since there was more choice in commercial software than ever before, it was more likely that buying off-the-shelf products would increase. This was likely to be more cost effective to many organisations as opposed to developing tailored IT solutions which were high risk and expensive. This is reinforced in the growing literature on IT/IS failures in both the commercial and public sectors (Abdel-Hamid and Madnick, 1990. Sauer, 1993. Brooks, 1987. Friedman, 1989).

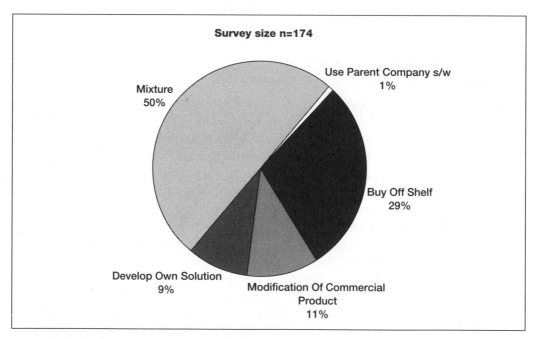

Figure 8.7 Preferences for IT solutions

Concluding remarks

One salient conclusion from the questionnaire and case study research into managing IT in three sectors was the emerging nature of IT strategies over time. There were no hard and fast rules for IT strategy formation and implementation. In all sectors, it seemed that

IT strategies were developed *ad hoc*, largely as a consequence of external (environmental) and internal (structural) changes. There seemed to be a wide gap between strategy (the vision) and implementation (the reality). Whilst the majority of respondents claimed their organisation had an IT strategy, few could elaborate on how it was aligned to the corporate strategy. Indeed, conversations with IT managers confirmed that IT was often the victim of cost-cutting measures, even though there were 'strong arguments' to suggest that, in times of recession, IT should be supported to generate new business development and information efficiencies.

Public sector entities were undergoing major changes, perhaps more so than their manufacturing and financial service sector counterparts. Indeed, a number of public sector IT managers said they could not even guarantee if their department would survive the post 1996 CCT measures. Many were of the view that 'the big boys (large consultancies) would swallow them up'. Clearly, the 1990s is an exciting time for IT, although doubts could be cast as to whether some of the changes would generate efficiency gains. Outsourcing was no doubt one of the hot topics for management. Yet the straightforward choice of internal (in-house) versus external (outsourcing) proved too simplistic in the light of so many other considerations. In chapter nine, we continue our discussion of the questionnaire survey by examining the findings on IT evaluation, performance measurement and management control in the three sectors.

Case study

The political nature of systems development work

A system was written by a senior analyst/programmer at a UK financial services institution using a DOS package called Clipper. The risk assessment program provided details on financial investments made by companies. For example, the program tracked those companies which posed the greatest financial risk to the bank should they collapse (e.g. the loss generated by the collapse of Maxwell Enterprises, Mirror Group News Papers and so on). It also provided details about the investment interests of a company or group of companies in other commercial enterprises. This enabled financial institutions to better assess the credit risk of their clients. A working example of this is given in Figure 8.8.

From this figure Company X was given an upper credit limit by the Bank of England. Whilst Company X's credit limit was £15m, it only had a loan of £10m. Company X also held 50% and 75% holdings in companies Y and Z respectively. Since Company X has investments in two other companies, it is liable for its pro-

portion of their credit arrangement. Thus, Company Y represents 50% of £5m (£2.5m) and Company Z represents 75% of £10m (£7.5m). In total Company X has a credit responsibility of £20m, £5m more than the limit imposed by the Bank of England. Such a situation posed a considerable financial threat to the

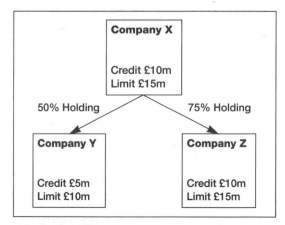

Figure 8.8 The structure of company X's distributed debt

bank given that Company X's credit limit was fixed at only £15m.

Due to the bad debt problem brought about by economic recession and other factors, the Bank of England decided to reduce the credit limit they monitored from £10m to only £1m. This meant that an information system had to be written to incorporate the new guidelines. The new system was to comprise a much larger database with far greater processing power. The new reporting limit of £1m would also mean that the number of companies being monitored would possibly increase by many thousands.

The proposed system was technically very complex and would involve systems development work in two UK cities. The original time scale was for eight months, with a budget of only £50k.

The original system had been developed in city 2. However, it was decided that the proposed system would be developed with a new team in city 1. Given that the financial institution did not have the available skilled IT staff to undertake work on the new system, a contract analyst/programmer was hired to develop the technical specification. This individual did not have any project experience of the programming language in which the system would be written. However, the project manager held the view that the contractor's previous experience of other database and 3GL programming languages would reduce the learning curve.

Throughout the initial two months period of the project, the contractor flew weekly to the client site to clarify their requirements for the system. After about four months, the financial institution became unhappy since the project had not progressed according to their target release date. In an attempt to redress the situation, the developer of the original system was brought in to give advice and guidance. Although this individual had a very strong IT background, he was not experienced in the programming language in which the system was being developed.

This problem was compounded by the political tensions between the two developers. The contract programmer resented the intervention of the original system developer, and the latter was unable to make improvements to the project given his lack of knowledge about the programming language. Neither fully understood the semantics of the language, and rather than working together they pursued their own development work.

After five months, the project was still far from completion. Technical and political problems were further compounded by the announcement that the project owner (the client) and principal user were moving to other jobs within the organisation. This meant that the project was essentially without 'an owner' to steer the decision-making about the desired end-functionality.

After some deliberations, the project was allocated a new 'owner' (located at the client department). The new owner decided to move the systems development work to another city (2) and appoint two experienced contract analyst/programmers to complete the project.

At this point, the project was now into its seventh month. The project manager was also concerned that the person who had been developing the system should impart his knowledge to the new team. As a result, his contract was renewed for two further months so that he could hold regular meetings with the new team (in city 2) to discuss the systems functional specifications.

After five meetings the city 2 team decided that this arrangement was not productive. Politically, the contractor who had been developing the system did not wish to impart his technical knowledge to the new team. He was also reluctant to admit any mistakes in his own code. This posed problems to the new team since they were of the opinion that the code presented to them was inadequate and would need to be re-written. The original contractor was unhappy with this arrangement since he felt it would reflect badly on his professional reputation and future employment prospects. He argued that, 'if the team had ever read any books about programming, they would know the number one rule that you do not re-write other programmers' code'. The team, however,

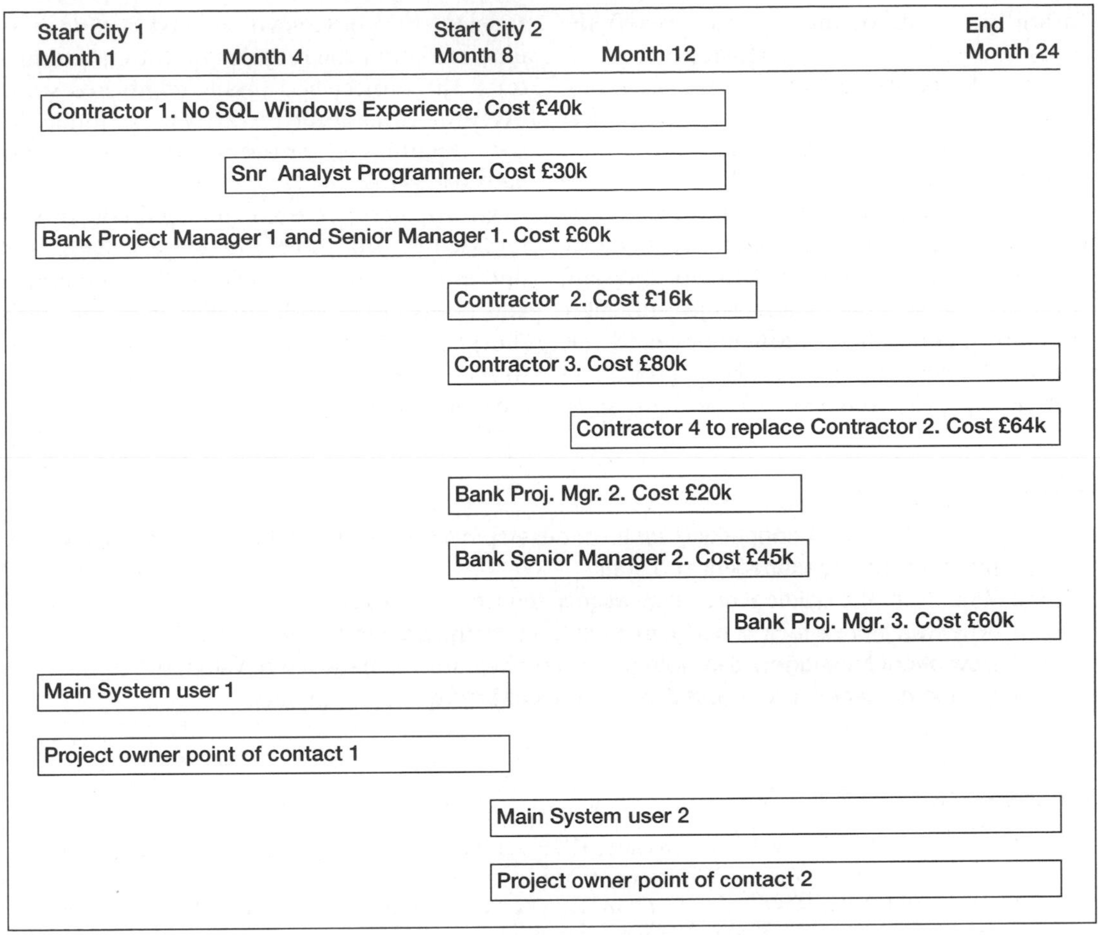

Start City 1		Start City 2			End
Month 1	Month 4	Month 8	Month 12		Month 24

Contractor 1. No SQL Windows Experience. Cost £40k

Snr Analyst Programmer. Cost £30k

Bank Project Manager 1 and Senior Manager 1. Cost £60k

Contractor 2. Cost £16k

Contractor 3. Cost £80k

Contractor 4 to replace Contractor 2. Cost £64k

Bank Proj. Mgr. 2. Cost £20k

Bank Senior Manager 2. Cost £45k

Bank Proj. Mgr. 3. Cost £60k

Main System user 1

Project owner point of contact 1

Main System user 2

Project owner point of contact 2

Figure 8.9 Employee change throughout project development

rewrote the entire program. For example, they reduced one module from 2,700 lines of code to only 300 lines, without losing any functionality.

Just before the end of his contract, the original contractor wrote to the project owner and senior development manager to stress the reasons why the project was 'in trouble'. His main argument was that the project lacked any structure, and that the two new contractors were unnecessarily rewriting his code. Politically, the situation became rather invidious, since the two contractors appointed to work on the project were forced to defend their actions. This state of affairs encouraged managers to re-focus their attention on the project. They concluded, however, that the new team were working effectively

and should continue to rewrite the code.

As a result, the two contractors embarked on a total rewrite of the system. The project had already cost some £130k (three times the project's original estimated cost). This money was written off on the basis that the project did not have a formal budget anyway! Managers reasoned that since the project had to be written under the directive of the Bank of England, and presented savings of tens of millions of pounds, a few hundred thousand pounds was 'chicken feed'.

The rewrite extended not only the financial cost of the project, but also its delivery date. The new team also had to take into account the revised requirements of the new project owner.

In addition, one of the contractors left the organisation, and had to be replaced.

Given the early disastrous history of the project, managers were adamant that the project should finally succeed. This created undue pressure on the contractors to work at a fast pace and deliver an effective system. The organisation was also undergoing a compulsory redundancy scheme to displace some 50 managers and staff. Both the senior manager and project manager were given compulsory redundancy, and this imposed further disruption to the IT project.

A new project manager was brought in to replace the above two managers, and was unaware about the project's objectives and history. The project was finally completed some twelve months after his arrival. In total, the project had lasted for twenty four months, and had cost £415k.

Whilst there were no financial constraints imposed on the project or project team, it is interesting to note that the staff fluctuations and political turmoil, coupled with the skills shortages of managers and staff, all contributed to the project exceeding its estimated delivery date and budget.

Discussion questions

1 Do you think that conducting systems development work at two locations poses any serious problems to managers and staff?
2 What were the political problems associated with this project?
3 Why was there a lack of budgetary control over the project?
4 How should managers deal with interpersonal problems between developers?
5 Should managers be removed from a project before it is completed?

References 8

Adler, P., McDonald, D. W., McDonald, F. (1992) 'Strategic management of technical functions'. *Sloan Management Review*, Winter, pp. 19–37.

Abdel-Hamid, T.K., Madnick, S.E. (1990) 'The elusive silver lining; how we fail to learn from software development failures'. *Sloan Management Review*, 39, Fall.

Allen, T. J., Scott-Morton, M.S. (eds.) (1994) *Information technology and the corporation of the 1990s*. Oxford University Press.

Andreu, R., Richart, J.E., Valor, J. (1994) 'Information systems planning at the corporate level', pp. 25–52, in C. Ciborra and T. Jelassi (eds) *Strategic information systems*. Wiley.

Boynton, A.C., Jacobs, G. C., Zmud, R.W. (1992) 'Whose responsibility is IT management? *Sloan Management Review*, Summer, pp. 32–38.

Brooks, F. (1987) 'No silver bullet: essence and accidents of software engineering', *IEEE Computer*, 20, pp. 10–19.

Ciborra, C., Jelassi, T. (1994) *Strategic information systems*. Wiley.

Currie, W. (1994a) *Comparative Management of AMT*. CIMA: London.

Currie, W. (1994b) 'The management of large scale IT projects in the financial services sector'. *New Technology, Work and Employment*, Vol, 9, No. 1. March, pp. 19–29.

Currie, W (1994c) 'Outsourcing, friend or foe?' Paper presented at the Cost A4 International Research Workshop – Management and New Technology, Grenoble, France, 16–17 June.

Currie, W., Bryson, C. (1994) 'Managing IT projects in the financial services, manufacturing industry and public sector'. Working paper, Department of Management and Organisation, University of Stirling, UK.

Currie, W., Fincham, R., Hallier, J. (1993) 'Strategy, evaluation and career development in the management of IT projects: a research framework', pp. 200-230, in A. Francis., S. Horte and J.L. Pedersen, *Cost A3 Management and New Technology: Designs, networks and strategies*, Commission of the European Communities.

Davenport, T. H., Eccles, R. G., Prusak, L. (1992) 'Information politics'. *Sloan Management Review*, p.53–65.

Deutsch, S. (1994) 'Outsourcing', Parts 1,2, and 3, *Computing*, 12 and 19 May, 2 June.

Earl, M (1989) *Managerial strategies for IT*. Prentice Hall.

Farbey, B., Land, F., Targett, D. (1993) *IT investment: a study of methods and practice*. Butterworth-Heinemann.

Friedman, A. with Cornford, D. (1989) *Computer systems development: history, organisation and implementation*. Wiley.

Grindley, K. (1991) *Managing IT at board level*. Pitman.

Hayes, R.H., Pisano, G.P. (1994) 'Beyond world class: the new manufacturing strategy'. *Harvard Business Review*, Jan/Feb, pp. 77–86.

HMSO (1993) *Realising our potential: a strategy for science, engineering and technology*. HMSO, London.

HMSO (1994) *Competitiveness: Helping business to win*. HMSO, London.

Jones, C., Currie, W., Dugdale, D. (1993) 'Accounting and technology in Britain and Japan: learning from field research'. *Management Accounting Research*. Vol, 4, pp. 109–137.

Lacity, M. C., Hirschheim, R. (1993) *Information systems outsourcing*. Wiley.

Mintzberg, H. (1993) *The rise and fall of strategic planning*. Prentice Hall.

NEDO (1989) *AMT: a strategy for success*. NEDO, London.

Porter, M. (1985) *Competitive Advantage: Creating and Sustaining Superior Performance*. Harvard Business Review.

Robey, D., Markhus, M. L. (1984) 'Rituals in information system design'. *MIS Quarterly*, pp. 5–15.

Rowe, C., Herbert, B. (1990) 'IT in the boardroom: the growth of computer awareness among chief executives'. *Journal of General Management*, Vol, 15, No. 4, Summer, pp. 32–44.

Sauer, C. (1993) *Why information systems fail: a case study approach*. Alfred Waller, Henley on Thames, UK.

Schein, E. (1994) 'The role of the CEO in the management of change: The case of information technology', pp. 325-345, in T. J. Allen and M. S. Scott-Morton (eds) *Information Technology and the Corporation of the 1990s*, Oxford University Press, Oxford.

Shank, J. K., Govindarajan, V. (1992) 'Strategic cost analysis of technological investments'. *Sloan Management Review*, Fall, pp. 39–51.

Starbuck, W.H. (1985) 'Acting first and thinking later: theory versus reality in strategic change', pp. 336-372, in J.M. Pennings and Associates, *Organisational Strategy and Change*, San Francisco: Jossey Bass.

Yazel, L. (1994) 'Farewell to arms ends FM fight'. *Computing*, 26 May, p. 26.

CHAPTER 9

Managing IT in the Private and Public Sectors: Evaluation, Performance Measurement and Control

Introduction

This chapter continues our discussion of the results of the questionnaire survey which was introduced in chapter seven. Here we are interested in the themes of evaluation, performance measurement and control of IT. The rationale for examining these topics was based on growing evidence of the difficulties facing contemporary managers in evaluating IT in qualitative and quantitative terms (Shank and Govindarajan, 1992. DeCotis and Dyer, 1979. Currie and Seddon, 1992. Barwise et al, 1989 Finnie, 1988). A significant proportion of the literature in this area stems from the finance and accounting field. This is because evaluating IT tends to involve the application of financial methods and techniques to measure operating performance. The relevant literature on this topic and the key debates are covered in some detail in chapter four.

Management and financial control

The issue of evaluation and performance measurement of IT has been examined from a number of inter-disciplinary angles, though the field of finance and accounting is dominant. From the management accounting arena, North American academics (Kaplan, 1984,1985,1986,1990. Cooper, 1989) have argued that traditional management accounting theory and practice is inappropriate for evaluating IT and AMT. They recommend a radical rethinking of management accounting methods and techniques and propose a replacement in the form of Activity Based Costing (ABC) which, they argue, identifies important cost drivers in organisations. In essence, they argue that ABC is better placed to measure costs in the key categories of direct labour, direct materials and, perhaps more important, burgeoning overhead costs (including IT).

In Britain, the problems associated with evaluating the costs and benefits of IT in industry and commerce have led some writers to speculate that a 'crisis in management accounting' exists (Bromwich and Bhimani, 1989. Dugdale and Jones, 1991. Currie, 1991). The crisis stems from the use of inappropriate (traditional) accounting methods and techniques to measure the performance of contemporary organisations. For example, using DCF techniques to measure IT and AMT, even though many of the benefits may be qualitative (non-financial).

Other research on evaluation considers the broader topic of how the various 'stakeholder' groups manage technical change in contemporary organisations (Currie, 1989abc, Currie and Seddon, 1992. Jones et al, 1993. Barwise et al, 1989. Eccles, 1991. Jaikumar, 1986. Hayes and Jaikumar, 1988. Drucker, 1988, 1990). Much of this work links the financial and human resource issues in the areas of IT strategy, implementation and evaluation.

Other writers focus on the difficulties of aligning IT strategies with business objectives and stress the poor performance, or even failure, of many IT projects (Sauer, 1993. Brooks, 1987. Allen and Scott-Morton, 1994). In recent years the subject of performance measurement has gained wide attention from managers, academics and the government. In the recent government publication on competitiveness of industry, the British government recommended that greater attention should be placed on performance measurement and benchmarking (HMSO, 1994). Whilst the government argues that it is important for industry and commerce to compare their economic performance with their international competitors, academics on the other hand are more concerned to examine the relevance of specific performance indicators for rapidly changing business conditions (Blenkinsop and Burns, 1992).

In this chapter we consider the results from the questionnaire survey on the theme of IT evaluation, performance measurement and control. Key issues relating to this theme consider the extent to which financial controls are imposed upon IT expenditure in the three sectors; the organisational level and position of key decision makers engaged in the investment appraisal process; the methods and techniques used in investment appraisal for IT; and the perceptions of managers on whether these methods and techniques are adequate for evaluating IT.

One of the key issues relating to IT is the extent to which managers quantify the benefits from investing in IT. As we saw in chapter four, a number of research studies have been published which question the validity and purpose of measuring the benefits from IT, particularly insofar as these measures are based on 'gut feelings', yet presented in the form of 'hard' financial data. Whilst contributions from the management accounting literature stress the need to develop revised performance indicators for evaluating IT, other writers argue that many of important benefits from IT are inherently difficult to quantify since they are qualitative: for example, a better service to customers; improved product quality; more efficient information generation capacity for decision making; ability to manipulate data for information generation purposes, etc.

Research conducted in the last decade has shown that new technology in the form of CAD/CAM, FMS, KBS, DSS and EIS etc, has become more complex and is now embedded into the core and support processes of organisations (Davenport, 1993. Earl, 1994). Traditional performance indicators such as labour-centred measures and productivity indices have therefore become increasingly irrelevant (Hayes and Jaikumar, 1988. Drucker, 1988, 1990). For example, Hayes and Jaikumar (1988, p.77-78) argue that the replacement of dedicated or old technology with new technology could not be undertaken by relying on the same logic since 'Executives are discovering that acquiring an FMS or any of the other advanced manufacturing systems is more like replacing that old car with a helicopter. If you fail to understand and prepare for the revolutionary capabilities of these systems, they will become as much an inconvenience as a benefit – and a lot more expensive'.

Similarly in the financial services sector, a recent study suggests that in spite of the high project failure rate of IT (most notably, the International London Stock Exchange TAURUS disaster at £400 million, cancelled in 1993; and the Prudential's Plato project at £40 million, cancelled in 1994), some 57 percent of finance businesses plan to increase their investment in IT over the next twelve months, in contrast to only 30 percent in 1993 (Price Waterhouse survey – quoted in *Computing*, 1994). The survey shows that more than eighty-two banks, building societies and insurance companies questioned said that fewer than 50 percent of their projects ended successfully last year. Many of these institutions said the key problems were caused by a failure to integrate systems, escalating costs and underestimating system delivery times. Yet within this context of poor IT performance, some 51 percent of financial institutions forecast significant changes in their IT applications with 47 percent planning to implement major changes in technology over the year (*Computing*, 1994).

Quantifying the benefits of IT in three sectors

The task of quantifying the benefits of IT was a high priority to the managers in the questionnaire survey which was introduced in chapter seven A number of IT managers confirmed that pressure from 'the top' was becoming more acute as the success rate of IT projects was considered unacceptably low by corporate executives. Common failures were very similar to those mentioned in the Price Waterhouse survey mentioned above (see *Computing*, 1994), and were largely due to the difficulties of managing technology in a constantly changing business environment. A number of IT managers confirmed that traditional evaluation methods were inappropriate because 'technology is embedded into core and support business processes'. It was therefore difficult to untangle the complex web of technology for the purpose of applying performance measures. For example, IT managers were keen to stress that evaluating IT is 'not just about measuring the cost of hardware and software'.

In the past, they argued that it was possible to measure the performance of inputs and outputs from computers because of the *stand-alone* or singular nature of the tasks which they performed. Nowadays, however, the rapid progress and move to 'integration' of PCs and the rethinking of business processes creates immense difficulties for those involved in evaluation and performance measurement. An example of this was the widespread use of electronic mail. One IT manager said that, 'Whilst some people use EM very efficiently, others merely use it to disseminate 'junk mail'. If we are trying to measure the effectiveness of this service to our internal and external customers, we come up against the problem that we don't have a useful yardstick from which to compare success or failure. EM is a revolution in the administrative functioning of a business. We know it has many advantages, but trying to measure them is not easy'.

This quote is along the same lines as the example given above where FMS used to replace dedicated technology is akin to replacing an old car with a helicopter, and therefore difficult to compare. Similarly, the replacement of a paper-driven administrative system with electronic mail is also difficult to compare as qualitative considerations are an important feature of the change. In turn, the change to electronic mail as with other PC applications software demands a new skills set which is yet another consideration in the evaluation of IT.

Faced with these challenges, the questionnaire survey asked respondents in the three sectors if they attempted to quantify the benefits of investing in IT. Figure 9.1 gives a breakdown of the responses from the three sectors. It is interesting to note that given that the financial services sector is by far the largest investor in commercial IT applications, some 93 percent of respondents in this sector said they quantified the benefits of IT against only 7 percent claiming they did not. A closer examination of these figures suggested that a relationship existed between annual IT spend and managements' decision whether or not to quantify the benefits from IT. In short, the greater the annual IT spend, the more likely it was for management to demand quantitative information about IT projects from IT divisions/departments.

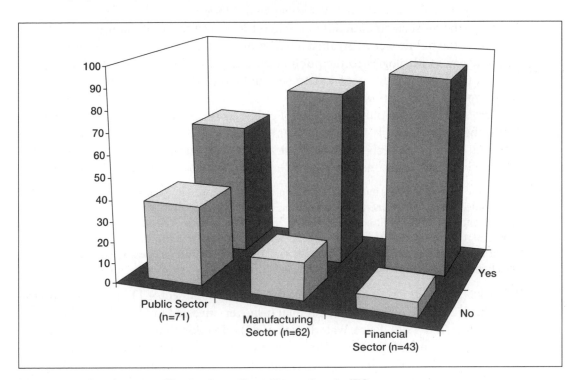

Figure 9.1 Do you quantify the benefits of investing in IT?

Those who claimed not to quantify the benefits of IT were unlikely to be in charge of large IT budgets. One IT manager at a small branch of à UK bank said that his IT annual budget was only £300k. As a result he was not required to provide his bosses with financial information to justify how the money was spent.

In the manufacturing sector, some 88 percent of firms claimed to quantify the benefits from technology. Reflecting on this topic, a number of managers said they were 'sceptical' of undertaking cost-benefit analysis on new technology because they believed that traditional performance indicators were 'outdated' for the new manufacturing environment. They said that technologies such as CAD, FMS, robots coupled with a whole variety of software applications for information generation had changed the traditional face of production. In addition, changes in business practices initiated by business process re-engineering (BPR), just-in-time (JIT) production management, manufacturing resource planning (MRP II) and total quality management (TQM) demanded new performance measures and techniques.

One engineering manager said, 'What is the point of quantifying CAD on the traditional grounds of number of production drawings, labour and machine costs, etc, when CAD is the only tool on which to do the job? Without CAD we simply couldn't undertake complex electrical design work. And without the designers, we wouldn't be able to use CAD. The old way of measuring technology in terms of headcount reduction and productivity gains is old hat. What we need are new measures which take into account quality and reliability. We also need to be able to measure the performance of one designer against another. It's not just about technology'.

Perhaps the most significant difference in the level and scope of quantification for IT occurred in the public sector. Against a background of attempts to transfer private sector management ideologies to the public sector, a number of managers admitted that stringent financial management was to be rapidly introduced, albeit not as quickly as some corporate managers would like.

Figure 9.1 shows that only 62 percent of public sector organisations claimed to quantify the benefits from IT, with 38 percent claiming they did not. This finding was surprising in some respects given the vast amounts of public money spent on IT and associated services (e.g. consultants). For example, Willcocks (1992, p. 170) claims that

'IT is now very big business in UK public administration. According to the Trade and Industry Select Committee, central government IT spend for the financial year 1987-88, excluding MOD operational equipment, was £1800 million and rising. This represented 1 percent of total public expenditure and a rise of 16 percent over the previous year. Within this total picture the Department of Social Security (DSS) is spending £1749 million between 1982 and 1999 on its operational strategy, though this figure has a history of being revised upwards'.

Willcocks (1992) argues that the massive rise in the public sector IT spend is comparable to the £12 billion (1.2 percent of annual turnover) invested in IT in the private sector (see also Kearney 1990. Price Waterhouse, 1990). He adds that since IT is now such a large investment in both the private and public sectors, managers and policy makers continue to question whether they are getting value for money in addition to demanding new performance indicators to better access how effectively resources for IT are used.

Continuing this theme, follow-up interviews with public sector IT managers at NHS trusts, local authorities and government agencies, among others, confirmed that greater pressure was now being placed upon them as 'service providers' to demonstrate value for money to both their superiors and customers. A new internal market was set up to reconfigure IT services in some instances. In fact, some IT managers seemed confused as to whether they were a purchaser, provider, adviser or seller of IT services – or even a mixture of all four.

In the past, IT budgets were centralised and IT managers were allocated an annual sum of money to spend before the end of the following financial year. A number of IT managers said that, 'We didn't have too much freedom about how the money would be spent because the money was earmarked for specific projects, equipment and staffing resources. All we knew is that we, as a department, had to spend all the money because any left over would be taken away from us'.

The traditional budgetary arrangements were now in a process of change. These changes were comprehensive and would affect the entire structure of service provision. One important change concerned the phenomenon of compulsory competitive tendering (CCT). This would mean that all service providers such as IT would have to compete for business along similar commercial lines as the private sector. Interviews with IT managers showed that a new language was being learned which adopted key words such as 'customer, competitiveness, money management, benchmarking, market testing and performance'.

A number of interviewees voiced their concerns about how successful these 'initiatives' would be, given the historical differences between managing in the private and public sectors. This issue has also been addressed in the academic literature. Willcocks (1992, p. 51) states that one concern

> 'is the extent of transferability of management practices across and between organisations, given the potential for organisational variation both within and between public sector organisations. Thus, some private 'solutions' may be inappropriate in some public services. More generally, they may not provide these solutions within the expected – and demanded – timescales; and where private sector prescriptions have worked in one public services organisation, they may not in another, or even in another sector of a large organisation'.

A number of public sector managers said that the transition from being a public service provider to a 'quasi-private sector company' was supported by 'dogma and ideology' and many were concerned about where all the changes and restructuring would lead. Others, however, were more optimistic in their approach and believed that by becoming more 'independent and accountable', this would be synonymous with 'new opportunities and reward structures', especially for the managers in question.

IT managers in the public sector therefore claimed that 'money management' was now the 'number one priority'. Unlike in the past when managers were likely to spend their entire resource allocation because 'it could not be carried over to next year's budget', attempts were now being made to rationalise departments to give the appearance of efficiency and cost effectiveness. One public sector IT manager said that his department was 'gearing itself up to meet the challenge of CCT' because he knew that external suppliers would also be competing for his business. He was particularly concerned about the threat from external management consultants whom, he said, were 'sniffing around for business'.

Yet faced with these fresh challenges, the emphasis on routine IT cost control in the public sector was less evident than in the private sector. As many as 38 percent of public sector managers said that no formal (financial) evaluation of IT was carried out, although in the current cost-conscious environment one would suspect the majority of medium and large size IT public sector departments to become more financially accountable, especially since their survival carried no guarantee.

IT and investment appraisal techniques

The gap between theory and practice in investment appraisal and IT has been well documented in the literature (Scapens, 1983. 1988. Dugdale, 1991. Dugdale and Jones, 1991. Currie, 1991). Whilst the textbooks on management accounting emphasise the theoretical techniques of investment appraisal, demonstrating, for example, the superiority of the more complicated NPV method over the less onerous 'payback' technique, empirical research suggests that practising managers commonly employ the latter approach since it is more easily understood across managerial functions (Dugdale and Jones, 1991).

This finding was reinforced by our questionnaire survey. Here it was found that in spite of an economic climate of capital rationing coupled with the relentless pressure from corporate executives on divisional managers to maximise the benefits from IT, over half the sample (63.2%) used the simple 'payback' technique rather than the more complex NPV, ARR or IRR methods.

Whilst a number of managers conceded that NPV was 'more superior' than using payback or other investment appraisal techniques, they claimed that 'not all managers understood the calculations required for NPV'. Again, this finding is reinforced by other writers (Drury, 1985. Dugdale and Jones, 1991. Pike, 1983). The payback method is described by Drury (1985, p. 378) as

'the length of time which is required for a stream of cash proceeds from an investment to recover the original cash outlay by the investment. If the stream of cash flows from the investment is constant each year, the payback period can be calculated by dividing the total initial cash outlay by the amount of the expected annual cash proceeds'.

One of the problems in justifying IT on the basis of using simple payback, according to several managers in the survey, was that it fails to take into account the time value of money and is therefore less effective than the NPV method. But on the plus side, payback was easily understood by the majority of managers, and was considered 'less onerous' than other financial methods.

Figure 9.2 shows that other accounting techniques were used such as ARR, NPV, IRR and DCF, although not in vast numbers. A small proportion of organisations (0.7 percent) used quality as a criteria for justifying IT. However, managers said that financial resource allocation for IT had to be justified on the strength of financial measures and techniques, taken from management accounting theory and practice. Quality measures were therefore *not credible*, particularly to senior managers who relied on financial information for decision making and planning.

Payback periods

Respondents were also asked to give information on the timescales used in IT investment appraisal. Figure 9.3 gives a breakdown of the three sectors and shows that common payback periods were three and five years. In the financial services sector, the average optimal payback period was usually three years, although some of the more sophisticated IT project work demanded a longer timescale of five-years. Perhaps the most striking finding was in the public sector. In this sector, it was common for IT projects to

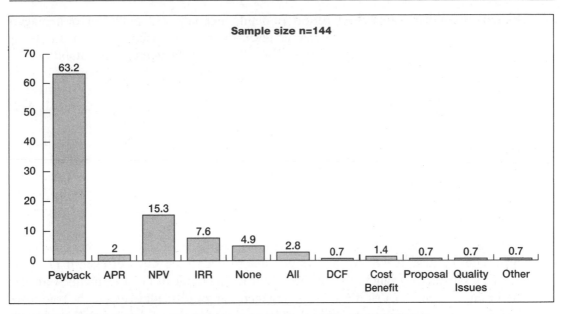

Figure 9.2 Management accounting techniques used in organisations

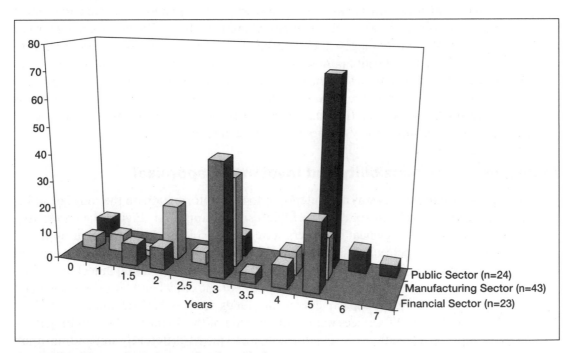

Figure 9.3 Upper limit for payback period

be accorded a five-year payback period. In-depth interviews with public sector managers suggested that this was likely to change given the new financial arrangements being foisted on public sector departments, e.g. devolved budgets, tighter accountability.

The long-term payback period for IT projects common in nearly 70 percent of public sector organisations was because of 'historical factors' according to a number of managers. They stressed that traditional accounting and auditing arrangements were 'not motivated by shareholder profits' or 'short-term financial planning'.

However, managers in the public sector believed that payback periods were likely to become shorter as they continued to change their financial accounting systems to emulate those of the private sector. The results from the survey suggested that decisions concerning the choice of payback period for IT projects in all sectors seemed to be driven by the financial arrangements governing the organisation rather than the nature and scope of IT investments.

Several managers said that payback periods irrespective of timescale were now 'inappropriate' because it was not always possible to determine when or even if IT could return a satisfactory sum to the business. Indeed, the range of IT investments were also becoming so complex that it was becoming increasingly difficult to assess the true costs. For example, the purchase of networked PCs across a range of departments could generate cost savings through efficiency and better information generation, but conversely create problems where staff required training to undertake new working practices.

Evaluating IT investments through payback was also difficult where core and support business processes underwent vast changes. Comments from the questionnaire survey and follow-up interviews suggested that problems were also associated with quantitative techniques for IT investment appraisal given that 'a wider array of performance indicators should be included to determine the success rate (or failure rate) of IT'. Additional performance indicators were more likely to be non-financial considerations such as improved quality of service (internally and externally), better information, improved management and supervisory control and skills enhancement.

Management responsibility and investment appraisal

The questionnaire survey was also interested to elicit information on the range of stakeholders responsible for preparing the IT investment appraisal. Figure 9.4 shows that about 34 percent of technical managers were responsible for IT investment appraisal compared with 20 percent of non-technical managers and 18 percent of management accountants. The influence of the management accounting profession in technical decision making is largely historical and is indicative of the era when IT was managed and controlled by accounting departments in the 1960s and 1970s (Friedman, 1989). In a number of instances, IT services were a sub-division of the finance and accounting function of large organisations. This situation was viewed differently depending upon stakeholder interests. For example, management accountants who controlled IT services usually justified this arrangement on the grounds that, 'It is important to impose tight controls on IT managers because they can easily let costs get out of hand'. The counter argument to this from IT managers was usually that, 'IT departments should be controlled and managed by IT managers who understand the technical needs of their

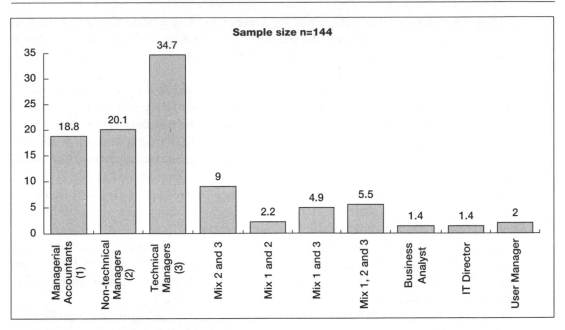

Figure 9.4 Responsibility for IT appraisal

customers. Accountants often misunderstand why certain costs should be incurred. You can't always justify everything on a cost-benefit basis'.

Whilst cost control in general was an important consideration in all the sectors, the more specific activity of investment appraisal was not given equal status by all managers. At the risk of over-generalisation, IT departments which were controlled by management accountants usually placed a high premium on investment appraisal for IT. On the other hand, IT departments run by IT managers were more concerned to satisfy the technical requirements of their customers. Having said this, it was common for IT managers to lose their technical skills once having become a manager and instead to spend most of their time on budgets and forecasts. However, a number of IT managers who had gained promotion from a technical background (previously having worked as programmers/analysts) were arguably more 'in tune' with the technical aspects of their department than was the case where management accountants were in charge of IT.

Whilst variations obviously occur both within and between sectors, other considerations also influenced the level and scope of financial controls over IT departments, e.g. nature of the business/organisation; level of expenditure on IT; skills profile of IT staff; IT strategies; legislative framework (CCT); profit/cost centre status; outsourcing arrangements; and size of IT department in relation to the organisation.

At one UK bank, investment appraisal was considered 'central to the financial evaluation of all bank-wide IT expenditure and investment'. This interview with a senior IT manager indicated that since the annual IT spend was over £50 million, 'all IT projects have to undergo a thorough vetting to determine if they are viable or not'. To achieve this, the NPV method was used with an upper payback period of five years. It was pointed out that, 'Since a whole variety of IT project proposals hit the desk of the steering committee (comprising senior bank executives), it is important given the time constraints to be able to prioritise the project proposals. A good financial case is important, although some projects are accepted because they are 'strategic' yet financially indefensible'.

Such a statement seemed to be a contradiction in terms. At the time of interview, the largest project being undertaken at the bank was at a cost of £100 million over five years. Since this was described as a 'strategic project' by corporate executives, the requirement for a 'sound financial case' was somewhat reduced. One IT manager working on the project described its budget as a 'bottomless pit' since no expense was spared in the overall objective of completing the project on time, albeit not necessarily on budget.

Interviews with a range of managers in the three sectors suggested a gap between formal policy for IT evaluation and practical reality. Whilst many senior managers confirmed that financial controls were 'imperative to ensure value for money from IT', those projects which were considered 'strategic to the business' seemed to require less formal, quantitative justification. This was surprising given that vast sums of money were 'thrown' at strategic projects, even though they were high-risk, technologically challenging and uncertain.

One manager at a manufacturing plant said that, 'If you can't apply cost justification methods to IT projects, then you call them strategic. As long as you demonstrate a good business case, you can usually get the resources you need to go ahead'. The survey results suggested that provided corporate executives were committed to a particular IT project based on their perception that it would add 'strategic value to the business', the requirement for stringent financial controls was lessened. Interestingly, a number of the respondents, irrespective of sector, suggested that whereas vast sums of money were allocated to 'high risk' strategic IT projects (without the guarantee of success), tight financial controls were often imposed upon heads of IT departments and project managers for relatively low levels of expenditure. This led one public sector manager to comment that, 'In my organisation we often save on the pennies and waste the pounds'. If these comments were anything to go by, then they may go some way to explaining some of the recent IT disasters such as TAURUS and the Prudential system, and even the poor results of many other IT development projects (Willcocks and Harrow, 1992).

A further breakdown of Figure 9.4 into the three sectors highlights differences between stakeholder roles in the IT investment appraisal process. Figure 9.5 shows that technical managers (with the exception of the manufacturing sector) were more likely to be in charge of IT investment appraisal than either non-technical managers or management accountants. The process of investment appraisal, however, was commonly described by managers in all sectors as an 'administrative hurdle' to overcome.

In the majority of organisations, irrespective of sector, those in charge of investment appraisal would prioritise proposed investment decisions and conduct a cost-benefit analysis for each project (item of proposed expenditure). Requests for expenditure could come from many sources (e.g. managers and staff), and it was the task of the head of department to prioritise competing requests and decide whether to include or exclude them from the budget. The investment appraisal document would then be dispatched to the next level up for scrutiny by a senior manager.

Eventually, board level executives would assess the investment appraisal document

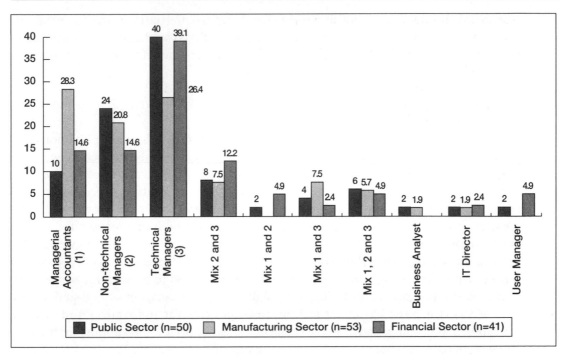

Figure 9.5 Responsibility for investment appraisal by sector

and allocate resources accordingly to the divisions/departments or units in question. At this stage, the 'architects' of the investment appraisal document would be informed which projects were to be financed and which had been rejected by the board. The criteria for selection and rejection was almost entirely based on a cost-benefit analysis, although the justification for proposed expenditure was given by the head or representative of the division/department or unit requesting the resources.

Whilst administrative differences occurred in the investment appraisal system between sectors, the nature and scope of the process was similar. Managers in all sectors admitted to manipulating data for the purpose of supporting their case for resources, and the whole process was highly political and subjective. The questionnaire data further suggested that the priorities of corporate executives concerning resource allocation decisions were also becoming more 'financially focused'.

This was particularly the case in the public sector. Here managers responsible for IT budgets suggested that a 'cost-conscious revolution was sweeping through public organisations'. A number of public sector managers claimed that their bosses demanded they become 'more business-like' in their approach to technology and people management. Many public sector managers equated business-like behaviour with 'financial awareness'. In this capacity many were now attending 'business training' on accounting and budgeting, performance measurement and cost control. Financial skills seemed to be accorded greater priority over people and technology management. Indeed, the term project management was also seen by many public sector managers in charge of IT departments as resource management (not necessarily human resources).

In the manufacturing sector, management accountants were more likely to be responsible for IT investment appraisal than their counterparts in the financial and public sectors. This finding is interesting in the light of past studies on the evaluation of technology which suggest a tension between the often contradictory priorities of manufacturing and finance managers (Currie, 1989abc).

IT and short-termism

Here the tension is concerned with the failure on the part of the finance function (usually senior managers) to understand the practical application of new technologies and how best to evaluate their performance. Engineers, on the other hand, often resent the intervention of accountants in the formal quantitative evaluation process since they argue that many of the real benefits from CAD and FMS, etc, are qualitative and therefore not amenable to 'traditional financial evaluation methods and techniques' (Currie and Seddon, 1992). Whilst this suggests the problem is simply a misunderstanding between those who understand financial matters against those who possess technical skills, the problem is of course much more complicated and to do with the wider issues of the financial arrangements for business; skills profile of management and staff; organisation structure; the nature of the business; policies for innovation and change; education and training; and even government industrial policy and support for industry and commerce as a whole.

However, it may be argued that the dominant function responsible for strategic investment decisions on technology (e.g. technical managers, non-technical managers, management accountants, among others) may nonetheless influence the choice and application of performance measures used to justify proposed IT projects. This is a common cry in the relationship between the city and industry, where the latter criticise the UK banking system for being too short-term with regard to expected returns from business investments. In the case of managing innovation, the argument is one which assumes that a short-term managerialist approach to evaluating and implementing new technologies (driven by shareholder and top management pressures) leaves little time for sufficient benefits to be achieved to make any real difference to performance. Such a short-term view on the part of both the city and top managers may reflect badly on R & D and technology investments, and may influence future resource allocation decisions for capital projects.

A relevant example is in the sphere of AMT where the short-term performance expectations of senior executives detract from the long-term perspective of those involved in its implementation (Currie, 1989abc). This is particularly the case in Anglo/American companies, where the annual management and staff performance appraisal system demands tangible results which are not always beneficial to the long-term health of the organisation. Top managements' demands for quantitative results from technology which are demanded from divisional managers also fuel inter-management competition for scarce resources. Again, this may not be conducive to good performance as managers resort to behaving politically by protecting their departments through the manipulation of information for top management consumption.

In the CAD study conducted in the late 1980s, it was found that the formal-rational approach to evaluating technology operated alongside an informal-political system.

The latter was characterised by a series of policies designed by managers to achieve 'departmental protectionism'. In the case of the engineering department, managers would deliberately distort budgets for the purpose of securing resources for their technology projects. This would be achieved by 'massaging' the figures to give the appearance that proposed investments in technology would return a healthy profit to both the department and, of course, the business in general. Budgets would be deliberately inflated by divisional managers and the expected benefits from proposed investments in technology were always likely to be grossly exaggerated (Currie, 1989abc).

In the area of financial evaluation for technology, one of the key findings from this study was that in spite of financial control being an important priority of senior managers, a certain amount of duplicity and manipulation characterised the whole capital budgeting process. Divisional managers therefore learned to 'play the game' of budgetary control and 'massage the figures' to meet their own resourcing priorities. This suggested that the veneer of financial control and performance measurement of technology was not as formal or rigid as one might suspect from a more superficial reading of the situation. Rather, the entire budgeting process was one of political infighting and internal competition both within and between departments. Little wonder that the over-optimistic approach adopted by divisional managers in relation to the perceived benefits from technology rarely translated into tangible benefits in practice (e.g. post-implementation). Yet the well-documented failure of IT to meet corporate expectations is problematic to IT budget holders as past IT disasters seems to have fuelled an even greater desire on the part of corporate managers to impose tighter financial controls on future IT investment (Willcocks, 1992).

Financial versus 'strategic' IT investment decisions

The finding from the questionnaire survey (see above) that the majority of organisations in all sectors attempted to quantify the benefits from IT suggested that financial control was an important requirement of corporate management. This finding reinforces other recent studies which suggest that large IT investors (e.g. banks, building societies, insurance companies, public sector organisations, industrial companies, etc) are attempting to impose more financial controls over their IT investments (Willcocks and Harrow, 1992. Grindley, 1991. *Computing* 1994. Sauer, 1993. Allen and Scott-Morton, 1994). However, over half the sample claimed to use the more simple payback technique of investment appraisal for IT than the complicated NPV, DCF or IRR methods because it was easier for managers to understand. This would suggest that, as opposed to devising more effective and efficient methods for measuring IT investment and performance, organisations were instead interpreting financial control in the same light as management control.

For example, in all of the sectors involved, managers in charge of IT departments said they were under greater pressure to demonstrate financial benefits from their IT investments. In many instances, career progression was becoming inextricably linked with performance more than ever before. Several managers in the financial and public sectors said that 'pressure from above' led them to behave 'single-mindedly'. In a number of instances this created problems as IT departments sought new ways to meet the ever more demanding requirements of their 'customers' (from other internal departments). The common problem that 'we give the customer what they ask for even though it is not always what they require as a technical solution' had become a more acute problem, particularly to the IT department with a reputation to both preserve and build in the new competitive environment.

The important issues of accountability and responsibility for IT services were being tackled head on by many IT service providers in all sectors. Several IT managers stressed the need to 'evaluate their customer base' along with the requests they receive for IT services. For example, IT managers said that although they give their customers a range of advice and guidance on their IT requirements, customers were becoming 'too demanding' as a result of financial pressures from within their own departments. At one public sector organisation, a senior IT manager said that he was now devising service-level agreements (SLAs) for his own staff as well as his customers. He commented that in the past supplier-customer relationships were 'more informal' and that 'my staff would often design and implement systems without dotting the i's and crossing the t's'. IT professionals would liaise with their customers and attend to problems accordingly.

However, the historical problem of IS systems poor performance and even failure was no longer tolerated by corporate executives, who threatened to cut resources to departments which were perceived to 'waste money'. As a result, the IT department was becoming more closely scrutinised and its customers were now beginning to 'pass the buck' back to the IT department if IS systems did not meet with their approval. The IT manager argued that, 'It is all about 'ownership' of IS. The trouble is, my team develop systems according to the client's requirement. If the client gets it wrong, they blame us. They don't want to own the problem, they just want to blame someone else. We are, it seems, the convenient scapegoat'.

As a consequence of this state of affairs, the new SLA was designed to act as a binding contract which detailed the type of IS required by the customer and how it would be developed by the IT department. It also detailed costs and post-implementation maintenance and support.

A common theme which seemed to arise from reviewing the questionnaire data and from the interviews was management control, more specifically the problem of management control concerning IT. This theme is discussed in some detail in the following section.

Management and the problem of control

Whilst managers in all sectors indicated that financial control of IT was becoming more important in the light of expanding IT budgets, they also pointed out that controlling IT costs was a serious problem. A number of managers simply perceived the whole process of investment in IT as 'an act of faith' and argued that investment appraisal techniques (however complex) could not ensure IT success or even satisfactorily measure performance.

Comments from several managers in all sectors seemed to suggest that managing innovation was a complex process and could not be simplified by imposing tighter and more restrictive financial controls. However, a number of managers perceived financial control as a ritualistic process supported by corporate executives. One IT manager said that, 'Top managers can control IT expenditure even if they can't control IT project development work. Resource allocation decisions seem to be driven by top managements' perception of the success of IT. If they think things are going well, then I get more money. If they think things are going badly, my budget is cut'.

This scenario was not seen as logical by this individual who claimed that managing IT was a 'complex activity, fraught with difficulties and problems'. His department was a sub-set of a large IS department and was largely involved in complex IS development work for internal customers. He claimed that IS development work was not simply a straightforward, linear process. Instead, he saw it as 'partly experimental and partly routine'. However, corporate executives were unhappy to allocate resources for 'IS experiments', since they demanded 'value for money from all IS undertakings'.

The survey findings suggested that the problem of evaluation and performance measurement was really a management control problem. Whilst a large proportion of the academic literature seems to confine IT evaluation narrowly in terms of formal quantitative techniques, the survey results suggested that the entire process was marked by political game playing between IT stakeholder groups. This finding is reinforced in the interpretive literature on IT evaluation (Walsham, 1993. Hirschheim and Smithson, 1988. Ginzberg and Zmud, 1988. Davis and Hamann, 1988).

A significant number of managers said that although formal evaluative techniques were used to measure IT performance, such as payback, NPV, DCF, etc, they fell short of providing managers with sufficient information regarding IT investment. Figure 9.6 shows that out of the three sectors, about a quarter of public sector managers said that investment appraisal techniques for IT were inadequate compared with as many as 35 percent of manufacturing managers and 15 percent of financial services managers.

In-depth interviews with financial services managers elicited some interesting insights into formal evaluation techniques for IT. A substantial proportion of managers in this sector said that provided an IT project was perceived as 'strategic', by virtue of it being

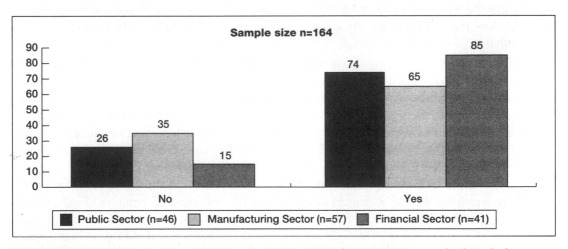

Figure 9.6 Percentage of companies who believe that investment appraisal techniques are adequate

'integral to the business', the release of resources was not a problem. Interviews with a leading UK bank suggested that huge sums of money were released for, often ill-defined, IT project development work. It was not unusual in this situation for tens of thousands of pounds to be allocated to 'strategically viable IT projects' even though many fell within the category of 'pure research', and did not have a guaranteed commercial outlet.

An IT contractor at the bank said that, 'You would be amazed at the amount of money invested in these (IT) projects. I am currently working on a project which will interface mainframe and PC data. It is partly experimental. So far this week, about £20k has been spent on flying up a few additional consultants from company X. It seems that money is no object when a project is considered important'.

Prior to the release of resources for IT projects, most organisations carried out some form of formal evaluation of the expected costs and benefits. But as we saw in Figure 9.6 a number of managers perceived this activity to be inappropriate. The reasons for this were multifaceted. But they largely concerned the difficulty of using traditional management accounting techniques to measure IT in contemporary industrial and commercial settings (Jones et al, 1993).

Perhaps a surprising finding from the questionnaire survey related to the decision by managers to allocate resources to IT in spite of a negative investment appraisal. Given that the majority of those involved in capital budgeting for IT were required to demonstrate the benefits of investing in IT, it was interesting to note that as many as 63 percent of respondents said that senior managers would allocate resources to IT even if the project was unlikely to give a satisfactory return on the capital.

This finding seemed to contradict the culture of 'money management' which prevailed in all sectors. Again, the reason for allocating resources to IT projects which were perceived to offer a negative return on capital was given as 'strategic'. To this effect it was stressed that, 'Projects with a negative NPV are possibly more important than those with a positive one. Quite often, a large-scale IT spend on a negative NPV project will have strategic importance to the business. For example, over time it may save vast amounts of money because it changes a key business process. But the savings may not be known at the time the resources are allocated. At other times, a negative NPV project will be a total disaster. We can never tell'.

Since the use of traditional management accounting investment appraisal techniques were only likely to capture the tangible aspects of IT projects (e.g. the cost of hardware/software, labour, materials, licenses, maintenance costs, etc), managers in all sectors were seeking to incorporate qualitative information into the formal evaluation process. This has been the subject of much speculation and debate within academic and professional circles (McNair et al, 1990. Bromwich and Bhimani, 1989. Blenkinsop and Burns, 1992. Currie, 1991. Drucker, 1988. 1989. Finnie, 1988. Waldron, 1988).

The desire to measure quality was perhaps more acute in the manufacturing sector. Here, virtually all the managers interviewed said that the real benefits of AMT were quality related. For example, better quality of information; improved process and product performance; ease of design, retrieval and modification (CAD drawings); space saving and greater simplicity of work organisation; customer satisfaction; skills development; enhanced flexibility; and teamworking (Currie and Seddon, 1992).

In fact, as many as 85.5 percent of managers said they believed non-financial (qualitative) benefits were just as important as financial performance indicators (see Figure 9.7). However, in-depth interviews with managers from the three sectors found that senior executives tended to place a higher premium on financial information for evaluating new technology than non-financial (qualitative) data. This was found to be more common in the manufacturing sector where managers operated in a climate of scarce resources, economic recession and capital rationing. Against a background of these constraints, it was evident that any investment in new technology had to be supported by a 'sound financial case'.

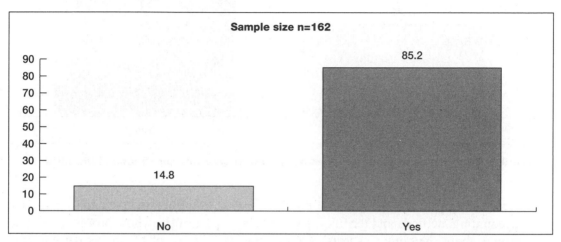

Figure 9.7 Percentage of companies who believe that non-financial benefits are as important as financial benefits

Although it was not surprising to find that over 80 percent of managers believed that non-financial benefits from IT were equally important as financial benefits, Figure 9.8 shows that only about 53 percent claimed to quantify non-financial benefits. For example, qualitative benefits such as customer services (e.g. complaints, delivery, satisfaction, return orders, etc) were given a financial value by many organisations. Other non-financial benefits included better quality information for management decision making. Several organisations were now using IT to speed up response times to customers, and this information was also of benefit to those involved in the development of new services to customers.

Conversely, some 46 percent of respondents said they did not attempt to quantify the qualitative benefits from IT. The reasons for this were twofold. First it was pointed out by a large proportion of IT managers that senior executives did not require this information for financial reporting purposes. Many pointed to the fact that traditional management accounting and financial reporting systems 'had not kept pace' with the technological, administrative and information systems which were currently in use. The same comment was made on several occasions that managing technology was 'not just about mainframes and PCs', but about management, co-ordination, planning and resource allocation. Second, a significant proportion of respondents said that the task of quantifying qualitative benefits from IT was not easy. Since many felt that existing

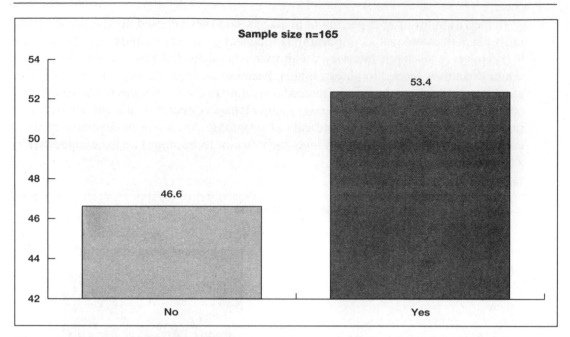

Figure 9.8 Percentage of companies who attempt to quantify non-financial benefits

financial appraisal theory was 'outdated' they were reluctant to introduce revised accounting methods and techniques when 'a large part of the whole process of evaluation is about the human aspects'. For example, the success of IT project development work depended largely on the skills of the project managers, analyst/programmers and other key personnel, and was not simply driven by resource allocation decisions from senior executives or accountants.

Respondents were also asked to prioritise their reasons for investment in IT. Figure 9.9 gives the top six key reasons for IT investment decisions in the three sectors. The financial services sector reported that the use of IT to support business needs was the most important reason for investment, followed by pressures of increased competition.

Equal weighting was given to the changes in regulatory requirements, a desire to maximise qualitative benefits and strategic advantages. A significant number of financial services companies from banks, building societies to insurance firms were currently rethinking the nature of their business. IT was seen as an important catalyst for change. This was exemplified by the new client-server environment, multimedia technology and a range of other new technological developments. The term 'mission critical systems' was used by financial services managers to embrace IT systems which were integral to the functioning of the business. It was reported by many financial services companies that changes in the way they do business had brought about an 'identity crisis', particularly insofar as banks were becoming more like building societies and vice versa.

In the manufacturing sector, strategic advantages were seen as the key criteria for investment in technology. In conjunction with other manufacturing initiatives such as JIT, TQM, MRP, MRP II, among others, UK manufacturers were attempting to pursue key objectives of enhanced productivity, cost reduction, flexible and leaner production, flatter organisation structures and better quality service to customers, to name but a few. Regulatory requirements were given priority by some manufacturers because of the new EC changes in procurement arrangements, standards, competition and markets.

As Figure 9.9 shows, the public sector tended to have different priorities for IT investment compared with the other two sectors. Against a background of market testing, compulsory competitive tendering and the shift from a purely 'service provider' status to a quasi-business operation, the majority of public sector organisations placed 'business needs' as their key priority. Many were introducing IT to improve financial reporting along similar lines to the private sector. Interestingly, the strategic use of IT was not seen as a priority in the public sector, and this may reflect the different language and terminology used within this sector as much as its traditional community service orientation.

Similarly, the changes in the regulatory requirements affecting public sector organisations also underpinned IT investment decisions. European community laws and directives imposed significant challenges to public sector organisations, and new information systems were required accordingly.

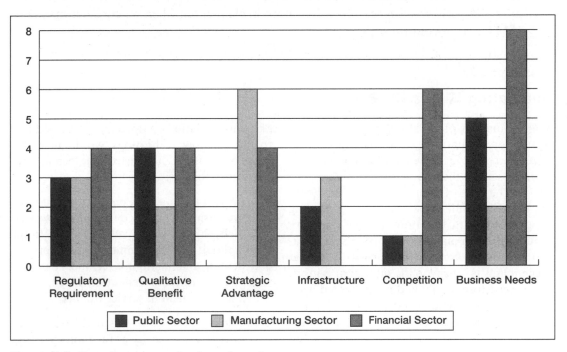

Figure 9.9 Top six reasons for investment

Concluding remarks

The issue of evaluating IT for performance improvement and control continued to be important in the private sector, and was becoming more critical to the public sector. In a number of cases, senior public sector managers were streamlining their IT departments to challenge the outsourcing threat. Indeed, the impending CCT arrangements would mean that some 70 percent of IT work would be put out to tender (*Computing* 1995).

One notable observation in all sectors was the lack of qualitative measures used for evaluating IT. Few managers attempted to make the connection between IT skill levels and project performance. In this context, the value of tacit skills of project managers and technical specialists was rarely formally evaluated. Rather, it seemed that evaluation continued to be a *numbers game* which encouraged managers to manipulate the figures to reflect IT projects in a more favourable light. Usually, the only significant performance indicator of IT project success was if they finished on time and within budget. Indeed, once projects were *signed off*, the evaluation process seemed to end. After this point in time, the users would complain to the technical team if they encountered problems, and in some cases, the system would be scrapped. Interestingly, a number of IT departments, especially in the financial services and public sectors, would initially undertake IS applications development work with a view to delivering a workable system at the end of the project. In several cases, however, this work simply ended up as a *prototype* and was labelled phase 1 of the project. Phase 2 would therefore be commissioned once the finances were in place. Perhaps unsurprisingly, a considerable amount of ex-post (after the event) rationalisation went into the evaluation process. The theme of evaluation and performance measure is continued in chapter ten when we consider managing AMT in four countries.

Case study

Evaluating IT at a UK Bank

The evaluation of IT at a UK Bank proved equally problematic to senior managers compared with the experience of engineers and managers in the manufacturing sector (see page 98). At the time of interview in the mid-1990s, the Bank had undergone a major re-structuring programme with the announcement of fifty redundancies in managerial positions. A document produced for senior managers said that 'Technology is crucial to the survival of Bank x. In the past technology had not delivered what the business required. There is now a need for people to manage complex projects and that the re-structuring had recreated new, more demanding roles and jobs, and up-skilling of the work force was required. Through the assessment process some staff have been judged to have skills which are not interchangeable with the new skills the new jobs require'. Skills deficiencies were seen to exist in both managerial and technical staff, and this was perceived to threaten the competitive position of the business.

To ensure that technology delivered business-orientated solutions, a document was produced to outline how technology would meet the needs of the Bank. It asserted that technology's role was as follows:

- to provide a pro-active, responsive and innovative business systems development service
- to deliver secure and reliable operational computing and telecommunications services
- to develop and maintain a technical base that enables continuous reduction in unit costs and improvement in service quality

Technology at the Bank was divided into five key processes headed by a Technology Director. The processes included services delivery; technical services; development; resource management; and planning and control. The responsibilities of the five areas were described as follows:

- **Services delivery**: Responsible for the computer operations centres, networks and branch services.
- **Technical services**: Responsible for technical

research, technical strategy and support to both services delivery and systems development

- **Development**: Responsible for the development of new systems and the maintenance and enhancement of existing systems
- **Resource management**: Responsible for planning the recruitment, career development and projected deployment of staff
- **Planning and control**: Responsible for providing technology management and other parts of the Bank with the information needed to effectively plan, control and explain the technology department's use of resources

According to the Technology Director, 'This year (1993/4) the Technology First Financial Forecast (FFF) has differed significantly from its predecessors in a number of ways. For the first time it has really been driven by the business, not just for systems development where the business drivers are more immediately visible but also for all the other areas of technology where the knock-on effect of these systems projects will ultimately be felt. In addition, the FFF has been prepared in a lot more detail than ever before, reflecting the significant effort put into the systems plans for project X and the definition of the infrastructure requirements necessary to support these plans. As a result, we are far better placed to articulate our forecast to the Executive and the quality of discussion which ensued was far higher than would ever previously have been possible. It also leaves us much better positioned for the budget, enabling us to concentrate on the key issues which have already been flagged in the FFF'.

The financial expenditure on technology and all its associated cost burdens were immense. The Bank invested as much as £50 million per annum on systems development work alone. This figure was estimated to correspond to 495 man years of development effort. However, it was further estimated that, for the following year, the total demand for development work would be 575 man years of effort, leading to a resource shortfall of around 78 man years. Other cost areas were the data centre, at £30

million per annum; networks, at £23 million per annum; and the infrastructure costs amounting to £5 million per annum. In the past year, expenditure on these four areas had increased by a total of £9 million and was expected to increase further in future years.

Developing a formal-rational evaluation process for managing technology

The role of technology at the Bank was considered to be strategic for two reasons. First, the vast annual financial commitment in technology meant that it was best managed by senior executives. To this effect, an IT Director was responsible for overseeing that financial investment in systems development, data centres, networks and infrastructures was managed according to a top-down strategy. Second, it was stressed that, 'we have a huge opportunity to demonstrate technology as a major contributor – a competitive advantage'. Technology could no longer be seen as a 'support function' since it was now embedded into nearly every key process of the Bank's activities.

However, the related tasks of strategy formation, evaluation, implementation and maintenance of technology, continued to pose fresh challenges to managers and technical staff at all levels. Since greater pressure from above was placed on managers to demonstrate the attainment of business benefits from technology, the IT Director had initiated the development of a formal-rational strategic planning process, to be adhered to by all Bank personnel, external and internal (contractors) consultants.

In-depth interviews with a number of Bank personnel were conducted ranging from senior and middle level managers, IT project managers, analyst/programmers to end users. A document was obtained from the Bank which outlined the formal strategic planning process for managing IT, together with the aims and objectives of the various stakeholders. The development of a formal structure for managerial decision making was seen as crucial in the attainment of competitive advantage from technology. The formal structure is given in Table 9.1.

Executive Management Guidance and Control	Sound planning and control of systems development must be ensured for the entire organisation. This requires that the department have a formal direct reporting relationship with executive management.
Organisational Commitment	Without a clear demonstration of the organisation's commitment, proper resources may never be allocated to the project.
Business Management Direction	Primary responsibility for the functional success of a new system should be placed with its major beneficiaries. Business management should therefore be in a position to provide clear guidance on project scope and direction to the project team.
Accountability of IT Project Management	The IT team must be clearly accountable for delivery of the agreed functionality. The organisation structure must allow the team to involve business management in all key decisions affecting a project, to resolve conflicts within the team and gain access to computing resources.

Table 9.1 Formal objectives and overall structure for IT

The structure is largely concerned with financial control and formal reporting arrangements and 'covers all projects initiated on behalf of business divisions and also projects initiated by technology in order to improve service levels or quality of the IT service'.

The document is unconcerned with the day-to-day management of IT projects and their associated rule-book methodologies and standards for IT project management. Nor does it mention the relationship between skills enhancement of IT professionals and the formal organisational objectives of the IT Division.

Executive management responsibility and control of IT expenditure for the Technology Department was provided by a two-tier committee structure: 1) An Executive Management Committee and 2) A Group Technology Steering Committee.

The first Committee was responsible for the allocation of financial resources to selected projects. The role of the second Committee was to assist in the management of the IT function by:

- participating in the planning process
- monitoring the progress of projects
- ensuring adequate user commitment

- resolving conflicting priorities for IT resource where necessary

The Group Technology Steering Committee had a number of responsibilities which included:

- the development of organisation policies for IT
- to serve as Project Steering Committee for long-range information planning projects
- to approve initiation of all projects above £1m budgeted expenditure and above £0.2m unbudgeted expenditure (IT projects over £5m require approval from the Board of Directors)
- to monitor progress of all development projects
- to set priorities and settle user disputes

Figure 9.10 outlines the structure of IT project management at the Bank. The Technology Steering Committee was responsible for all the IT projects undertaken by the IT Division. The Divisional Steering Committee acted within the policies and architectures set out by the Group Technology Steering Committee. Its key responsibilities included: the agreement of annual technology budgets and quarterly revisions; approval of all significant projects (or budget

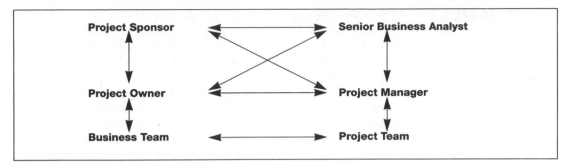

Figure 9.10 Key personnel in IT project management

allocations in the case of smaller grouped activities such as support/maintenance); ensuring that the business was adequately supported by production systems (this included any new business areas or products); prioritising of technology budgeted resources available to the division; regular review and monitoring of all major activities; submissions to the Group Technology Steering Committee as required, the resolution of conflicts, issues and problems raised by the Project Control Committees; justification of material variances from Group strategic aims; establishing a Project Control Committee to execute and control specific division projects or portions of the budget and, finally, to ensure adequate business staff were made available to support technology projects. This itemised list of key responsibilities of the Divisional Steering Committee focused primarily on the financial monitoring and control of the Bank's IT activities.

The emphasis on financial control of IT was highlighted as a key managerial responsibility and was further reinforced by examining the duties of the Project Control Committee (PCC). The PCC adopted a 'less strategic' and 'more operational' role in IT project management. The PCC was primarily concerned with the approval, review, monitoring and control of project scope, plans and budgets; the submission of proposals and progress reports to the Divisional Technology Steering Committee; the overall management of the progress of IT projects to ensure that problems do not amplify; to sign off and approve all agreed milestones throughout the life of the project; to ensure the

commitment of qualified business personnel; to ensure that work is constrained while continuing to meet the original business objectives; to deliver the project or system, including the co-ordination of all related activities outside Technology; the control and testing, conversion and installation tasks, to 'sign off' the system before 'going live' and to establish Project Working Groups to execute and control specific segments of the project as required.

Interviews with IT project managers at the bank suggested a clear division between the 'strategic' responsibilities of senior managers and the 'operational' duties of senior/middle level IT managers. Strategic management of IT was synonymous with financial control, and great efforts were made to identify appropriate financial performance indicators for evaluating IT. Technology projects were evaluated according to their perceived return on investment (ROI) and quantitative advantage. IT project managers were generally responsible for staffing. This included hiring permanent and contract analyst/programmers and associated staff. They were also responsible for the evaluation of the most appropriate software for the project, the co-ordination of development work (coding, testing, re-coding, etc), training, liaising with the client (the department which requested the system), and the 'sign off' and delivery of the system.

According to one IT project manager, many of these responsibilities were 'strategic in nature' because they influenced the future direction of the Technology Division. For example, the evaluation and implementation of specific software packages and associated training would 'move the department in the direction of that technology' and influence future IT projects. In one division, contract programmers said that, 'Since our project manager does not understand the software we are using, we tend to carry out the evaluation and feasibility of software for the projects we do. I suppose we steer the technology decisions rather than senior managers'.

Evaluation of IT projects

An organisation chart was produced to steer the process by which IT projects were managed at the Bank. The rational for the structure was to ensure that people at all levels were given clearly defined management and technical roles. Given that past investment in IT was deemed not to have provided tangible business benefits, all future investment was to be carefully managed and co-ordinated. Demarcation lines were drawn between responsibilities and tasks. Managers and technical staff were encouraged to get together and discuss possible technology projects and evaluate them on the basis of a formal-rational methodology. 'Acts of faith' evaluation was discouraged. The bank had created a four-box grid to evaluate and manage IT projects. Within each grid, a senior manager was responsible for certain functions and activities. The purpose of this structure was to 'form a marriage' between the technical specialists and the business managers.

The Project Sponsor (the client) was responsible for identifying specific business problems which required a technical solution. This person was described as 'an internal customer' and would discuss requirements with a Senior Business Analyst – a person who was expected to have dual skills in the form of technical and business awareness.

Having agreed on the type of IT project required, the Project Sponsor would then delegate the management and control responsibilities to a Project Owner (a business manager). This person would negotiate the day-to-day management of the project with the IT Project Manager on the technical side and would tend to discuss the business requirements of the system rather than its technical complexities. Neither the Senior Business Analyst nor the Project Owner were technical specialists.

Whilst the technical complexities were intended (theoretically) to be discussed by the Senior Business Analyst with the client, in practice the technical problems were delegated to the IT Project Manager. The role of the IT Project Manager was central to all IT activities undertaken at the Bank. This person was responsible for all the day-to-day management aspects of the project, its 'agreed functionality, time scales and budget; the creation of a work plan specifying resource requirements; the arrangement of the appropriate skills training for team members; the reinforcement of effective relationships with end users; the documentation of reporting relationships; the control of the project.' The IT Project Manager's role was described as one of 'constant fire-fighting' since it dealt with all the problems from resourcing the project to the training of programmers, possible skills shortages, managing technical specialists, identifying (unforeseen) faults in the selected software packages and developing problem solving 'remedies'.

A discussion about the division of labour between non-technical and technical managers led the IT Project Manager to suggest that a common problem was in the identification of the most appropriate technical solution for the business problem. He said that, 'We give the customer what they have asked for. Sometimes, though, the system we have developed is not what they need.... It is up to the business side to tell us what they want – not the role of technology to tell them what they need. But the business is not always certain about what it needs. Negotiations between the business and technology usually start with us asking, 'What do you want?' Then the business replies, 'What have you got?' We need to forge a greater understanding between the business managers and the technology division. But this is difficult because very few senior managers understand technology – even at its most elementary level'.

Managerial responsibility for IT project work was shared between the business (client) and technology (technical managers). Yet the Project Sponsor was responsible for the overall financial commitment to the project. A common complaint at the Bank was that 'technology does not always deliver what the business wants'. This had led senior executives at the Bank to demand greater managerial control over all aspects of technology expenditure.

Discussion questions

1 How has the bank attempted to formalise the IT evaluation process?
2 Do you think the bank has created hybrid managers?
3 What is the role of technical specialists in the evaluation process?
4 Describe the problems of the formal evaluation process?
5 Who is finally accountable if IT projects fail?
6 Should there be more stakeholders in the evaluation process?

References 9

Allen, T.J., Scott-Morton, M.S. eds (1994) *Information technology and the corporation of the 1990s.* Oxford University Press.

Blenkinsop, S.A., Burns, N. (1992) 'Performance measurement revisited'. *International Journal of Production and Operations Management,* Vol. 12, No. 10, pp. 16–25.

Bromwich, M., Bhimani, A. (1989) *Management Accounting: Evolution not revolution*, CIMA: London.

Brooks, F. (1987) 'No silver bullet: essence and accidents of software engineering'. *IEEE Computing*, 20.

Chew, W.B. (1988) 'No nonsense guide to measuring productivity'. *Harvard Business Review*, January/February, pp. 110–118.

Computing (1994) 'Finance firms raise IT spend', 2 June, p. 4.

Cooper, R. (1989) 'You need a new cost system when.' *Harvard Business Review*, January/February, pp. 77–82.

Crockett, F. (1992) 'Revitalizing executive information systems'. *Sloan Management Review,* Summer.

Currie, W. (1989a) *Managerial strategies for new technology*. Gower, Aldershot.

Currie, W. (1989b) 'The art of justifying new technology to top management'. *OMEGA – The International Journal of Management Science*, Vol, 17, No. 5, pp. 409–418.

Currie, W. (1989c) 'Investing in CAD: a case of ad-hoc decision making'. *Long Range Planning*, Vol, 22, No. 6, pp. 85–91.

Currie, W. (1991) 'Managing technology: a crisis in management accounting? *Management Accounting*, Vol, 69, No. 7, July.

Currie, W., Seddon, J. (1992) 'Managing AMT in a JIT environment in the UK and Japan'. *British Journal of Management*, Vol, 3, No. 3, pp. 123–136.

Davenport, T.H. (1993) *Process Innovation: re-engineering work through information technology*, Harvard Business School Press, Boston.

Davis, G.B., Hamann, J.R. (1988) 'In-context information systems assessment: a proposal and an evaluation', in N. Bjorn-Andersen and G.B. Davis (eds) *Information systems assessment: issues and challenges*, Proceedings of the IFIP WG 8.2 Working Conference on Information Systems Assessment, Noordwijkerhout, The Netherlands, 27–29 August 1986, North Holland, Amsterdam.

DeCotiis, T.A., Dyer, L. (1979) 'Defining and measuring project performance'. *Research Management*, pp. 17–22.

Drucker, P. (1988) 'The coming of the new organisation'. *Harvard Business Review*, January/February.

Drucker, P. (1990) 'The emerging theory of manufacturing'. *Harvard Business Review*, May/June.

Drury, C. (1985) *Management and cost accounting*. Prentice Hall.

Dugdale, D. (1991) 'Is there a 'correct' method of investment appraisal?'. *Management Accounting*, May, pp. 46–48.

Dugdale, D., Jones, T.C. (1991) 'Discordant voices: accounting views of investment appraisal'. *Management Accounting*, November/December, pp. 54–9.

Earl, M. (1994) 'The new and the old of business process redesign'. *Journal of Information Systems*, Vol, 3, No. 1, pp. 5–22.

Eccles, R. G. (1991) 'The performance measurement manifesto'. *Harvard Business Review*, January/February, pp. 131–137.

Eilon, S. (1993) 'Editorial: Measuring quality of information systems'. *OMEGA: International Journal of Management Science.* Vol. 21, No, 2, pp. 135–138.

Finnie, J. (1988) 'The role of financial appraisal in decisions to acquire advanced manufacturing technology'. *Accounting and Business Research*, Vol. 18. No. 70, pp. 133–139.

Ginzberg, M. J., Zmud, R. W. (1988) 'Evolving criteria for information systems assessment', in N. Bjorn-Andersen and G.B. Davis (eds) *Information systems assessment: issues and challenges*, Proceedings of the IFIP WG 8.2 Working Conference on Information Systems Assessment, Noordwijkerhout, The Netherlands, 27-29 August 1986, North Holland, Amsterdam.

Haas, E.A. (1987) 'Breakthrough manufacturing'. *Harvard Business Review*, March/April, pp. 75–99.

Hayes, R.H., Jaikumar, R. (1988) 'Manufacturing's crisis: new technologies, obsolete organisations'. *Harvard Business Review*, September/October, pp. 77–85.

Hirschheim, R.S., Smithson, S. (1988) 'A critical analysis of information systems evaluation', in N. Bjorn-Andersen and G.B. Davis (eds) *Information systems assessment: issues and challenges*, Proceedings of the IFIP WG 8.2 Working Conference on Information Systems Assessment, Noordwijkerhout, The Netherlands, 27-29 August 1986, North Holland, Amsterdam.

Jaikumar, R. (1986) 'Postindustrial manufacturing'. *Harvard Business Review*, November/December.

Jones, C., Currie, W., Dugdale, D. (1993) 'Accounting and technology in Britain and Japan: learning from field research'. *Management Accounting Research*. Vol, 4, pp. 109–137.

Kaplan, R. (1984) 'Yesterday's accounting undermines production'. *Harvard Business Review*, July/August, pp. 95–101.

Kaplan, R. (1985) 'Accounting lag: the obsolescence of cost accounting systems', in K. Clark., R. Hayes and C. Lorenze, *Technology and Productivity: The Uneasy Alliance*, Harvard Business School Press.

Kaplan, R (1986) 'Must CIM be justified by faith alone?' *Harvard Business Review*, March/April.

Kaplan, R. (1990) *Measures for manufacturing excellence*, Harvard Business School Press.

McNair, C.J., Lynch, R.L., Cross, K.F. (1990) 'Do financial and non-financial performance measures have to agree?' *Management Accounting*, Vol. 72, No. 5, pp. 28–36.

Moules, J. (1995) 'Tender is the fight', *Computing*, January 5, pp. 16–17.

Nixon, B., Sundgaard, E., Sinclair, D. (1993) 'Industry and the city: is R & D the key?' *Accountancy*, January.

Pike, R. (1983) 'A review of recent trends in formal capital budgeting processes'. *Accounting and Business Research*, Summer.

Sauer, C. (1993) *Why information systems fail*. Alfred Waller: Henley on Thames, UK.

Scapens, R. W. (1983) 'Closing the gap between theory and practice'. *Management Accounting*, pp. 34–36.

Scapens, R.W. (1988) 'Research into management accounting practice'. *Management Accounting*, December, pp. 26–28.

Shank, J. K., Govindarajan, V. (1992) 'Strategic cost analysis of technological investments'. *Sloan Management Review*, Fall, pp. 39–51.

Udo, G.J. (1993) 'Managing organisational bias in the post-audit of MIS projects'. *Industrial Management and Data Systems*, Vol. 93. No. 3. pp. 26–30.

Waldron, D. (1988) 'Accounting for CIM: the new yardsticks'. *Industrial Computing*, EMAP, February, pp. 36–37.

Walsham, G. (1993) *Interpreting information systems*. Wiley.

Wheelwright, S.C., Clark, K.B. (1992) 'Creating project plans to focus'. *Harvard Business Review*, March/April, pp. 70–82.

Willcocks, L. (1992) 'The manager as technologist'. L. Willcocks and J. Harrow (eds) *Rediscovering the public services*. McGraw Hill.

CHAPTER 10

Managing AMT in Four Countries: Some East-West Comparisons

Introduction

The background to this article is the debate on the choice and utilisation of costing and investment appraisal methods and techniques for advanced manufacturing technology (AMT). It is part of a wider debate on the industrial decline of Anglo/American manufacturing industry (Hayes and Abernathy, 1980. Hayes and Wheelright, 1984. Thompson, 1989. Williams et al, 1983). Searching for solutions to the problems of western manufacturing, academics and practitioners have focused attention on the Japanese 'miracle' of recent decades (Pascale and Athos, 1981. Fruin, 1993. Czinkota and Kotabe, 1993). The impetus behind some of this work is to identify appropriate Japanese practices for adoption in the west. Yet questions arise about the suitability of Japanese *solutions* since the business and management areas which are deemed problematic by western academics (management accounting) are not those considered important to the Japanese, particularly with regard to AMT strategy formulation and implementation (Jones et al, 1993). This article draws from empirical work on cross-national comparisons of AMT and management accounting in twenty four companies operating in four countries (Currie, 1994).

Evaluating AMT in Japan

The last decade has witnessed a plethora of academic and practitioner literature on the 'art of Japanese management' (Pascale and Athos, 1981). A large proportion of this literature addresses two inter-related debates. The first considers the decline of Anglo/American manufacturing and the consequent threat to those economies (Hayes and Abernathy, 1980. Williams et al, 1983. Thompson, 1989. Hayes and Wheelright, 1984. Vernon, 1986). The second focuses attention on the success of the Japanese enterprise system and questions the extent to which Japanese management methods can be transported to the west (Fruin, 1993. Khabanda and Stallworthy, 1991. Currie, 1991bc. Currie and Seddon, 1992. Williams et al, 1991. Schonberger, 1986).

In attributing Japanese economic success to their effective exploitation of 'new manufacturing methods and techniques', research has focused upon the implementation of JIT, MRP, MRP II, TQM, TPM, SPC and QCs and so on (Gilbert, 1989. Imaud Lee, 1989. Inman and Mehra, 1990. Cobb, 1991. Zipkin, 1991. Voss and Robinson, 1987), although many of these 'new' methods originated in the post-war period in the west, notably the USA.

In conjunction with examining Japanese manufacturing processes, researchers have further considered Japanese management development and training (Pascale and Athos, 1981. Crump, 1989. Suzuki, 1989. Williams et al, 1990. Abbegglen and Stalk, 1985. Yang, 1992). Here, managers are seen as creating a 'multi-skilled' or 'polyvalent' labour force with the accent on 'team-working', loyalty to one's company and high motivation (Kumazawa and Yamada, 1989. Storey, 1991. Currie, 1994). Forceful arguments have therefore been advanced to encourage western managers to adopt 'Japanese' management practices to enhance their international and domestic competitive position, a process which may lead to the 'Japanization' of Anglo/American industry (Oliver and Wilkinson, 1987. Jones et al, 1993).

In parallel with the literature on the 'new' manufacturing methods and human resource practices in Japan, an important area has been the adoption and implementation of 'new' information and advanced manufacturing technologies (IT and AMT). They refer to DSS, MIS, LANs, client-server technology, open systems, CAD/CAM, FMS, NC, CIM and robotics, among others (Currie, 1994). The Japanese, however, are reluctant to refer to any form of technology as 'new' since they perceive technology development and diffusion as an evolutionary and 'on-going' activity. In the case of AMT, Japanese manufacturing managers prefer the term 'production technology' or 'factory automation'. As a result, the exploitation of CAD/CAM and robots, etc, in Japanese manufacturing firms is not perceived as a 'quick-fix' panacea to cure problems of low productivity and profitability. Instead, technology diffusion is simply one aspect of an all-embracing corporate/manufacturing strategy planned over a three to five year period (Currie, 1994). Yet the very fact that 'technology decisions' are taken at board level is indicative of the importance senior managers attach to technology as a tool to enhance organisational performance and competitive position.

A further line of enquiry into reasons which underpin Japanese economic success has been to analyse their use of accounting methods and techniques (Hiromoto, 1988. Yoshikawa, et al, 1989. Sakurai, 1990). Whilst research into this area is sparse, it is important if only because the growing preoccupation with identifying new management accounting techniques for Anglo/American businesses (in the form of Activity Based Costing and Throughput accounting) elevates accounting theory and practice to centre stage.

Much of the current academic critique of Anglo/American management accounting stems from the US accounting literature. Focusing upon 'traditional' or 'conventional' accounting practice, two key problems are identified. The first is in the area of costing systems and the second investment appraisal (Kaplan, 1984, 1985, 1986, 1990).

Cost systems

The underlying assumption of this critique into Anglo/American companies is that accounting information is the

'dominant, indeed the sole, determinant of decisions to adopt AMT. It further assumes that AMT is crucial for successful manufacturing performance. Thus problems in existing UK accounting practice, discovered in its measurements and techniques, are held to generate inadequate or incorrect accounting information which has central significance for UK manufacturing' (Jones et al, 1993).

Critics of conventional accounting practice cite examples where managers rely on distorted accounting information on the cost of particular production processes and profitability of products. Kaplan (1990) cites five key areas of cost system distortions. First, costs may be allocated to products that have little relation to the products being produced. For example, research and development costs, excess capacity costs and corporate overhead costs such as pensions. Second, costs may not be attributed to certain products being produced or to customers serviced. They include marketing, sales, general, admin and warranty costs. Third, 'distortion can be introduced by costing only a subset of the outputs of the firm as products'. Here, Kaplan differentiates between 'tangible' (manufactured) and 'intangible' (service) products, in that costs may only be assigned to the former. Fourth, distortion occurs where costs are 'inaccurately' assigned to products. Kaplan highlights two forms by which this may occur. The first is price distortion. This may occur 'when the cost system is too aggregated and average prices are used instead of specific prices. For example, some cost systems use an average price per direct labour hour despite wide differences in actual wage rates for both skilled and unskilled individuals'. Quantity distortions, on the other hand, occur when costs are 'indirectly assigned to products using a basis that is not perfectly proportional to the actual consumption of resources by products'. He points out that labour-intensive products are often 'overcosted when direct labour hours are used to assign all overhead costs to products' (Kaplan, 1990, p.4).

Interviews with Japanese engineers and accountants confirmed the use of 'conventional' management accounting techniques in eight Japanese manufacturing firms (Currie and Seddon, 1992. Currie, 1994). This is also confirmed by other research on Japanese management accounting (Williams et al, 1991. Yoshikawa et al, 1989. Morgan and Weerakoon, 1989). In turn, many of the inadequacies of traditional management accounting outlined above were reinforced by Japanese managers. The reduction of direct labour and enhanced productivity through AMT were seen as two key performance goals. Japanese managers were also keen to reduce costs as a consequence of capital rationing and facilitating management philosophies such as JIT and TQM. As Williams et al (1991, p. 14) point out, 'As far as one can judge, there is no general retreat from labour centred measures'. Many Japanese firms remain preoccupied with the reduction of (direct and indirect) labour hours. However, Japanese firms, unlike their western counterparts, were disinterested in the 'new' management accounting techniques such as ABC (Currie, 1994). One or two managers had heard of ABC but showed little interest in exploring it further. They felt that knowledge that some products were more expensive to produce than others was not in itself important to determine product strategy decisions (Currie and Seddon, 1992). On the contrary, expensive products were likely to have real strategic importance to the company and their elimination on the basis of simple product costing information could prove disastrous.

Where Japanese companies differed largely from their western counterparts was in the areas of cost management, investment appraisal, market orientation and strategic awareness of AMT. In the area of cost management, Japanese firms mentioned the importance of *target costing*. Japanese managers said that it was important to identify the correct price of a product for the marketplace at the pre-manufacturing stage. Financial planning for the entire product life-cycle was therefore carried out prior to manufacturing.

This is reinforced in the work of Yoshikawa et al (1989, p.22) who state that, 'Japanese companies show more attention to product costing at the pre-manufacturing stages with earlier and more sustained attempts at target costing and reduction. They also make positive use of quality control feedback'. Similarly, Kharbanda and Stallworthy (1991) claim that, as opposed to cost control being the sole responsibility of the accounting function, in Japan it is 'everyone's job'. Relating this to cost control in product development, the authors claim that Japanese manufacturers 'develop the cost of a design and then establish the market price'. Prices are fixed according to what the market will bear. Thus the Japanese 'work backwards to the basic cost of the product' and design it to an 'acceptable quality' at the right cost.

Investment appraisal

Investment appraisal is another area where dissimilarities occur between Japanese and western managers. In recent years, the 'failure' of traditional investment appraisal techniques has been well documented (Dugdale and Jones, 1990, 1991, 1993. Currie, 1989ab. Motteram and Sizer, 1992). The fixation on labour costs by perceiving the range of new technologies as *labour saving* has distorted the real strategic advantages of this form of capital investment (Currie, 1994a). The continuing decline in direct labour costs as a proportion of total manufacturing costs has rendered the focus on this performance indicator somewhat meaningless. It has also eliminated one of the key reasons for justifying AMT.

Whilst western managers appear over-concerned with the quantitative advantages of AMT investment, Japanese managers instead include a wider array of performance indicators when assessing the benefits from production technologies (Currie, 1994). Some Japanese managers claimed to quantify the *qualitative* benefits from AMT, with particular attention on quality control costs, scrap, rework, warranty, service costs, wastage and machine downtime, etc. This is also advocated for western managers (Primrose, 1988, 1989). Interviews with Japanese managers confirm the difficulty of quantifying the so-called *intangibles*, but it was stressed on a number of occasions that *payback* from AMT was geared to the long term (two to five years). This differs from the Anglo/American tendency to adopt short-term performance targets which invariably over-estimate the cost of capital leading to too-high DCF hurdles (see Kaplan, 1986. Pike, 1983. Woods et al, 1984).

One notable difference between Japanese and western management accounting practices was the level of responsibility for capital budgets and investment appraisal. Indeed, it was difficult to discuss preferences for management accounting techniques in isolation of other important considerations. For example, the notion that individuals could be responsible for departmental capital budgets (as is the case in the west) seemed surprising to many Japanese managers, who instead emphasised the value of teamworking and co-operation. Out of eight large Japanese manufacturing firms, only two middle managers were given budgetary responsibility, albeit at levels of only £400 and £2000 per annum respectively. The 'technical champion' – a term sometimes applied to the individual effort of a highly skilled technical expert in the west – was not recognised by Japanese managers (Currie, 1994).

In six of the eight case studies, expenditure on AMT was decided at *management meetings* comprising the president, board level directors and associated expert teams from the organisation. Technology strategy was not devolved to even senior level management where board levels directors simply served to *rubber stamp* capital budgets. One reason for the centralisation of the capital budgeting process was indeed the vast cost of introducing AMT. All Japanese companies confirmed an increase in the annual level of expenditure of AMT in the five years to 1990. Further, expenditure on AMT was commonly planned over five years where investment was likely to exceed several £millions.

Japanese manufacturing firms' use of management accounting techniques for investment appraisal of AMT was also surprising. Table 10.1 shows that in spite of large-scale annual expenditure on AMT, only one company used the more sophisticated technique of DCF. All companies, however, used some form of simple *payback* (see also Sakurai, 1990).

Case No.	Capital Budget Per Annum Company £ millions	AMT Investment Site £ millions	Discounted Cash Flow (DCF)	Payback
1	–	2	No	Yes
2	500	40	No	Yes
3	–	4	No	Yes
4	268	–	Yes	Yes
5	1296	29	No	Yes
6	14.8	3.2	No	Yes
7	217.1	40	No	Yes
8	135.1	4	No	Yes

Table 10.1 Management accounting and AMT in Japan

The use of accounting techniques in Japan

Payback periods of 2–3 years were typical but Japanese managers said that the ever-decreasing life expectancy of products and process technology meant that traditional accounting techniques including DCF were inappropriate. It was stressed that accounting measures for hardware and labour costs tended to exclude other important costs such as software development, training and vendor support services. Some Japanese managers expressed the difficulty in identifying the *real costs* of software and associated research and development activities. Commenting on software development, one Japanese manager said that the new PC-based languages and packages required new programming skills.

Although investment appraisal criteria in Japanese companies emphasised labour-centred measures, several managers reported a severe skills shortage in systems engineering. One Japanese manager at an automobile plant said that, 'You have to be careful when you talk about eliminating jobs through technology. Here, we do not get rid of people. We move them to another area if their job has become redundant'. As part of a major JIT programme, this company had 're-engineered' the plant and reduced forty control rooms to only one and organisational functions from seventy-eight to forty (Currie, 1994). Whilst this manager conceded that some jobs were 'in the past', he said that new technology was both a threat and a challenge. On the one hand, it threatened the status quo and people would have to learn new skills and, on the other, it posed a challenge to managers and staff as new *broader* skills were constantly demanded. He said that 'good systems engineers' were at a premium in Japan (e.g. the writers of programmes which drive industrial robots, CAD to point-of-sale stock control, etc).

This comment is reinforced by a *Financial Times* survey on Japanese industry which stresses 'The shortage of systems engineers has been a subject of popular complaint by (Japanese) employers'. Part of the shortage is related to employer perceptions of the software engineer. As the FT survey demonstrates, employers wish to groom software engineers with wider business skills than simply being proficient at programming. 'Engineers must understand the business of clients and be able to give them consultation' (*Financial Times*, 16 December 1991, p.5).

Whilst Japanese companies were committed to training and skills development, they agreed that it was 'difficult to quantify' the advantages which accrue from high calibre staff. However, the realisation that technology demanded re-training and re-skilling of the workforce did not discourage high-level capital investment. To realise strategic goals from AMT, managers in the majority of Japanese companies stressed the importance of having 'an all embracing strategic plan'.

AMT strategy and implementation

The commitment to the development and implementation of AMT strategy was company-wide and not simply a middle-level management responsibility as is the case largely in the UK (Currie, 1994). Important technology decisions such as level of expenditure on AMT, cost savings, market share objectives, procurement, vendor contracts, maintenance and training formed part of the corporate strategic plan for AMT. Moreover, AMT strategy was not simply a 'mission statement' to guide middle management decision-making. Rather, it was an 'all encompassing' strategic plan incorprating guidance on implementation and performance milestones.

A plant manager at a company which manufactured automatic control device equipment said that in recent years upper management had 'formalised' the strategic and operational decision making process for AMT. Starting with a Long Range Strategic Plan (LRSP) board level managers discussed the perceived advantages and disadvantages of AMT with a 'multi-disciplinary' 'expert' team from the organisation (Figure 10.1). The LRSP covered a five-year period. Performance criteria for AMT included financial and non-financial objectives. For example, detailed financial information was presented to the board in the form of perceived payback from AMT in addition to non-financial benefits such as increased flexibility, improved quality of process and product technology, better customer service, reduced waste and space savings. The plant manager said that sometimes qualitative benefits would be quantified, but this was not always possible in a five-year plan.

Where the Japanese approach differed significantly from Anglo/American approaches

Level		Term	
Top Management	T O P	Long range strategic plan	5 Years
Director	D O W N	Long range operational plan	3 Years
Manager		Annual operational plan	1 Year

Figure 10.1 Business planning architecture

to strategy formulation was in their emphasis upon implementation (Currie, 1994). Once the LRSP was agreed, a Long Range Operational Plan (LROP) was developed to cover all aspects of implementation. This plan was implemented under the direction of upper management and covered a three-year period. Although the strategic planning process was described as 'top down', it was actually a company-wide commitment and junior and middle level managers were expected to plan their activities to meet the overall corporate strategy.

Writing on the US strategy formulation process, Mintzberg and McHugh (1985, p.160) claim that

'Strategy making still tends to be equated with planning – with the systematic 'formulation' and articulation of deliberate, premeditated strategies, which are then 'implemented'.... This view of strategy, however, is unnecessarily restrictive; it is inconsistent with more contemporary forms of structure and sometimes with the conventional forms as well.... If strategy is defined only with intention, the researcher is reduced to studying perceptions, devoid of behaviour. Defining strategy with respect to realisation, however, enables the researcher to track the rise and fall of strategies in empirical terms'.

The authors therefore argue that empirical investigation should differentiate between deliberate strategies (intentions realised) and emergent strategies (patterns realised despite or in the absence of intentions).

Empirical research into Japanese companies (Currie, 1994) confirmed a strict adherence to a corporate strategic plan, although Japanese managers said that *ad hoc* sub-strategies emerged as a result of shifting markets for products and the rapid pace of technological change. For example, the Annual Operational Plan (AOP) was designed to track the progress of the LRSP and LROP. Whilst the AOP was largely introduced to monitor expenditure on capital equipment, labour and overhead, it also served to inform senior managers of necessary changes to the original performance milestones of the LRSP and LROP.

What was clear about the Japanese approach to strategy formulation and implementation was their commitment to working as part of a team. Individual ego was eclipsed by a desire to work towards a shared goal rather than for personal financial gain or promotion. Two important cultural explanations reinforced the stability of teamworking and cohesion. First, the tradition of life-time employment (at least in the large Japanese corporations comprising about 10% of the labour market) encouraged a long-term view of one's career goals and conduct. One interviewee said that 'a person loses something if he/she leaves to join another (rival) company). Indeed, the loss could be significant as the individual may lose all their accrued benefits and may be treated like a junior at their new company and re-trained accordingly. Second, the route to promotion was length of service, seniority and loyalty to one's company. Individualism and eagerness to 'shine' in addition to 'fast track' promotions were unusual' (Fruin, 1993).

Strategy formulation for AMT was further achieved by the effective restructuring of organisations. One Japanese electronics giant which was split into nineteen business groups had restructured to facilitate innovation, growth and market leadership (Figure 10.2). This company believed that technical innovation was too important to be managed in isolation of other activities. The company therefore 'pooled' technical expertise to assist in the formation, implementation and management of AMT strategy. As Figure 10.2 shows, the matrix structure was designed to provide the nineteen business groups with technical expertise from the Computer Aided Engineering (CAE) Division comprising 100 technical specialists, the Factory Automation (FA) Division comprising 1400 people and operating as a profit centre in its own right, and an Investment Committee where 20 directors and senior management considered a range of investment proposals from the various business groups. One manager said that, 'The business groups are encouraged to buy production technology from FA. If they want to go to West Germany for equipment, they are discouraged by the Investment Committee. This sometimes makes our lives difficult, but we are one of the most successful companies in Japan!'

The CAE and FA Divisions were described as 'internal consultancy'. However, individuals appointed to these Divisions were expected to act for the corporation by ensuring that the appropriate technology was installed in the business groups. On the subject of external management consultants, some Japanese managers were surprised that

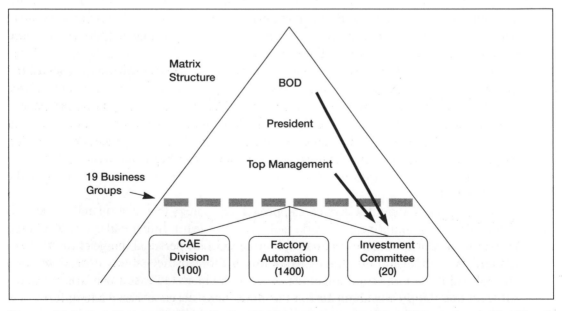

Figure 10.2 Creating a structure for technology management in a Japanese multinational

Anglo/American companies even considered using 'outsiders' for advice and guidance, particularly in crucial matters such as AMT strategy and implementation. Many Japanese companies 'outsourced' small IT projects, but their concern to retain control ensured that strategic decision making was kept strictly in-house.

Evaluating AMT in Japan

The significant reason for the scant attention paid to Japanese management accounting, particularly in the USA and UK, is because the methods and techniques used are 'traditional' and do not, in isolation, explain the Japanese 'miracle' or Japan's position as a 'world class manufacturer'. Indeed, Japanese management accounting has arguably played little part in Japan's post-war pursuit of economic success (Fruin, 1993). In fact, some Japanese managers described management accounting activities simply as 'good housekeeping'. Even the focus on cost reduction through the redeployment of direct labour suggests that while traditional accounting may *influence* rather than simply *inform* decision-makers (Hiromoto, 1988) manufacturing goals were nevertheless achieved by an all-embracing corporate strategy and not by cost-cutting alone. Japanese companies focused upon a wide array of multi-disciplinary financial and non-financial performance indicators and a strong 'engineering voice' was present at board level (Currie, 1994). Japanese managers' definition of JIT also differs from UK managers since it incorporates production management methods, Total Quality Management (TQM) and Total Preventive Maintenance (TPM). JIT was described as a 'simple all-embracing manufacturing philosophy' designed to continually improve manufacturing and reduce costs. Inventory control was just as important as preventive maintenance strategies. Many Japanese managers stressed that post-production-run maintenance shifts ensured the smooth running of the JIT system. Machine breakdown was addressed immediately and communicated to operators through the loud ringing of alarm bells. Indeed, operators were expected to carry out routine machine repairs and only alert maintenance staff if necessary (Currie and Seddon, 1991). Performance targets and achievements were also displayed on the shopfloor in many Japanese firms suggesting that JIT was more than a 'toolbox of techniques' (Cobb, 1991) or a system for inventory control (Lubben, 1988, Trick, 1990. Tidman, 1990).

Field research in Japan confirmed the view of Williams et al (1991) that deficiencies in management accounting addressed by Anglo/American academics and consultants are not considered important to Japanese practitioners. The following section considers this issue in relation to field work into five US manufacturing companies visited by the author in 1991.

Evaluating AMT in American manufacturing firms

Interviews with managers in five north-eastern US companies ranging from only forty employees to three thousand five hundred found that a three-year strategic plan for AMT was followed in only two companies (Currie, 1992). This signalled an immediate difference between US and Japanese manufacturing firms regarding strategic timescales for AMT implementation. Even where US companies were spending over $1million per annum on AMT, payback and/or ROI was expected within a year in two cases.

Interviewing the Treasurer (a management accountant) at a paper-making company, recently taken over by a Finnish firm, it was stressed that capital rationing had made it difficult to raise money for *new* equipment as opposed to *replacement* equipment. Advanced manufacturing technologies such as CAD and FMS, for example, were perceived by upper management as new technologies, whereas an investment in a paper-making machine was described as *replacement technology*. According to the Treasurer, 'The stringent demand for cost justification of AMT is a disincentive to innovation'. He gave the example (below) of the investment appraisal process for CAD.

Identifying productivity savings from CAD

The investment appraisal process at this company was administratively simple since a positive NPV was seen as adequate financial justification. Capital expenditure exceeding $50k required a signature from the president and all investments in AMT had to demonstrate their worth post-implementation. Five years ago the company invested in a CAD system to reduce manufacturing costs. This particular experience of CAD had proved unsatisfactory as 'the vendor subsequently went out of business'. As novices in CAD technology, lack of trained personnel and no supplier resulted in a 'support nightmare'. On reflection, the Treasurer said that ongoing vendor support was crucial and should have been considered in the investment appraisal process.

To avoid a recurrence of this situation the company had moved away from the *act of faith* approach to AMT investment in favour of a *methodical* and more stringent financial approach. Investment appraisal of CAD was therefore assessed by comparing the cost of manual drawing to automated design. However, the selection of performance indicators could be described as 'spurious'.

According to the Treasurer, 'Specific estimates of savings are based upon a combination of practical experience, and on experience gained during the pilot project. This company generates approximately 2000 drawings per year. Estimated time to generate a new drawing varies from two hours to a maximum approaching 80 hours, with an average of approximately 6 hours. Without the use of CAD software, it is estimated that design modification of an existing drawing (when practical) results in a 50 per cent saving (three hours based on the average drawing but higher for more complex shapes). CAD software has features which facilitate geometry modifications (i.e. stretching, re-positioning and associated re-dimensioning). With the use of CAD software the estimated savings resulting from design modification increases to 85 per cent (approximately five hours on average). It is estimated that successful retrievals will occur in approximately 15 per cent without the use of CAD software, and in approximately 50 per cent with the use of CAD software' (Currie, 1992). (See also Case Study p. 98.)

The Treasurer said that CAD was introduced to enhance performance in the following areas:

- enhance design retrieval
- improve design standardisation
- standardise process planning

- enhance production process (work cell formulation)
- enhance production scheduling

Engineers at the company were sceptical of this approach and described it as 'mechanical' and 'narrow in orientation'. They also pointed out that it was 'too quantitative' and 'failed to consider the quality of design work'. The fact that it was possible to 'retrieve' drawings was not important in isolation of design quality and customer requirements. This approach also 'failed to consider the skill and flair of individual engineers' and assumed equal status and ability of the design team.

Evaluating CAD

The Treasurer stressed that investment in CAD was only possible if a 'cast iron' financial case could be put to upper management. Using a Group Technology (GT) database, automated design work (CAD) had several cost advantages. He reflected on the *philosophy* behind the GT database. 'The basic philosophy of group technology is to analyse a collection of manufactured items and classify them into subsets (families) based on common attributes. A single manufactured item is readily identified as a member of a given subset by a GT code. There is a wide base of knowledge regarding how to formulate a GT classification. Perhaps the foremost criterion for determining the structure of a GT cost is its intended purpose' (Currie, 1992ab).

Table 10.2 gives the figures based upon the estimated time savings (man hours) using manual and automated (CAD) design work on the GT database. The time saving cost is deducted from the cost of using the GT database – the latter remaining fixed in both cases. The estimated cost savings using CAD against manual methods are much higher. The Treasurer conceded that, 'Because CAD typically permits more complex modifications to be performed in a simpler manner, a higher percentage of drawings are modifiable. This leads to a greater retrieval rate'.

Activity	Manual Drawings Using Group Technology Database	CAD Drawings and Group Technology Database
Cost GT DAtabase	$ (6,900)	$ (6,900)
Drawing Savings	12,600	98,700
BOM/Routing Saving	8,500	28,500
Total	**14,200 PA**	**120,300 PA**

Table 10.2 Estimated savings from group technology and CAD

The GT database cost $6,900. This figure was calculated from a 'ten minute search' for a drawing on the database. This is equal to 330 man-hours at a cost of $21 per hour ($6,930) or 2000 (drawings) multiplied by ten minutes (1/6th hour). Similar calculations were made for the time saving advantages of the GT database whilst undertaking manual and CAD design work in addition to the time savings in modifications of existing drawings stored on the GT database (i.e. stretching, re-positioning and associated re-dimensioning).

The Treasurer produced a document which concluded that, 'In either case of a CAD or non-CAD environment some additional benefits will also occur in the manufacturing area. Manufacturing engineering and pre-production planning review engineering drawings and prepare Bill of Materials and Routings. At this company six people are involved with this process approximately thirty per cent of their time. The other seventy per cent involves similar work on non-company x designs and on miscellaneous support activities. When BOM and associated routings can be retrieved and modified, a conservative estimate is that between sixty and seventy per cent savings can be achieved. With a fifteen per cent retrieval rate (non-CAD environment) the estimated savings are 390 man hours (approximately $8,500). With a fifty per cent retrieval rate (CAD environment) the estimated savings are 1,300 man hours (approximately $28,000)'. Figure 10.3 gives a comparison between estimated manual drawing times and proposed options (using CAD).

In spite of attempts to quantify some of the qualitative advantages from CAD, engineering managers felt that the real justification for CAD was fivefold: process innovation, product innovation, better quality, ability to undertake complex design work and ease of modification/retrieval. One engineer said, 'Without CAD, we simply couldn't produce complex mechanical and electrical design drawings – which means we wouldn't be able to compete in the domestic, let alone international marketplace'. A further criticism by engineers was the 'short-term payback' from CAD expected by upper management. It was stressed that, 'Any new purchase of software requires a learning period. In the case of CAD, it takes nine months to become proficient in using it. This

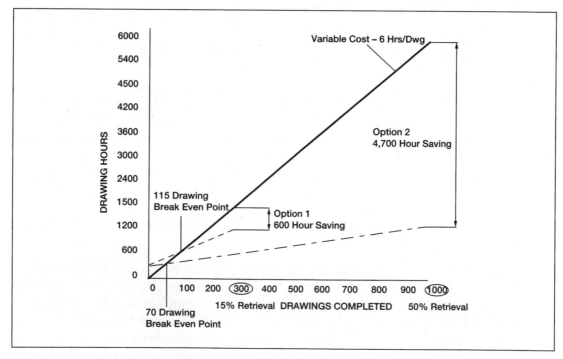

Figure 10.3 Comparison between manual drawing times and proposed options

means you have a further three months to meet the payback period'. The present investment appraisal process for CAD also assumed a fixity in skills profile and productivity rates of engineers, customer orders, competition, annual number and quality of drawings, delivery times and obsolescence of hardware/software. Given these factors, engineers argued it was difficult to produce hard statistics about likely productivity gains from CAD in an ever-changing organisational and external climate (Currie, 1994).

Evaluating AMT in British manufacturing firms

Research into five UK manufacturing companies on accounting and AMT strategy highlighted many dissimilarities with the Japanese experience. Capital rationing programmes in three companies affecting all functional areas had forced accountants and production engineers to identify cost savings through AMT. In parallel with the US company described above, the capital budgetary framework in UK companies signalled strategic intentions. Yet the relationship between strategic aspiration and practical implementation was somewhat tenuous. This was also the case in an earlier study into the evaluation and implementation of CAD in twenty UK companies between 1985-88 (Currie, 1989a).

Peculiar to the British experience was the perception of engineering managers that capital budgeting for AMT was an *art form* characterised by *game playing* and numerical manipulation. Two reasons were paramount. First, the strong 'accounting voice' at senior management level reflected a lack of understanding about the strategic capabilities of AMT for manufacturing. Engineers were keen to stress that whilst the techniques of investment appraisal for CAD equipment were 'easy to understand and apply', upper managements' preference for a narrow range of financial performance indicators excluded important non-financial considerations. In parallel with Japanese manufacturers, UK companies emphasised labour-centred measures but, unlike the former, imposed short-term payback periods for CAD investment.

Second, strategic evaluation of AMT omitted associated costs such as training, skills development (including project management skills), vendor services (maintenance/support contracts) and software updates. To circumvent what was described as a 'narrow financial focus' by senior managers, engineers said that necessary AMT-related expenditure would be allocated to other budgets. For example, a two-day software update course would be met by a centralised training budget, although this form of expenditure was strictly AMT related. More serious problems arose when engineers wished to purchase the latest software update and found that money was unavailable until the next financial period. The study therefore concluded that capital budgeting for AMT was a fragmented and *ad hoc* managerial activity with little cross-fertilisation between functional or hierarchical levels. Payback periods for AMT were particularly short and failed to address issues of skills shortages (i.e. programming languages), training needs and vendor/clients relationships relating to support (Currie, 1989abc). These findings are reinforced by other academic studies on UK management accounting (Dugdale and Jones, 1990, 1991. NEDO, 1989).

Applying investment appraisal at a British car plant

An interesting empirical observation on the UK experience was the tendency to employ simple payback methods rather than the more complicated DCF techniques in evaluating AMT (Jones et al, 1993. Dugdale and Jones, 1990, 1991). At a UK automobile plant, a senior production engineer said that greater financial controls were now imposed on all capital expenditure. In the case of AMT, a sound financial case was the single most important factor in investment appraisal. Whilst he was not opposed to providing detailed financial evaluation for proposed expenditure on AMT, he was highly critical of the 'fragmented approach' adopted by the organisation. Figure 10.4 outlines the key stages in the investment appraisal process for AMT. First the project engineer devises a cost proposal which forecasts the benefits of investing in, say, a new CAD system. This is discussed with the engineering manager who assesses the proposed investment according to its strategic importance to the department/plant. The cost proposal is then sent to a project analyser (who may be a trainee management accountant) for scrutiny. Cost proposals exceeding $1 million are sent to the USA for approval (rubber stamping). The accounting function checks the figures and records the expected cost savings before proceeding with the order.

According to the senior production engineer, the whole process may last nine months and sometimes a year. He pointed out that often the project analyser failed to grasp the meaning behind engineering terminology used to justify the proposed expenditure. Information was thus 'diluted' to facilitate understanding and occasionally lost its meaning. Apparently, poor communication characterised the investment appraisal process since accountants and engineers occupied 'separate buildings' and used 'different canteens'. As Jones et al (1993, p.125) argue,

> 'Divisions between accountants and engineers tend to fragment AMT decision making and, although organisational patterns differ, even the most integrated forms of middle management decision-making do not correspond to Japanese 'team management'. Accountants are either remote from production, or are restricted in their participation in planning teams by their narrowly specialised knowledge and skills'.

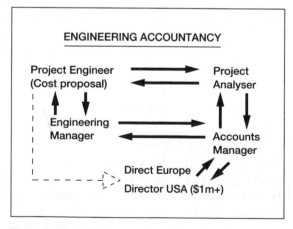

Figure 10.4 The process of capital budgeting at a British car plant

AMT and JIT

The fragmentation of AMT decision making was no more apparent than in the pursuit of *new manufacturing philosophies* such as JIT. Unlike the Japanese approach which perceived JIT as an holistic (company-wide) approach to world class manufacturing status, many UK companies saw JIT as an inventory control system (Currie and Seddon, 1992). Indeed, one or two UK companies had confined JIT implementation to the responsibility of an individual engineering manager (Currie, 1991b). At the UK automobile manufacturer (described above), JIT appeared to be perceived separately from technology decisions. For example, preventive maintenance (PM) was carried out in isolation of a wider manufacturing plan and was the sole responsibility of the maintenance department. In recent months maintenance had been streamlined in line with the corporate labour elimination policy. Such measures had significantly affected the service offered to production (see Figure 10.5). According to one maintenance manager, 'They (upper management) seem to like it when a machine breaks down because they see us working. They don't like the idea of us reading newspapers in the maintenance crib'. Such short-sightedness on the part of senior management had resulted in a firefighting approach taken by maintenance, where preventive work had given way to simply fixing machines at the point of breakdown (usually several hours after). Maintenance costs were treated as 'overhead' and, whilst production engineers received monthly reports on machine breakdown, this information was not costed and highlighted in accounting reports. Nor was it required by senior executives.

Whilst many academic studies urge the need for effective maintenance policies (More, 1987. Hughes, 1988. Kruger, 1988. Stevens, 1989. Pintleton and Van Wassenhove, 1990. Willmott, 1990ab) the UK experience suggests an absence of Japanese-style TPM. Even Anglo/American and Japanese comparative studies show that the two-shift production

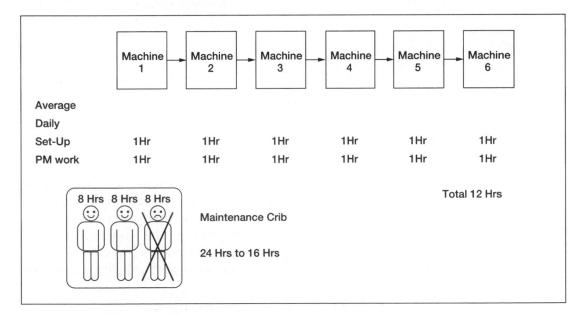

Figure 10.5 Labour elimination in the maintenance function

system adopted by Toyota, Kamigo is more productive (inventory, products, operators, wages, line rate/day, labour engines/hours) than the three-shift system of the UK car manufacturer (Schonberger, 1986. Currie, 1994). Part of the reason is the emphasis upon TPM and the importance attached to short maintenance shifts following production runs.

The failure to support maintenance activities at the UK car plant became apparent over time as PM actions decreased (e.g. to maintain equipment) in conjunction with an increase in machine failure (see Figure 10.6). The shortfall of maintenance personnel meant that only 90 per cent of PM work could be carried out according to an agreed schedule. Over time the decrease in PM work was reflected by an increase in machine failure, so that downtime increased to 61 per cent. Even at the end of the year, downtime was running at 58 per cent (uptime = 42 per cent) although the forecast year end uptime was 60 per cent (Figure 10.7).

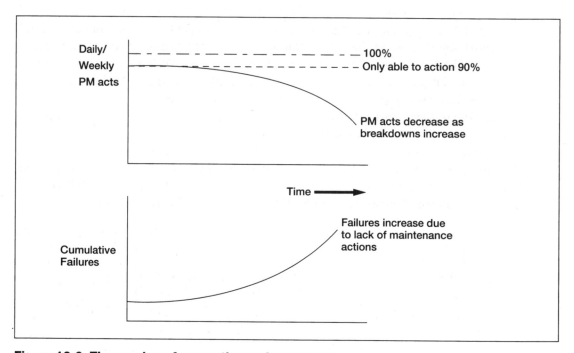

Figure 10.6 The erosion of preventive maintenance

This example reflected the difference between strategic intentions and actual practice and suggested that key performance indicators were not communicated to management accountants and senior executives. In addition, the pursuit of labour elimination went little way to increase production efficiency. On the contrary, the tendency of senior executives to view production problems of labour shortages, poor machine performance and lack of capital investment as issues for production managers highlighted an absence of a manufacturing strategy.

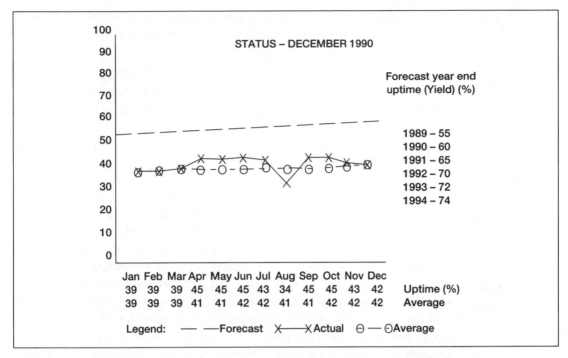

Figure 10.7 Production line uptime at an automotive manufacturer (*Source:* Currie and Seddon, 1991)

Management accounting and AMT in West Germany

Management accounting in West German companies has gained little attention in academic and business circles, although several studies focus upon production methods and techniques (Schonberger, 1986, 1989. Williams et al, 1989. Lawrence, 1980. Campbell et al, 1989). Much of this research emphasises the strong *engineering voice* at the apex of West German manufacturing firms and their underlying commitment to capital investment and R & D (Hirst and Zeitlin, 1989. Sorge and Warner, 1986. Glover and Kelly, 1992). The recent preoccupation by western academics with the *Japanese miracle* is similar to past interests in the success of West German manufacturing industry (Finniston, 1978. Sorge, 1979). The impetus behind these studies is to explain the relative decline of UK manufacturing compared with other industrialised nations (Thompson, 1989. Williams et al, 1983). But instead of management accounting theory and practice occupying centre stage, researchers have attributed economic success to industrial policy, manufacturing techniques, human resource practice, the education system and even the backgound of senior managers.

A recent comparative study on West German and UK management accounting concluded that

'A comparison with German theory and practice in engineering suggests that British management accounting overemphasises the single-minded pursuit of profit. This may have contributed to

Britain's relative industrial decline. German management accounting was found to be more modest in its goals, more restricted in its use and more accurate in content' (Strange, 1991).

In a recent comparative study on management accounting and AMT in six West German manufacturing companies with similar Anglo/American and Japanese firms, it was found that the role of management accounting neither helped nor inhibited AMT strategy. In fact, the practice of management accounting in West Germany was similar to the Japanese experience.

For example, DCF was used in only two of the five West German companies (and in only one out of eight Japanese firms). One West German engineering manager said that, 'Ten years ago we installed CAD. At the time it was a bit of an experiment as nobody knew much about CAD, or what it could achieve. After about a year, two of our senior designers became very knowledgeable about it. They designed a database (i.e. a collection of all our production drawings). Initially we thought CAD was an expensive toy and we could not demonstrate that it had any cost advantages whatsoever. However, after about eighteen months, we saw the real benefits. We could retrieve and modify drawings from our newly acquired database. This helped to reduce design lead times as our drawings reached production much more quickly. In short, CAD has been vital in design and production. But it is impossible to quantify the many hours of intellectual effort and the painstaking attention to detail of our engineers. This is why a DCF is not appropriate to capital projects of this type. Implementing new technology costs more than the price of the hardware and software packages. Perhaps if the true costs of AMT were known, there would not be any future investment!'

West German companies devised AMT strategies at senior executive level where engineers often outnumbered finance directors (Table 10.3). Long-term (five year) strategies were also implemented as part of an all-embracing manufacturing strategy (incorporating JIT, TQM, SPC, etc). Interestingly, cost justification for AMT was often undertaken by engineers in West German firms because 'it is important to understand the technical

	(1) Machine Tools For Sheet Metal	(2) Consumer Goods (Plastics, Detergents and Food)	(3) Components For Textile Industry	(4) Textiles	(5) Components For Automobile Industry	(6) Control Units For Machine Tools
How are decisions taken by management to acquire AMT, e.g. committees/ working groups/ project teams/ functional heads/ individuals etc?	Project teams reporting to the Board	Interdisciplinary work groups	Director level (engineering)	Director level (engineering)	Steering group (engineers, accounting, sales and planning)	Director level (engineering)
How many levels of management hierarchy are involved in capital budgeting for AMT?	5	3	2	2–3	1	2
Do you use Discounted Cash Flow for AMT? (if yes, please give time period in years)	Not used	2 years	3 years	Not used	Not used	Not used

Table 10.3 Management of AMT in West Germany

capabilities of technology which lead to competitive advantage'. Unlike the Japanese, however, West German managers were keen to differentiate between *new* and *dedicated* (traditional) technology. They argued that whilst conventional management accounting was more easily applied to the latter, it was unsuitable for cost justification of AMT.

AMT and performance measures

West German and Japanese manufacturing firms also shared a similar choice of performance indicators for AMT. Only one West German manager at a textiles firm said that labour elimination strategies were expected from AMT investment (Table 10.4). This same company also hoped to increase productivity through AMT unlike the remaining five who claimed that productivity was not a key performance indicator. Instead there was a great emphasis on the reduction of product lead times through CAD, FMS and robots in the two countries. JIT was also part of a wide-ranging manufacturing strategy and not to be confused as a technique for inventory control. Like Japanese companies, West German manufacturers prided themselves on possessing a thorough understanding of production and information technology. Skills development and training at all levels were a key priority. One West German manager commented, 'If I believed everything I read in vendor literature, I would have invested in every CAD system or CNC machine I had come across. The truth is, you need a lot of skill and judgement when you do a feasibility study on AMT. Many of our engineers know more about CNC machines than the vendors, and more importantly, the shortcomings of the machines'.

What are the criteria for assessing the benefits of from AMT?	(1) Machine Tools For Sheet Metal	(2) Consumer Goods (Plastics, Detergents and Food)	(3) Components For Textile Industry	(4) Textiles	(5) Components For Automobile Industry	(6) Control Units For Machine Tools
(1) Increase productivity	No	No	No	Yes	No	No
(2) Minimise capital in work-in-progress	Yes	No	No	No	No	No
(3) Shorten lead times	Yes	Yes	Yes	Yes	Yes	No
(4) Increase flexibility	Yes	Yes	Yes	Yes	Yes	Yes
(5) Improve quality of manufactured components	Yes	No	No	No	Yes	No
(6) Delivery to customers	Yes	Yes	Yes	Yes	Yes	Yes
(7) Reduce headcount	No	No	No	Yes	No	No
(8) Develop process technology	Yes	Yes	Yes	No	Yes	Yes
(9) Reduce R&D costs	Yes	Yes	Yes	No	Yes	Yes

Table 10.4 Performance measurement of AMT

Recognising the pitfalls of conventional management accounting theory and practice, West German companies had no plans to introduce ABC or any other *new cost management system*. Alternatively, most said that accounting information had to be used in conjunction with non-financial (qualitative) considerations. An interesting observation from the West German study (and one which is reinforced in the work of Strange, 1991) was that management accountants were trained in production engineering cost accounting techniques and seemed to agree with engineers about the full range of strategic (financial and non-financial) benefits from AMT.

Concluding remarks

Comparative field research in Japan, the USA, UK and West Germany highlights many similarities and dissimilarities regarding strategy formulation, evaluation and implementation of new manufacturing technology. While it is unwise to offer general explanations in isolation of the wider organisational and societal context, some tentative conclusions will nevertheless be put forward. In respect of the US and UK interest in identifying a *problem* with traditional accounting and proposing a *solution* to develop new accounting methods and techniques, Japanese and West German managers did not perceive this as a worthwhile challenge. In particular, Japanese managers used management accounting to assist in developing AMT strategy to achieve a variety of short- and long-term benefits relating to lead times, market share, process and product innovation, skills development, space reduction, waste and maintenance. The US and UK, on the other hand, seemed more determined to pursue short-term profit and labour elimination through technology (Gerwin, 1982. Drucker, 1988, 1990. Hayes and Jaikumar, 1988).

A significant finding was also the comparative occupational status of management accountants in the four countries. Whilst the UK (and to a lesser extent the USA) placed accounting at centre stage, where they enjoyed a trusted and influential position (Armstrong, 1985, 1987ab), technology decisions in Japan were taken by multidisciplinary (technical) expert teams and, in West Germany, predominantly by engineers (many of whom occupying board level positions).

Comparative observations on the use of management accounting methods and techniques showed that Japanese and West German firms tended to use simple payback. Anglo/American companies also used payback but also attempted DCF for the more expensive forms of AMT investment. As one UK car manufacturer stressed, high capital expenditure on production technology and increased risk had forced senior executives to impose tighter financial controls. Similarly, the desire to achieve financial returns from CAD equipment at a US firm produced some creative accounting of labour productivity and design output (see Pike, 1983).

The fusing of technology decisions with manufacturing methods (JIT, TQM, TPM) further pointed to cross-national differences. The Japanese emphasis on LRSP, LROP and AOP using JIT and production technology as two important factors in achieving business goals was dissimilar to the more fragmented approaches adopted by Anglo/American and even West German companies. Moreover, JIT practised in Japan was a team effort and not driven by a figurehead personality as is often the case in Anglo/American firms.

In conclusion it is argued that detailed comparative field research is an appropriate research method for attaining insights into the strategic goals and practices of contemporary organisations. However, as the chapter demonstrates, any discussion of management accounting practice and AMT strategy needs to be placed in a wider organisational and societal context. Recommendations for future research may therefore address comparative cross-national differences of management accounting theory and practice, AMT strategy and implementation and occupational groupings (accountants, engineers, human resources, etc) at both the company, institutional and governmental levels.

Case study

Developing a decision support system (DSS) for a UK car manufacturer

Background

This company was facing severe global competition, particularly from the Japanese car manufacturing industry which was now operating successfully in the UK. To face growing competition head-on, management had embarked upon a number of *change programmes* such as TQM and JIT, among others. Japanese management methods were looked upon favourably by management, yet the company struggled to replace rigid structures with more flexible ways of working. One such flexible system was perceived as the JIT *philosophy*. JIT comprises three essential components. It is a set of production management methods and techniques; a total quality assurance system; and a total preventive maintenance (TPM) system. It is argued that such an holistic approach to JIT will only succeed if all the components are given adequate attention (Wu et al, 1992). However, JIT is interpreted differently by academics and practitioners alike. Some see JIT in narrow terms, such as inventory control, whereas others consider JIT to be more ambitious in its aims and objectives. Generally, JIT is concerned to improve performance by reducing costs, increasing work flows and decreasing waste. In this case study, we consider only one area of JIT – TPM. The purpose of the case study is to illustrate the key issues in the development and implementation of a DSS to enhance production efficiency through adequate machine maintenance methods.

Using a DSS for TPM

Over the past thirty years there have been significant changes in customer requirements and expectations. These can be seen as high reliability, high quality and low cost. The only way the product can meet this is through a more technologically advanced manufacturing environment. Just as the manufacturing process has changed, so too have machine failure patterns. For example, traditional dedicated technologies have now been replaced by advanced manufacturing technologies in the form of Computer Aided Design/Computer Aided Manufacturing, Flexible Manufacturing Systems, Computer Numerical Control Systems, Robots, and others. This means that the maintenance requirements and schedules must also change. For if technology is to be maintained adequately, costly occurrences caused by machine downtime, scrap and rework are avoided. In other words, the accent is on *right-first-time*.

But maintenance of technology is neither a glamorous nor particularly interesting aspect of production. This was found to be the case at the company concerned, where senior management delegated the development of maintenance schedules to production managers and operators. Similarly, information technology to record and monitor machine performance was also under the domain of these individuals. Seemingly, senior managers were disinterested in machine performance statistics, even though persistent problems of machine downtime affected bottom-line financial performance of the company.

Over the past few years, this company found that machine downtime was persistently high, sometimes as much as 60 per cent of the time. Every time a machine stopped working, crucial work-in-progress schedules were seriously affected, leading to massive bottlenecks in production. This not only affected internal production scheduling, but also the delivery of incoming *raw* materials and outgoing finished or partially-finished products. In turn, machine downtime was particularly damaging to staff morale, as production managers sometimes blamed the operators for the problems. Maintenance staff were also accused of poor machine maintenance practices, leading to persistent breakdowns.

Whilst the problem was complex and many faceted, it seemed that old practices needed to be replaced by new ones. In other words, a total re-thinking of the maintenance process.

The commonly held belief of a time-dependent failure can only be associated with a simple machine (see Figure 10.8).

As seen in the figure, these simple machines belong to the first technological stage. These machines were built from standardised components which meant only a few different failure modes existed. In an attempt to remove such modes, parts were over-engineered. The reliability inherent with a complex production line (technological levels IV and V) are very different to those from this earlier stage. A report published by the Federal Aviation Authority (FAA) stated, '...after careful consideration, the committee is convinced that reliability and overhaul time control are not necessarily related topics' (Nolan and Heap, 1979). The reasons for this statement can be seen in Figure 10.9.

Whereas the original belief in replacing parts before a certain time made sense with simple equipment, it worsened the condition for the more complex. The curves show that 89% of all component failures observed with advanced equipment would not benefit by a planned maintenance action.

The fundamental question of whether the appropriate maintenance methodology was being used was asked by the company concerned. In an attempt to answer it, a DSS was developed. The two most significant influences upon determining an appropriate maintenance action are:

1. Does it matter if the part fails? If so, what are the costs?
2. What is the interval between warning of possible failure and failure occurring?

The only way these questions can be answered when historical volumes of data are low is through a dynamic database. The failure of each item can be compared with the current preventive maintenance schedule and previous similar failures. Through the analysis of such events, future preventive maintenance actions can be

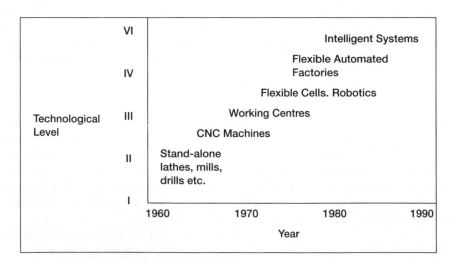

Figure 10.8 Technological developments in manufacturing
(*Courtesy:* Milacic and McWaters, 1987)

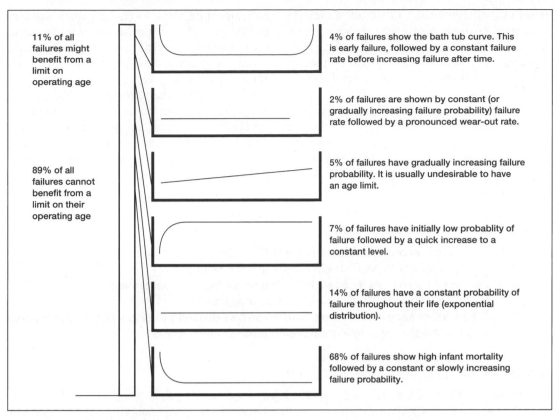

11% of all failures might benefit from a limit on operating age

89% of all failures cannot benefit from a limit on their operating age

4% of failures show the bath tub curve. This is early failure, followed by a constant failure rate before increasing failure after time.

2% of failures are shown by constant (or gradually increasing failure probability) failure rate followed by a pronounced wear-out rate.

5% of failures have gradually increasing failure probability. It is usually undesirable to have an age limit.

7% of failures have initially low probablity of failure followed by a quick increase to a constant level.

14% of failures have a constant probability of failure throughout their life (exponential distribution).

68% of failures show high infant mortality followed by a constant or slowly increasing failure probability.

Figure 10.9 Complete set of age-reliability curves (*Courtesy:* Nowlan and Heap, 1979)

developed. The purpose of the DSS was to have all the information associated with each machine, accessible by the engineers. The maintenance of each machine follows a continuous loop of:

1. Planning what actions need to be undertaken
2. Carrying out these tasks
3. Comparison of failures against previous actions

This DSS was to complement the work which was currently undertaken. Rather than attempt to impose any new structure to their work, the methods currently used were to be optimised. The existing Preventive Maintenance (PM) policy was used to define all the potential failure conditions which existed. This information had key words which related to failure types. Clearly the description of an electrical failure contains different words to that of a hydraulic failure.

For each of these failure conditions, the system would select key words from the text which was entered by the operator and match them against pre-defined terms and relations of words. If the user was specific in defining a particular part number, then the database could be searched for previous occurrences. On the other hand, if a general error text was used, for example 'water hose burst', then the error had to be further enhanced. The system would match previous failures using the terms used and display groups related to them. These could be 'machine clamping head', 'machine slide', and 'machine eject system'.

Having selected the sub-set, the process would, if possible, show a list of similar failures and the preventive maintenance rules which should have prevented the failure from occurring. If the new failure matched any, the details are saved in the associated table. If not, they are saved in a different area. Based upon the data contained in these tables, the preventive maintenance acts can be constructively revised. Data contained in the latter table would be used to define new actions which are currently not in existence.

The DSS was to provide a direct feedback to the operators' information which can then be used to alter their previous acts. In a dynamic cycle the maintenance team are involved in all stages of the development process. The use of such a system enhanced maintenance actions in two important ways. First, their work was seen as having a direct input to the manufacturing cycle. Their failure reports were used in a structured way rather than being ignored. Their activities became a key part to the machine's reliability, rather than providing a fire-fighting cover. Second, the status of the maintenance function increased as information about machine downtime and failure could be used strategically. In this respect, accountants were provided with information for cost control purposes.

Discussion questions

1 What was the rationale for developing a DSS for the maintenance function?
2 Why is it important to prevent failure from occurring?
3 Should senior managers receive information about machine performance?
4 How can accountants use the information strategically?
5 List the performance improvements which can be obtained by using a DSS of this nature.
6 How is knowledge, information and data organised using a DSS?

References 10

Abegglen, J. C., Stalk, G. (1985) *Kaisha: The Japanese Corporation*, Basic Books.

Armstrong, P. (1985) 'Changing managerial control strategies: the role of competition between accounting and other organisational professions'. *Accounting, Organisations and Society*, Vol. 10, No. 2, pp. 192–148.

Armstrong, P. (1987a) 'Engineers, management and trust', *Work Employment and Society*, No. 4, pp. 1–28.

Armstrong, P. (1987b) 'The rise of accounting controls in British capitalist enterprises', *Accounting, Organisations and Society*, Vol. 12, No. 5, pp. 415–436.

Bromwich, M. (1991) 'Accounting Information For Strategic Excellence'. Paper presented at the Management Accounting Research Conference, LSE, April.

Bhimani, A. and Bromwich, M. (1989) *Management Accounting: Evolution Not Revolution*, CIMA.

Blankinsop, S.A. and Burns, N. (1992) 'Performance measurement revisited', *International Journal of Operations and Production Management*, Vol, 12, No. 10. pp. 16–25.

Cobb, I. (1991). 'Understanding and working with JIT'. *Management Accounting*, 69, 2, pp 44–46.

Cooper, R. and Kaplan, R. (1988) 'Measure costs right: make the right decisions', *Harvard Business Review*, Sept/Oct, pp.96–103.

Cooper, R. (1989) 'You need a new cost system when.', *Harvard Business Review*, Jan/Feb, pp. 77–82.

Cooper, R. (1991) 'Explicating the logic of ABC'. *Management Accounting*, 68, 10.

Coulhurst, N. (1989) 'Justifying the new factory'. *Management Accounting*, 68, 4, pp. 26–28.

Crump, L. (1989) 'Japanese managers, western workers: cross-cultural training as development issues', *Management Development*, 8 (4), 48–55.

Currie, W.L. (1989a) *Managerial Strategies For New Technology*, Aldershot, Gower.

Currie, W.L. (1989b) 'The art of justifying new technology to top managers', *OMEGA: The International Journal of Management Science*, 17, 5, pp. 409–418.

Currie, W.L. (1991a) 'Managing Technology: a crisis in management accounting?' *Management Accounting*, February, pp. 24–27.

Currie, W.L. (1991b) 'Managing production technology in Japan'. *Management Accounting*,

July/August, 6.

Currie, W.L. and Seddon, J. (1991) 'Developing management information systems for manufacturing', paper presented to the Northeast Manufacturing Technology Centre, Rensellaer Polytechnic Institute, Troy, New York State, USA, July.

Currie, W.L. and Seddon, J. (1992) 'Managing AMT in a JIT environment in the UK and Japan'. *British Journal of Management*, September.

Currie, W.L. (1992a) 'The strategic management of AMT in Japan, the USA, the UK and West Germany', Part 1: Developing a performance measurement system for CAD in a US manufacturing company', *Management Accounting*, November. Vol, 70, No. 11.

Currie, W.L. (1992b) 'The Strategic Management of AMT in Japan, the USA, the UK and West Germany: Managing AMT in a UK automotive plant', *Management Accounting*, December. Vol, 70, No. 12.

Currie, W.L. (1993a) 'The Strategic Management of AMT in Japan, the USA, the UK and West Germany: Developing AMT strategy for world class manufacturing', *Management Accounting*, January. Vol, 71, No. 1.

Currie, W.L. (1994) *The Strategic Management of AMT*. CIMA: London.

Czinkota, M. R. and Kotabe, M. eds. (1993) *The Japanese Distribution System*, Probus Publishing Company: Cambridge, UK.

Drucker, P. (1988) 'The coming of the new organisation'. *Harvard Business Review*, Jan/Feb.

Drucker, P. (1990) 'The emerging theory of manufacturing'. *Harvard Business Review*, May/June.

Drury, C (1989) 'Activity based costing', *Management Accounting*, September.

Dugdale, D., and Jones, T.C. (1990) Accountants' perceptions of investment appraisal, Management Accounting Research Conference, Aston, September.

Dugdale, D., and Jones, T. C. (1991) 'Discordant voices: accounting views of investment appraisal', *Management Accounting*, November, 54–59.

Ferguson, P (1988) 'Accounting for JIT: sorting out conflicting advice', *Management Accounting*, December.

Financial Times (1991) Survey on Computerised Manufacturing, 14th May.

Finniston, M. (1978) *Engineering Our Future*, HMSO, London.

Fruin, W. M. (1993) *The Japanese Enterprise System*. Oxford: Clarendon Press.

Gerwin, D. (1982) 'Do's and dont's of computerised manufacturing'. *Harvard Business Review*, March/April, pp. 107–116.

Gilbert, J.P. (1989). 'The state of JIT implementation and development in the USA'. *International Journal of Production Research*, 28, 6, pp. 1099–1109.

Glover, I. and Kelly, M. P. (1992) 'Engineering better management: sociology and the Finniston Report', in G. Payne and M. Cross (eds) *Sociology In Action*, MacMillan: London.

Hayes, R. H. and Abernathy, W.J. (1980) 'Managing our way to economic decline'. *Harvard Business Review*. July/August.

Hayes, R. H. and Jaikumar, R. (1988) 'Manufacturing's crisis: new technologies, obsolete organisations'. *Harvard Business Review*, Sept/Oct.

Hayes, R.H. and Wheelright, S. C. (1984) *Restoring Our Competitive Edge: Competing Through Manufacturing*, Wiley.

Hiromoto, T. (1988) 'Another hidden edge: Japanese management accounting', *Harvard Business Review*, July/August.

Hughes, W., 1988 Developments in reliability centred maintenance and its application to achieve cost effective maintenance in the process industry. *The 1988 Maintenance Management Convention Proceedings*, in association with P-E Corporate Services SA (PTY) Ltd.

Im, J.H. and Lee, S.M. (1989) 'Implementation of just-in-time systems in US manufacturing firms'. *International Journal of Operations and Production Management*, 9, pp. 5–14.

Inman, R.A. and Mehra, S. (1990). 'The transferability of just-in-time concepts to American small businesses'. *Interfaces*, 20, 2, pp. 30–37.

Jones, A.K.V. (1990) 'Quality Management the Nissan Way', B.G. Plunkett and J.J. Dale, (eds.), *Managing Quality*, London: Philip Allen.

Jones, C., Currie, W. Dugdale, D. (1993) 'Accounting and technology in Britain and Japan: learning from field research'. *Management Accounting Research*. Vol, 4, pp. 109–137.

Kaplan, R. (1984) 'Yesterday's accounting undermines production'. *Harvard Business Review*, July/August, pp. 95–101.

Kaplan, R. (1985) 'Accounting lag: the obsolescence of cost accounting systems', in Clark, K. and Lorenze, C. (eds.), *Technology and Productivity: The Uneasy Alliance*. Harvard Business School.

Kaplan, R. (1986) 'Must CIM be justified by faith alone?' *Harvard Business Review*, March/April.

Kelly, A. (1991). 'An overview of organisational change and human factors in maintenance management'. 14th National Maintenance Management Show 1991.

Kharbanda, O. and Stallworthy, E. (1991) 'Let's learn from Japan'. *Management Accounting*, 69, 3.

King, W.R. and Sethi, V. (1993) 'Developing transitional information systems: a case study', *OMEGA: International Journal of Management Science*, Vol, 21. No. 1.

Kruger, T.C.B. (1988). 'Management of the total maintenance system with special reference to the quality of maintenance'. SA Airways.

Kumazawa, M. and Yamada, J. (1989) 'Jobs and skills under the lifelong Nenko employment practice', in Wood, S. (ed), *The Transformation of Work?*, London, Unwin Hyman, pp. 103–126.

Lawrence, P. (1980) *Managers and Management in West Germany*. St Martin's Press.

Lubben, R (1988) *Just-In-Time Manufacturing*. McGraw-Hill.

March Consultancy (1989). *The DTI report on Maintenance*.

Maskell, B (1989) 'Performance measurement for world class manufacturing', *Management Accounting*. Part IV, September.

Milacic, V. R. and McWaters, J. F. (1987) *Diagnostic and Preventative Maintenance Strategies in Manufacturing Systems*. Berlin: North Holland.

Mintzberg, H. and McHugh, A. (1985) 'Strategy formation in an adhocracy', *Administrative Science Quarterly*, 30, pp. 160–197.

More, J. (1987). 'Apathy jeopardises AMT investment'. *Production Engineer*, 66, 9, pp. 21–22.

Morgan, M. and Weerakoon, P. (1989) *Japanese Management Accounting: Its Contribution to the Japanese Economic Miracle*. Penguin.

Moyes, J (1988) 'The dangers of JIT'. *Management Accounting*, February.

Nakajima, S. (1988). *Introduction to TPM*. Productivity Press.

Nixon, B. Sundgaard, E. Sinclair, D. (1993) 'Industry and the City: is R&D the key?', *Accountancy*, Jan.

Noble, J. (1989) 'Techniques for cost justifying CIM'. *The Journal Of Business Strategy,* Jan/Feb.

Oliver, N. and Wilkinson, B (1987) 'Just-in-time, just-too-soon?' *Industrial Society Magazine*, Sept.

Pang, K.K. and Oliver, N. (1988) 'Personnel strategy in eleven Japanese manufacturing companies in the UK', *Personnel Review*, 17, 3, pp. 16–21.

Pascale, R. and Athos, A. (1981) *The Art of Japanese Management*, Penguin.

Pavitt, K. (1991) 'Key characteristics of the large innovating firm'. *British Journal of Management*, 2, 1, pp. 41–50.

Phillips, J. (1992) 'Understanding profitability in the insurance industry'. *CMA Magazine*, November.

Pike, R.H. (1983) 'A review of recent trends in formal capital budgeting processes', *Accounting and Business Research*, Summer, 201–208.

Pintelton, L.M. and Van Wassenhove, L.N. (1990) 'A maintenance management tool'. *OMEGA: International Journal of Management Science*, 18, 1, pp. 59–70.

Ramsey, J. (1985) 'Just too late', *Purchasing Supply Management*, pp. 22-23.

Sakurai, M. (1990) 'The influence of factory automation on management accounting practices: a study of Japanese companies', pp. 45–57, in R. Kaplan (ed) *Measures for manufacturing excellence*, Harvard Business School Press.

Schonberger, R. (1982). *Japanese Manufacturing Techniques: nine hidden lessons in simplicity*. New York: The Free Press.

Schonberger, R. (1986). *World Class Manufacturing*. The Free Press.

Schonberger, R. (1990). *Building a Chain of Customers*. Hutchinson Business Books.

Scicon Ltd. (1990). COMPASS Product Description. Issue 2.0.

Sepehri, M. (1986). *Just In Time: Not Just In Japan*. American Production and Inventory Control Society.

Seddon, J.J.M. and Currie, W (1991) 'Developing a maintenance strategy at a major automotive manufacturer in the UK', paper presented at the Management Information Systems Conference at Groupe ESC, Grenoble, France, October.

Senker, P. (1984) 'Implications of CAD/CAM for management', *OMEGA: International Journal of Management Science*. 12, 4, pp. 341–355.

Shank, J.K. and Govindarajan, V. (1992) 'Strategic cost analysis of technological investments', *Sloan Management Review*, Fall.

Sharp, F. (1989). 'The way forward in predictive maintenance'. *Production Engineer*, 69, 5, pp. 37–9.

Shingo, S. (1989) *A study of the Toyota production system*. Productivity Press.

Simmonds, P. and Senker, P. (1991) 'Changing technology and design work in the British engineering industry, 1981–1988'. *New Technology, Work and Employment*.

Sirkin, H. and Stalk, G. (1990). 'Fix the process not the problem'. *Harvard Business Review*, July–August, pp. 26–33.

Sorge, A. (1989) 'Engineers in management: a study of British, German and French traditions', *Journal of General Management*, 5, 46–57.

Sorge, A. and Warner, M. (1986) *Comparative Factory Management*, Gower.

Stevens, B. (1989) *The reliability approach to maintenance optimisation in manufacturing industries*. UKAEA Publication.

Stevens, B., (1989) *The reliability approach to maintenance optimisation in manufacturing industries* (National Centre of Systems Reliability).

Suzuki, N. (1989) 'The attributes of Japanese CEOs: can they be trained?', *Journal of Management Development*, 8 (4), 5–11.

Storey, J. (1991) 'Do the Japanese make better managers', *Personnel Management*, Aug, 24–28.

Thompson, G. (1989) 'The American industrial policy debate', in *Industrial Policy: USA and UK Debates*. G. Thompson (ed). London: RKP.

Tidman, G.G. (1990) 'Organisational aspects of implementing Just-In-Time', *Journal of the Oil and Colour Chemists Association*, 73, Part Two, pp. 65–70, 77.

Trick, R.R. (1990) 'Introduction to the Just-In-Time philosophy', *Journal of the Oil and Colour Chemists Association*, 73, Part Two, pp.71–3.

Voss, C.A. and Harrison, A. (1987) 'JIT in the corporate strategy', *4th European Conference on Automated Manufacture*, IFS.

Voss, C.A. and Robinson, S.J. (1987). 'Applications of Just-In-Time manufacturing techniques in the United Kingdom'. *International Journal of Operations and Production Management*, 7, 4, pp. 46–52.

Williams, K., Mitsui, I. and Haslam, C. (1990) 'How far from Japan? a case study of management calculations and practice in car press shops.' Dept. Economics, University of Wales.

Williams, K., Haslam, C. and Williams, J. (1991) The Western Problematic against the Japanese Application, 3rd Interdisciplinary Perspectives on Accounting Conference, Manchester University.

Williams, K., Williams, J., and Thomas, D., (1993) *Why are the British Bad at Manufacturing?*, RKP.

Willmott, P. J. (1990a). 'Managing maintenance'. *Manufacturing Engineer*, 65, 4, pp. 28–30.

Willmott, P. J. (1990b). 'Maintaining profitability'. *Manufacturing Engineer*, 65, 5, pp. 30–33.

Wood, S. (1991) 'Japanisation or Toyotaism?', *Work, Employment and Society*, 5 (4) 567–600.

Woods, M., Pokorny, M., Linterner, V. and Blinkhorn, M. (1984) 'Investment appraisal in the mechanical engineering industry', *Management Accounting*, October, 36–37.

Wu, B. (1991). *Fundamentals of manufacturing systems design and analysis*. Chapman and Hall.

Wu, B., Seddon, J., Currie, W. (1992) 'Computer-aided dynamic preventive maintenance within the manufacturing environment'. *International Journal of Production Research*, Vol, 30, No. 11. pp. 2683–2696.

Yang, J.Z. (1992). 'Americanisation or Japanisation of human resource management policies: a study of Japanese manufacturing and service firms in the USA'. *Advances in International Comparative Management*, Vol, 17, pp. 77–115.

Yoshikawa, T., Innes, J. and Mitchell, F. (1989) 'Japanese management accounting: a comparative survey', *Management Accounting*, 68, 11, pp. 20–23.

Zipkin, P. H. (1991). 'Does manufacturing need a JIT revolution?' *Harvard Business Review,* Jan-Feb.

CHAPTER 11

Managing IT in Japan

Introduction

The Japanese miracle (Johnson, 1982) has been examined from a variety of disciplinary perspectives. Whilst some writers have concentrated on Japanese production techniques such as Just-In-Time (Schongerger, 1982. Oliver and Wilkinson, 1987. Cobb, 1991. Zipkin, 1991), others have looked at Japanese management methods and human resources policies and practices (Pascale and Athos, 1981. Suzuki, 1989. Kumazawa and Yamada, 1989. Storey, 1991. Yang, 1992). As we saw in the previous chapter, contributions from the field of management accounting question whether Japanese accounting practices differ from those adopted in the West (Jones et al, 1993. Yoshikawa et al, 1989. Sakarai, 1990). A common theme running through many of these contributions is the debate about transferability. More importantly, whether the west can 'learn from Japan' (Kharbanda and Stallworthy, 1991).

This chapter continues this debate and is divided into three parts. First it considers some of the literature which attempts to explain Japanese corporate success over the last two decades. Second, it considers some recent studies on the problems which afflict Japanese companies, most notably the burgeoning white collar sector, and the reluctance to give 'soft loans' to companies as a result of the 'bad debt' problem of the last few years. Third, the discussion draws upon the findings of a recent field study carried out in Tokyo on the management of IT projects in three sectors. This study was funded by the Carnegie Trust, and continued the research outlined in the previous chapter.

Learning from Japan

Throughout the 1980s, interest in Japanese management methods and practices intensified as the Japanese economy went from strength to strength. The widening of the trade gap between Japan and the US, and Japan's aggressive overseas investments, led many writers to search for solutions to the problem of economic decline in Western industrialised nations (Thompson, 1989). Coupled with this, many attempts were made to explain unprecedented Japanese economic success. Some writers looked at the Japanese economy and industrial policy, particularly the role of the Ministry of International Trade and Industry: MITI (Johnson, 1982. Thompson, 1989. Fruin, 1993). Others examined Japanese management practices at the level of the organisation (Clark, 1979. Schonberger, 1982. Abegglen and Stalk, 1985). In doing so, convincing arguments were put forward to demonstrate the superiority of Japanese practices compared with those of their Western counterparts (Schonberger, 1982).

In particular, Abegglen and Stalk (1985, p.5) identified four 'competitive fundamentals' which explain the success of the Japanese Kaisha (Japan's companies). They include:

- a growth bias
- a preoccupation with actions of competitors
- the creation and ruthless exploitation of competitive advantage
- focused corporate financial and personnel policies

First, the authors claim that the strong growth bias of many Japanese firms is inextricably linked to their desire to survive in a fierce competitive environment. Thus

'The desire to survive by growing is heightened by the standards of the Japanese society. Wholesale layoffs by a company in response to a weakening demand for a product are unheard of in post-war Japan. It is considered the task of management to increase demand or to find another product in which the capacity of the industrial organisation can be utilised' (p.6).

An obvious way to grow is for a company to diversify into new businesses. Canon, for example, has pursued such a strategy by diversifying into printers, computers, word processors, facsimile machines, copiers, and semiconductor manufacturing equipment.

A study conducted in the early 1990s found that many Japanese companies placed a higher premium on achieving market share growth than profit (Currie, 1994). This is an interesting contrast with manufacturing firms in the West who emphasise profit maximisation, cash flow management and return on capital employed (ROCE) as three key (financial) performance indicators. In fact, many Japanese companies have been noted to expand their production and labour capacities ahead of demand.

Second, the Japanese keep a close eye on competitors. Abegglen and Stalk (1985) state that falling behind a competitor is regarded by many leading Japanese companies as a much greater threat than low profits. This suggests that the Japanese take a longer-term view of corporate performance, since profits are likely to be sacrificed in favour of sustaining or improving market share. In the area of R&D expenditure, Japanese firms often commit significant resources to this activity even in times of recession.

Third, the success of Japanese manufacturing firms has received much attention in the last decade. Against a background of declining western profits from manufacturing and deindustrialisation (Hayes and Abernathy, 1980), many western academics began to 'look east' for the reasons behind the Japanese 'assault on world markets'. Hayes and Pisano (1994) explain that, 'their secret weapon turned out to be sheer manufacturing virtuosity'.

Fourth, the Japanese corporate financial and personnel policies are seen to facilitate high growth, competitive advantage and manufacturing and technological success. Abegglen and Stalk (1985, p.14) claim the key differences between Japanese and Western companies are 'in the amounts (the former) borrow and in their attitudes towards dividends and profits'. Japanese companies 'rely much more on debt financing than do their Western counterparts'. Although this exposes them to greater financial risks, their all-important competitive risks are reduced. If the competitive fundamentals are correctly chosen, a highly leveraged company can aggressively use debt to fund growth at significantly higher rates, even with lower profitability, than can a more conservatively financed company with higher profits. This means that the more aggressive company can 'spend profits by shaving prices, accepting higher manufacturing costs, or investing more heavily in expense items such as R&D and market development and still grow faster than a conservatively financed counterpart'.

Japanese employment policies are a further attribute to successful commercial enterprises. Traditional human resources policies have favoured life-time employment, cross-functional training, promotion according to seniority and length of service and teamworking.

Similarly, Fruin (1993, p. 2) cites five interpretations underlying the success of Japanese companies. They include:

- human resource practices
- institutional control and financial interrelations
- late development, technological catch-up, advantages of backwardness
- industrial policy, government-business relations, and the capitalist development state
- an accent on the efficiency and utility of native economic institutions

First, there are several explanations for Japanese corporate success from a human resources perspective. Many writers have focused upon the Japanese tradition of offering life-time employment to their workforce, particularly in the large Japanese corporations. It is contended that life-time employment facilitates company loyalty among managers and staff. In addition, 'job-hopping' from company to company is discouraged, and even frowned upon. As one manager put it, 'a person loses something when he/she leaves a company to join a competitor' (Currie, 1994). The loss may comprise a company pension, status, position and bonuses. Indeed, the individual may have to start at the bottom of the organisation hierarchy as promotion in many Japanese companies is based on length of service as well as seniority.

Japanese management styles have often been labelled as 'paternalistic'. Individualism and personal initiative are not part of the Japanese enterprise culture. Conversely, teamworking and consensus (group) decision making are encouraged as opposed to ruthless single-minded behaviour. The trade union structure is also markedly different in Japan compared with the West.

Second, Japanese companies over time developed their financial accounting systems and interlocking financial arrangements with banking institutions and their suppliers. Many of these accounting control systems were adapted from Western style methods and practices to suit their own institutional structures (Jones et al, 1993). As Fruin (1993, p.26) points out

'Large industrial firms in pre-war Japan lacked sophisticated management accounting controls. Standardised accounting systems came later in the 1950s and 1960s. This, as much as anything else, may account for the longer time horizon of Japanese firms in evaluating financial performance, and it may well be connected to slower promotion ladders for executives. Without detailed financial information by which to evaluate short-term performance, managers cannot easily demonstrate the differences that they make. Managing, by the numbers, proves impractical'.

To reiterate a point made above, many Japanese firms place a higher premium on growth measured by increased market share than on profit maximisation. As we saw in chapter ten, the Japanese also adopt longer-term strategic plans vis a vis AMT implementation and return on investment (ROI). This is perhaps more appropriate compared with shorter-term expectations from technical change, as research studies have shown that AMT (CAD/CAM, FMS, robots, etc) like other technologies is not a quick-fix panacea (Currie, 1994. Burnes and Weekes, 1989).

A further factor which is attributed to Japanese corporate success also relates to performance measurement. Here, Japanese managers measure performance at levels below a division, most often at the factory level. A recent study found that, unlike many British manufacturing companies, Japanese manufacturers develop stringent measures for maintenance performance levels (Currie and Yoshikawa, 1994). Having developed a system of Total Preventive Maintenance (TPM) as part of the JIT *philosophy*, Japanese manufacturers regularly measure machine downtime, capacity, output, etc, to determine maintenance schedules. Consequently, the problem of machine downtime is reduced as technology is maintained frequently and effectively. According to many Japanese managers, the act of measuring operational performance is important since it is one factor which directly relates to overall profitability.

Third, Japanese corporate success has also been attributed to their late development and 'catch-up' with the West. Transferability was an important part of the development of the Japanese enterprise system. The Japanese transferred from the West, organisational models, managerial methods, and production and distribution systems. This effort began in the latter half of the nineteenth century. In fact, many so-called 'Japanese techniques' such as TQM and JIT originated in the West and were adopted by Japanese companies and adapted to suit their institutional structures and working practices. This is sometimes forgotten by some Western academics, who continue to perceive the transferability debate as one-dimensional, e.g. from Japan to the West. This is clearly inappropriate given that historical studies of the Japanese enterprise system are full of examples where the Japanese were exposed to numerous Western-style management methods and techniques from accounting to production (Fruin, 1983. 1993. Hirschmeier and Tsunehito, 1981).

Fourth, the role of the Japanese government in developing a focused industrial policy for economic growth should not be underestimated. In the post-war period, the Japanese government set out to create an institutional framework to facilitate economic growth and prosperity. The Ministry of International Trade and Industry (MITI) was formed.

The Japanese banking and financial institutions also played a large part in the policy by facilitating corporate growth through 'soft loans' (e.g. long-term loans at lower interest rates). The fusing of factories, firms and networks was equally important in creating the institutional foundations of industrialised capitalism in post-war Japan. These linkages helped in the areas of technology transfer, R&D, product and process innovation, engineering, manufacturing, cost accounting, distribution channels, sales and marketing and personnel practices.

Fruin (1993, p. 82) states that

'...the later development of the firm in Japan, in comparison with the Western corporation, has emphasised the importance of organisational learning, or the importance of Western knowledge and its transformation into Japanese practice... Organisational learning is, above all, a process of institutional differentiation: to the extent that institutions depend on organisational learning, they become increasingly adept at managing change and increasingly different as a result of change. Distinctive company cultures result' (p. 121).

An important facet of organisational learning is in the act of 'doing' rather than 'thinking'. Fruin (1993, p. 41) explains this well, thus

'While organisational learning has been characterised as routine-based, history-dependent, and target-orientated, such characterisations tend to view organisational learning in the short run. In the long run, organisational learning is limited only by the speed with which general knowledge can be transformed reliably into applied or firm-specific knowledge. In circumstances of nearly complete dependence on foreign technology transfer (late development), organisational learning (the firm-specific capacity to use knowledge) accumulated operationally in Japan, more often at the level of the shop-floor rather than in corporate level offices. Theoretical knowledge was and is of limited value. In these circumstances, organisational learning includes both 'learning by doing' or so-called 'experience curves' (more efficient effort as a function of accumulated output) as well as what are sometimes referred to as generalised or categorical scripts'.

Japanese companies facilitated organisational learning in a number of ways. Education and training were given a high priority. This was effected largely by in-house cross-functional training. In addition, the factory, firm and network system offered a fertile training ground as knowledge was shared and exploited through the tangible assets of technology and new product development.

Fifth, and related to the concept of organisational learning was Japan's impressive exploitation of technology. The development of technology has been a crucial factor in Japanese manufacturing success. Where firms decided not to manufacture in-house, they located and cultivated a network of suppliers to manufacture for them, and assisted the process by offering capital, labour, equipment and training. Technical knowledge was seen as important in the development of Japan's manufacturing companies. In this respect, technology strategies were developed at board level (Currie, 1994).

The transition from bubble economy to corporate restructuring

During the last two decades, Japan has become prominent in many fields, especially in advanced technology. However, like the situation in the West, Japan has scaled down many of its less competitive industries such as shipbuilding and steel. Between 1986-1989, some of the largest steel producers, shipbuilding companies, mining concerns, textile mills, and other 'smokestack' industries were closed with the elimination of thousands of jobs. Since the mid-1980s, Japanese overseas investment has significantly increased, particularly in the United States and Europe. In the three-year period between 1986 and 1989, total direct investment by Japanese investors more than doubled. In 1988, Japan became the largest foreign investor in US assets. Some of these investments were politically contentious in the US.

Other smaller direct investments have been in computers, semiconductors, scientific instruments, construction and the retail business. Japanese firms have also invested in petrochemicals in the middle east, electronic assembly in south east Asia and agriculture in Latin America.

Demographic trends in Japan have also given rise to a radical rethinking of some of the traditional employment and management practices (see below). For example, by the year 2000, the Japanese population will have the largest percentage of people over 65 years of age in the world. This will pose serious threats to the welfare system, labour supply, retirement age and labour productivity.

Bitter trade disputes between Japan and the US continue. Between 1986–1989, the Japanese Yen appreciated more than 50% against the US dollar. This drastic change in the exchange rate resulted in a substantial drop in profits for major Japanese multinational firms. Whereas the early 1980s saw Japanese firms going from strength to strength, the late 1980s saw Japan enter an economic downturn. During 1988, many Japanese firms experienced a sharp decline in their profits ranging from 30% to 50% from the previous financial year. This factor, coupled with the record-breaking appreciation of the Japanese Yen, forced Japanese firms to reorganise their international business strategies.

At an exchange rate of US $1 = ¥105 (and higher), Japanese manufacturing wages became the highest world-wide. For example, many Japanese companies were paying their employees an average of US $13 per hour compared with only US $10.50 in the United States. In many south east Asian countries, the hourly rate was less than US $2. This led many Japanese manufacturers to look east to their Pacific rim neighbours for possible business opportunities.

Japanese firms also tend to operate with a high debt-equity ratio. They were largely financed by bank debt rather than equity. In 1989, of the total net increase in the supply of operating capital and capital equipment investment in major corporations, less than 20% was from stock and debentures, while more than 80% was from loans. Of the debts, about 85% came from private financial institutions. Large firms are closely related to the banks and the latter retain equity in the firms they finance. In this respect, banks are generally involved in the major long-term decisions of their large corporate customers. Fruin (1993, 202) argues that the debt owed to the financial institutions was more like equity because 'loans were rarely called in or paid off'.

Commercial banks provide about 80% of the short-term funds for firms. Finance is also common between manufacturers and their subcontractors or suppliers. Fruin (1993, p. 190) claims that

'Since the oil shocks of the mid-1970s, the ways in which companies raise capital have changed noticeably. Self-financing through retained earnings and share participations has increased. With the liberalisation of capital markets at home and abroad from the early 1970s, Japanese companies have gone directly to financial markets with increasing frequency. They now have much more latitude than in the past as to what capital instruments and currencies they use, where to raise funds, and in general how to increase capital. Companies, even those enmeshed within an interfirm network, are now more than ever free to choose their own financial future'.

In the past five years, many of Japan's leading corporations have been severely challenged by the world-wide economic recession. Some writers argue that structural weaknesses highlighted by Japan's economic recession would lead to long-term changes in many of Japan's large companies. For example, recent reports show that despite Japan's low unemployment rate of 2.5 % (compared with levels of 10–16% in European countries), there are an estimated 800,000–1.2 million employees who are surplus to companies, yet still retained on the payroll (*Financial Times*, 7 October 1993; 3 December 1993). In a recent study, Japanese managers claimed that 'unemployment is kept in-house'. This was a deliberate personnel policy to retain the culture of life-time employment (Currie, 1994).

However, many sources suggest that traditional employment practices are undergoing significant changes, as many companies announce job cuts (*Financial Times*, 12 January 1993, 15 December 1993). Toshiba electronics group announced that it was to cut 5,000 jobs; Honda, the car maker 3,000; and Kawasaki Steel, 3,200 (*Financial Times*, 3 December 1993). Other companies embarking on job cuts include: Fujitsu, 6,000 jobs; Nippon Trust Bank to reduce its staff by a third from 2,300 to 1,500 through reduced recruiting; and NTT by as many as 32,000 staff (Hori, 1993, p.167). Extensive job cutting is unprecedented in Japan, and a phenomenon that will undoubtedly alter the traditional life-time employment culture for some 35% of Japan's labour market (Hori, 1993).

The way in which Japan chooses to tackle its over-staffing problem, however, is significantly different from the strategies adopted in the West. A recent survey of 18 industries conducted in 1993 found that the steel, electrical appliances, securities and information service industries felt they had too many employees on their payrolls (*Financial Times*, 12 January 1993). To reduce staffing levels, many of these companies reject Western-style compulsory redundancy schemes, and instead seek a variety of measures including cutting bonuses and overtime hours, freezing recruitment and laying off part-time workers. Indeed, it is often the latter 'peripheral' (part-time) work force who suffer as large Japanese corporations transfer the cost burden to their smaller suppliers.

One important factor in relation to job reduction strategies in leading Japanese corporations concerns the disproportionately high levels of white collar work compared with production jobs. Against a backdrop of manufacturing efficiency and technology exploitation in Japanese manufacturing companies (Hayes and Pisano, 1994) the phenomenon of 'lean production' suggests that manufacturing is already streamlined in terms of staffing levels. Indeed, many writers suggest that whilst Japanese manufacturers have concentrated on efficiency gains and cost cutting by slashing blue collar jobs through automation, the same has not yet occurred in the white collar sector (Hori, 1993. Currie, 1994. Hayes and Pisano, 1994. Hunt and Targett, 1995).

One reason is because white collar workers have traditionally enjoyed life-time employment, bonus payments and have been located in the 'core' labour market. As one Japanese businessman put it, it is 'socially unacceptable' to embark upon Western-style job reduction programmes in Japan, since secure employment has been the embodiment of successful Japanese institutions and economic development (*Financial Times*, 15 December 1993). Recent trends, however, show that Japanese companies are now targeting their job reduction programmes on the white collar sector.

The Japanese white collar labour market

Faced with the most severe recession for some twenty years (*Financial Times*, 3 December 1993) coupled with the 'bad debt' problem facing Japan's financial institutions (*Financial Times*, 30 September 1993), leading Japanese corporations are forced to address some of their internal weaknesses as raising capital becomes more difficult in the current environment (Hori, 1993). During the bubble economy of the 1980s, it seems that few Japanese firms were concerned to address the issue of over-staffing, even though they were aware that labour surpluses existed. As Hori (1993, p.158) points out

> 'During their struggles to grow fast enough to keep up with the expanding market for their products, few Japanese companies paid attention to the fact that overhead personnel costs were increasing much faster than other costs. When what had seemed to be perpetual market growth stopped, sales could no longer support Japan's huge fixed-cost burden. As a result, for the first time in decades, Japanese businesses must rethink their fundamental priorities. They must focus on improving the productivity and innovativeness of white collar workers with the same level of commitment and vigour they directed at becoming highly productive quality and customer-orientated manufacturers'.

Figure 11.1 shows the trends in occupational sectors in Japan from 1960 to 1990. The figure shows that the white collar sector has risen from comprising 31.7% of the labour market in 1960 to 48.6% in 1990, with a compound annual growth rate of 2.7%.

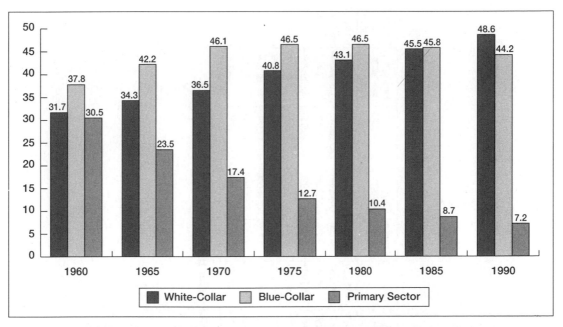

Figure 11.1 White collar shift: occupational changes in the Japanese work force (Adapted from Hori, 1993, p.160)

Hori (1993) states that worker productivity is low in Japan's domestic service sector. Recent comparative studies between Japan and the US show that a productivity gap exists which is estimated to be as high as 40% in industries including airlines, telecommunications, retail banking, general merchandise and restaurants. The author points out that 'methodological difficulties' arise in conducting cross-national industry comparisons since there are many important contextual variable to consider. Nevertheless, poor productivity in Japan's service industries has been noted by many writers on Japanese industry (Fruin, 1993. Abegglen and Stalk, 1985. Hori, 1993).

Hori (1993) has also said that throughout the 1980s, many leading Japanese companies enlarged their corporate and headquarters functions to cope with domestic

Company	Canon	Dai Nippon Computing	Fuji Film	Hitachi	Kanebo	Kirin Brewery	Matsushita Electrical Industrial	Mitsubishi Electrical	NEC	Nissan	Sony	Tato	Toyota
1992 Sales (M ¥)	1,073,403	1,092,649	914,849	3,925,250	524,918	1,315,742	4,994,719	2,611,139	3,049,450	4,270,523	1,979,061	417,606	8,564,040
1984 Sales (M ¥)	374,126	569,304	545,057	2,648,207	269,296	1,069,841	2,718,812	1,587,690	1,459,738	3,450,124	770,074	159,741	4,892,653
% Growth	187%	92%	66%	48%	81%	23%	84%	64%	109%	23%	157%	161%	75%
1992 Manf Personnel	10,164	6,563	8,441	63,999	5,659	4,926	29,654	39,296	27,730	37,991	11,935	8,035	44,496
1984 Manf Personnel	9,205	6,237	9,272	51,469	3,618	5,659	26,656	40,958	27,383	43,524	11,214	5,697	32,901
% Change	10%	5%	-9%	4 %	56%	-29%	10%	-4%	1%	-13%	6%	20%	35%
1992 OH Personnel	7,213	6,847	3,488	16,998	4,712	4,060	17,980	10,270	12,175	17,575	7,876	2,195	30,770
1984 OH Personnel	3,754	4,060	1,925	14,080	2,552	1,907	12,235	7,236	7,464	16,091	3,290	1,079	28,566
% Change	92 %	69%	81%	21 %	85%	113%	47%	42%	63%	9%	139%	104%	16%

Table 11.1 Blue collar success pays, white collar bills (*Source:* Hori, 1993, p. 162.)

and overseas expansion. This boosted white collar recruitment and added to fixed labour cost burden. Hori cites a study which considers the comparative levels of manufacturing and overhead (white collar) personnel in 1984 and 1992 in a selection of large Japanese firms.

In four of the companies (Fuji Film, Kirin Breweries, Mitsubishi Electric and Nissan) manufacturing personnel declined in the eight-year period. Conversely. manufacturing personnel rose by as much as 56% in one company (Kanebo). Comparing these figures with the levels of overhead personnel shows that all companies increased employment levels in this area. Indeed, some companies (Kirin Breweries, Sony and Toto) increased overhead personnel by more than 100%. Whilst business expansion is likely to account for the increases in both manufacturing and overhead personnel levels, it is interesting to note the relative high increases in the latter area. For example, whilst Sony only increased its manufacturing personnel by 6%, its overhead personnel rose by a massive 139%. One might expect equal increases or decreases in both areas over the eight-year period, or at least similar percentage changes.

Hori (1993) states that the impressive manufacturing improvements have in fact subsidised the burgeoning white collar sector. But given there are few savings to be made in production areas, declining company profits mean that Japanese managers must now look for savings elsewhere. This has given rise to the current wave of restructuring, downsizing and BPR.

Business process re-engineering in Japanese companies: the latest trend

A recent article in the *Japan Times* (7 February 1994, p.7) claims that 're-engineering' only began to be used by Japanese managers in 1993. The authors of the article claim that three important factors are behind the need for re-engineering in Japanese companies. They include:

- the factory productivity gap
- white collar weaknesses
- distribution systems which cannot meet consumers needs

The factory productivity gap has already been considered (above) and relates to the efficiency gains made by Japanese manufacturers in production. The relatively low cost of labour coupled with large investment in R&D, technology (i.e. robotics, etc) and effective working practices such as TQM and JIT, all contributed to the Japanese economic 'miracle'. However, as the productivity gap began to close as a consequence of rising Japanese domestic labour costs (which reduced the competitive advantage of some firms) and the focused strategies of overseas competitors (choosing to invest in countries where labour is cheap), Japanese firms have begun to consider restructuring and downsizing. White collar weaknesses do not only relate to over-staffing and large 'overhead' labour costs. According to one US academic, 'Japanese office workers have only one-quarter the usage of electronic devices such as workstations, faxes and scanners as do their US counterparts. Only about 3% of Japanese PCs are networked, compared with more than 50% in the US'.

Whilst the debate about job reduction through technology is contentious, the prospect of re-engineering through technology suggests that core and service business processes may become more efficient. Examples are Electronic Data Interchange (EDI), strategic databases and networks, etc.

A radical rethinking of Japan's distribution channels is also required. This is due to the relative high prices in Japan coupled with poor value for money. Thus, 'Manufacturers still hold disproportionate power over distributors and have inhibited the growth of efficient distribution approaches.... Discounters overall share of Japan's $1.2 trillion retail market remains tiny – little more than 3%. Prices are high in Japan; assortment is poor. Consumers have become aware that they are not getting value for their purchases'. This is likely to change as 'value added chains' make inroads into certain markets. This will 'create value at the point of purchase and establish new innovative distribution channels' (*Japan Times*, 7 February 1994, p.7).

It is contended that to facilitate changes in the white collar sector and distribution channels will require investment in 'white collar' technology. This includes PCs, networks, databases and telecommunications equipment, etc. In the following section, the results from a study on managing IT in ten Japanese companies are considered in the light of BPR.

Managing IT in ten Japanese companies

A grant was obtained from the Carnegie Trust to carry out field work in Japan in private and public sector organisations on the management of IT (Currie and Yoshikawa, 1994). Interviews were conducted with Japanese managers, usually senior managers responsible for IT investment and systems development work. A questionnaire was used during the interviews. It served primarily as a guiding framework for interdisciplinary questions on IT strategy, the structuring and co-ordination of IT activities, financial evaluation of IT, implementation, outsourcing, performance measurement and human resource issues. The questionnaire was similar to the one adopted for the interdisciplinary UK study on managing IT in the financial services, manufacturing industry and public sector (see chapters seven, eight and nine). The responses obtained from the interviews were the perceptions and priorities of the managers in question, and not the formal policy of the companies.

The sample of companies in the Japanese study comprised both private and public sector organisations. Interviews were carried out at an airline company and also in manufacturing companies. A financial institution was also included. Although the sample was small, the objective of the interviews was to provide some up-to-date information on the management of IT following Japan's worst economic recession for twenty years. The research would also enable some comparisons with a previous study conducted by the author into the management of AMT (Currie, 1994).

Restructuring and re-engineering in Japan

Interviews with a number of senior Japanese managers in the IS/IT area confirmed recent reports of the current wave of restructuring and re-engineering in leading Japanese companies (*Japan Times*, 7 February 1994, p.7). Whilst the sample companies had clearly survived the economic turbulence of the recession, they were all reconsidering how they manage their key business processes.

Unsurprisingly, many of the problems which afflict Western companies vis a vis IT management also posed serious threats to Japanese firms. For example, IT was perceived by the majority of managers as a cost burden which occasionally went out of control. Rapid technological developments, and the desire to undertake complex IS development work to improve business processes, constituted a major challenge to management. Skills shortages were common in Japanese companies, particularly in the areas of client-server, database management, networking, etc.

Business process re-engineering was also viewed as a significant challenge, and one which was thought to be more difficult than restructuring. One manager said that, 'It's easy to reduce budgets by 10% or move people from headquarters to branch offices. But it's more difficult to change the way you do things'.

The need to restructure and re-engineer was determined by 'growing red ink'. In other words, low growth, poor profits and the difficulties in raising capital from increasingly cautious banking institutions. At one company, it was confirmed that the Nenko system of employment (e.g. full-time, life-time employment with annual bonuses, a good pension, etc) was coming under threat. This situation was due to the recession, and also because of the emerging markets of the Pacific rim and China. Cheap overseas labour was leading corporate executives to relocate to countries like Taiwan, Malaysia and South Korea and use local labour for production and unskilled work.

Some managers said that the time had arrived to 'run a comb through white collar areas' and scale down these activities. This was producing ripple effects within many corporations as corporate restructuring had become a euphemism for 'Kata-Tataki' – the 'tap on the shoulder' which precedes early retirement. However, interviews with a number of managers confirmed that job losses through restructuring would be achieved by 1) a freeze on recruitment, and 2) natural wastage and early retirement. Aggressive compulsory redundancy was perceived as too threatening, particularly for those embarking on careers and others in mid-term career.

Restructuring and IT

In a climate of economic turbulence, severe global competition, low profits and rapid technological change, it was interesting to observe how this was affecting the structure of organisations in the sample companies. As many as nine out of ten companies said they had been restructured in the past five years. A further five said IT had played a part in the restructuring process. Asked whether the company was structured according to a functional or matrix/product structure (or other), six out of the ten said they had a traditional functional structure. Interviews with managers confirmed that, even in organisations with a matrix/product structure, the clerical and administrative functions tended to remain functionally structured. (See Table 11.2.)

	Bank1	Man.1	Man.2	Service1	Man.3	Man.4	Airline1	Man.5	Man.6	Service2
Has company been restructured in past 5 yrs?	Y	Y	Y	Y	Y	Y	Y	N	Y	Y
Has IT played a part in this restructuring?	Y	N	Y	Y	N	Y	Y		Y	Y
What organisational structure do you have?	Func Struc	Func Struc	Matrix	Matrix	Matrix Product	Func Struc	Func Struc	Func Struc	Prod Struc	Func Struc

Table 11.2 Restructuring in ten Japanese companies

	Bank1	Man.1	Man.2	Service1	Man.3	Man.4	Airline1	Man.5	Man.6	Service2
Do you have an IT division?	Y	Y	Y	Y	Y	Y	Y	Y	Y	Y
How many people work in this division?	460/890	200	60	1,113		100	300	83	100	300
Who is in charge of IT projects?	IT Director	IT Manager	IT Manager	IT Director	IT Director	IT Director	All IT Managers	IT Director	IT Director	Division Directors

Table 11.3 Organisation structure and IT

Organisation structure and IT: the parent/subsidiary relationship

The structure of the organisation is important in the context of how IT activities are managed. Companies who claim to operate within a matrix/product organisation could be assumed to possess multiple IT units to serve each product area. However, a closer examination of the results proved otherwise. Every company in the sample said they possessed a single IS/IT division/department. Many of these divisions/departments were quite substantial, with some possessing in excess of 200 staff. In addition, many were run by an IT Director – a person who was likely to be senior in terms of age, experience and length of service to the organisation. (See Table 11.3.)

Whilst some of these findings suggest similarities with British companies, an important difference concerned the financial arrangements of the IT division/department. For example, the majority of them were subsidiaries of the parent company. They were therefore profit centres who worked primarily for the parent. This could be in the capacity of designing, developing, implementing and maintaining information systems for customers at headquarters or the business divisions/units. In one organisation (Service1), a subsidiary of the parent comprising over 1000 people was run as a profit centre where 30% of its sales were from the parent. The remaining 70% were for external companies. They could be suppliers to the parent or other commercial enterprises, possibly even competitors of the parent. The parent company did not possess an IT division or undertake any systems development work in-house. Clearly, the subsidiary was obliged to carry out work for the parent, and acted as a consultancy with in-depth knowledge of the parent's activities.

Other organisations also structured their IT activities in a similar way. Whilst IT was seen as a cost burden, the fact that subsidiaries were set up to supply IT services to the parent, as well as other customers, forged an independence which is absent in the traditional in-house IT division/department of many British companies. This is because, the subsidiaries in Japan acted as profit centres with their own budgets and performance measurement systems.

One manager said that the reason for the parent/IS subsidiary division was twofold. First, the subsidiary was accountable for its own profit and loss record. Second, personnel at the subsidiary understood the business of the parent and the industry in which it operates. This meant that 'expert advice' could be obtained in addition to good support for legacy systems. Indeed, the after-delivery maintenance of IS was seen as crucial.

At an airline company an IS/IT subsidiary had been set up ten years ago to serve the parent. About 80% of its business came from the parent, and the remaining 20% from external companies. Similarly, the financial separation between parent and subsidiary coupled with the fusing of business knowledge were important prerequisites for a successful partnership. Having said that, problems arose when the subsidiary felt disinclined to embark on certain projects which were proposed by the parent (or other internal customers). In many cases, the subsidiary was at a disadvantage as the set-up meant that, 'We (the parent) can control our subsidiaries, even though they are profit centres'.

A key advantage for the subsidiary, however, was a capital injection from the parent should they perform badly. There were few circumstances where a parent would not 'bail out' one of its subsidiaries, particularly a subsidiary responsible for the majority of its IS development work! Employees from the parent or subsidiary could also be 'borrowed' according to project demands and deadlines. This facilitates the process of organisational learning as knowledge becomes a commodity in the form of output from the IT subsidiary. Indeed, 'knowledge of the business' was seen as crucial in the process of developing workable information systems for use throughout the business areas.

A strategic approach to IT?

Whilst the academic literature espouses the view that IT is a strategic device, many Western companies continue to perceive IT as a support function and treat it as a cost centre accordingly (see chapter seven). Interviews with Japanese managers found that in all the companies, IT was perceived as a strategic device which could enhance performance. IT was also managed according to a strategic plan and, in eight companies, IT plans were aligned to the corporate strategy. Where IT was not linked to the corporate strategy (in two manufacturing companies) it was likely that IT was differentiated from AMT. Respondents perceived IT more in terms of office automation and AMT as production automation. But as we have observed above, Japanese companies have been much more inclined to streamline production through AMT than rationalise white collar work through IT. IT may not therefore be perceived as important to the successful realisation of the corporate strategy in these two companies. (See Table 11.4.)

Reinforcing a previous study on AMT in Japan (see chapter ten) found that IT strategies tended to be developed and implemented by senior-level managers. Although Japanese companies are associated with bottom-up decision making, the crafting of IT strategy was perceived as the domain of senior personnel. Board level personnel were likely to be senior managers with proper managerial roles. IT strategies were also likely to be medium (up to three years) to long term (up to five years). IT strategies were not perceived to be cast in stone. Instead, they were seen to evolve in line with other changes in, for example, technology, the economy, competitor strategies, labour/skills shortages, product development requirements, budgets, etc. Only one company said that IT strategy could not keep up with technological changes. Indeed, some managers said they felt technology was upgraded too quickly, and this posed a problem for those responsible for developing IT strategies.

Strategic benefits of IT

Managers were also asked to identify the key strategic benefits from IT. They were presented with a list of some 22 potential benefits and asked to rank them in order of importance (1 = most important, 22 = least important). Obviously, some benefits were seen as equally important. Given this, managers could give an equal weighting to those benefits which they perceived as equally important (this means that comparisons can only be made by considering how each company ranks all the benefits, rather than simply comparing the number ranking of one company with that of another). (See Table 11.5.)

	Bank1	Man.1	Man.2	Service1	Man.3	Man.4	Airline1	Man.5	Man.6	Service2
How long is the strategic plan?	Medium	Medium	Long Term	Medium	Long Term	Medium	Long Term	Medium	Long Term	Medium
Who is responsible for developing the IT strategy?	Senior Managers	Board Level	Senior Managers	Board	Senior Managers	Senior Managers	Middle Managers	Board	Board	Senior Managers
Who is responsible for implementing the IT strategy?	Middle Managers	Middle Managers	Senior Executives	Board	Middle Managers	Senior Executives	Board	Senior Executives	Senior Executives	Middle Managers
Do you use external management consultants to develop IT strategy?	N	Y	N	Y	Y	N	N	N	N	Y
Can your IT strategy keep pace with the corporate strategy?	Y	Y	Y	Y	Y	Y	Y	N	Y	Y
Is the IT strategy linked with the corporate strategy?	Y	Y	Y	Y	N	Y	Y	N	Y	Y

Table 11.4 Strategy and IT in Japanese companies

	Bank1	Man.1	Man.2	Service1	Man.3	Man.4	Airline1	Man.5	Service2
(a) Competitive advantage in a global market	7	19	1	22	12	1	2	14	22
(b) Competitive advantage in a domestic market	1	6	1	4	5	2	1	1	2
(c) Strategic alliances	6	7		20	12	4	4	6	13
(d) Movement towards facilities management		11	5	19	12	13	2	11	19
(e) Reduced organisational functions	8	1	5	6	3	14	1	10	1
(f) Reduce staff	9	5	5	14	5	15	1	8	9
(g) Reduce operating/unit costs	11	2	4	3	5	16	2	5	6
(h) Process/product innovation	11	3	2	13	3	3	3	3	3
(i) Faster supplier delivery times	11	12	3	5	12	6	4	4	15
(j) Shorter product cycles	11	4	2	2	5	5	4	3	14
(k) Enhanced flexibility	11	14	3	19	12	7	4	5	19
(l) Faster customer delivery times	2	10	3	9	5	16	4	2	16
(m) Improved information	14	8	4	9	1	10	2	7	8
(n) Organisational learning	5	20	4	1	5	21	3	9	10
(o) Skills development	3	9	4	8	2	9	3	12	9
(p) Continuous improvement/quality	4	18	4	11	5	12	3	2	5
(q) Gain leverage over suppliers	15	16	3	12	12	17	4	13	18
(r) Reduce number of suppliers	15	19	5	10	12	18	4	13	21
(s) Reduce customer costs	13	15	4	15	12	19	2	5	20
(t) Identify new potential customers	12		5		12	20	3	1	4
(u) Raise entry cost of potential competitors	12	21	5	21	12	11	4	3	11
(v) Identify a new market niche	10	20	5	18	12	8	4	1	12

Table 11.5 Management priorities and performance measurement in Japanese companies

Whereas IT as a means of attaining competitive advantage in a global market (a) was seen as the most important strategic benefit by two manufacturing companies (3 and 6), it was perceived to be the least important benefit by another two companies (4 and 9). Part of the reason for the latter was likely to involve whether these companies served the international market or only the domestic market. As we can see, their response to (b) regarding the domestic market shows that it was the fourth and second most important benefit respectively (4 and 9). Whilst there was no comparable pattern regarding the range of priorities managers attach to the itemised list of benefits between the companies, the most important benefits were listed as

- competitive advantage in the domestic market
- competitive advantage in the global market
- reduction in organisational functions
- organisational learning
- improved information
- staff reduction
- identify potential new customers
- identify new market niche

The above potential strategic benefits from IT seem to reinforce existing literature on the changes currently taking place in Japanese enterprises (Fruin, 1993. Currie, 1994). The literature on business process re-engineering also highlights many of the above benefits as crucial in the link between IT and re-engineering (Davenport, 1993). However, the Japanese emphasis upon organisational learning as a key benefit is not echoed in Britain. Paradoxically it seems that many British companies experience the problem of skills shortages, yet place skills development at the bottom of their priorities! This is also rein-forced in the literature on the lack of education and training opportunities in British companies (Senker and Beesley, 1986. Hirst and Zeitlin, 1989. Thaimhain, 1992. Garvin, 1993. Skills and Enterprise, 1993. Stata, 1989).

At an airline company staff reduction was their key priority (at least according to the respondents to the questionnaire). This organisation had recently announced a five-year job-reduction scheme where 1,200-2,000 ground staff jobs would be eliminated. Jobs would also be cut through a recruitment freeze, voluntary retirement, and by one -year paid-absence programmes (Hori, 1993, p. 167). Strategic benefits from IT which were given low priority by managers included:

- raise entry costs of potential competitors
- identify potential new customers
- organisational learning
- identify new market niche
- competitive advantage in a global market
- reduce number of suppliers

Some of these benefits were of low importance to some companies, yet highly important in others (see above). Interviews with managers found that controlling suppliers was important, but not necessarily an area which required re-adjustment. Gaining leverage over suppliers was also given low priority by many organisations, as most of them had already achieved this objective.

The key problems in developing and implementing an IT strategy

Respondents were asked to identify they key problems in developing and implementing their IT strategies. By far the biggest problem was in the rapid rate of technological change. In addition, a poor perceived financial return also acted as an impediment to developing and implementing the IT strategy. A number of managers said that the economic recession and low profits had reduced capital for IT projects, and many companies were cutting their IT budgets as a result. (See Table 11.6.)

In spite of the Japanese record on education and training, the rapid pace of technological change had created skills shortages. But Japanese companies did not hire in contract labour, as is the case in Europe and the US. Rather, they felt that individuals would have to undergo a learning curve and develop the latest skills. Japanese managers were critical of the notion of hiring contract labour for short-term periods since they believed it was important for individuals to have an in-depth understanding of the business. Personal contacts throughout the organisation were perceived as crucial in the learning process. The notion that a contractor could be hired to start work on day one on a major IS project was seen as astonishing.

IT managers: experience, training and skills

One of the key debates in the West is about the skills levels required to manage IT activities. Whilst some writers espouse the advantages of 'hybrid managers' (ie people with both business and technical skills), in reality it seems that individuals seeking promotion move away from their technical specialism and into general management. Promotion prospects for technical specialists seem few and far between in Western companies, given the widespread view that 'technical people don't make good managers'.

In Japanese companies, managers confirmed there were some difficulties facing technical people to move from their specialisms into other functional management areas. However, the problem was seemingly not so entrenched in Japan. Respondents were asked about the skill set required for managing IT. Seven companies said that it was important for IT managers to understand the business since they were engaged in developing business systems. Respondents were also asked if they possessed 'hybrid managers'. Clearly this was translated for a Japanese audience and the term 'multi-skilled' was used instead. Only three companies claimed to have multi-skilled managers, although the meaning attached to this term encapsulated individuals with business and technical skills (possibly long serving members of staff).

In addition, all the companies claimed it was possible for IT managers to gain promotion to senior management positions, and possibly beyond (director level). One advantage for individuals in the Japanese corporation was the prospect of moving around the functional areas. This avoided the possibility of being labelled, 'a boffin'. (See Table 11.7.)

Respondents were also asked to rank what they believed were the most important

What are the key problems in developing and implementing an IT strategy?	Bank1	Man.1	Man.2	Service1	Man.3	Man.4	Airline1	Man.5	Man.6	Service2
(a) Shortage of funds	Y	N	N	N	Y	Y	Y	N	N	N
(b) Rapid pace of technology change	Y	Y	Y	Y	Y	N	Y	N	Y	Y
(c) Skills shortage	Y	Y	N	Y	N	Y	N	N	N	N
(d) Poor perceived financial return	N	N	Y	Y	Y	N	N	Y	Y	Y
(e) Changes in the market	N	N	N	N	N	Y	N	N	Y	N

Table 11.6 Implementation and IT in Japanese companies

	Bank1	Man.1	Man.2	Service1	Man.3	Man.4	Airline1	Man.5	Man.6	Service2
Is it important for senior IT executives to understand IT?	Y	Y	Y	N	Y	N	Y	N	Y	Y
Do IT professionals gain promotion to senior management?	Y	Y	Y	Y	Y	Y	Y	Y	Y	Y
Are senior IT managers multi-skilled?	N	N	N	Y	N	N	Y	N	Y	N
What are the most important skills to manage IT?										
(a) Technical expertise	7	6	1	4	1	5	2	8	2	8
(b) Project management skills	3	4	1	3	2	2	1	7	2	5
(c) Co-ordination skills	5	8	2	2	4	7	1	5	2	4
(d) Communication skills	4	7	2	3	5	6	2	6	2	7
(e) Financial awareness	8	5	3	3	5	5	3	4	2	2
(f) Business awareness	1	1	3	1	5	1	2	1	2	1
(g) Leadership of team	2	2	3	2	3	4	1	2	2	6
(h) Networking	6	3	3	5		3	2	3	2	3
(i) Other										

Table 11.7 Management skills and IT

skills for IT managers (1 = most important, 8 = least important). Again, some managers gave equal weighting to some skill groups.

Interestingly, business awareness was seen to be the most important skill in six of the ten companies. When questioned why this was the case, respondents tended to give the same answer. They argued that since competition is becoming increasingly severe, it is crucial that IT plays a part in re-engineering core business processes to make them more efficient and cost effective. Although technical expertise was given the lowest priority by two companies, and low priority by a further three companies, two companies actually placed it first on the list. Some managers said that whilst it was not important for project managers to possess state-of-the-art technical skills, they should at least be in a position to determine who, in their team, are the technical experts. As a result, one company only promoted individuals to project management positions after ten years systems development experience. The idea of bringing someone in from marketing or finance to manage projects was, in this example, seen as misguided.

Interestingly, leadership of the team was given high priority by many respondents. This is perhaps unsurprising given the emphasis in Japanese companies on teamworking and consensus decision making. Project management skills were also given high priority. However, when questioned about the meaning attached to the term project management, Japanese managers said that it involved planning, co-ordinating, assessing and advising the technical team. Financial management was only a small part of the project management remit.

Achieving the benefits from IT

Managers were also asked to prioritise the benefits directly attributable to IT. As opposed to corporate-wide strategic benefits from IT, along the lines of business process re-engineering, the following benefits related to functional improvements. (See Table 11.8.)

The two most common benefits were lead time reduction and increased flexibility. Clearly, the two go hand in hand, since enhanced flexibility through the use of IT is likely to result in the faster delivery time to market. One company (Airline1) only listed two key benefits from IT: staff reduction and increased management control. These objectives seemed to reflect the current strategy of the corporation to downsize.

Another company (Man.1) placed administration improvements through IT as its key priority. This company was aware of over-staffing in its white collar areas and claimed that it could reduce white collar jobs by 30% just by installing E-mail. This company was also pursuing labour elimination, but recognised that organisation culture did not permit 'shock therapy'.

Despite the teamworking approach in Japanese companies, many respondents were keen to increase management control through IT. Impediments to this objective were again grounded in the organisational culture. Interviews with managers confirmed that it was easier to introduce changes in production than in white collar work. The latter was perceived as rigid and traditional. The paperless office was certainly not evident in the white collar areas of Japanese companies.

One Japanese manager said that, 'We must be careful about imposing a formal struc-

What are the benefits of IT?	Bank1	Man.1	Man.2	Man.3	Man.4	Airline1	Man.5	Man.6	Service2
(a) Reduced inventory	11	6	3	7	1		1	2	10
(b) Lead time reduction	5	7	2	4	1		6	1	1
(c) Improved quality	6	5	3	3	5		9	2	4
(d) Reduced scrap/rework	7	10		5	2		8	2	11
(e) Reduced set-up time	4	11	4	7	9		7	1	2
(f) Improved administration	3	1	2	7	3		2	2	7
(g) Improved management control	1	3	2	7	3	1	4		6
(h) Staff reduction	9	2	2	7	4	1	3	2	8
(i) Increased flexibility	2	4	1	9	1		5	1	9
(j) Reductions in space	10	12	4	7	8		12	2	
(k) Skills development	9	9	4	1	6		10	1	3
(l) Improved quality	8	8	4	2	7		11	1	5

Table 11.8 Business benefits and IT in Japanese companies

ture on an informal business culture. In Japan, we spend a lot of time talking informally about business problems. The introduction of databases, E-mail and formal administrative systems could destroy the informal culture. Trust is important in Japanese companies'.

The implication of this statement was interesting in the light of the cultural differences between the formal (performance appraisal, payment by results) system adopted in the West, and the informal (group decision making, shared responsibility, teamworking) approach followed in Japan. Whilst the West seemingly criticises Japan for its inflated white collar sector, the task of restructuring Japanese companies is perhaps more difficult from a societal and cultural perspective.

Concluding remarks

This chapter has considered some of the significant changes affecting Japanese industry and commerce, most notably re-engineering, continuing technical change and a rethinking of the life-time employment system. As we saw, many of these changes are brought about by structural movements in both the global and domestic economy. Faced with a world-wide economic recession, and a massive trade surplus with the US, Japanese goods have become expensive and uncompetitive. As a result, Japanese companies have opened subsidiaries abroad to take advantage of cheap labour and possible new market opportunities.

Domestic companies, however, have found that their profits have declined as a consequence of recession and, what some writers perceive as, the burgeoning white collar sector (Hori, 1993). Field research has found that, in the light of challenging economic conditions, Japanese managers now seek to restructure the white collar sector using technology as a key player in the process. However, the case studies suggest that vast changes to Japanese corporations are likely to engender cultural problems as the life-time employment system is replaced by an alternative system.

Case Study

Bank1, Tokyo, Japan

Like many other banks in Japan, Bank1 had suffered the turbulence of the recent economic downturn. Bad debts were a serious problem, and this had led to greater caution in dealing with existing and new customers. IS was seen as a cost burden, and the senior executive interviewed at the bank said the annual IS spend was about $164 million (this figure was a reduction from the previous year). At the same time, IS was seen as a strategic tool to reduce operating costs. About 20% of company costs were on IS facilities. An optimum figure was felt to be 15%, but new technical developments kept the figure higher.

A subsidiary was owned by the bank comprising two IS divisions. About 890 people worked at this company, and there were a further 460 people working in IS at headquarters. The organisation was described as 'functionally structured' comprising four major business areas.

The company adopted a three-year strategic plan for IS, and was currently engaged in some very complex IS development work. Decision making was described as 'bottom-up', and flowed from middle-level management to board level.

		Off-Line Systems 1955–1964	1st Generation On-Line System 1965–1974	2nd Generation On-Line System 1975–1984	3rd Generation On-Line System 1985–Present
System Characteristics	*Objectives*	Saving labour	Effectivity	Marketing	Profitability
	Scope of on-line system		Bookkeeping	Office work of customer counters at branches, a part of operations at head offices	All office work at branches operations at head office
	Type	Batch processing	Single items in line	Deposit, loan and exchange integrated on-line system	Integrated systems for account processing and international systems
System Functions	*Customer management*		Using ledger by subject and office	Management by CIF including all customers	Diversification of customer information management
	Co-operation			Automatic connection amongst accounts	Co-operation amongst systems
Trends in services	*Expansion of locations*	Only opening accounts	Network services for all branches	Co-operative links with all branches of other banks–NCS, BANKS, other)	Corporations and households making transactions
	Service times	9:00 – 15.00		8:45 – 18:00	Extension of service times including bank holidays
	Automation		Cash dispensers	Automatic equipment (ATM, OTM, ARS)	Firm banking, bank POS, home banking
	Diversification		Automatic debit for public utility charges	New service using computer programs	Information consultancy
Software Development	*File techniques*	Magnetic tape (sequential processing)	File (sequential, random processing)	File and database	Database
	Language	Assembly	Assembly	Compiler (COBOL, PL/I)	Compiler
	Design techniques			Structured techniques	Software modularization
Hardware	*Recording media*	Magnetic tape	Low-capacity disks	Medium-capacity disks	Large-capacity disks
	Terminal		Exclusive-use terminal	General-purpose terminal (dot printing)	Diversification (laser printing)
	Automatic equipment		Cash dispensers	ATM (deposits)	Multi-purpose ATM (money exchange, tax)

Table 11.9 IT system functions and structural progress

External consultants were not used by the bank, although it was pointed out that 'strong support' was given by IBM – the bank's major supplier of equipment. IBM also supplied training and technical advice. Training for people in IS was not given priority. Generally, individuals acquired their knowledge through on-the-job training by working on IS projects.

Some IS development work was outsourced to specialist software houses. The bank used about twenty-five different companies. A major criterion for hiring these firms was their size in conjunction with annual turnover. Many were quoted on the Tokyo Stock Market, and were also listed in Fortune 500.

But the vast majority was undertaken in-house. IS development was described as 'becoming more complex, day by day'. Table 11.9 gives a technological development of the banking system over the past few decades.

Skills shortages affected the scope by which complex IS work could be carried out. There was also a reluctance to embark on open-ended, high-risk IS projects, given their uncertainty of outcome and high capital outlay. This emulates the situation in many British financial institutions discussed in previous chapters.

Key skills requirements were in the areas of:

- project management
- business awareness
- communication skills
- home banking
- multi-media technology

- system development
  - case tools
  - maintenance methods
  - re-engineering (using existing systems to renew business processes and using IS/IT to develop new business processes)
  - database management

Whilst project managers generally had ten years experience of IS development work, they were also required to possess knowledge about budgeting and planning. Project managers were expected to work closely with their clients on all matters relating to the project. The fusing of technical and commercial knowledge was seen as crucial to the successful completion of IS projects.

One important development was in the area of client-server. A support system was being developed for portfolio managers which would cost ¥2 million over three years, comprising 1000 man hours.

A key problem for management was the evaluation of IS projects. Senior managers pointed out that traditional performance evaluation methods and techniques were inappropriate, and this served as an impediment to innovation within the organisation. It was pointed out that, senior management 'gut feeling' was an important criterion for approving IS project proposals. Another factor was 'to undertake IS development work if our competitors were doing it'. IS projects were deemed a success if the users perceived them to be adequate.

Discussion questions

1 What are the major technical changes of the last few decades?
2 What do you think are the key skills for project managers?
3 Should technical or non-technical managers run IS departments?
4 How should you evaluate IS project success?
5 What are the key advantages of retaining an IS subsidiary company?
6 Can white collar labour be reduced through re-engineering using IT?

References 11

Abegglen, J.C., Stalk, G. (1985) *Kaisha: the Japanese Corporation.* Basic Books, USA.
Burnes, B and Weekes, B (1989) *AMT: a strategy for success?* NEDO Technical Communications.
Campbell, A., Currie, W., Warner, M (1989) 'Innovation, skills and training: micro-electronics and

manpower in the United Kingdom and West Germany', in Hirst, P. and Zeitlin, J. *Reversing industrial decline*. Berg Press, London.

Cobb, I. (1991). 'Understanding and working with JIT'. *Management Accounting*, 69, 2, pp 44–46.

Currie, W. (1994) *The Strategic Management of AMT*. CIMA, London.

Currie, W. and Yoshikawa, T. (1994) 'Restructuring IT departments: Japanese problems and western solutions?', working paper Stirling University.

Drucker, P. F. (1988) 'The coming of the new organisation'. *Harvard Business Review*, January/February.

Fruin, M (1983) *Kikkoman: Company, Clan and Community*. Harvard University Press.

Fruin, M. (1993) *The Japanese Enterprise System*. Clarendon Press, Oxford.

Garvin, D.A (1993) 'Building a learning organisation'. *Harvard Business Review*. July/August.

Hall, R. (1983) *Zero inventories*. Dow Jones-Irwin.

Hayes, R.H., Pisano, G.P. (1994) 'Beyond world class: the new manufacturing strategy'. *Harvard Business Review*, Jan/Feb, pp. 77–86.

Hirst, P. and Zeitlin, J. (1989) *Reversing industrial decline*. Berg Press, London.

Hirschmeier, J. and Tsunehito, Y (1981) *The Development of Japanese Business*. George Allen & Unwin.

Hori, S. (1993) 'Fixing Japan's white collar economy: a personal view'. *Harvard Business Review*, November/December, pp. 157–172.

Hunt, B., Targett, D. (1995) *The Japanese Advantage?*, Butterworth-Heinemann.

Japan Times (1994) 'Re-engineering revolution comes to Japan', 7 February, p. 7. Developing a new vision for Japan for the 21st century, p. 7.

Johnson, C. (1982) *MITI and the Japanese miracle*. Stanford University Press.

Kharbanda, O. and Stallworthy, E. (1991) 'Let's learn from Japan'. *Management Accounting*, 69, 3.

Kumazawa, M. and Yamada, J. (1989) 'Jobs and skills under the lifelong Nenko employment practice', in Wood, S. (ed), *The Transformation Of Work?*, London, Unwin Hyman, pp. 103–126.

Oliver, N. and Wilkinson, B (1987) 'Just-in-time, just-too-soon?' *Industrial Society Magazine*, Sept.

Pang, K.K. and Oliver, N. (1988) 'Personnel strategy in eleven Japanese manufacturing companies in the UK', *Personnel Review*, 17, 3, pp. 16–21.

Pascale, R. and Athos, A. (1981) *The Art of Japanese Management*, Penguin.

Sakurai, M. (1990) 'The influence of factory automation on management accounting practices: a study of Japanese companies', pp. 45–57, in R. Kaplan (ed) *Measures for manufacturing excellence*, Harvard Business School Press.

Schonberger, R. (1982). *Japanese Manufacturing Techniques: nine hidden lessons in simplicity*. New York Free Press.

Senker, P. and Beesley, M (1986) 'The need for skills in the factory of the future', *New Technology, Work and Employment*, Vol, 1, No. 1, pp. 9–17.

Skills and Enterprise Briefing (1993) 'Lack of IT skills: a barrier to growth'. Issue 27/93, September.

Stata, R (1989) 'Organisational learning – the key to management innovation'. *Sloan Management Review*, Spring, pp. 63–74.

Suzuki, N. (1989) 'The attributes of Japanese CEOs: can they be trained?', *Journal of Management Development*, 8 (4), 5–11.

Storey, J. (1991) 'Do the Japanese make better managers', *Personnel Management*, Aug, 24–28.

Thamhain, H. J (1992) 'Developing the skills you need'. *Research, Technology Management*, March/April.

Thompson, G. (1989) 'The American industrial policy debate: any lessons for the UK?' in G. Thompson (ed), *Industrial Policy: USA and UK Debates*, Routledge, pp. 11–83.

Yang, J.Z. (1992). 'Americanisation or Japanisation of human resource management policies: a study of Japanese manufacturing and service firms in the USA'. *Advances in International Comparative Management*, Vol, 17, pp. 77–115.

Yoshikawa, T., Innes, J. and Mitchell, F. (1989) 'Japanese management accounting: a comparative survey', *Management Accounting*, 68, 11, pp. 20–23.

Zipkin, P. H. (1991). 'Does manufacturing need a JIT revolution?' *Harvard Business Review*, Jan-Feb.

CHAPTER 12

Organisational Learning as a Competitive Strategy

Introduction

In recent years attention has focused on the need for organisations to place a higher premium on skills development and learning (Garratt, 1987). A relationship may be postulated between organisational learning and competitive advantage. This link becomes more evident in the context of research which suggests that poor management skills are an impediment to technical change – an important prerequisite for competitive advantage (Currie and Bryson, 1995).

This chapter discusses the relevant literature on skills, knowledge acquisition and learning in the context of IT. The fundamental argument is that new skills are required for both managing and developing IT in all industrial and public sector settings. Organisations need to establish more appropriate ways to reward their high-calibre technical professionals, rather than continue to view these individuals as second-tier organisational members. Indeed, a closer examination of managerial work in relation to IT projects suggests that, for the most part, low-grade administrative tasks are executed by project managers. Caution is therefore needed regarding the view that generalist managers should run large-scale, complex and high-risk IT projects, since a lack of technical awareness is likely to render these individuals devoid of the appropriate analytical tools for performance measurement.

Organisational knowledge, IT skills shortages and competitive advantage

The issue of IT skills development has gained much attention over the past decade from the academic community, industry, commerce, and the government. In the early 1980s, the debate about skill requirements for IT diverged into optimistic and pessimist scenarios (Currie, 1989). On the one hand, many writers argued that IT would eliminate dull and monotonous jobs and, in turn, create new types of employment. The optimistic scenario also perceived IT as a major force behind economic growth and prosperity. Demands were therefore made to increase the skills of the work force for the information age (Forester, 1980. 1985. MSC, 1985ab, 1987. Senker, 1984ab, 1985. Campbell et al, 1989). The pessimistic scenario, on the other hand, cautioned against the 'collapse of work' through unbridled technical change (Jenkins, 1979, 1980. Cooley, 1980. Wood, 1982). Here, IT was seen largely as a management tool to displace and deskill the work force.

Whilst the debate on the extent to which IT develops or degrades skills continues, recent studies highlight the continuing IT skills shortages which serve as an impediment to companies trying to maximise their competitive advantage (Skills and Enterprise, 1993. Thaimhain, 1992. HMSO, 1993, 1994). Many of these studies locate this problem in the wider context of businesses operating in a global market, characterised by the emerging markets of China, the Pacific rim and central and eastern Europe (HMSO, 1994. Drucker, 1988. Porter, 1992). Skills shortages in the IT field appear to afflict all mature and newly industrialised nations. As we saw in the previous chapter, many Japanese companies recognise the problem of IT skills shortages, particularly in the new fields of client-server, multi-media, open systems, etc. Despite the impressive record for training and development within Japanese firms (Fruin, 1993) the rapid pace of technological change guarantees a constant need for retraining to acquire new skills.

In a recent survey of 700 private sector employers in the UK by the West London Training and Enterprise Council (1993) shortfalls in IT skills were seen as a significant barrier to business growth. The survey claimed that, 'unskilful introduction and use of IT will inhibit sales, slow expansion and reduce profitability', and that between £10-20 billion is needed to remedy the problem. Many of the 'best-equipped organisations' were found to be 'struggling to exploit IT' since 'employees at all levels were lacking in these critical skills'.

The survey claimed that since specialist and user roles were now merging, the traditional centralised IT department containing specialist staff engaged in the design, implementation and maintenance of IT systems was becoming the 'exception rather than the rule'. Only 10% of organisations which used IT had a specialist IT function, with the remaining 90% having no specialist IT staff engaged in design work or even working in an advisory capacity. However, of the 700 organisations surveyed, only 38% said they had introduced 'some form of IT'. This suggests that the large proportion of the sample were small private sector companies. A further 13% said they planned to use some form of IT in the near future.

The survey also claimed that in the 90% of organisations with no IT department, the users were responsible for selecting, implementing and running IT-based information systems. Moreover, of the 7 million people who currently use IT in British firms, users were seen to outnumber IT specialists by thirteen to one.

Given the absence of specialist IT departments in the majority of the firms, it was unsurprising that the survey found that, 'the acquisition of IT skills is a very desirable asset to companies of all sizes in all sectors. Senior managers believe that any shortfall in IT skills depresses turnover, inhibits business expansion and reduces profitability. Some even think that, in practice, lack of IT skills could drive them out of business'.

Whilst there is disagreement in the literature about the definition of IT skills, the survey found that twelve areas of skill deficiency were common:

- business skills of IT staff
- top managers understanding of IT
- greater care over implementing IT
- administration of departmental systems
- interpersonal skills of IT people

- implementation of PC-based systems
- out-of-date skills of IT people
- IT skills of junior and middle managers
- technical skills in specific areas of IT
- expertise in specific tools for applications development
- keeping abreast of fast-moving technology
- IT skills of IT users

The above itemised list is a mixture of business and technical skills, and implies a need for formal training in most of these areas. Yet only 35% of the organisations surveyed said they provided formal IT training. Whilst the majority of firms who did not provide training were small, the survey found that as many as 20% of the large organisations also provided no IT training for their staff.

Of the organisations who did provide IT training, IT staff received, on average, 29 days of training per year, whereas IT users received only 8-9 days. The survey found that large organisations, unlike their smaller counterparts, were more likely to use external training providers such as IT manufacturers and dealers. In-house training facilities and commercial training firms were also used extensively. Very few private sector firms used public sector IT training providers. This was because some employers believed that IT training offered by the universities and colleges was 'irrelevant, invisible or outdated' (West London Training and Enterprise Council, 1993).

The survey concludes by offering four recommendations to help resolve the problem of IT/business skills shortages. First, it is argued that organisations must identify and clarify the skills which they require. Different groups within an organisation should undertake this task given the variety of technical solutions required for business problems. Second, it is contended that organisations should develop and deliver intensive training to bring high-leverage personnel to a high standard of competence. High-cost training is required for specialist IT personnel to develop state-of-the-art skills. This is preferred to on-the-job-training. Third, organisations should develop and deliver low-cost approaches to bring other personnel to satisfactory minimum standards. It is contended that, 'other groups of employees are larger in number and developing their IT skills must be addressed by a low-cost approach which doesn't make unrealistic demands on their time'. A satisfactory minimum standard is sought. The survey suggests distance learning materials as an appropriate option. Fourth, organisations should upgrade the education of their employees 'of the future' to a high standard. A key role should be played by schools, colleges and universities. It is suggested that courses should 'meet the needs and priorities of employers'.

This study, like many others in the area, seemingly offers a common-sense approach to the development of appropriate IT skills for private and public sector organisations. However, there are two important problems with this approach which relate to the content and process of IT training. First, the measure of how many hours individuals spend on training is arguably a worthless indicator in isolation of other factors. Although numerous articles in the IT field suggest a need for IT training and skills development, many of them fail to address the relationship between the content and quality of training. One of the key problems in identifying training for IT specialists, managers and staff is the confusion about what constitutes appropriate training for a rapidly changing business environment. New languages and packages enter the commercial market at alarming frequency. As a result, even IT specialists are faced with the prospect of continuous retraining to meet the demands of state-of-the-art technology. To a lesser extent, users are also frequently confronted with software upgrades as IT business applications become more sophisticated and complex. This situation often leaves managers and staff floundering in a state of ongoing confusion which is little helped by an IT industry renowned for its jargon and hype. Identifying the training requirements of departments or individuals is therefore highly challenging as those involved in the process have few yardsticks to go by in the design and development of appropriate IT training programmes.

Second, a question mark hangs over whether formal IT training is indeed the best way forward. Arguably, the majority of IT specialists as well as users learn their IT skills through constant exposure to IT. In other words – on-the-job-training. Whilst it is recognised that training for IT is important, IT professionals develop their skills almost entirely through working on IT projects.

In a recent questionnaire survey, Currie and Bryson (1995) found that IT contractors working for large financial services institutions (notably, banking and insurance) placed a higher premium on experiential learning than on formal IT training courses. Several contractors argued that listing formal IT training courses on C.V.s was inappropriate since employers were only interested in work experience on large and medium sized IT projects. One contractor working for a bank with a PhD in information systems claimed that, 'After I finished university, I thought my PhD would guarantee me a job in IT. I then found to my surprise that my PhD was not even recognised by employers as a useful or worthwhile qualification. I was rejected from many companies on the basis that I didn't have practical experience. This was in spite of the fact that my PhD was developed for and funded by a leading UK car manufacturer. In the end, I took the PhD off my C.V. and told companies simply that I had worked for the car manufacturer in their IT division. Having removed the PhD from my C.V. I found that companies were bending over backwards to offer me employment. I now work for a bank as an IT contractor. The contract has been renewed four times. I don't tell the bank that I have a PhD – If I did, they may terminate my contract!'

This experience was not uncommon. IT professionals interviewed claimed that formal educational qualifications in IT were not as important as work experience. Similarly, formal training for IT was perceived as relevant, although many highly trained IT professionals working as contractors for large organisations were critical of some of the training programmes offered by external IT suppliers and commercial training companies. Their main criticism was that, on many occasions when they had attended external IT training courses, they found their experience of the language or package to be greater than the person running the course. According to one IT analyst/programmer, 'I eat and breath IT day in day out. A lot of these training courses are expensive – large on presentation and short on content. I would rather spend time learning an application in my own time. Nearly all training is undertaken on the job. You can't spend a day or two on a training course and expect to become proficient on a specific language or package. You only become proficient after months of experience'.

Interviews with IT professionals suggested that a wide gap existed between power and responsibility with regard to IT professionals and their managers. Whilst a key problem in managing the IT function has often been cited as the difficulty of co-ordinating and controlling the activities of technical specialists field research suggested that little progress had been made to resolve the problem. On the contrary, the problem of managing the 'knowledge-worker' persisted in many organisations which was indicative of a crisis in management control (Currie and Bryson, 1995).

Managing the knowledge worker: a crisis in management control?

The perception of IT professionals as 'knowledge-workers' who are instrumental in maximising the potential of IT has gained prominence in recent years. Indeed, it is generally recognised that hardware alone is insufficient in gaining competitive advantage since specialist IT skills and business awareness are two crucial prerequisites of this goal. But the notion that knowledge is a commodity which can be exploited for commercial gain, in much the same way as PCs, databases, and the like, is difficult to conceptualise. Nonaka (1991, p.96) states that

> 'In an economy where the only certainty is uncertainty, the one sure source of lasting competitive advantage is knowledge. When markets shift, technologies proliferate, competitors multiply, and products become obsolete almost overnight, successful companies are those that consistently create new knowledge, disseminate it widely throughout the organisation, and quickly embody it in new technologies and products. These activities define the 'knowledge-creating' company, whose sole business is continuous innovation'. Yet few companies, he argues, understand the nature of the knowledge-creating company and how it should be managed.

The knowledge-creating company is seemingly one which adopts a different interpretation of knowledge, and how it can be exploited. As opposed to knowledge constituting formal and systematic and hard quantifiable data, obtained through bureaucratic and codified procedures, knowledge is instead embodied in a company's ability to adapt to new market conditions, create new products, exploit technology and respond to customers' needs. Examples of Japanese knowledge-creating companies are Canon, Honda, Kao and Sharp, among others. Writing on the topic of organisational knowledge, Tricker (1992, p.21) claims that, 'Managing organisational knowledge accepts the notion that organisations learn as they adapt to changing environments. That learning takes place as a result of acquiring knowledge. Moreover, the process has to be managed if it is to be effective in a complex organisation'. But definitions of knowledge vary. For example, organisational knowledge may exist in the form of databases, files, records, reports, minutes, letters, etc (Tricker, 1992), and also in the somewhat invisible form of peoples' memories, experience, rules of thumb approaches to problem solving, heuristics, gut-feeling and intuition.

Nonaka (1991) divides knowledge into two forms: *explicit* and *tacit* knowledge. He claims that explicit knowledge is formal and systematic. It is therefore easily communicated and shared throughout the organisation. For example, explicit knowledge is embodied in a computer program or set of procedures for hiring staff, etc. Organisations are full of examples of explicit knowledge, indicated by their various administrative procedures and controls. Tacit knowledge, on the other hand, is defined as 'highly personal' and not amenable to formalisation and standardisation. In addition, tacit knowledge is not easily communicated to others. Nonaka (1991, p. 98) claims that

'Tacit knowledge is also deeply rooted in action and in an individual's commitment to a specific context – a craft or profession, a particular technology or product market, or the activities of a work group or team. Tacit knowledge consists partly of technical skills – the kind of informal, hard to pin down skills captured in the term "know-how". A master craftsman after years of experience develops a wealth of expertise "at his finger-tips". But he is often unable to articulate the scientific or technical principles behind what he knows'.

Nonaka (1991) argues that the knowledge-creating company should attempt to make tacit knowledge explicit. This is likely to be achieved in the ubiquitous team approach adopted by Japanese companies where individuals work together in an attempt to create and share knowledge for product development and technological innovation.

In a recent study Currie and Bryson (1995) found that one of the most pressing issues confronting management concerns the control of IT professionals (project managers, systems analysts, analyst/programmers, database administrators, etc). Using a semi-structured questionnaire, both technical and non-technical IT managers were interviewed to elicit information on how they control the activities of the IT professionals they manage. The researchers were keen to interview both managers and IT professionals for comparative purposes.

An important distinction was made between managers with IT backgrounds and those without. For example, some managers in charge of IT departments and IT projects were brought in on the basis of their business knowledge either internal or external to the organisation. Some managers claimed that 'an important requirement' was that they understood the business. Here, specialist IT skills were perceived by the upper echelons of management as 'less critical' compared with business awareness. The generalist manager was therefore favoured against the specialist or technologist.

Conversely, other organisations had promoted their technical people to managerial positions. Promotion of technical specialists to IT management positions depended largely on the career structure adopted by organisations. Whereas some organisations had a single spine structure, others adopted a dual one which separated technical and managerial personnel. The latter structure was becoming less common as many organisations were following the trend of reducing their management hierarchies, thus creating flatter structures.

Figure 12.1 shows that out of 174 organisations surveyed, just over half (52%) had a single spine salary/career structure. However, as many as two-fifths (39%) had a separate but overlapping salary/career structure. The remaining organisations (9%) had a separate, non-overlapping salary/career structure. Interviews with a number of managers in the organisations found that separate salary/career structures for IT professionals had emerged because of the 'historical separation of IT and management career paths'.

Interviews with managers in the various organisations highlighted a common tendency to refer to managers as generalists and technical personnel as specialists. In some of the organisations, the technical salary grading system ended well below the managerial grades. Yet interviews with managers and IT professionals showed that educational qualifications of the two groups could be similar. For example, it was common for both

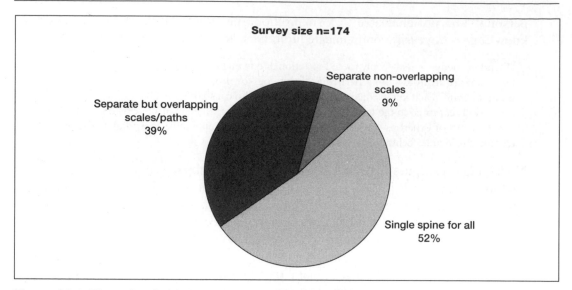

Figure 12.1 The salary/career structure for IT professionals

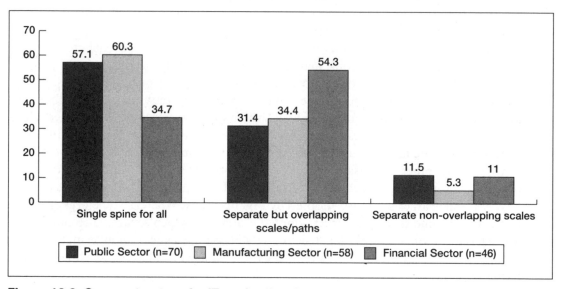

Figure 12.2 Career structure for IT professionals

senior-level analyst/programmers and middle-level managers on a separate salary/career spine to possess a degree. But the same individuals were unlikely to be on equal salary/career grades. Thus, a middle manager in mid-thirties could be earning much more than a senior analyst/programmer of the same age and educational background.

Whilst those in middle-level managerial positions were likely to argue that their role carries greater responsibility and authority than specialist (technical) positions, a closer examination of the situation suggested the contrary. In the financial services industry, for example, the separation of managerial and technical personnel tended to engender poor relations between the two groups reflected by a 'them' and 'us' attitude. Senior analyst/programmers also argued that their role was becoming 'more and more responsible'. This was exemplified by their informal role as 'internal technical consultants' where their advice on highly technical matters tended to steer the future technological direction of the organisation. As one senior analyst/programmer put it, 'I recently advised my manager on client-server technology. My department is now moving to this direction, and the total investment is likely to exceed £4 million. I believe I was instrumental in the decision making on client-server. Actually, my manager is completely uninformed about it'.

In a number of organisations it was found that the IT department did not sit comfortably with the various business departments. A common cry was that, 'IT people don't communicate well with the users'. There were many stories about poor systems development projects where the users (in the various business departments) had received a product (an IT system) which was deemed unsuitable for their particular business requirements. A number of respondents confirmed that while the 'hybrid manager' was an ideal (which did not necessarily exist in reality) some attempts had been made to align IT with the business strategy. Some organisations had created new positions such as 'relationship manager' and 'business analyst' with the intention of merging business and technical awareness. Such a move appeared to be an attempt to make tacit knowledge explicit, and usable in a practical sense.

Yet interviews with managers and IT staff in a range of organisations indicated that the multi-skilled manager operated less effectively in practice than in theory. Whereas a number of managers (non-technical) in charge of IT projects were supportive of the theory behind the multi-skilled manager, IT staff usually embraced a different view. The following comments were received from a project manager (non-technical background) and a contract senior IT analyst/programmer (with a PhD in information systems).

'My degree was in history. I'm not really interested in computers, but you don't need to be technically knowledgeable to manage IT projects. My main duties are to set deadlines for my technical team, manage the project budget, liaise with the project owner (person who commissioned the systems development work), and deliver the system on time and within budget. If I need some advice on technical matters, I can hire in external management consultants or ask my technical team. For example, two of my contract IT programmers recently advised me about client-server technology. That's what they get paid for"'

IT project manager (Bank)

'Although a project manager runs the project in theory, I consider that I manage my own work. Usually, the project manager will ask me how long it will take for me to complete a particular stage in the systems development phase. Every project is date-driven. The quality issues are left until last, usually at the system sign-off phase. One of the problems of being managed by a non-technical person is poor communication. When I talk about technical concepts, he (the project manager) simply doesn't understand me. The cliché that technical people can't communicate is false. I think the business managers should learn about the new technology. After all, the bank spends millions on it, and so many systems are developed which do not meet user requirements – even though they are developed to user specifications'.

Senior analyst/programmer (Bank)

Clearly, the two views were diametrically opposed in terms of each individual's perception of the skills required for managing IT project work. The project manager viewed managerial work as 'non-technical in nature'. The analyst/programmer, on the other hand, believed that those in charge of managing IT projects should possess some technical awareness since the nature of systems development work was, by definition, highly technical.

One of the key management issues was the division of labour between the project manager and IT specialist. Many project managers interpreted their work as planning, co-ordinating and controlling. A large proportion of the project manager's role seemingly involved administering the IT project budget. Once a project was commissioned, the project manager defined performance targets and deadlines, and kept the project on time and within budget. Indeed, many project managers said they were judged according to this criteria.

Analyst/programmers and other members of the technical team were given deadlines to meet, which were either imposed upon them or negotiated with the project manager. A number of project managers appeared to perceive systems development work as following a linear process, with each stage carefully delineated by checklists and performance targets. Certainly, this was the case in terms of how the budget was structured, e.g. resources being allocated at various stages of the project.

But technical personnel, particularly those involved in writing/coding the system, adopted an alternative viewpoint. According to several technical staff, IT systems development was a dynamic activity which was iterative as opposed to linear in nature. One analyst/programmer commented that

> 'It is difficult to think of systems development work in linear terms. Knowledge is acquired through constant exposure to various languages and packages. Clients frequently change their mind. The business changes. Legal frameworks change. This means that a project specification may undergo several alterations. Also, as an analyst/programmer, I am constantly learning new skills. I make mistakes. I learn from those mistakes. When I got this job, I bluffed my way in. I told management that I had two years experience of SQL Windows. Since they didn't know the product well, they believed me. When I started, I had to work like crazy to understand how to program in this language. I think I survived because I really enjoy programming and working with computers. But I know a lot of programmers who would like to be doing something else. People with non-technical backgrounds can't really supervise programmers because they don't know how to measure our efficiency. Charts, tables and graphs are ineffective as a form of management control'.

Analyst/programmer (Bank)

Whereas managers were unlikely to admit to a management control problem in setting goals and evaluating the performance targets of their technical team, anecdotal evidence from technical specialists suggested that control was a key issue. The majority of technical specialists interviewed argued that IT disasters usually resulted for two reasons. First, managers responsible for assessing the potential risk factor of proposed IT projects often failed to do so adequately. This was certainly the case with the TAURUS disaster (Currie, 1994). Second, lack of project management skills led to management control problems. In many cases it seemed that managers imposed administrative and budgetary controls upon technical specialists to give the appearance of being in control. These controls took the form of preparing GANTT charts where IT project work was broken down into various parts and allocated a performance target accordingly. Although this approach was common to many IT projects, technical personnel argued that it failed to guarantee success. They said that 'arbitrary deadlines' imposed on analyst/programmers by managers simply forced them to conduct their work at a rapid pace to meet these deadlines. Yet working quickly encouraged them to cut corners, particularly in the writing of programs. This resulted in poor quality programs, as they were pressured to complete their work and move on to the next stage in the development process. The date-driven approach was common in the majority of organisations, and meeting deadlines within budget was perceived by senior managers as indicative of the project being 'on course'. Problems usually arose down stream; sometimes at the project 'sign-off' stage, but also at the later stage of implementation.

Several technical personnel said that it was common to 'completely rewrite a system', even though it may have already cost tens of thousands of pounds. In fact, the subject of IT systems failure tended to evoke embarrassment amongst managers and technical personnel, and several respondents admitted that very few IT systems could be described as a 'resounding success to the business'. Respondents were asked what they believed were the key ingredients of successful IT projects. Interestingly, managers and IT staff often gave conflicting opinions. For example, it was common for many project managers to think of success in terms of meeting time and budget deadlines. Signing off a system and handing it over to the client on time and within budget demonstrated to managers that it was successful. Future problems relating to the functionality of the system were described by managers as 'matters for technical staff'. Many managers said that, 'all systems are maintained and it is up to the technical team to do this work'. Conversely technical staff believed that successful IT projects were almost entirely dependent upon two factors. First, that the client had thought through what was required as a business application. Second, that highly trained technical personnel were brought in to design, develop and implement the intended system. This point is reinforced by Samson (1994, p. 7) who writes:

'The bulk of IT work is analysis and programming and one way in which this activity is different from most other skills is in the wide range of abilities of those involved. Studies have shown that the best analyst/programmers can be ten or twenty times more productive than the average. At first sight this seems hard to believe but it makes more sense if the relatively high failure rate of IT developments is taken into account. The high rewards of IT and the skills shortage attract a fair number of people into IT jobs who have no great aptitude for the work. Observing how someone less talented tackles finding a bug in a system, for instance, can be very revealing in this connection. It may take them days or even weeks to resolve a problem that a real techie could crack in minutes. If this divergence is extrapolated into the life of a project, it's as if the skilled individual is making a journey by car while the less gifted are on foot. Minor glitches can be real show-stoppers for the employee who does not really have a good grasp of the technicalities they are dealing with. Without wishing to be unkind to the less proficient employee, there are probably tasks they will not be able to complete no matter how long they spend on them'.

Whilst the above comments suggest that it would be reasonable to recommend the promotion of technical personnel to managerial positions, the normative academic literature rarely advocates this as a viable option. Indeed, there is plenty of evidence which supports the view that technical specialists rarely make good managers. Whilst this view has arguably reached mythical proportions, technical specialists themselves were often reluctant to relinquish their technical expertise by becoming managers. Instead, many

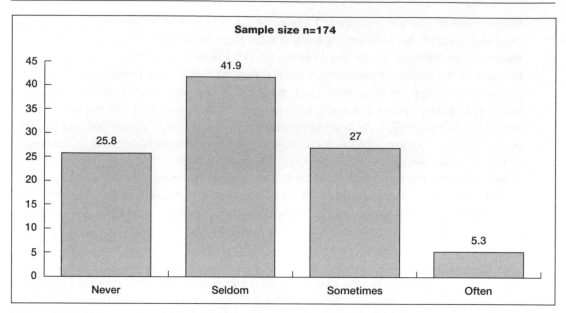

Figure 12.3 Frequency of IT professionals to senior management

technical staff opted for an alternative to remaining in relatively low paid permanent positions by becoming freelance contract IT staff. A large number of technical personnel called for a revision of managerial skills for IT project management as they argued that traditional definitions were 'outdated'.

One important area where managers were seen to be lacking in skills was their ability to evaluate the performance of technical personnel. Using Nonaka's (1991) definitions of explicit and tacit knowledge, technical personnel suggested that managers were often unable to place a value on the latter. For example, tacit skills were demonstrated by an analyst/programmer's ability to embark on complex systems development work, the success of which depended largely upon the flair, understanding and experience acquired by the individual. Yet many analyst/programmers were concerned by their perception that managers merely saw them as 'dispensable technicians'. This was clearly the case in one organisation which had developed a policy of 'skills scraping'. One analyst/programmer summed up the policy:

> 'The other contract analyst/programmer and myself have now worked here for two years. We believe we are indispensable to the company. Recently, the company tried to hire two permanent people from outside to be trained to do our jobs on half our salary. I was asked to interview them which I found surprising. One person had never programmed in SQL Windows before, and the other was also learning and had a mainframe background. A policy was recently developed by managers called 'IT skills scraping'. The general idea is to get contract programmers to impart their knowledge to trainee programmers or even to permanent staff whose skills are out of date. In truth, I am not going to impart all my gems of knowledge to people that could ultimately put me out of a job. But I don't think I have to worry too much because some people never become good programmers anyway'.

Interviews with a range of analyst/programmers suggested that a pecking order existed between contract (freelance) and permanent technical staff. In fact, many permanent staff in both private and public sector organisations were keen to become 'freelancers' as they could earn much more money. They were unconcerned by less job security associated with contract work as they believed their jobs were not secure anyway. Also, permanent IT staff were concerned by the lack of promotion prospects of technical staff to managerial grades. They considered their job to be more skilled in some areas than management roles. One analyst/programmer commented that

> My manager simply draws up a project budget and tries to keep expenditure within its parameters. As project manager, the client for whom we are developing a system should liaise with him. In truth, the client liaises almost entirely with us (the technical team). When we finished our last project, the client said it was completed 'in spite of Mr S (the project manager).
>
> *Analyst/programmer* (Bank)

Figure 12.4 gives the results of a questionnaire survey into 174 UK private and public sector organisations on the extent to which IT staff gain promotion to senior management. Although a management hierarchy existed within the IT departments of these organisations, promotion to senior management was likely to involve the individual moving away from their technical specialism to one of the business departments (e.g. marketing, HRM) or to a general management position.

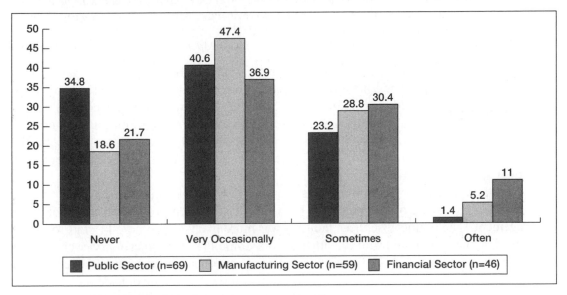

Figure 12.4 Staff promotions to senior management

As we can see from Figure 12.3, some 42% of respondents said that IT staff seldom gained promotion to senior management. This compared with only 5% claiming that IT staff often moved into senior management positions. In-depth interviews carried out with managers of IT departments in various private and public sector organisational settings confirmed that as IT staff tended to move away from their technical specialism to managerial positions, managers from other functional areas (either internal or external) were often brought in to manage IT. For example, many organisations confirmed that their IT director did not have a technical background, but a business background instead. The latter was often seen as a prerequisite for managerial work. Key requirements for management were seen by managers as *communication skills, business awareness and budgeting*.

Managing people was also seen as an important skill. Yet interviews with technical staff suggested a wide gap in the perceptions of this group and managers in how this was to be achieved. On the one hand, technical staff usually saw themselves as working autonomously and independent of management. In a number of cases, highly skilled technical staff looked upon their non-technical managers with some disdain as they were unable to discuss technical concepts pertaining to systems development work. On the other hand, managers tended to overstate the ease by which they could impose performance controls and targets on their technical team. They claimed that IT projects are 'better managed' by non-technical (general) managers, and past failures in systems development work were often perceived as the fault of technical staff. The views of several managers were summed by one senior manager at an engineering company who pointed out that

'When technical people manage IT projects, they lose control of the budget and get bogged down in the technology. They enjoy playing with new toys and forget the needs of the users. General managers make sure that systems are developed with the business in mind. After all, the users are paying for the systems development work, and IT is only a service'.

Senior Manager, Accounting (Engineering firm)

The survey research on managing IT in the three sectors accentuated many power struggles between management and technical personnel. Interviews with the two groups elicited many contradictory statements about the skills and abilities needed to run IT projects. Professional and managerial protectionism was evident, although interviews with technical staff suggested that IT failures continued to be common, despite the trend of assigning larger numbers of general managers to control IT departments and their range of activities.

Although the above sample represents only 174 UK organisations, it none the less gives an indication of the frequency by which IT staff gain promotion to senior management. The financial services industry was more likely to promote IT staff to senior management compared with the other sectors. Some 11% of financial service companies said they promoted IT staff to senior management often, and a further 30% claimed it was sometimes. Senior management positions could be within or outside the IT department. Usually, in the banking sector, there were opportunities to rise up the management hierarchy within IT, although many people saw greater managerial opportunities outside of IT. The survey also found that the financial services industry tended to have the highest annual IT spend compared with the other sectors, and it was common to find IT departments with over 600 IT staff, especially in banking and insurance.

IT staff in the public sector appeared to offer fewer senior management opportunities to IT staff. Only 1% of public sector organisations claimed they often promoted IT staff to senior management roles, which implied a career bottleneck for this group. Pay scales for IT staff in the public sector were also much lower than in the private sector. Coupled with this, many public sector IT departments were slower to upgrade their IT facilities. Consequently, the public sector found it more difficult to attract IT professionals with state-of-the-art skills, as they could command higher pay rates in the private sector. This led to skills shortages in many public sector organisations. In the event of undertaking complex systems development work, it seemed that the public sector opted to hire external management consultants, even though the cost of doing so was extremely high.

Manufacturing firms were also reluctant to promote IT staff to senior management positions, particularly in large organisations. In a number of cases, IT staff in the manufacturing sector were highly critical of the lack of a technical voice at the apex of their organisation. This reinforces earlier studies on the poor promotion chances of technical personnel in the manufacturing sector (Finniston, 1978. Currie, 1994. Glover and Kelly, 1987). However, an important factor in determining promotion of technical people within the manufacturing sector appeared to be company size. The survey results coupled with an earlier study (Currie, 1989) suggested that small engineering firms comprising highly specialised technical personnel were more likely to have technical people in senior management and board level positions than their larger manufacturing counterparts (e.g. car manufacturers and avionics firms, etc).

The questionnaire survey also asked respondents if senior managers responsible for IT retained direct IT roles. Direct IT roles was interpreted by the researchers as the capacity of senior managers to have a good working knowledge of the technology used by the technical team. Although this did not mean programming to an expert level, it did mean a thorough understanding of the concepts, parameters and application of the various technologies.

The 178 respondents who answered the question in Figure 12.5 appeared to contradict the findings from the in-depth interviews. For example, even though 56% said that senior IT managers retain direct IT roles (with 44% claiming they did not) interpretations of 'direct IT roles' differed within and between the three sectors. Follow-up interviews with a number of senior IT managers suggested that very few possessed a

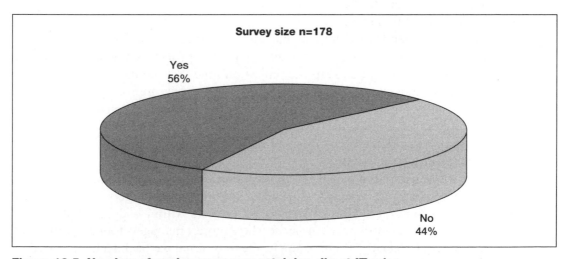

Figure 12.5 Number of senior managers retaining direct IT roles

good working knowledge of the technology used by their technical teams. In fact, those who did possess a good working knowledge were likely to have a technical background. One manager at a local authority said that

> 'I run a very large IT department with about 500 people. As I rose through the ranks from being a programmer in the early 1970s to a senior manager now, I have seen technical changes. I believe that you have to understand all the technical changes to be able to manage IT projects. My lads know they can't pull the wool over my eyes about deadlines and targets, because I know the technology they are working with. I make sure I keep up to date. Besides, a senior IT manager should understand the technology. We can talk glibly about re-engineering the business, but if you don't understand the technology, you can't even begin to think about how you will change business processes'.
>
> *IT Director* (Scottish Local Authority)

Very few organisations irrespective of sector commented on the link between IT success and organisational learning as a continuous process. Interviews with a range of managers (especially those with non-technical backgrounds) reinforced the view that the IT department was simply another service provider. Users would therefore place an order for a system and the technical team (comprising the project manager, analyst/programmers and other personnel) would simply develop and deliver it on time and within budget.

The issue of how to make tacit skills explicit in the organisation was rarely addressed. In most organisations, a rigid division of labour existed between managerial and technical grades. Even managers working in technical departments were keen to repackage themselves as *managers* for promotion and, by doing so, avoid being labelled *a techie, egghead or boffin*. Whilst this career strategy made sense to those seeking managerial positions, it tended to widen the skills gap between managers and technical staff which culminated in the absence of a common language. Technical staff were often labelled *bad communicators* by the managers and users. Equally, managers and users were looked upon with some disdain by technical staff for their 'total lack of understanding of today's technology'.

Poor systems development work was often described as a 'technical failure', and rarely one of managerial incompetence. Users often complained that 'the IT department rarely develops what we want'. In defence, the IT department would say, 'But we gave you what you asked for'. In short, there appeared to exist a crisis in management control over IT which was multifarious.

First, managers tended to embrace bureaucratic forms of control over IT staff by imposing stringent time allocations for the completion of technical work (e.g. writing code). This was an attempt to keep the project on time. Yet the date-driven approach tended to force analyst/programmers to adopt a piecework approach to their work, which often resulted in poor quality results even though it was completed on time. Since project managers were unlikely to have the skills to carry out quality checks on the work, software faults (in the form of bugs or simply poor quality code) would be brought into the next stage of the project.

Second, it seemed that managing the project budget was one of the most important tasks of being a project manager. Indeed, many project managers said they were appraised on their success rates of keeping IT projects within budget. Whilst this is important, financial control problems arose where project managers found it difficult (if not impossible) to evaluate IT. For example, the traditional payback technique used by management accountants to evaluate IT was deemed inappropriate by several project managers. Also, the task of allocating a value on expected financial benefits from IT project work was equally viewed as 'spurious' (e.g. speed up information flows by 10% = saving of £350k; headcount reduction by 2% = saving of £200k, etc).

Third, human resource control problems were to do with managing the knowledge worker for the exploitation of tacit knowledge. In many organisations it was implicit that *technical whiz kids* were critically important in IT project work. Yet few organisations had any formal mechanism for rewarding technical staff. On the contrary, formal administrative grading procedures tended to penalise technical staff, particularly where a dual career/salary spine operated. Promoting technical experts into management was not the answer, since these skills were usually scarce as a consequence of the ongoing IT skills shortage, although many IT staff with state-of-the-art skills were reluctant to relinquish their technical leverage to become *paper-pushers*. The answer seemed to be a re-evaluation on the part of organisations to upgrade highly skilled IT staff to make their remuneration and reward structure commensurate with managerial grades. Whilst this was beginning to occur in some organisations, notably in the financial services and manufacturing sectors, the issue had not been addressed in the public sector.

The ability to exploit tacit skills was also a problem where organisations tended to favour outsourcing and the contracting in of IT staff. In several organisations where a significant number of IT staff were *on-contract*, project managers were keen to renew the contracts of highly skilled people. One project manager said that

> 'We talk a lot these days about teamworking and the learning organisation. I now have to contract in IT staff to work on highly complex systems. The trouble is, once they have finished, they leave the company. I not only lose a colleague, but also the skills, experience and knowledge they possess. They take it all away with them. Contracting might save the company money, but it is disastrous for skills retainment'.

> *IT project manager* (Insurance)

Clearly, one of the most important issues for project managers in IT concerned the development and retainment of skilled IT labour. The growing trend of outsourcing and reducing employment contracts, however, did not bode well with the desire to retain scarce skills. Indeed, the piecemeal, stage by stage (as opposed to holistic) approach of managing IT projects demonstrated that skills were perceived as dispensable commodities, at least by upper management. To this effect, one contract analyst/programmer said that

> 'The idea with a contractor is that managers can 'turn you on and off like a tap'. What is forgotten is that IT project work is a dynamic process which involves interaction with people at all levels of the company. You need to get to know people and find out what they want. Communication is much easier if you have established a working relationship with someone. Now you are expected to come in on day one and just start programming. But people interpret things differently. This is why so many IT systems crash. People get confused about what they want and what they have asked for. Its an organisational and management problem – not a technical problem'.

Organisational learning and competitive advantage

The concept of organisational learning is difficult to define since it embodies intangible processes of knowledge and skills generation, and shared insights, experiences and memory (Stata, 1989. Argyris, 1977. Huber, 1991. Garvin, 1993. Fiol and Lyles, 1985). Garvin (1993, p.80) states that, 'a learning organisation is an organisation skilled at creating, acquiring, and transferring knowledge, and at modifying its behaviour to reflect new knowledge and insights'.

Clearly the challenge for management in creating a learning organisation is immense. Other definitions of organisational learning are as follows:

- 'Organisational learning means the process of improving actions through better knowledge and understanding' (C. M. Fiol and M. A. Lyles, 1985).
- 'An entity learns if, through its processing of information, the range of its potential behaviours is changed' (G. P. Huber, 1991).
- 'Organisations are seen as learning by encoding inferences from history into routines that guide behaviour' (Levitt and March, 1988).
- 'Organisational learning is a process of detracting and correcting error (Argyris, 1977).
- 'Organisational learning occurs through shared insights, knowledge, and mental models ... (and) builds on past knowledge and experience – that is, on memory' (Stata, 1989).

(Source: Stata, 1993)

The subject of organisational learning has become important in recent years as many industrialised nations have experienced economic decline. Much attention has focused on new product and process developments to sustain competitive advantage (Porter, 1985). Companies have been advised to invest heavily in technology, take advantage of cheap overseas labour, revise employment contracts to favour short-term arrangements, *downsize or rightsize* their organisation structures to enhance efficiency, and much more.

But the subject of managing innovation for competitive success has not been well researched, according to Stata (1993). He argues that the link between theory and practice in managing innovation needs to be more fully addressed. In particular, managers need to consider how organisations learn, and how knowledge and experience can be exploited for competitive advantage. Indeed, he claims that

'I would argue that the rate at which individuals and organisations learn may become the only sustainable competitive advantage, especially in knowledge-intensive industries' (p.64).

He differentiates between organisational and individual learning in two important respects:

'First, organisational learning occurs through shared insights, knowledge, and mental models. Thus organisations can learn only as fast as the slowest link learns. Change is blocked unless all of the major decision makers learn together, come to share beliefs and goals, and are committed to take the actions necessary for change. Second, learning builds on past knowledge and experience – that is, on memory. Organisational memory depends on institutional mechanisms (e.g. policies, strategies, and explicit models) used to retain knowledge. Of course, organisations depend on the memory of individuals' (Stata, 1993, p.64).

Organisational learning and knowledge protectionism

The results of the questionnaire survey outlined above suggested that organisational learning was not an explicit goal of IT project managers. Nor was it part of an ongoing policy of continuous improvement. Conversely, many organisations were pursuing policies to appoint staff on short-term contracts. IT departments were especially threatened by this since they were perceived as service providers. Also, the workloads within IT departments were subject to internal market fluctuations, a factor which had led many companies to consider outsourcing as a viable option. Numerous IT departments practised a policy of hiring in contract IT staff, and many were considering stepping up this activity. In some public sector settings, managers were uncertain if their IT department would survive CCT and rationalisation. Yet interviews with a range of managers in both the private and public sectors indicated that very few of them adopted a labour market perspective on outsourcing and contracting in, and instead simply concentrated on reaching financial performance targets.

Several managers were unconcerned about the prospect of losing contract IT staff at the end of a project. They argued that, 'We can ring the agency and advertise for the same skills-set when new projects are commissioned'. However, others were critical of the 'ongoing IT skills haemorrhage', as contractors moved from one job to another and took their knowledge with them. Obviously, highly skilled IT contractors could negotiate a new contract (assuming their was more work). But the individual nature of working *on contract* tended to suggest individual learning for self-improvement as opposed to organisational learning for company-wide benefits. Permanent IT staff were less mobile, although those wishing to become managers were almost certain to lose their technical skills.

Many IT contractors saw themselves as *portfolio workers* who had acquired technical expertise and business experience from a range of commercial and/or public sector settings. Many openly admitted to being protective about their knowledge to rival contractors and management consultants. This scenario indicated an absence of organisational learning as individual knowledge, expertise and skills were traded on the IT labour market. Moreover, IT contractors and permanent staff often admitted to 'enjoying the status of being the expert in x'. They were thus disinclined to impart their knowledge and expertise through a process of *skills scraping* or mentoring. Rather it was their intention to make themselves indispensable in a competitive individualist working environment.

Concluding remarks

The transfer of knowledge and experience from one person to another is a highly complex process, and one which is not easily researched. Findings from the case study interviews in the private and public sectors suggested that project managers seemed to value IT project experience more highly than academic achievement. Managements' perceptions of IT project success appeared to be based upon two factors. They were: a) the ability to complete IT projects on time and within budget and, to a lesser extent, b) if the team worked well together. Indeed, political in-fighting among managers, IT staff, users and other 'stakeholders' should not be underestimated as more evidence is coming to light which associates IT failure with poor management practices as opposed to being technical malfunctions (Galliers, 1991, 1992. Currie, 1994. Boynton, 1992. Murray, 1989).

Whilst organisational learning was perceived by managers as theoretically important, very few of them had developed practical methods designed to retain and exploit the knowledge base of their organisation. This finding is also confirmed in the recent literature on organisational learning and innovation (Stata, 1989, 1993. Nonaka, 1991. Garvin, 1993). But in a climate of decreasing costs of computer technology, scarce IT skills, poor success rates in systems development work and intense global competition, managers it seems will be forced to identify more effective ways to manage the knowledge worker and how to translate organisational knowledge into competitive advantage. This is arguably going to be the key IS issue for the twenty-first century.

Case study

The development of a nationwide management information system (MIS)

The accounting division of a large financial services company established a requirement for an MS Windows based system which would enable all project costs to be tracked and forecasted to enhance financial control of IT expenditure. This type of system did not currently exist at the company, but was seen as vital if IT project costs were to be properly administered and controlled. Technologically, the proposed system arose from the application of new development languages and databases. The system was to operate using all the benefits of a client-server environment, with copies of the program being installed on all PCs whilst the data was to exist within a centralised database. As such the PCs would communicate across their local area network (LAN) and onto the server via a wide area network (WAN). This would enable every branch within the United Kingdom to input and to select and manipulate data from the same set of details.

The development package deemed most appropriate was SQLWindows/SQLBase. This was a 4th generation language (4GL) and associated database. This represented the most advanced client-server development tools available at the time. Whilst this product enabled fast prototyping coupled with reduced development lead times, the main drawback of using it was the shortfall of skilled developers with experience of the product. Consequently, the trend to migrate many services towards the PC arena in an environment of state-of-the-art skills shortages forced the company to request tenders from external consultancies.

The selected software house was currently engaged in the development of the technical specifications of the proposed multi-user IT system, and the contract to develop it was worth a total of over £500k. To meet the development projections, two consultant programmers from the software house began development at the client site. The project was expected to be completed within four months and was to be overseen by a manager at the client company.

At the end of this period the system was signed-off and installed, after which the software house left. Soon after, a variety of human and technical problems with the MIS emerged. An important point to note is that, although the system had been *briefly* tested by the two developers (employed by the software house), it had not been thoroughly tested by a third party (namely, the client or client's representative). It was not standard practice for individuals to fully test their own code for the purpose of removing any subtle bugs or to correct logical anomalies. However, the date-driven approach encouraged the two developers to cut corners and conduct *ad hoc* tests of their own work. Thus the absence of an independent analysis of the work allowed many mistakes to go unnoticed until the implementation stage.

Sometime after implementation, the system was deemed unusable for a variety of reasons.

For example, the database structure was believed to be inadequate. The fact that multiusers were accessing the same data sets proved difficult in practice. Some individuals found they were unable to gain access to vital areas of the database, and once records had been updated, they could not be selected and used by other individuals. This was not conducive to the aim to create a shared database (containing reference tables, etc), and so the ambition of moving to client-server in this respect was lost.

Since the users of this system were to be senior managers, the problem had to be rectified as soon as possible. Ironically, the system was intended to improve financial control of IT; yet it embodied all the common problems associated with IT systems development work. In this respect, it simply added to the statistics of unsatisfactory IT projects throughout the organisation.

Given that the database structure was believed to be the most serious problem, two external contract programmers were employed to rectify the problem. They were employed in the first instance on short-term contracts (6 months). Within days it became clear to these individuals that the problems were more serious than had been anticipated by managers. Not only was the database full of errors, a factor which seriously slowed down its performance, sections of the code were virtually un-maintainable.

It was evident from the style of the coding that the two software house employees had 'learned on the job'. No effort had been made to write compact modular code using functions and structured techniques. Indeed, as much as 40% of all the code was unnecessarily repeated. Where there was an error, a work-around had

then been written, rather than the problem being removed altogether. This code had then been cut and pasted into other similar modules. In short any attempt to follow the logical flow within the program was almost impossible for the two contract programmers. The database was far from being normalised. Not only were values replicated in many tables, but they were also repeated within the same tables. There was so much data repetition that almost 80% of the 300Mb database was repeated information, indexes, and temporary tables.

Technically, the problems with the system were twofold. First, the immense size of the database tended to slow operating performance as individuals tried to access data. Second, the database contained incorrect use of indexes. As such an index will speed up data retrieval by pointing to all the data of a specific type. But the downside is the minor degradation in performance whenever a record is changed or deleted. One table which contained 30,000 records and grew at 5,000 each month contained over seventeen different indexes. Not only did every column have an index, but so to did many of their combinations. The net result was that each month 85,000 (5,000 ∗ 17) references to the records had to be stored and maintained. This represented an additional overhead after six months of about 340Kb!

Whilst the original system developers were presented to the client as *experts*, their work on the system suggested otherwise. Also, the project managers responsible for the systems development work were technically uninformed about the selected language and package. Although project managers are not required to fully understand the subtleties of the programming language, they should be able to discern whether the code written by the programmers is usable.

Since the two contract programmers were unhappy with the code presented to them, they spent a great deal of time in re-writing vast sections of the programme. This was the only feasible option if the system was to work effectively. As a result, managers manipulated the situation to make it *politically acceptable* to write off the initial investment as a 'prototype' and start again. The scale of these problems was so great that the changes took many more months than the timescale presented in the initial project estimate. After ten man months of work, two individuals were brought in to test both the original and revised code. Despite the re-write, some 120 documented errors were present. These ranged from the trivial (date shown as mm-dd-yy but searched for in the order dd-mm-yy) to the not so trivial (the inability to delete a record).

Once the system had been satisfactorily 'patched up' (and ignoring the recorded errors) the system was re-released at an extra cost of £250k, 50% more than the initial budget and five months late. The next six months were spent with just one contract programmer removing as many bugs (errors) as possible before embarking on the third stage of the development work which was intended to enhance the system to improve its features and functionality.

Discussion questions

1 Do you think the problems are technical, managerial or organisational in nature?
2 Are project managers effective in managing the systems development process?
3 Can the concept of organisational learning be applied to this case study?
4 How would you evaluate the performance of the software house originally brought in to do the programming work?
5 What are the management control problems of the case study?
6 Was the company right to hire additional IT contractors to re-write the program?
7 Describe the skills shortages (if any) which exist at the company?

References 12

Argyris, C. (1977) 'Double loop learning in organisations'. *Harvard Business Review*, September/October.

Boynton, A. C., Jacobs, G. C., Zmud, R. W. (1992) 'Whose responsibility is IT management? *Sloan Management Review*, Summer, pp. 32–38.

Campbell, A., Currie, W., Warner, M (1989) 'Innovation, skills and training: micro-electronics and manpower in the United Kingdom and West Germany', in Hirst, P. and Zeitlin, J. *Reversing industrial decline*. Berg Press, London.

Cooley, M. (1980) *Architect or bee?* Langley Technical Services, Slough, UK.

Currie, W. (1989)'The art of justifying new technology to top management'. *OMEGA - The International Journal of Management Science*. October, Vol, 17, No. 5. pp. 409–418.

Currie, W. (1994) 'The strategic management of large scale IT projects in the financial services sector'. *New Technology, Work and Employment*, Vol, 9, No. 1. pp. 19–29.

Currie, W., Bryson, C. (1995) Managing IT professionals: a crisis in management control? in Glover, I and Hughes, M (eds) *The professional-managerial class*, Avebury, Aldershot (forthcoming).

Drucker, P. (1988) 'The coming of the new organisation'. *Harvard Business Review*, January/February, pp. 45–53.

Fiol, C.M., Lyles, M.A. (1985) 'Organisational learning'. *Academy of Management Review*, October.

Forester, T. (1980) *The micro-electronics revolution*. Blackwell, Oxford.

Forester, T. (1985) *The information technology revolution*, Oxford University Press.

Fruin, W. M. (1993) *The Japanese Enterprise System*. Oxford: Clarendon Press.

Garratt, R. (1987) *The learning organisation*. Fontana Collins.

Garvin, D.A. (1993) 'Building a learning organisation'. *Harvard Business Review*, July/August, pp. 78–91.

Glover, I., Kelly, M. (1987) *Engineers in Britain: a sociological study of the engineering dimension.* Allen and Unwin.

HMSO (1993) *Realising our potential: a strategy for science, engineering and technology.* Cm2250.

HMSO (1994) *Competitiveness: helping business to win.* Cm2563.

Huber, G.P. (1991) 'Organisational learning: the contributing processes and the literatures'. *Organisation Science*, February.

Jenkins, C. (1979) *The collapse of work.* Methuen.

Jenkins, C. (1980) *The leisure shock*, Longman.

Levitt, B., March, J.G. (1988) 'Organisational learning'. *American Review of Sociology*, Vol, 14.

Maccoby, M. (1993) 'What should learning organisations learn?' *Research & Technology Management*, May/June, pp. 49–52.

MSC (1985a) *The impact of new technological skills in manufacturing and services.* Moorfoot, Sheffield.

MSC (1985b) *A challenge to complacency: changing attitudes to training.* Moorfoot, Sheffield.

MSC (1987) *The making of managers: A report on management education in the USA, West Germany, France, Japan and the UK.* NEDO, London.

Murray, F. (1989) 'The organisational politics of information technology: studies from the UK financial services industry'. *Technology Analysis & Strategic Management*, Col, 1, No. 3, pp. 285–298.

Nonaka, I. (1991) 'The knowledge-creating company'. *Harvard Business Review*, November/December, pp. 96–104.

Porter, M (1985) *Competitive advantage: creating and sustaining superior performance.* Free Press, New York.

Porter, M. (1992) *The competitive advantage of nations.* McMillan: London.

Samson, J (1994) 'The greasy pole'. *Computer Contractor*, 19 August, p.7.

Senker, P. (1984a) 'Implications of CAD/CAM for management'. *OMEGA: The International Journal of Management Science*, Vol, 12, No, 3. pp. 225–231 .

Senker, P. (1984b) 'Training for automation', in M. Warner (ed) *Microprocessors, manpower and society*, Gower.

Stata, R. (1993) 'Building a learning organisation'. *Harvard Business Review*. July/August, pp. 78–91.

Stata, R. (1989) 'Organisational learning – The key to management innovation'. *Sloan Management Review*, Spring, pp. 63–74.

Thamhain, H.J. (1992) 'Developing the skills you need'. *Research & Technology Management*, March/April, pp. 42–47.

Tricker, R. I. (1992) 'The management of organisational knowledge', in R. Galliers (ed) *Information Systems Research*. Alfred Waller, Henley on Thames, pp. 14–27.

West London Training and Enterprise Council (1993) *IT skills in the 1990s – overcoming obstacles to growth*, Hounslow, Middlesex. See also *Skills and Enterprise briefing – Lack of IT skills: a barrier to growth*, Issue, 27/93, September, published by Skills and Enterprise Network, Nottingham, UK.

Wood, S. (1982) *The degradation of work.* Hutchinson.

CHAPTER 13

Summary and Conclusions

This book began by considering the key developments in corporate information systems over the last two decades. It was observed that moves from traditional mainframe technology to PC-based client-server systems call for a radical rethinking in management methods and practices. For example, the use of formal methodologies to guide complex information systems development work tends to favour a linear approach. Yet field research on the design and implementation of information systems in a client-server environment suggests that an iterative approach is perhaps more appropriate. This would suggest that traditional project management methodologies which favour a linear, as opposed to a processual or iterative, approach require some adjustment, if not a radical revision. This is further reinforced by comments from systems developers (project managers and analyst programmers, etc), as many are critical of the *command and control* management style adopted in their organisation.

A matrix was introduced in chapter one to illustrate the organisational use of IT (see Figure 13.1). It was suggested that as technology becomes more complex, the knowledge base of professional and managerial personnel, together with administrators and clerical

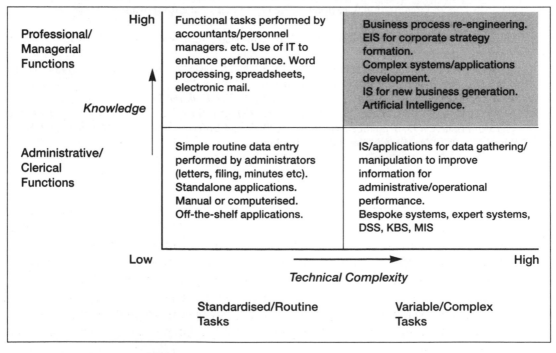

Figure 13.1 The organisational use of IT

workers' may become embedded into computer technology. In other words, simple administrative systems may be automated and thus reduce some of the skill element of the administrative or clerical job.

By the same token, some elements of professional/managerial knowledge may be embedded in a computer program with the inevitable consequence that less qualified personnel may be able to execute the program. An example of this is where production operators use a decision support system to measure and monitor information within the maintenance department. Here important financial information may be collected to monitor the performance of advanced manufacturing technology. This information may then be used by managers for preventive maintenance purposes to improve future technical performance. Other examples are where medical staff use a computer program for symptom diagnosis of a patient. Consequently, the knowledge of a professional doctor could be embedded in the computer program, yet be used by less qualified medical person, such as nursing staff.

Arguably, the increased complexity of technology enables knowledge to be manipulated and stored within a computer program, and utilised by individuals who are able to operate the technology. This clearly has ramifications for skills levels at both professional/managerial and administrative/clerical levels of personnel.

The matrix differentiates between high level and low levels of technical complexity. Less complex technologies are those which execute relatively simple tasks. For example, an accountant may use a popular spreadsheet package, or a secretary a word processing package. But as technology becomes more complex, ambitious systems development projects are initiated for business process re-engineering (BPR), process innovation, and to implement other strategic change programmes. In this instance, software is developed with a clear purpose in mind, although the outcome of such projects may be uncertain and high risk. This is because the more complex the technology, the more difficult it becomes to manage and control technical change. As a result, ambitious IS development projects may result in failure.

Notable examples of IS failures are the TAURUS and London Ambulance projects in the UK. Whilst these projects are extreme examples of IS failures, it is likely that many other large and medium sized IS projects equally fail to meet the desired expectations of management. A recent study found that some 25 percent of companies interviewed by Price Waterhouse believed that most of their IT systems were unsuccessful either because they were delivered too late and over budget, or because they did not meet user requirements (*FT*, 1994).

The topic of IS failure clearly poses a problem for social science researchers, as IT failures reflect badly on the company, not to mention those who commission them. Senior managers are therefore more inclined to speak optimistically about technical change than relay stories about a series of high-cost IT catastrophies! But it is important to remember that IS projects reflect the management priorities, principles, procedures and practices of the individual and wider organisation, and are not simply products of contemporary technological capability. Indeed, poorly constructed IT architectures/ strategies or ill-thought-through IS projects exemplify human mis-management more so than technical failure.

In-depth interviews with IT managers and analyst/programmers reinforce the managerial and political difficulties relating to systems development projects. In this context, the unquestioning relationship between IT and competitive strategy becomes even more dubious. Moreover, it is suggested that glib prescriptions that IT automatically translates into higher profits and increased market share are too simplistic, particularly in the context of the inherent complexities and dynamics of managing technical change.

Similarly, the advocacy of formal-rational strategic frameworks for managing IT must also be treated with caution, since it is implicit in some models that behaviour in organisations is easily managed and controlled. Simple models and prescriptive solutions for devising IT strategies become less relevant in the context of field research on managing IT in three sectors: the financial services, public sector and manufacturing industry. Interviews with a number of IT managers suggest that significant changes are taking place which will revolutionise the status and position of large IT departments and the way in which IS projects are managed and controlled.

One such change is clearly the outsourcing phenomenon. Three types of outsourcing are identified which consist of short-term contracts to IT (freelance) staff, project management outsourcing where an independent company designs and implements a system, and total outsourcing where a company assumes the management and control of the IT facility.

In the public sector, total outsourcing is likely to become more commonplace. This is because of the current trend of market testing and compulsory competitive tendering (CCT). Research undertaken in the public sector suggests that IT managers are now competing for their own jobs with external IT providers. In fact, many individuals currently working within this sector are unable to say whether their job will exist in two years time. Or even if the IT department will survive the changes.

One of the major issues confronting large IT departments in all sectors concerns the evaluation and performance measurement of IT services. The provider-purchaser split in the public sector means that individuals seeking IT services are given greater powers to choose their suppliers – with the in-house IT team also competing for business. This move is enabled by the growing trend to devolve budgets in the public sector, making managers at lower levels more accountable for their expenditure across a range of activities.

In some ways, the concentration on evaluating and monitoring IT is encouraging a wholesale move towards outsourcing, as many senior executives believe the *better value for money* rhetoric of the external IT providers. The idea of purchaser choice is also attractive to budget holders. This is undoubtedly encouraging the growth in outsourcing. Outsourcing is also a popular option for those who perceive IT as a troublesome function.

Yet some evidence suggests that legal and logistical issues continue to pose problems for companies who opt for outsourcing. For example, the failure to scrutinise the outsourcing contract prior to signing it may result in the client having to pay additional costs at a later date for services originally thought to be included in the contract. In addition, outsourcing may pose serious problems about confidentiality, as companies find their intellectual capital (e.g. customer information, profitability forecasts, business strategy, etc) is readily available to the outsourcing *partner*.

Cross-national comparisons of managing IT suggest that problems are not confined only to western (Anglo/American) business cultures. Indeed, Japanese, Australian and other European companies also experience similar problems. These include budget and project over-runs, skills shortages and the failure to align IT and business strategies. Research in Japan highlights the serious problem of the burgeoning white collar sector; and many Japanese companies admit the value system of life-time employment is being threatened. Indeed, the Japanese research shows that whereas manufacturing managers have ruthlessly pursued cost reduction from advanced manufacturing technologies, the office (white collar) sector has not been revolutionised by technology. However, this is now changing as Japanese companies have embraced the fundamental principles of BPR, and are contemplating mass rationalisation of white collar work. Although unlike many North American and European companies, Japanese IT is often provided by a subsidiary company with profit centre status. As a result, the prospect of outsourcing is less likely given that, by and large, the principle of the provider-purchaser split is already in place.

The threat to in-house IT departments from external competition in the form of outsourcing is not simply driven by internal management pressures to seek better value for money. It is also spurred on by external economic constraints and growing international competition. This issue is perhaps more pressing in North America and Europe, where the growth in IT costs, especially in the financial services sector, is forcing senior executives to fixed -price outsourcing contracts (*FT*, 1994).

But the extent to which companies are achieving performance improvements through outsourcing or rationalisation of IT departments is subject to debate. Many outsourcing contracts are still in their infancy – or honeymoon period. Yet the continuing trend to place IT professionals on short-term contracts (managers and staff) is perhaps not entirely conducive to organisational learning and skills development. Indeed, the growth in the IT contract labour market is creating a dynamic situation where IT professionals trade their knowledge and experience for higher annual salaries as *freelancers*, although the responsibility of who should instigate and pay for the training and skills development of freelance IT professionals is unresolved. Whilst companies increasingly move towards short-term contracts and performance-related pay (PRP) schemes, the reluctance to train *temporary staff* is possibly contributing to the international IT skills shortage problem. Permanent staff with skills that are perceived to be out of date are not usually retrained for the new IT environment. So whereas this situation seemingly favours the bargaining power of IT professionals with *state-of-the-art skills*, it contributes little to improving the skills set of IT staff with traditional skills.

This state of affairs is also likely to influence the success rate of systems development projects. In this context, project managers who are unfamiliar with some of the newer forms of IT are unlikely to be able to manage or evaluate the skills set of their technical team. This suggests that project managers equally require ongoing retraining to enable them to manage large-scale IS projects.

Indeed, the unsatisfactory outcome of IS projects is now becoming a major issue, as companies realise that technical malfunctions can no longer be attributed simply to IT personnel. Management too must also share the responsibility. A plausible solution to the problem (notwithstanding the political dimension of managing IS projects) is a greater accent on developing multi-disciplinary teams by emphasising shared learning experiences and knowledge creation, rather than simply evaluating individual skill levels from an itemised list of professional/technical qualifications on a c.v. Such a proposal is clearly at odds with the short-term perspective adopted by management in evaluating and monitoring IS projects. Currently management perceive IS project success as synonymous with meeting project deadlines according to timescales and budget. Qualitative aspects such as skills acquisition, knowledge attainment, system quality, user satisfaction and business relevance, and improved information seemingly take second place. Whilst qualitative factors are given lower priority to the financial (quantitative) imperatives of IS projects, it is likely that more attention to nurturing managerial and technical skills would greatly enhance the success rate of IS projects. However, the current trend to hire IT professionals on a short-term basis, and dispense with these skills at the end of a project, fails to develop the stability, continuity and shared learning among individuals assigned to the project team.

One observation from the case study research is that IS failures tend to engender more management control in the form of tighter project deadlines, capital rationing and more stringent performance targets. While this response is unsurprising given the current accent on performance measurement and control, it is seemingly at odds with contemporary thinking on organisational learning and the creation of the knowledge worker.

In this context, tacit knowledge is all important, yet few companies recognise, let alone measure, its value. This is apparent in each of the three sectors studied. For even though managers reaffirm the importance of building a learning organisation with improved information flows, formal-rational procedures continue to stress the linear approach to managing IS projects. This overlooks the value of the processual approach and, more importantly, the utilisation of knowledge as a competitive advantage. In conclusion, it would seem that one of the critical issues for management in the next few years concerns the search for appropriate performance indicators which evaluate both quantitative and qualitative factors.

References 13

Financial Times (1994) Computers in Finance, Survey. 15 November.

INDEX